Also by Scott O'Brien:

Kay Francis – I Can't Wait to Be Forgotten (2006)

Classic Images Magazine – "Best Books of 2006" Laura Wagner— "O'Brien has a way with words as he beautifully examines Kay's films. He treats her private life with respect, without shying away from some unpleasantries. He skillfully uses Kay's own diary to paint a picture of an independent woman ahead of her time."

Russian River Monthly – "A meticulously researched, well-written biography of one of the most interesting, intelligent actresses of all time."

Virginia Bruce – Under My Skin (2008)

Daeida Magazine – David Ybarra (editor) – "O'Brien successfully brings Virginia Bruce to life in a way that is believable, intelligent and never pitiable. [He] triumphs in making her more than an actress. . . . *Under My Skin* is by no means a "love letter" to Bruce, but it is a well-researched, tactful, and skilled examination into the tragedy of a talented, beautiful and popular figure in film history, desperate to fall in love and stay in love at any cost. Highly recommended."

Classic Images Magazine – Laura Wagner – "This book is long overdue and luckily Scott O'Brien is the one who wrote it. There is an elegance to O'Brien's writing. . . . Perfectly in tune with his subject, the author also makes a very strong case for her acting. . . . *Under My Skin* is fascinating as it chronicles Bruce's successes and devastating failures, both on and off screen. . . . a roller-coaster of emotions not easily forgotten."

Ann Harding

Cinema's Gallant Lady

A Biography by Scott O'Brien

Published in the USA by:
BearManor Media
P O Box 71426
Albany, Georgia 31708
www.bearmanormedia.com

Printed in the United States of America
ISBN 1-59393-535-8
     13: 978-1-59393-535-1

Book & cover design and layout by Darlene & Dan Swanson • www.van-garde.com

Contents

In memory of my parents –

Bette Morgan O'Brien
and
Eugene LeRoy O'Brien

Ann Harding (c. 1933) (RKO)

Ann Harding
by Mick LaSalle

Lots of minor stars from the 1920s and '30s deserve to be better known. Their names are forgotten, and yet their films would please people. Perhaps their obscurity is of no great loss to culture. Perhaps their contributions to art and civilization were minor. No matter. Modern audiences would like them. Resurrecting their memory might not be a big deal in the grand scheme, but it would sure be great if it were to happen.

That's all very nice. But *Ann Harding is not in that minor league category.*

Make no mistake: The book you have in your hand is not just another book by a fan. Scott O'Brien did not just go out and pick an obscure actress that he happens to like, so that he could build a biography around her. On the contrary, he has given us a book about someone essential, an overlooked master. He has written the life story of one of the greatest actresses in the entire history of American cinema

That's the essential point to realize. The loss of Ann Harding to history is not something akin to the relative obscurity of, say, Madge Evans, a completely charming actress of the same era. In terms of talent, this is more as if Bette Davis were somehow to be forgotten. Harding's body of work was small. Her luck in terms of studios was nonexistent, and the coming of the Production Code eliminated the sex drama, the genre in which she thrived. For these reasons, most people have never seen an Ann Harding movie. But the talent was enormous – and apparent to anyone within 10 minutes of watching her on screen.

Ann Harding is the missing link between the theatrical style of her own day and the more introspective acting style that followed a generation later, in the wake of Marlon Brando and the Actors Studio. Like many of the stars of her own time, Harding, who was trained for the stage, had a cultivated voice and speaking style. But unlike the actors of her day, she put the emphasis on the thought, not the word.

Her technique was utterly suited to the screen. Her onscreen close-up showed that she was always, always thinking. Old-time actors – that is, the good ones, who bothered to think at all – tended to think *throughout* a line of dialogue. Today's actors tend to think *before* a line. They pause, they reflect, they find the words. Harding was an actress in the modern mode, at least a generation, perhaps two generations, ahead of her time.

With Harding you always got the impression of a whole world of experience behind the dialogue, what modern actors call a back-story. Take, for example, that marvelous scene at the end of *When Ladies Meet* (1933). Harding is getting rid of her pathetic, cheating husband, and she's explaining why she has stopped loving him. Her pauses and expressions, her eyes and her thinking all tell a story far more detailed than the words on the page. She remembers years of humiliation and struggle, grapples with the new understanding that meeting his latest lover has given her, and marvels (and to some degree celebrates) that she's finally free, that she no longer loves this guy.

Harding does much more than simply say the words in a convincing way. She gives you an entire life.

Harding was an actress of our time, who just happened to be working in the early sound era. She was a woman of our time, who just happened to be living three generations ago. She was a pioneer in the art of acting who, through either instinct, intellect or some inspired combination of the two, pointed the way to an entirely new way of being on screen. It's time to reclaim her legacy, not for her sake but for ours.

Ann Harding and Myrna Loy in
When Ladies Meet (1933). (MGM)

Portrait from RKO's *Animal Kingdom* (1932).

Introduction

When Ann Harding arrived in Hollywood in 1929, she was ready for a change. "The thought of going back to the stage sends shivers of horror up and down my spine," she told a reporter in 1930. "The stage is a terrific grind."[1] She found the challenges of working before the camera "exciting," but just as important was her spectacular new hilltop home. "A home that is really mine," Ann declared, "fresh air and sunshine—all the pleasant things in life." A few months later, Ann began to change her tune. Questions were being asked. Fan magazines wanted interviews. "Nobody likes to live in a goldfish bowl," Ann gently protested. "Whatever charm and dignity an actor may possess are ruined if delved into too deeply."[2] She discovered there was a pricetag attached to her new life: an adoring public with an insatiable appetite to know *everything* about her. All this adoration gave her pause. "It is perhaps flattering to any actress, stage or screen, to be persuaded that her views on anything and everything, from radishes to relativity, should have a cosmic significance," Ann stated. "But personally I find this … removed from certain ideas I cherish about what constitutes an actress's job. I also feel that an actress is under something of an obligation to try to preserve the illusion of the profession."[3] Over the next two years Ann was obliging to the press, and even penned a few articles detailing her early life. She was a writer, and a darn good one—as you will discover in her article, "When I Was an Army Girl." In numerous articles and interviews, Ann enthusiastically offered her formula for a happy marriage. Then came 1932. Her "blissful" relationship with actor Harry Bannister came to an abrupt end. Fans were skeptical of the couples' self-declared "friendly divorce," and eager to devour the *real* details of their troubled relationship. The type of scandal that befell Ann's friend, Mary Astor, a few years later, could well have booted Ann out of Hollywood in 1933. On the advice of her agent, Harry Edington (who also managed the reclusive Greta Garbo), Ann found an answer to her dilemma. She stopped offering interviews. Her battle with Harry Bannister, and his threats of blackmail, however, would go on for years. Ann resigned herself to the confines of her home and sanctuary overlooking the San Fernando Valley.

Ann took *acting* seriously, not stardom. She didn't need close-ups, or preferred camera angles. She didn't fuss over costumes and demand fabulous gowns. Staircase scenes a la Norma Desmond? You won't find them in an Ann Harding film. Watch her descend the stairs in *The Fountain* and you'll see a human being approaching the camera. Real acting and stardom, for Ann, did not mix. Co-stars were surprised when she suggested building up their roles at the cost of her own. She felt films were as good as their weakest link. According to Ann, every single role in the story had import. Her ideas put her at odds with her employer, RKO. She fought over scripts, and frequently found herself, due to contractual obligations, conceding to do films she thought meaningless. Ann offered to buy the negative to RKO's *Prestige* (1931) and have it destroyed. By 1933, she felt a prisoner at her studio, as well as her home.

Ann Harding was composed of two, seemingly conflicting, personalities. The fearless and soldierly qualities of army life were instilled in her from birth, and she held them close to her heart. At the same time, she realized that for a woman, the army atmosphere was stifling. So, the "Daughter of the Regiment" opted to create her own life as an actress. After Ann's escape to England in 1936 (ex-husband Bannister had sworn out a warrant for her arrest), her character was succinctly summed up by Freda Bruce Lockhart, a longtime English film critic. "Ann's individuality," wrote Lockhart, "seems to be made up of two people—Ann Harding, and [Dorothy] Gatley, the actress and the General's daughter. In all her conversation one feels the force of these two stresses, as if her business in life were to reconcile them."[4] To back up her theory, Lockhart recalled asking Ann if there was anything she specially wanted to do. "Yes," Ann nodded. "Sit under a palm tree in Hawaii!" "For good?" Lockhart queried. "I think for good," Ann hesitated. "But I know that after a few months I'd get a sort of itch and want to know what was going on back in the world." It was the fall of 1936, and Ann had recently finished her contract with RKO. She was in the process of redefining what her life was about. The previous fall she had seriously considered marrying Major Benjamin Sawbridge, who was stationed on Oahu. Ann was torn between what he represented, which was exactly what she had rebelled against in her youth, and her creative ambitions as an actress. "I went to Hawaii a year ago," Ann told Lockhart, "and stayed with my father's regiment. It was like being sixteen again, as if I'd gone right back to where I'd begun. I was just General Gatley's daughter—nobody cared a thing for Hollywood, Ann Harding or spotlights."

While in England, Ann attempted to establish a new identity. "Pleasure always ends in work," Ann observed. "Work's a vice, and if it gets into your blood you're licked. I don't mean I want to go on acting until my face drops and I have to lift it up and carry it on to the set. Acting may be the hardest work in the world, but it isn't the only work." Soon after her interview with Lockhart, Ann gave up on films—for nearly six years. She returned to the stage in Shaw's *Candida* in England and the United States, and made a job of being an orchestra conductor's wife.

Ann was repelled by the thought of perpetually playing romantic leads, as many of the great screen divas insisted on doing long past their youthful bloom. She returned to films in 1942, content to look her age—and act it. Ann had her hopes set on playing opposite Spencer Tracy in MGM's *The Yearling*. "My ambition was to come back in the role of Ma Baxter in *The Yearling*," Ann stated. "There's a *real* part!" According to the interviewer, "Ann wasn't smiling when she said that. She meant it."[5] No doubt, Ann desired a complete turnabout in the portrayals for which she was known.

While her acting had intelligence, depth and weight, and she had the innate ability to lose herself in a variety of characters, it seems unfair that Ann Harding is mostly remembered for being only "noble." For those who had witnessed Ann's work on stage, their overall impression of her was more diverse. After all, on stage she had portrayed tarnished women and gold-diggers. She originated the role of Mary Dugan in the Broadway hit *The Trial of Mary Dugan* (1927). In that play, Ann found herself on the witness stand, defending herself and justifying the "gifts" she received from her murdered sugar-daddy, including a Rolls-Royce. Upon leaving Hollywood in 1936, Ann admitted that her gallant lady-like screen persona was partly her own fault ... and undoing. She tried to rectify this image when she returned to the stage in 1948. Her new repertoire would take her onto much edgier turf, such as Tennessee Williams' *Suddenly, Last Summer*.

In person, many found Ann to be the antitheses of her screen roles. She also showed no interest in looking fashionable. Popular columnists deemed her dowdy and unrecognizable on the street. Author David Chierichetti talked to a former RKO employee whose out-of-town guests from back east insisted on meeting Ann Harding. When she arrived at the studio, Ann had just completed a round of morning golf. Her hair was disheveled, her complexion ruddy. She came across as tough and athletic-looking. As she approached them, they looked quizzically at their friend before asking, "That's Ann Harding?"[6]

My own "romance" with Ann Harding began in the 1960s. As a teenager, I remember watching *Devotion* on television, turning to my dad and asking, "Who's that amazing-looking actress?" My dad, who was named after silent screen idol Eugene O'Brien, knew every actor, every bit player and all the popular songs that had ever been written since 1910. "That's Ann Harding," he said. "She's one of the best." I was com-

Leslie Howard found Ann "completely devoid of mental shams."
Critics found the duo "perfect teammates" in
Devotion (1931). (RKO-Pathé)

pletely mesmerized by Ann's angelic warmth, her unique blonde looks, her voice ... and that hair! "Ethereal" was the word that kept entering my fifteen-year-old mind. In the fall of 1963, I saw *Peter Ibbetson* and that nailed it. There was no one else like Ann Harding. She had molded herself perfectly to play the formidable Duchess of Towers, who softens graciously to Gary Cooper's mystical and subdued Ibbetson. This exquisite film has remained my favorite of hers.

While Ann was married to actor Harry Bannister, a group of their friends gathered at their home. During the course of the evening the question came up as to how to determine, from your deathbed, if you had succeeded or failed in life. Someone suggested one's service to humanity was the obvious answer. Ann's throaty, pulsating voice burst forth saying, "Boloney! With me, it would be whether or not I had achieved personal happiness."[7] Ann Harding had no idea how difficult it would be for an actor who becomes a celebrity to achieve her definition of "success." But, one thing is for sure, in spite of the drawbacks (and there were many), she stretched her humanity in the process of developing her art.

(Endnotes)

1   "The Girl on the Cover," *Photoplay*, June 1930
2   Harrison Carroll, "Behind the Scenes in Hollywood," *San Mateo Times*, 10/16/30
3   Elza Schallert, "Why I have Kept Silent for Two Years," circa 1934, article from *Hedgerow Theatre Collection*, UC Berkeley, Bancroft Library
4   Freda Bruce Lockhart, "Lunch With Ann Harding," *Film Weekly*, 11/21/36
5   Connie Curtis, "The Return of Ann Harding, " *Hollywood*, September 1942
6   Phone conversation with David Chierichetti, 9/21/2009
7   Myrtle Gebhart, "The Happiest Woman in Hollywood," *Picture Play*, March 1931

Acknowledgements

Except for the self-deluded, no one accomplishes anything on their own. I was buoyed with wonderful support and generous assistance from many kindred souls in the writing and telling of Ann Harding's story.

Graceann Macleod, a talented writer, Apex Award Winner (twice), and Ann Harding fan, heard it through the vintage cinema grapevine that I was working on Ann's biography. She volunteered to proof and edit my manuscript. Graceann's eagle eye for error and keen suggestions were a godsend. As I wrapped things up, my good luck charm and friend Martha Hunt, who proofed my books on Kay Francis and Virginia Bruce, gave the manuscript an appreciated and scrupulous final perusal.

My connection with theatre archivist/preservationist, Gail Cohen, was essential in delving into the legendary Provincetown Players, Hedgerow Theatre, and Jasper Deeter. In 1976, Gail was offered an NEH grant to organize, document and preserve, the Hedgerow Theatre Collection for Boston University. Gail is a fighter and a fountain of knowledge. And, she definitely helped put Ann's retirement years in perspective.

I was aware that writer/film critic Mick LaSalle greatly admired

Ann's talent. LaSalle has kept the legacy of classic film actors alive in his expertly researched and revealing *Complicated Women* and *Dangerous Men*. So, I was pleased when he agreed to write the foreword. LaSalle was influential in nudging me to write my first book, *Kay Francis – I Can't Wait to be Forgotten*.

The prolific writer of Hollywood lore, James Robert Parish, was behind me one hundred percent, just as he had been for my previous book: *Virginia Bruce – Under My Skin*. Parish's *RKO Gals* (1974), was a bible-of-sorts. His chapter on Ann Harding proved a pivot point for my own research. Canadian writer Joseph Worrell (*Asian Cinema Journal*) offered his insight as well as providing numerous articles on Ann. Archivist and film historian/professor Richard Jewell (*The RKO Story*) sent me box-office results for Ann's films. Publisher G.D. Hamann's *Ann Harding in the 1930's* chronicled news coverage from the Los Angeles area. Hamann was always available to answer questions as he had been with my projects on Virginia Bruce and Kay Francis. Assistant Professor of Theatre Arts at Arcadia University, Jonathan Shandell, kindly forwarded me the guide to the Hedgerow Theatre Collection held at UC Berkeley's Bancroft Library. A special thank you to Howard and Ron Mandelbaum of Photofest. They provided many rare photos from Ann's career on stage and television. Howard made the keen observation, "Ann was a great listener with a beautiful voice and intelligent manner: a perfect combination." Hedgerow Theatre publicist, Margie Royal, sent excerpts from the company's files, and photo scans. Actor/director Paul Aaron shared his impressions of working with his and Ann's mentor, Jasper Deeter. Mike Rinella offered his collection of reviews of Ann's stage appearances. Other fellow writers/biographers involved were David Noh, Andre Soares, Jay Blotcher, and Matthew Kennedy. Author David Chierichetti, who had the opportunity to meet Ann, shared some interesting and appreciated anecdotes. My friends Jenny Paxson and husband Larry Smith were generous in providing DVDs and stills from their own amazing collection. And, special thanks to film-maker Carole Summers, co-worker Ken Converse, and cellist Sherrill Roberts. For his emotional support, watching a marathon of Ann Harding films, and scanning dozens of photos, I owe thanks to my partner, Joel Bellagio. Ann's co-workers were harder to come by. My lengthy interview with Robert Brown, who co-starred with Ann in one of her favorite stage vehicles, *The Corn is Green*, provided invaluable insight into how Ann co-created her role with a fellow artist. Brown had worked with the "greats" and he includes "Annie" among the best. The prolific scenarist, Sam Hall, worked with Ann in two 1950's television dramas. His vivid recollections of knowing Ann, on and off the set, were priceless. Other co-stars who shared memories of Ann were: Joan Leslie, Jimmy Lydon, Marlyn Mason, Piper Laurie, and the wonderful Peter Mark Richman. Of course, there were dozens of other celebrities I sent inquiries who chose not respond. When you ask someone to recall events from 45-75 years ago, I can understand why.

I am especially grateful to the friends and family members of Ann and her daughter Jane Harding Otto. Those who were kind enough to share memories include: Lynn Stickrod (Ann's step-granddaughter), Aaron Perillat (Ann's great-grandson), Grace Kaye (Ann's adopted daughter), Mary Gibson and Jeanie Barry (life-long friends of Jane). Ann's namesake and niece, Dorothy Nash MacKenzie Wylder Wagar, according to her daughter Fay Ellen Wylder, was not available to be interviewed. This came as a surprise, as Gail Cohen had informed me that Dorothy "really likes to talk about Ann." Fay Ellen, who also declined to talk to me, has been researching her own project on Ann and Ann's sister Edith (Dorothy's mother). I do want to give special thanks to the daughter of Mary Astor, Marylyn Roh, whose candid comments about her mother's retirement years seemed to parallel Ann's own experience.

Just as they had for *Virginia Bruce – Under My Skin,* Dan and Darlene Swanson (Van-garde Imagery) have created another stunning, eye-catching cover for Ann Harding. As BearManor Media approaches the celebration of its first decade, it remains committed to preserving film history and the stories of performers and artists who made it happen. The library that publisher Ben Ohmart has created is unusual in that it focuses on talents that have been overlooked by major publishers, but are so very deserving of having their stories told. From silent stars such as Francis X. Bushman, George O'Brien, Baby Peggy, Harold Lloyd, and Lon Chaney, to Ann Harding, Kay Francis, Virginia Bruce, Fred MacMurray, Ann Sothern, Betty Hutton, Agnes Moorehead, Don Ameche, George Raft, Joan Davis, Judy Canova, Sybil Jason, and "Our Gang's" Buckwheat—BearManor deserves a special bow.

Jasper Deeter greets Ann upon her return to Hedgerow in 1933. Ann claimed to have been a "model prisoner" at RKO, getting time off for "good behavior."

Cornerstones
Inheritors & Hedgerow

It was Summer, 1931. After a grueling day at the studio, Ann kept her scheduled appointment with the young syndicated columnist Robbin Coons, asking him to follow her home. A private audience with RKO-Pathé's top female star? Coons was ecstatic! Harding's residence atop Pyramid Drive, replete with swimming pool, and chiseled into a high stone ridge, was the Valhalla of Hollywood homes. You couldn't get a better view of Hollywood from an airplane. As Coons later wagged, "Ann and Harry swim at an altitude in which others fly." Her husband, actor Harry Bannister, along with Ann, had designed the home and done all the landscaping. There was nothing ostentatious about it. "We simply want comfort," Ann had insisted. "There must be a place to flop in every room."[1] In fact, the dining room only sat a party of six. Ann could see no point in having more than four dinner guests at a time. For Ann, her home was a sanctuary from the world below. "I like living on top of the mountain because of the perspective it gives me," she said. "Harry and I see a violent storm hang over Santa Monica Bay while there is a bright sun flooding San Fernando Valley at the very same moment. Up here neither the storm nor the sun seems important. It's quiet here. It slows down the tempo, the mad pace, that governs life below. When I go shopping

I feel annoyed, confused by the rush and racket. I get back up here and it's all like a bad dream that doesn't exist."[2] Ann liked referring to Hollywood as "the carbon monoxide area."[3]

Upon entering the living room which Ann had furnished herself, Coons admired the cozy interior, and gazed out at the picture window's panoramic views. Ann, admitting she was tired, sat down, picked up a book, and after leafing through it, asked if he would mind if she read something to him. Coons readily accepted, considering it an unusual treat. Ann selected an excerpt from her first stage success, *Inheritors*, written by the Pulitzer Prize-winning playwright Susan Glaspell. In 1921, Ann had played the lead in the play's premier, a college student named Madeline Morton, who stands up for the rights of Hindu students protesting for a free India. Her character also comes to the defense of her friend, a conscientious objector, who refused to fight in WWI. Ann, the daughter of a Brigadier General, was initially horrified at the idea. She was blunt with the play's director, Jasper Deeter. "My rearing as a general's daughter rebelled against some of the lines," Ann later recalled. "I told Mr. Deeter I would say the lines the way he wanted me to, but I couldn't feel them … because I didn't believe in slackers. Jasper just looked at me for about 30 seconds, sighed … and called off the rehearsal. And then we sat down for a long talk – he pulled back my blinders as an actress … and as a person too."[4] By the time the play opened, Ann's anger had cooled. She made a complete about-turn regarding the subject. "It was my first actual education," Ann acknowledged, "the first revelation of a broad world outside my own narrow track."[5] The impact of the play affected her deeply.

Glaspell's *Inheritors* used dialogue with intellect and headed straight for the heart. While Madeline establishes a stirring defense for free speech, she also jeopardizes state funding for the college, an institution that her late grandfather, Silas Morton, had founded. A visiting senator, holding the coveted purse-strings, is seeking evidence of patriotism at the school. Ann read Coons a passage in which Madeline voices her ideals, and her feelings about the Hindu students whom the college is about to expel. As she read, the tiredness seemed to lift from her. The text proved to be an elixir for her soul.

> They're people from the other side of the world who
> came here believing in us, drawn from the far side
> of the world by things we say about ourselves. Well,
> I'm going to pretend – just for fun – that the things
> we say about ourselves are true. I thought America
> was a democracy.[6]

When Madeline's uncle Felix, a banker and president of the college board, argues that America had just fought a great war for democracy, Madeline counters, "Well, is that any reason for not having it?"

Madeline points out that Felix's father, a Hungarian revolutionist, had escaped to America, and that her grandfather Silas had laid the country at his feet. Together, the two men envisioned a college rising up from the thoughts and soil of the earth. Silas gave up the most valuable land in the area for a place of learning - on the crest of a hill - a hill Silas' father and Blackhawk had climbed together. That was before Blackhawk knew how many white men there really were. Relinquish all claim to his beloved hill? Silas saw it as atonement for the white man's slaughter of Native Americans. "Maybe I can lie under the same sod as the red boys," Silas had declared, "and not be ashamed."

Susan Glaspell's "earth consciousness" underscores the very core and meaning behind *Inheritors*. Something more primal than democracy raises its head up out of rich, life-giving soil. After a long pause, Madeline finds herself thinking out loud:

> I took a walk late yesterday afternoon. Night came, and for some reason I thought of how moonlight made this country beautiful before any man knew that moonlight was beautiful. It gave me a feeling of coming from something a long way back. Moving toward – what will be here when I'm not here. Moving. We seem here, now, in America, to have forgotten we're moving. Think it's just us – just now. Of *course*, that would make us afraid, and – ridiculous.

The last act of *Inheritors* takes place in the old Morton homestead kitchen. Madeline listens to her father Ira's pent up bitterness about life. He lost his son in WWI. Adding insult to injury, the improved strain of corn he had developed after *years* of hard work, was now benefiting neighbors he hated. "Not even the corn stays at home," cries Ira, "If only the wind wouldn't blow! Why can't I keep what's mine? … I've made corn *more*! … the golden dust it blows, in the sunshine and of nights – blows from corn to corn like a gift." The idea hurts him. His is a mind burned to one idea. Madeline listens as if heavenly mists are parting with his every word. She later reflects, "I have to be – the most I can be. I want the wind to have something to carry."

When Madeline contemplates the fate of Fred Jordan, the conscientious objector who had been in solitary confinement for two years, she takes a piece of chalk, and sits down on the floor. She makes an outline the size of his prison cell. She envisions herself being penned up in such a hole. As the scene progresses, one of her favorite professors pays a visit. He warns Madeline of the consequences of doing the "big, brave thing," and ending up in prison for her beliefs. But, Madeline appears preoccupied, distracted, and offers an apology.

> I'm sorry. I was listening to what you were saying
> – but all the time – something else was happen-
> ing. Grandfather Morton, big and –oh, terrible. He
> was *here*. And we went to that walled-up hole in the
> ground – (rising and pointing down at the chalked
> cell) – where they keep Fred Jordan on bread and
> water because he couldn't be a part of nations of
> men killing each other –and Silas Morton tore open
> that cell – it was his voice tore it open – his voice as
> he cried, "God damn you, this is America!"

Robbin Coons, Ann's captive audience, listened intently as she read. He intuited that Madeline's views mirrored those of the actress. When Ann had finished, she looked up at Coons, smiled warmly, glanced down again at the play, and stated, "*This* is my Bible." She had recently gone east to Hedgerow Theatre in Pennsylvania's Rose Valley, to repeat her role in *Inheritors*. Whenever Ann talked about Hedgerow, she did so in reverence -- reverence for what it was, and reverence for the man who had made it all possible: Jasper Deeter. Reflecting on his evening at Ann's, Coon's news report of their visit came to an obvious conclusion. After commenting on the inspired reading from her "Bible," Coons stated, "I think, in the same sense, that Hedgerow is her 'church.'"[7]

Jasper Deeter, a disorderly-looking individualist, took theatre seriously. His actors got no reward other than board and room. They received no billing, and no name on the program – only the satisfaction of performing their art. The troupe lived communally in three big houses. There was a garden and twelve sheep. From the sheep they averaged twelve blankets and four quilts a year. From the garden they received sustenance. Everything was shared: money, food, clothes, and work. Especially work. Everyone at Hedgerow was required to contribute something other than mere acting skill.[8] And for that, Deeter was a relentless taskmaster. "What he does first," said one of the older actors, "is break you down. You come in imagining you're somebody pretty important and by the end of a month you're considering suicide. After you're properly smashed, Deeter picks up the pieces and begins recreating you as an actor."[9] Beneath his discerning and enormous eyebrows, Deeter never saw stars, only truth. In 1924, he told the acclaimed Eva

On stage with Jasper Deeter for Ann's final appearance in Glaspell's *Inheritors*.

La Gallienne, a resident for many months at Hedgerow, that she ought to be arrested for the way she murdered Ibsen's *The Master Builder* on Broadway. In a rage, La Gallienne challenged him to allow her to repeat the role on even nights at Hedgerow, and let his "little pet" Ann Harding present it under Deeter's direction on odd nights. The odds won.

While at RKO, Ann referred to Hedgerow as a sanctuary. "I simply wait for vacation time to fly home to Hedgerow," she told one reporter. "I can work quietly in the little theater there. I have done a lot of work at Hedgerow and I have enjoyed every minute of it. The theater has no commercial ties, it does what it wants and with whom it wants, and it is great fun. What a pity we can't have more of them."[10] Ann was listed among the regular Hedgerow players from 1923-1926, and offered "surprise" guest appearances in the early thirties. She continues to be recognized as Hedgerow's most famous alumnus.

Upon resuming her theatrical career in the late 1940s, Ann echoed her earlier sentiments regarding little theatre: "There is apparently no longer any room for a merely 'successful play,'" observed Ann at the time. "A production in the American theater today has to be a smash hit or it is a flop. The economics of the theater now demand that a play catch on immediately and do excellent business from the beginning. Nothing less than overwhelming success can keep most plays going. The economic system of the theater apparently needs an overhauling. The theatergoing habits of the public … somehow have to be reformed."[11]

Hedgerow's non-commercial status explains why Ann never concerned herself about whether or not a theatrical project was going to be a "hit." One cannot underestimate the impact Deeter had on Ann Harding. He had discovered her. Much to Ann's amazement Deeter and Glaspell had selected Ann, a complete novice, for the premier of *Inheritors* in 1921. Her reviews were excellent. Ann's sister, Edith, recalled, "The audience stood on their feet and cheered, calling for 'Madeline.'"[12] The girl with the corn-yellow hair epitomized the theme of yellow corn, yellow pollen, and had a natural gift for being the most she could be. The play ran four weeks instead of the scheduled two. Ann referred to Deeter as, "the man who taught me all that I know about acting, about the theater, about my fellow men and women – about life."[13] At the height of her film career, Deeter still had a way of renewing her ambition and ability to lay bare a character's soul, and in so doing transport audiences into deeper understanding of the human experience. Ann was blunt in her assessment of Deeter. "I have a sort of Svengali in my life," she smiled. "Jasper Deeter who runs his little theater near Philadelphia. He is a hard task master – but when I feel myself acquiring cheap little stage tricks, I go back to him to be purged of them."[14] Ann had been involved from the beginning with Hedgerow. On June 14, 1923, Hedgerow's premier was a revival of *Inheritors*. Ann played her lead part as Madeline, and Deeter played her father, the mentally broken, corn-loving, Ira Morton.

What few people realize is that Jasper Deeter's cornerstone for Hedgerow was *Inheritors*. Together, he and Ann, who would eventually give Jasper the money to buy Rose Valley's little theatre outright in 1932, were buoyed spiritually by the play. Deeter credited *Inheritors* with why he founded Hedgerow, calling it, "the story of what life might be if people bring their caring directly to bear upon their ways of doing."[15] Hedgerow embodied Glaspell's story.

Ann was also energized and in tune with the area surrounding Hedgerow. During her visits, she spent her days walking through the wooded slopes and taking the footpaths that dotted the countryside. Sporting an old tweed skirt, plain blouse, and low-heeled, mud-caked shoes, Ann absorbed nature as spelled out in Glaspell's *Inheritors*, "It gives itself away all the time. The best corn a gift to other corn. What you are doesn't stay with you. Be the most you can be, so life will be more because you were ... Love could save the world if only you'd throw it to the winds." After her tramps though the woods, Ann might be spotted in the five-and-ten store in the village of Media, trying on something as unglamorous as a beret.

Ann was so taken with her Hedgerow experience of acting in anonymity, that stardom had initially repelled her. "When I was appearing at the Eltinge Theater in Al Woods's play *Stolen Fruit*," recalled Ann, "I went to the theater one day and saw my name being put up in lights. I went right into Mr. Woods's office and refused to go on until they took my name down."[16] The truth of the matter was, at that point in her career (1925), Ann felt undeserving, and under-prepared. Conserving her ammunition for a lengthy career, Ann pointed out, "My father was a general and I'm an Army brat. His advice to me was always; 'Don't go off half-cocked!'"[17]

Ann, the Army brat, did not *always* listen to the general's advice. In fact, she rarely did. As Ann put it, "I felt no filial obligation. Things rankled. More than all was the terrific warfare between the man of his generation, his traditions, his inherent beliefs and the woman of my generation, building new traditions, no longer in bondage. He was an individual. *So was I*. We never thought of the white flag of truce."[18] And, her mother? Ann's own assessment of her mother's life could be summed up in the chalk outline that Madeline Morton had drawn on the kitchen floor in the *Inheritors*. Ann put it bluntly, many times. "Army life is a narrow prison cell for the soul of a woman," she said, "she must restrict her thoughts, fold her wings."[19]

(Endnotes)

1   Lois Shirley, "The Story of Magic House," *Photoplay*, October 1930
2   Ben Lyon, "My Friend Ann Harding," *Screenplay*, September 1931
3   Willa Okker, "The Hollywood Parade," *San Mateo Times*, 10/16/35
4   Tex McCrary and Jinx Falkenburg, "New York Close-Up," *Oakland Tribune*, 11/1/49
5   Margaret Ried, "Blond-But Not Light," *Picture Play*, May 1930
6   Susan Glaspell, *Inheritors*, Cambridge University Press, c. 1921
7   Robbin Coons, "Hollywood Sights and Sounds," *Evening Tribune (MN)*, 4/18/32 (In this article Coons recalls his interview with Ann from the previous year)
8   Kyle Crichton, "Directed by Simon Legree," *Colliers*, 6/13/36
9   Richard Powell, "Broadway? Hollywood? 'Phooey' say Hedgerowians," *Edwardsville Intelligencer*, 1/24/40
10   Wood Soanes, "Ann Harding Says Stage Alone Gives Stimulation She Requires on Screen," *Oakland Tribune*, 5/15/32
11   Wood Soanes, "Catholic Theater Group to Hold Conference Here," *Oakland Tribune*, 2/1/50
12   Edith Gatley Nash, "My Sister, Ann Harding," *Photoplay*, April 1933
13   Gladys Hall, "The Hot Spot," *Motion Picture*, December 1930
14   Alma Whitaker, "Luck Pursues Ann Harding," *Los Angeles Times*, 8/25/29
15   Gail Cohen, "Provincetown Playhouse History, III," *The Clyde Fitch Report*, 5/8/2008
16   Steven H. Scheuer, "Ann Harding is Not 'Sold' on Live TV," *Syracuse Herald (NY)*, 5/3/56
17   Scheuer, "Ann Harding is Not …"
18   Hall, "The Hot Spot"
19   Ann Harding, "When I Was an Army Girl," *Los Angeles Times*, 5/5/31

1
When I Was An Army Girl

In the spring of 1933, Ann Harding, having survived film assignments at RKO, as well as the shark-infested waters off the shores
of Cuba after her skiff capsized, decided she would write a book
about her father, the late General George Grant Gatley. It had been
two years since he had passed away, and Ann admitted she was late
in realizing what a colorful character her father was. She began to interview soldiers and army officers who, according to news reports,
were "tickled to death to help her with her literary effort."[1] Actually,
there was much more behind Ann's decision. She and her father had
been estranged during the decade prior to General Gatley's demise at
San Francisco's Letterman Hospital on January 9, 1931. Gatley had
never seen his daughter perform as an actress on stage, or on film. He
adamantly refused to do so. According to Ann, he had disowned her.
"For years, he did not speak my name," she admitted.[2] Reconciliation
between father and daughter finally took place in September 1930.
After Ann told him that she loved him, America's authority on artillery fire rose up from his hospital bed and said, "Get me that damned
piece of wood I'm carving – why the blank-blank-blank-can't I find

my knife?"[3] He diligently held back any potential tear.

George Grant Gatley (spelled "Gathleigh" a couple of generations earlier) descended from a long line of New England seafaring stock. His parents, Richard and Sarah, resided in Portland, Maine, where George was born on September 10, 1868. He graduated from West Point in 1890 and was immediately assigned to the Presidio in San Francisco. Upon being promoted to 2nd Lieutenant, Gatley was stationed at an army post on nearby Alcatraz Island. It was there he met Ann's mother, Bessie Crabbe, daughter of an artillery officer. The couple wed after Gatley transferred to Fort Hamilton in New York. Gatley rapidly advanced in rank during the U.S. conflict in the Philippines (1903-05), and the intervention in the Mexican Revolution (1913-15). His first assignment, during WWI, was at Camp Sevier, South Carolina. Virtually none of the men in the outfit knew anything about artillery. It was a tough and trying situation for Gatley. According to army historian Arthur Lloyd Fletcher, the resourceful Gatley stuck to his task, and "out of the raw material ... welded together a great fighting machine."[4] Fletcher stressed that Gatley ruled with a rod of iron. "He was sharp of tongue, impatient and quick of temper," wrote Fletcher, "bubbling over with nervous energy and at all times bordering on an explosion. Nervous young officers ... in reach of the General had all of the sensations of walking over a volcano that had just erupted and was due to erupt some more at any moment. His method was to chasten without mercy and then chasten some more. He was chary of praise. Rarely did he drop a word of commendation. He permitted officers who were really doing fine work to believe that they were on the ragged edge of failure, ready to topple over."[5]

One of the men in Gatley's unit, Grant Dixon, who later became a syndicated columnist, recalled that when Gatley did him the honor of advancing his rank and assigning him to France, Gatley admonished the amateur soldier, "Just because I am doing this don't get the idea that you are any god damn Napoleon." Before leaving for overseas, Dixon approached Gatley's "warlike red head," thanked him, and told him he would do his best. Gatley bellowed, "What the hell do you think I am sending you over there for?"[6] As Dixon walked away, head in a slump, Gatley, completely out of charac-

George Grant Gatley. "Don't get the idea that you are any god damn Napoleon," the quick-tempered Gatley cautioned young recruits. The "volcanic" General welded a great fighting machine for the campaign in France (WWI).

ter, called after him, "God bless you boy! Take care of yourself."[7]

The highlight of Gatley's career was his promotion to Brigadier General. He left South Carolina on July 9, 1918, to command the 67th Field Artillery Brigade, 42nd (Rainbow) Division, in the Champagne region of France. He remained in command until the war ended the following year. After his passing in 1931, *The Field Artillery Journal* was generous when paying homage to the "holy terror" General George Grant Gatley:

General Gatley died at Letterman Hospital. By his death the Field Artillery has lost an institution. He was known and loved not only throughout the Field Artillery, but throughout the entire Army. He typified the Old Army. Those who have heard his stories and songs will always smile with a surge of pleasant reminiscence as thoughts of him come to mind. From duck shooting in Mindanao, one-armed flute players, Down East sea yarns, and imparting knowledge of the Spanish language to thirsty second lieutenants, he has ever striven to maintain *esprit de corps*. ... This was one side of his nature, for when occasion demanded he could be as inflexible in duty and as decisive in action as any man. His gruff exterior concealed a heart of gold.[8]

(c. 1913) Dorothy Gatley, age 11, promenading the sidewalks of East Orange, N.J., wearing one of her father's military caps.

There would be no book published on George Grant Gatley, although Ann was still promoting the idea while vacationing in Hawaii in the Spring of 1935. She was reported as "having a great time in the islands, visiting the army post and renewing friendships with friends of her late father."[9] No doubt her book would have discouraged many a recruit. "The glamour of army life," Ann once remarked, "makes a pretty tale, if you like fiction. ... I've seen army conditions at too close range."[10] In truth, Dorothy Walton Gatley, born August 7, 1902, in Fort Sam Houston, Texas, had already paid tribute to her father by her own accomplishments as a well-respected and acclaimed actress. She attributed her success to her upbringing and the influence of the very same father that rejected her career. After the General died, Ann consoled herself by wearing his wristwatch. It was an unusually large watch for a woman, but Ann was persistent in wearing it. The watch had gone with him to the Spanish-American War, to the Boxer Rebellion, and the Great War. She explained that it had timed "many a barrage" and had been under fire with her father on innumerable occasions.[11] Shortly after her father's death, Ann's memento ticked away as she detailed the story of her childhood to the *Los Angeles Times* reporter, Myrtle Gebhart. Gebhart, noted for her unvarnished accounts of celebrities, listened, and gave Ann all the credit for a childhood story "all tangled up with riding a horse." Ann's horsemanship was an acknowledged phenomenon on the army posts. At age seven, she begged to tame an incorrigible sorrel named "Sam Lewis." It wasn't long before Ann and Sam were galloping in the train of the cavalry and inspecting the fort with solemn dignity. Who else aside from Ann Harding herself could better detail her early life? So, from 1931, here she is, age 28, speaking in her own words.

When I Was an Army Girl

By Ann Harding

> I was brought up in a field artillery post. Discipline was written into my soul. To this day, every time a director gives me an order on a motion-picture set, my inclination is to salute and say, "Yes, sir! No, sir! Immediately, sir."

Two things I learned almost in the cradle: to obey orders; and never to acknowledge fear.

I could ride a horse almost as soon as I could walk. The memories of my girlhood are tangled up with riding a horse over the edge of a precipice, trying to keep up with the soldiers. Often I was so scared that my heart stopped beating. But there was one thing that frightened me more than the horse and the precipice; that was the fear that I would turn yellow. One of the things that you just are *not* in a field artillery regiment is afraid. It is a good deal the same philosophy of the Indians; you've got to die some time. It doesn't matter so much when you do it as how you do it.

My father was a famous rip-snorting, hard-riding, hard-swearing artilleryman. If I had turned out to be a timid, squealing, fainting type of girl, he probably would have drowned me in a rain barrel like the pups that didn't pan out. I adored him – and so did the rest of the cannoneers. His name was George Grant Gatley.

An Army Cradle Song

I was born at old Fort Sam Houston and the thunder and clank of the guns, the rattle-bang of the caissons and the pound of galloping feet were my cradle song. My playmate in my little-girl days was Rebel E. Goddard. He taught me how to ride and to love horses. He was a civilian, in charge of the remount depot. Taking along a bottle of liniment, we would ride all morning until we were tired and hungry, pick out a prosperous farm and tie up at the barn. Noseying around the stables, Rebel would find a horse with a little something wrong. "Wa-ll, now, friend. I'm downright glad we happened along," he would expand cordially to the farmer. "This here mare, she sure don't look none too chipper. But you won't have to send for a veterinary. I'll fix her up, Buddy." The grateful farmer would invite us in to dinner—fluffy biscuits, fried chicken, cakes that oozed chocolate icing. It worked fine, and it wasn't a fake, either, for Rebel really knew horses and their ailments. Of course, perhaps at times he did exaggerate the malady a trifle! No, they never caught onto us. In fact, all the countryside welcomed us.

My Troop Horse

But, as my mind goes back to those days, it seems to me that all the "human nature" which the machine muffles in the man is to be found in the horses. Sharp anger, the spirit of the frolic, an ingenuous display of affection – oh, I could talk of horses all day! Rebel taught me horsemanship and how to appraise horses shrewdly. I had my pets. Sam Lewis – the name came with him, it wasn't my choice—was a beautiful sorrel. He was practically my handiwork when I got through with him. Because it took five men to saddle him, a notion spread that he was fractious. He couldn't be ridden, they said. That was a challenge to my spunk. Besides, he looked too good to be drawing a buckboard. I made friends with him, always bringing him sugar and apples. He became so fond of me that when he saw me approaching he would stretch out and lower himself, to make it easier for me to mount. He would follow me all around. Once we were ready for a ride when I decided to go over to the Officers' Club, where a tea was in progress. A riding habit is acceptable attire anywhere in daylight hours, so, leaving him unhitched, I walked across and up the eight wide steps and into the building. A moment later I heard an awful clatter behind me. Before I could turn, I felt Sam Lewis's head placed softly on my shoulder. He was trembling, threatening to slip all over that polished oak floor, and whinnying—hurt because I had left him waiting. So, amid cheers and laughter, I mounted—and rode Sam Lewis down those steps very, very proudly. Later, I selected another mount and neglected Sam Lewis. The day of my departure I went all over the post looking for him and finally found him, in harness again. He started running toward me, dragging the lumbering buckboard. And when I reached him he stretched out, straining at his harness, for me to mount! I laid my head on his neck and we both had a grand cry.

An officer knows no home. The Army gives a commutation of quarters, a pittance on which families live, near by. In times of war, like the fracas in the Philippines, the border trouble with Mexico and the world conflict, relatives are excluded from the post. And there seemed to be a lot of war going on while I was growing up! Those nomadic years taught me the value of first impressions, and to make friends quickly. While other little girls were playing with dolls, I was pedaling my tricycle out to reveille and retreat. It was quite a lot of effort, what with keeping my cap on at the right angle and not dropping my wooden sword that one of the boys made for me.

But I had to be there, to see the flag furled at sunset, my corn-colored hair flying in the breeze. My small feet propelled my tricycle energetically in the wake of my father, at maneuvers and reviews. That he paid not the least attention to me, when on duty, was no deterrent. At Fort Sheridan, I grew from the tricycle to a bike. Then we were sent to Cuba, where my father instructed in artillery. I attended a Cuban school, studying geography and history in Spanish, and rode proudly in the parades on fete days.

My father was in command of the Brigade Post at Camp Knox, where recruits were trained. Horses were brought from the remount depot to the polo field … I worked with them, training the four-footed soldiers in canter, wheeling, short-stopping, and other maneuvers of their regimental training. I kept three or four people's horses exercised, rode my own entries in the Kentucky Army Horse Show, rode and raced with the men and loved the paper chases, something like "Hare and Hound." One would scatter papers ahead, with many misleading trails. Returning to camp, he would tie the gunnysack to a tree and the first one to pass under the branch after him got the "brush." The prize would be a riding-crop, spurs, something of the sort. I frequently got the "brush," but I had to work for it. Handicap? Not my army! I had to compete on my own merits.

I bossed and flirted with the twenty bachelor officers of the regiment, proposals being monotonously frequent. They had to stop the cutting-in system at hops for they couldn't get two steps! My sister and I were the only girls, so we were spoiled outrageously. Heart attack? One. I fell head over heels in love with an officer old enough to be my father. Colonel William Rucker. Loving the picturesque old mounted army, he had a violent antipathy toward motorization. I was crazy about him because he scolded me. He would call me a raw recruit, scoff at my riding, always digging into my pride.

I attended my first real hop at fourteen, my father then being on Governor's Island, in New York Harbor. It was an embarkation celebration in honor of the boys bound for the big war. All were gay; no shadow of the tragedy that awaited many of them touched us. Besides, death is a taboo topic in the Army, by tacit understanding seldom mentioned. You are in the Army to fight, not to die. Each thinks he will come back, though his buddy may "go West."

Going on the Stage

General Gatley was unsympathetic toward my thespic ambitions … to flounce around, making puppy-love on a stage before the people, bordered upon disgrace. Unwilling to accept his financial care while harboring notions at variance with his wishes, I set out to make my own way. Respecting always his fine qualities of character, there were times when I longed to be his little girl again. Whatever success I may be able to make as an actress or—later on—as a writer, I shall always be an army girl. In the trials of marriage, motherhood and home management, I have always felt grateful for the discipline I learned when "the battery was changing front."[12]

Ann ended her story here. Seeing life as being akin to an artillery unit, with the line of battle constantly changing position, may have been the very thing that allowed Ann to escape the fate of her mother, Bessie Crabbe Gatley. Ann discovered she did not especially enjoy taking over her mother's responsibilities. She stated, "Mother was ill when I was 16. So I became official hostess at Camp Knox and took precedence over women two or three times my age. I don't think I've ever been so important since! How scared I used to be when questions of what was what in social matters were referred to me! That's the custom in an army post, where the senior hostess is judge and jury in such things ... how dignified I tried to be and how terrified for fear I was wrong!"[13] No, Ann preferred being in the saddle, not behind a stove. "I cooked all summer in a hot kitchen under a tin roof," she recalled. "Colonels' wives were coaling their own old-fashioned stoves. Maneuvers were events, cards and teas diversions of which much must be made. Determined to avoid learning bridge, even if by the cowardly tactics of flight, I spent my days in the saddle."[14] Ann had little to say about her mother, other than "Army wives have a lot to put up with."[15] Her childhood was wrapped around her father, even though they were usually at odds, and he was often away on assignment. When he was around, Dorothy, and her sister Edith, were confused by his lack of affection. Shortly before his death Ann remarked, "The dolls houses and toys he used to make -- he loves to fool about with wood – always for other children. Never for us. *We never had one toy of my father's making.* I didn't believe then that my father loved me. He had some complex that would not permit him to show it."[16]

While the "rip-snorting, hard-swearing" General Gatley was out fighting for "democracy," the Bessie Gatleys of the world stayed home, couldn't vote, and God forbid they have an opinion on anything other than social etiquette. Ditto for any female offspring. Army life was all Bessie had ever known. She was a third-generation army brat. It would take an Ann Harding to break the mold, to escape the "narrow prison cell" of her mother's life.

The irony behind Bessie's story is that a good deal of her childhood was spent on the premises of one of the most notorious federal prisons: Alcatraz (the future residence of gangster-racketeer Al Capone). No wonder Ann saw army life as a sort of incarceration for a woman. Bessie was born February 1, 1876, at the historic Fort Barrancas overlooking Florida's Pensacola Bay. Arriving at San Francisco Bay in 1888, Bessie, age eleven, and her older sister Edith, came to make Alcatraz, an army post and military prison, their home. Their father, George W. Crabbe, Jr., an artillery officer, had been assigned to the island for many years. Captain Crabbe was a stern-looking, second-generation military man. Bessie and Edith's "fellow inmates" on Alcatraz consisted mostly of deserters, who busied themselves working around the 20-acre island. There were also Hopi Native Americans, whose only crime was refusing to allow their children to be sent off to government boarding schools.[17] Bessie made a point to befriend the Hopi inmates. The two sisters entertained themselves, along with a few other children, by hiking along the seawall, playing games, and flying kites on the parade ground where the soldiers drilled. Their small family was sadly diminished during an epidemic of scarlet fever. Edith died, and the blonde, delicate-looking Bessie was heartbroken. Then, as if ensuring her "captivity" in army life, at the age of 16, Bessie fell in love with the young 2nd Lt. George Gatley.

The culmination of this four-year courtship found Bessie at Fort Hamilton, New York, dressed in a white satin wedding gown, wearing a tulle veil, and holding a bouquet of lilies of the valley and white roses. Her husband-to-be, and future war hero, was in full dress uniform, wearing a helmet adorned with long red plumes. The military wedding, performed by Reverend Russell, took place on February 10, 1896, at the picturesque St. John's Chapel. *The New York Times* reported that the event was profusely decorated with the American flag. Fort Hamilton's colors were looped over the altar along with evergreens and white roses. A subsequent reception was held at the home of Captain Crabbe.

Bessie was well aware that her new husband, like her own father, was of the old school. Lt. Gatley believed in the iron heel where his wife was concerned. She was to cower to his every word. However, Bessie and her daughter Edith (born 1898) were to witness a "revolution" instigated by Dorothy, the couple's next child, against the man of the house. "When I disobeyed orders," stated Ann, "I presented myself at the parental court martial of my own volition. To have waited for father to find out about my misdemeanors from a third party would have meant losing caste with the family, and no child wants that. There were times when my spirit chafed against the strict code."[18] Ann chose the valiant fight, faced her father with square shoulders, and, as she put it, "took my medicine no matter how bitter the pill."

"We were exactly alike," she emphasized. "That was the trouble. He was talking from his generation. I was talking from mine. And *never* the twain shall meet."[19]

(Endnotes)

1   *Van Nuys News*, 7/4/33
2   Ann Harding, "When I Was an Army Girl," *Los Angeles Times*, 5/5/31
3   Gladys Hall, "The Hot Spot," *Motion Picture*, December 1930
4   Arthur Lloyd Fletcher, *History of the 113th Field Artillery 30th Division*, The History Committee of 113th F.A., Raleigh, N.C.
5   Arthur Lloyd Fletcher, "Brigadier General George G. Gatley," *History of the 113th Field Artillery – 30th Division*, The History Committee of 113th F.A., Raleigh N.C. c1920 pp 205-206
6   Grant Dixon, "Lights of New York," *Daily News Standard (PA)*, 3/11/31
7   Grant Dixon, "Lights of New York"
8   *The Field Artillery Journal*, March-April 1931, pg 139
9   "Why Ann Came Back," *Kingston Daily Freeman (NY)*, 4/30/35
10   Margaret Reid, "Blond-But Not Light," *Picture Play*, May 1930
11   "Ann's Wrist Watch," *San Antonio Light*, 3/15/31
12   Harding, Ann, "When I Was an Army Girl," *Los Angeles Times*, 5/5/31
13   Alice L. Tildesley, "What the Movie Stars Like to Talk About," *Oakland Tribune*, 9/18/32
14   Ann Harding, "When I Was …"
15   Lee Shippey, "The Lee Side of L.A.," *Los Angeles Times*, 12/14/30
16   Gladys Hall, "The Hot Spot," *Motion Picture*, December 1930
17   Claire Rudolf Murphy, *Children of Alcatraz*, Walker & Co., N.Y. c. 2006, pp 13-18
18   "Army Life of Ann Harding Made Her a 'Good Soldier,'" *Bismarck Tribune*, 8/22/32
19   Gladys Hall, "The Hot Spot"

(c. 1905) Dorothy, age 3, posing for tea. "I just
escaped being an albino," Ann claimed.

2

Complete About Turn

Ann referred to her childhood memories as "kaleidoscopic," a result of the various locations in which they occurred. She and Edith could never recall the exact sequence of places they had lived. Dorothy Gatley's first two years were most definitely spent in her birthplace at Ft. Sam Houston, Texas. The fort, built in 1876, maintained an harmonious relationship with the City of San Antonio. Edith, who was four years older than Dorothy, described her little sister as a "pink cherub" with white curls, a very pink scalp, and dark blue eyes that looked straight through you. Little Dorothy had a grand disposition, despite "an occasional outburst of rage at some imagined grievance, resulting invariably in pulling out diminutive handfuls of the white curls."[1] Edith clearly remembered walking along the Alamo plaza in San Antonio when a photographer rushed out of his studio begging Bessie Gatley for an opportunity to photograph the astonishingly lovely child who was holding her hand. "I will gladly give you any number of poses for the privilege of placing one portrait in my window," he pleaded. Edith said her mother responded rather frigidly, "Thank you, but of course, I could never dream of allowing my child's face to be displayed to the public!"[2]

When Captain Gatley and family were transferred to Ft. Sheridan, Illinois, on Lake Michigan, Dorothy was three. Edith recalled watching her sister, dressed in a dark blue chinchilla coat and leggings, struggling heroically with a snowball twice as big as herself. Dorothy was less enthusiastic when total strangers stopped Bessie to remark on her daughter's unusual white hair. Quickening their steps upon detecting an admiring gleam in approaching eyes was to no avail. There was no escaping the inevitable question, "Where did you get those beautiful curls? May I have one?" Edith claimed that Bessie had coached Ann in memorizing a polite rejoinder. "God gave 'em to me," she sniffed, "but I'd love to give 'em to you if I could."[3] When shopping in Chicago, Dorothy, now nicknamed "Dody," insisted on wearing a white piqué hat, which she persistently pulled down to hide her hair. Years later, Ann would jest at all the fuss made over her appearance, saying, "I just escaped being an albino. If my coloring had been just a little whiter and my eyes pink, I would have been in a circus instead of on the stage and screen."[4]

In 1907, Gatley was transferred back to San Antonio. Even with his advancement in rank, the family never had quite enough funds for a home or good clothes. "We had to skimp through," Ann admitted.[5] By the age of five, Dody excelled in tree-climbing. "Whenever I think of her as a child," recalled Edith, "the first picture that comes to me is that of a little figure swaying in the top of a tree, utterly content with her own quiet company."[6] Ann also remembered a weakness for climbing trees in the rain. She would prop herself, under an umbrella, amid the branches "to write reams of short stories."[7]

The family's real adventure began when they sailed to Cuba in

1909 to join Captain Gatley at Camp Columbia, an army post outside of Havana. He had been sent to the island to instruct the Cuban Army's field artillery. The two little blonde *Americanas* attracted much attention. And Dorothy, having observed her father in action, took complete charge of the situation. Wearing her father's military cap, and carrying a wooden sword one of the troops had made her, she "ripped out orders in fluent Spanish to a serious dark little squad of soldiers." "General Dody" was the acknowledged leader. Edith noted that Dorothy "reached the point where she spoke their language better than they, with ten times the force, and full accompaniment of Latin gesture."[8] When Ann returned to Cuba for a visit in 1931 (during the filming of *Prestige*), she commented that the surroundings were "scenes of some of my happiest childhood days."[9]

When her parents became concerned about their daughters' formal education, Dorothy "retired" as squad leader. By age nine, she had attended close to a dozen schools. It was decided that Bessie and the girls would leave the recently promoted *Major* Gatley, in September 1911. They embarked from Havana on the *SS Alleghany* for New York, where they temporarily made home with Bessie's mother, Elizabeth. (Her father, Captain Crabbe, had passed away while staying with them at Ft. Sheridan in the spring of 1907.) As Spanish had become Dorothy's easiest language, it took her awhile to assimilate. She insisted on calling her new home *Nueva* York. Visits with her father, now stationed at Fort Dix, were intermittent. "Each vacation," noted Ann, "we visited our father – at a different army post. Each time, he had stepped up a rung: Lieutenant-Colonel, Colonel, finally a Brigadier-General."[10]

Shortly before the outbreak of the World War (1914), Bessie,

Edith and Dorothy moved to the lovely, yet prosaic town of East Orange, New Jersey. Dorothy had the opportunity to attend the Baldwin School at Bryn Mawr in nearby Pennsylvania, where she elected to study languages, music and history. It was at Baldwin she had her first taste of "theatre." Mrs. Otis Skinner, wife of the noted Shakespearean actor, decided that the all-girls school should tackle the Bard's *Macbeth.* Dorothy was originally cast in a minor role as Ross. Skinner's daughter, Cornelia, who would also become a well-known writer and actress, played Lady Macbeth. "I had bands on my teeth," recalled Cornelia, "but, had the confidence of a Bernhardt. Our MacDuff was none other than Ann Harding whose blonde hair was hidden by a fearsome horned helmet and whose cherubic face emerged from a thicket of Scottish beard."[11] Indeed, two days before the production, the girl cast as MacDuff, who Ann referred to as a "big husky hockey player," contracted the measles. Dorothy's extraordinary talent for memorization landed her the role. "Mother and I arrived at the school shortly before the curtain was to go up," recalled Edith. "Our first sight of [Dorothy] was rather terrifying: heavy makeup, ferocious eyebrows and mustache, armor breastplate, enormous boots and clanking sword –and in one mailed fist, a tube of white Vaseline which she was swallowing as fast as possible. 'Lost my voice,' she croaked, 'trying to talk like a man. But I think I'll get it back in an hour if I can only swallow this stuff.' Sure enough, the well-oiled vocal chords responded to the heroic treatment and she got through the evening nobly."[12] Ann suspected the resonant quality of her voice may have been a result of this experience.[13]

Dorothy was disappointed when, for financial reasons, she had to continue her education at East Orange High. She was a quick study,

however, and finished her homework early, which gave her time to
see movies, or practice the piano
in the afternoons. Dorothy easily doubled up her schoolwork,
and she was able to complete the
last two years of her education in
just one. At school, she had the
reputation of a bookworm, a very
fussy one. One of her instructors
reprimanded Dorothy for poring
over a hidden book (*Ben-Hur*) in
lieu of listening the teacher's reading of *Les Miserables*. She told the
teacher she couldn't stand the Victor Hugo novel. She found it sordid and depressing. Outraged by the
teacher's rebuke, Dorothy marched
out of the classroom and into the prin-

(c.1916) Baldwin School.
Ann as MacDuff in Shakespeare's
Macbeth. She lost her voice
trying to "talk like a man."

cipal's office, and demanded justice. "She explained to him that *Les Miserables* gave her nightmares."[14] The principal listened to the very proper,
ethereal-looking young lady, and was sympathetic. He let her have her
way. Edith thought Dorothy a bit too proper, too "highbrow," and not
much fun at a party. This didn't faze Dorothy in the least. She fancied
herself becoming something laudable - a writer, not a party girl. It was
this ambition for which the name "Ann Harding" first reared its silvery-
blonde head. "At the age of 10, I decided that some day I would change

my parental cognomen," stated Ann,[15] "… a *nom de plume.* I wanted a short, first name, but musical. So, I picked Ann without the 'e.' For my last name, I borrowed that from my piano teacher – it was before Warren G. Harding made it famous."[16] Dorothy fancied the name would look good on book covers. After arriving in Hollywood, Ann's ambition as an author lingered. "There never has been a time when I haven't wanted to write," Ann explained. "As a child I used to think continually of story plots … I never had the courage to show them to anyone, so they usually found a grave in the fireplace. I loved to study faces on street cars, making up stories as to the past of each one. I am quite sure that if acting hadn't claimed me, I would be writing novels now."[17]

Ann also harbored ambitions for acting. She announced her intention of trying for the lead in the senior play at East Orange High. Garrett Fort, the play's author, thought Dorothy all wrong for the part of a languorous vamp, and begged her not to try out. "You know the faculty will give it to you," he exploded. "You're teacher's pet around here – but, doggone it – you'll ruin my play. This is a *vamp* part – do you realize that? Lord knows *you* haven't any 'jazz' in your elbows – it'll be a complete flop."[18] Dorothy agreed she was a wallflower, but took the part anyway. The night of the performance found Garrett slumped in a corner and feeling rather dismal. During rehearsals Dorothy fulfilled his worst fears, acting the proper young lady in every scene. When the curtain rose, Garrett sat up with a jerk. Dorothy sported a purple chiffon gown and, according to her sister, "the only marcel wave she was ever known to inflict upon her hair." She gave a bewitching portrayal based on one of the super-sirens of the screen. "Dody had been a devotee of the movies since grammar school days," recalled Edith. "She glided through the part with sinuous undulation of hip, half-closed, heavy-lidded eyes, and parted lips. The audience, unaccustomed as it was to anything like this coming from the senior class, stamped and cheered and howled ... [she] brought the audience right out of their seats."[19] Years later, Ann divulged that Garrett's play was a direct steal from two of the current Broadway hits, that she had little notion of sex and simply mimicked Theda Bara. "I'm afraid it was almost an indecent performance!" chuckled Ann. "Picture me innocently giving all the gestures of a love-tossed lady." By 1930, Garrett Fort would develop the unusual ability of blending the sinister with unexpected humor. He created some of the best remembered lines in classic horror films: "I never drink – *wine*," Count Dracula from Tod Browning's *Dracula* (1931); "Look, it's moving! It's alive, it's alive, it's alive!" Dr. Frankenstein, from James Whale's *Frankenstein* (1931).

Until her debut as a vamp, the only boy at school who had paid Dorothy any attention was the captain of the football team. She was content with what she referred to as "quality" rather than "quantity." Besides, the captain showed no interest in such mundane activities as petting. That suited Dorothy just fine. However, after Garrett's play, things changed. "When I stepped off the stage," recalled Ann, "I was met by all the social boys of the school. They had never given me a tumble before, so I waited until I got a bid to every fraternity dance. Then turned them all down. I'd proved that I could be a vamp! But I stuck to my own likes and dislikes, and soon had plenty of proposals of marriage. The boys would start weeping on my shoulder about their troubles with other girls, and end up by wanting to marry me! The kind of attention a vamp gets isn't the kind I, at least, wanted."[20]

After the World War ended, General Gatley, Bessie and Dorothy re-located to an army training school at Camp Knox, just south of Louisville, in Kentucky. Gatley was completely ignorant of his daughter's theatrical ventures. Approaching her seventeenth birthday, Dorothy was designated "Daughter of the Regiment." A great ball was given in her honor, and she was suddenly surrounded by 500 student officers. "I didn't lose my head," remembered Ann, "It was a great place to be the general's daughter, but if one married a second lieutenant she ceased to be the general's daughter socially. She took her husband's rank and got snubbed by the wife of a captain, who never liked her, anyway." It was during this time that Ann took over her mother's responsibilities, and was faced with such prestigious personalities as General John J. Pershing, the highest-ranking officer in the United States Army. "At Camp Knox," recalled Ann, "I entertained General Pershing, then on an inspection tour. As the senior hostess, by rank … I wouldn't let them see I was flustered. There was no time for proper preparations. I had been out on the polo field all morning. Only coarse china was available, even for officers' mess. 'But aren't we all in the Army?' I reasoned. 'He'll take pot luck and like it.' I served him a polo tea from the rolling kitchen. So tall and soldierly he looked, towering there above me; he was charmingly appreciative."[21] It was a poignant meeting. Pershing had lost his own three daughters shortly before the war. A fire at San Francisco's Presidio not only claimed their lives, but that of his wife. Those who knew him said he never really recovered from their deaths.

Ann's personal favorite was Major General Pelot Summerall, who had carried her around on his shoulder when she was a toddler. Ann described him as "a most human man, with many sentiments."[22] She had no doubt been dazzled by Summerall, "who liked to turn out in prewar dress uniform with copious medals, gilded sashes, and fringed epaulettes–suggesting a viceroy of India rather than a plain American officer."[23] Contrary to Ann's youthful impressions, military journalist Joseph E. Persico describes Summerall as "a severe, unsmiling, some said brutal man."[24] A contemporary of General Gatley, and Pershing, Summerall showed extraordinary heroism while serving on the front line in France during the Great War. But, to his *dis*credit, knowing that Armistice was only hours away, he took vainglorious action and ordered his men into battle for an area they could have walked freely upon the next day. The cost: thousands of casualties and several hundred deaths. Lives needlessly wasted … and, a Distinguished Service Cross for Summerall. Pershing influenced Summerall's clouded thinking, finding the idea of Armistice repugnant. He stated, "There can be no conclusion to this war until Germany is brought to her knees."[25] "Pershing," writes Persico, "saw his army akin to a fighter ready to deliver the knock-out punch who is told to quit with his opponent reeling but still standing."[26] With or without Pershing's "knock-out punch," Hitler and his party used the humiliation of defeat as reason to rebuild Germany.

During their time in Kentucky, Edith noticed a "seething restlessness" take hold of her sister. Thankfully, Rebel E. Goddard came into Dorothy's life at a crucial moment, and deepened her passion for horses. Riding helped assuage pent-up emotions, and pulled Dorothy back into her body with elemental force. She became grounded in the subtle communication and response – the thin veil between a rider and her horse. Goddard was superintendent of the Remount Depot (35,000 horses) at Camp Knox. When the nationally-known horseman was asked years later about his young blonde protégée, Rebel turned ecstatic, declaring, "Ann Harding was the sweetest angel who'd ever lived!"[27] When Rebel wasn't available, Edith and Dorothy ordered their horses for 8:30am, and ventured into the surrounding countryside. "This put us in great form for the Kentucky-Army horse show on the historic Churchill Downs track," said Edith. "In spite of the fact that we rode army nags, we both managed to capture ribbons."[28] Ann later recalled, "The biggest thrill was [taking] a horse over a jump without 'pulling leather.' I had been going over three and four-bar jumps for some time, but always grabbing the saddle when the leap came. But I was to take part in a horse show in Louisville … and pulling leather was just not done. So, scared to death, I rode out determined not to clutch for a saddle-horn if I could help it. And I didn't."[29]

The months flew by. Gatley finished his job at Camp Knox and was transferred to Washington, DC. The area was overrun with post-war activity. Gatley ordered Bessie to take the girls anywhere but there. So, they ventured back to New York, where Dorothy found her first real taste of independence. They located an overpriced flat in uptown Manhattan. "We went to a boarding-house," Ann recalled. "A horrible, red plush boarding-house. There was nothing to do there but sit on a red plush couch. I couldn't stand it."[30] Whenever possible, Dorothy and Edith escaped their dismal surroundings to explore the biggest city of them all. When Edith took a job as secretary in a brokerage office, Colonel Gatley stormed and fumed. By the time Dorothy secured a position at Metropolitan Life Insurance Co. ($12.50 a week, in the welfare division), he had simmered down.

Completely unaware of her next "dramatic" step, Dorothy trained herself to enunciate perfectly into the Dictaphone. She modulated her voice and accented the important syllables unobtrusively, so that whatever she relayed to typists could not be misconstrued. The clarity and timbre of her speech was unique. Before long she was demonstrating the proper use of the machine to company executives. According to Ann, most of her time was spent creating "little pamphlets about what to do when the baby has whooping cough."[31] "The typists told me that my voice registered better than anyone else's in the office," said Ann. "And that's when I began to think about going on the stage."[32] Dorothy also made extra money as a reader for Famous Players-Lasky (parent company of Paramount Pictures). She envisioned herself as a scenarist, visited the Long Island studio, and located the office of Harry Durant, a scenario editor. He thought she was a motion picture aspirant. "So you want to get into pictures?" Durant inquired. "Not at all," replied Ann. "I want it understood that I am not a silly girl looking for a chance on the screen. What I am here for is to get work in your reading department."[33] Taken completely aback, Durant automatically handed her four books to report on. After that, she took whatever books, plays, and original scenarios Durant handed her. She typed synopses and critiques from what she had read, and delivered them the next morning before reporting to the insurance office. "I would be a second Lois Weber," declared Ann. "I would revolutionize the business."[34] Weber, who tackled such daring subjects as birth control and capital punishment, was a prolific screenwriter, and the first woman to direct a feature-length film, *Merchant of Venice* (1914).

After three months of this routine, Bessie and Edith noted a distinct change in Dorothy. "For several days mother and I noticed that she was coming and going with a most detached air," remembered Edith. "She scarcely touched her food – lapsed into great silences – something was certainly brewing."[35] Erupting, to be exact. Dorothy had found the tedious monotony of taking subways from office to office not nearly as satisfying and grounding as riding horseback. She felt disconnected. She needed an alternative that would get into her blood. "I had to have adventure!" Ann later explained. She was restless, and eager to toss what she called the "special set of blinders" that had been instilled in her since birth.

> I read the newspaper ads. And I found one which said, "Inexperienced Girl Wanted." "An inexperienced girl" fitted me better than my one pair of gloves. The ad directed me to the Provincetown Theater in– Heavens above!—*Greenwich Village.* Undoubtedly I would meet up with Jack the Ripper, the Poisoned Needle and be a Fallen woman, whatever that might mean. I didn't know. I was full of muzzy names and labels. I didn't know a Fact. Not one Fact of Life. I had that perfect "innocence" that hides the ugly face of Ignorance. Still, I had heard that the Provincetown Players were "college people." That sounded sort of *safe.* Another point of comfort … they were known to be "amateurs." The first time I took a girlfriend of mine with me. I got to the door—and fled. We went uptown and were reckless enough to see "The Tavern." Which was the third play I had ever seen in my life. But I had to have that "Adventure." Jack the Ripper was preferable to being shoved about by another subway guard. The probable portals of the Inferno looked rosy compared to that red plush boarding house.[36]

Upon her return to Provincetown Players, Ann was met at the door by the play's author, Susan Glaspell. Ann thought Glaspell the image of a Dresden China Shepherdess. "As dainty and exquisite a woman as breathes," Ann declared. "With all the dignity, the refinement, the savoir faire I would expect from a colonel's wife."[37] After a kindly greeting, Glaspell, along with the director, Jasper Deeter, thought Ann might do a bit part in *Inheritors*. "It seemed they were in great need of a giggling girl," said Ann. "I had been feeling very dramatic. I went hoping they would maybe let me carry a spear. But I thought, 'Well, if *that's* the impression I give, I'll be a good sport and go through with it.'"[38] When they asked her name, she blurted out "Ann Harding" – her childhood *nom de plume*. Glaspell and Deeter asked her to come back the next day, and arrive before the other cast members. She did. Deeter talked to her for about a half an hour, while peering at her under his enormous eyebrows. Suddenly his face lit up. "Why, you can pay attention!" he smiled. "You can listen when you're being talked to! Read the last act of this play and in an hour or so we'll see what you can do with *Madeline*." During her reading, Ann was so moved by the dialogue, she found herself weeping at the finish. "I decided then that I was either a darn fool, or an actress," Ann stated.[39] She was offered the role. "Adventure" had arrived! Deeter discerned great promise in Ann – raw material, sprung from nowhere, that could be molded. Ann said she felt like "unspoiled clay" in Deeter's hands. She was fired with enthusiasm. Edith remembered her sister arriving home, and in more or less of a whisper, announcing, "I am going on the stage—I have a part and start rehearsal tomorrow."

"Mother and I were tremendously proud and excited," said Edith of Ann's bombshell, "but one word came simultaneously from three mouths: 'Father!'"[40]

Ann informed her mother that she would be moving to a chaperoned "girls club" near the theatre, maintained for aspirants who made less than $25 a week. She was preparing herself for General Gatley's outrage. As Ann pointed out, "My parents reared me with the idea that actors were not the sort of people one met socially."[41] Ann surmised, "I figured that, since I had gone against his will, I could not live under the roof, nor eat the bread his money was paying for."[42] During the first two weeks of rehearsals, Ann kept her day job and home-reader position with Famous Players. "But that couldn't last," Ann recalled, "so I kept the home reading and gave up the insurance."[43]

Provincetown Players began in 1915. A small group of writers and artists, mostly from Greenwich Village, decided to stage plays on the wharf while vacationing in Provincetown, Massachusetts. Susan Glaspell, already a recognized author, was one of the founding members. She arranged the first reading of a Eugene O'Neill play at Provincetown. Other notable participants were Edna St. Vincent Millay and Theodore Dreiser. These summer theatricals were transferred to New York in the fall of 1916. As a catalyst in the Little Theatre movement, the group provided a vital experimental venue. Political themes included everything from the plight of lower- and middle-class Americans, to anti-war plays demonstrating that America's moral rhetoric was really a cover for self-interest. There were also expressionist and surrealist presentations. Provincetown Players provided opportunities for black actors, and women were encouraged in both artistic and managerial positions. By the time Ann took on her role, the group had relocated to a permanent home at 139 Macdougal Street. The building had previously been an old stable and bottling plant. In November 1920, prior to *Inheritors*, the theatre had its first bona fide "hit," Eugene O'Neill's *Emperor Jones*. The number of subscribers soared. Audiences were responding to Provincetown Players' distinctly American voice.

Ann's debut as Madeline opened March 21, 1921. Critics were impressed with the play and especially her performance. *Inheritors* was extended for another two weeks. As a result of Ann's singularly earnest and sincere performance, she received calls for interviews from five producers: John Cromwell, Brock Pemberton, Dave Burton, Daniel Frohman and Adolph Klauber. Even though Provincetown Players was far, far from Broadway, producers kept an eagle-eye on new plays and performers coming out of Greenwich Village. Ann's first interview was with Dave Burton, who would later stage Broadway's *The Royal Family*. During the course of their conversation, Ann's old "bugaboo" reappeared. Bur-

(c. 1921) Ann, the girl with "corn-colored hair," felt like "unspoiled clay" in the hands of director Jasper Deeter.

ton kept staring at, what she referred to as, her "funny hair." It appeared that Burton was more impressed with it than her acting. While listening to him rave, Ann rose up from her chair, squared her shoulders and made a characteristic speech: "Mr. Burton, if it were possible to cut off my hair and present it to you on a silver platter, I would be very happy to do so, since that is apparently all you want of me as an actress."[44] She then walked directly to the door, and left Burton with his jaw agape. Ann felt the same way about producer Daniel Frohman. She later recalled, "I cut off a strand and sent it to Frohman with a note … that it was hair, not me, which seemed to be what he wanted."[45]

Ann's own perspective of her momentous transition into theater was interesting. "I never started out in life to be an actress," she emphasized. "My break with my environment did not come from being stage-struck. It was almost impossible that it should. I had never heard theater discussed. I had seen only three plays in my life. I had always been taught that actresses—well, my *dear* …voices dropped to a whisper when the dangerous topic reared its hydra-head. I simply wanted to be *free*. I wanted to be independent. I wanted to assert my Self. The Self that was in awful danger of being trampled out and extinguished. That the 'Inexperienced Girl Wanted' happened to be the Provincetown Theater was the merest toss of the dice. Or call it Fate."[46] The courage and truth Ann had learned as an army girl suddenly came to the fore. After accepting an offer from Adolph Klauber, and signing a contract at a hundred dollars a week, she finally decided it was time to write a letter to her father.

(Endnotes)

1   Edith Gatley Nash, "My Sister, Ann Harding," *Photoplay*, March 1933
2   Edith Gatley Nash, "My Sister …"

3   Edith Gatley Nash, "My Sister …"
4   Edith Dietz, "She's Through with Suffering," *Oakland Tribune*, 2/23/36
5   Lee Shippey, "Lee Side …"
6   Edith Gatley Nash, "My Sister …"
7   Alma Whitaker, "Luck Pursues Ann Harding," *Los Angeles Times*, 8/25/29
8   Edith Gatley Nash, "My Sister …"
9   "Ann Harding Sails On Cobb Today When Plane Doesn't Come," *Key West Citizen*, 12/11/31
10   Ann Harding, "When I Was An Army Girl"
11   Cornelia Otis Skinner, "Well, Here I Am!" *Los Angeles Times*, 5/7/39
12   Edith Gatley Nash, "My Sister …"
13   Gene Ringgold, "Ann Harding," *Films in Review*, March 1972
14   Harrison Carroll, "Ann Harding is Annoyed," *Los Angeles Evening Herald*, 9/12/31
15   "Ann Harding Changed Names And Wanted To Become An Author," *Capital News (MI)*, 8/23/31
16   Tex McCrary and Jinx Falkenburg, "New York Close –Up," *Oakland Tribune*, 11/1/49
17   "Ann Harding Changed …"
18   Edith Gatley Nash, "My Sister, Ann Harding"
19   Edith Gatley Nash, "My Sister, Ann Harding"
20   Ben Maddox, "Discovering Hollywood's Real Sophisticate—Ann Harding!" *Screenland*, November 1931
21   Ann Harding, "When I Was an Army Girl"
22   Ann Harding, "When I Was an Army Girl"
23   Joseph E. Persico, "World War I: Wasted Lives on Armistice Day," *MHQ: The Quarterly Journal of Military History*, Winter 2005
24   Joseph E. Persico, "World War I …"
25   Joseph E. Persico, "World War I …"
26   Joseph E. Persico, "World War I …"
27   Faeylyn Wylder, "Rebel Goddard," www.rootsweb.com c. 2006
28   Edith Gatley Nash, "My Sister …"
29   Louis Sobol, "Down Memory Lane with Ann Harding," New York paper dated 1/20/34, Hedgerow Theater Collection, UC Berkeley, Bancroft Library
30   Gladys Hall, "The Hot Spot," *Motion Picture*, December 1930
31   Alma Whitaker, "Luck Pursues Ann Harding"
32   Louis Sobol, "Down Memory Lane With Ann Harding," New York paper dated 1/20/1934, Hedgerow Theatre Collection, UC Berkeley, Bancroft Library
33   Margaret Reid, "Blond-but Not Light," *Picture Play*, May 1930
34   Gladys Hall, "The Hot Spot"
35   Edith Gatley Nash, "My Sister …"
36   Gladys Hall, "The Hot Spot"
37   Winifred Aydelotte, "Character," *Los Angeles Record*, 9/12/31
38   Gladys Hall, "The Hot Spot"
39   Margaret Reid, "Blond- But Not Light," *Picture Play*, May 1930
40   Edith Gatley Nash, "My Sister, Ann Harding"
41   Lee Shippey, "Lee Side of L.A.," *Los Angeles Times*, 12/14/30
42   Gladys Hall, "The Hot Spot"
43   Ruth Biery, "Sisters Under Their Biographies," circa 1929, in Hedgerow Theatre Collection at UC Berkeley, Bancroft Library
44   Edith Gatley Nash, "My Sister, Ann Harding"
45   Ruch Biery, "Sisters Under Their Biographies," circa 1929, Hedgerow Theatre Collection at UC Berkeley, Bancroft Library
46   Gladys Hall, "The Hot Spot" – "I went hoping maybe they would let me carry a spear" – from an interview by Muriel Babcock, "Ann Harding Likes Films," *Los Angeles Times*, 12/01/29

Ann's triumphant return to the New York stage in *Tarnish* (1923).

3

"The Straight and Inevitable Road to Hell"

After her four-weekend run in *Inheritors* Ann was eager to undertake a new role. Faced with multiple offers, she asked Deeter's opinion. "It's time for you to start making your own decisions," he said, "and mistakes."[1] Deeter's advice to the eighteen-year-old was a reflection of his own personal experience. Born in Mechanicsburg, Pennsylvania, in 1893, Jasper Deeter didn't exactly fit into a family of achievers. Expelled from Dickinson College, he took a stab at writing obituaries for the Harrisburg, Pennsylvania, *Patriot*. For starters, Deeter followed up his obit on a prominent judge by visiting the widow's home where he intended to inquire about his honor's memorial service. The *judge* answered the door. Deeter took a further nosedive as a newshound at the City News Bureau where his "inventive" reporting resulted in a libel suit against the Bureau, from a patent medicine company. The outcome for the Bureau looked rather grim until the owner of the firm died during trial. Deeter's sardonic news update stated, "We permit it to be known that he died in court from the shock of listening to his own lies."[2] Off the record, Deeter admitted the man died at home from pneumonia, but he just couldn't resist a clever barb.

After seeing actor James O'Neill as *The Count of Monte Cristo* on stage, Deeter turned to acting. A brief stint (he was fired) in Charles Coburn's 1918 stage hit, *The Better Ole*, was followed by a connection that stuck. That same year, he became fast friends with James O'Neill's son, Eugene, who was involved with Provincetown Players. Deeter took the lead in O'Neill's "lost" play *Exorcism* (1920). He later played the role of Smithers in O'Neill's *Emperor Jones*, which he also helped stage. Deeter convinced O'Neill to cast a black actor in the lead, and forego the tradition of casting a white actor in blackface. The breakthrough production outgrew Greenwich Village, and went "uptown" to Broadway. O'Neill's fame skyrocketed, and the disgruntled Deeter contemplated leaving New York. "If they'd kept [*Emperor Jones*] in repertory, as they always said they wanted to do," fumed Deeter, "they could have kept it going two nights a week for the rest of their lives. They got Broadway-Crazy and that was the beginning of the end for the Provincetown."[3] After *Inheritors*, the obstinate Deeter went on tour in *Emperor Jones* only to be fired in Baltimore. His frustration finally found release. He volunteered to bang iron pipes with a crowbar in the cellar of Provincetown Theatre, thus simulating engine-room noises for O'Neill's *The Hairy Ape*. Scene designer Max Gorelik, whose diary pictured O'Neill as a tall, slight, timid figure, was in awe, yet wary of Deeter. "Jasper is amazing," wrote Gorelik, "He is an extraordinary combination of brains, imagination, and self assurance. This assurance springs partly from a certain viciousness apparent in his small eyes. In short, he is a real leader, the most baffling and dangerous man I have ever come across."[4] Eventually, Deeter's love-hate contest with Provincetown was the catalyst that propelled him to create something completely unique: Hedgerow.

Ann was focused on establishing her independence as an actress. After signing with producer Adolph Klauber for a morality play titled *Like a King,* she wrote what she knew would be a farewell letter to her father. Ann stated simply that she had become an actress. She may just as well have told him she had adopted the "oldest profession in the world." His response began, "You have chosen the straight and inevitable road to Hell." Gatley asked her if she had no self-respect. And, what about *him?* Had she not considered that his daughter's "painted face would be on exhibition for the harlots and the perverts to jape at"?[5] Ann defended her position, and indicated that her "self-respect" was a matter of being "a producer and not a consumer of bread that was begrudged her." "It is too bad," she replied, "that you have never had a daughter and that I – have never had a father."[6] A curtain of silence fell between them. Her name was not to be spoken in Gatley's presence. Dorothy Walton Gatley no longer existed.

Ann received ample reinforcement from the variety of personalities and numerous world views that now surrounded her. "The army mind differs in its very basic forces and motivations from the civilian," said Ann. "No conversational dexterity, no verbal pondering of the many fascinating sides of human nature … they don't waste even small talk! Speech is materialistic and objective – about the job to be done. I never discovered the charm of conversation until I went to Greenwich Village to learn the rudiments of this colorful world of the arts."[7] Wherever she turned, Ann was propelled forward on her new path.

Ann's journey took an unexpected turn which proved to be a godsend. In April 1921, after a successful tryout of *Like a King* in Trenton, New Jersey, Ann had time on her hands, and no money in her pocket. *Like a King* would wait for its scheduled Broadway opening that fall.

She opted for some invaluable experience with a Buffalo stock company run by Jessie Bonstelle. At first, Ann had balked at Bonstelle's $25-a-week offer, and turned it down. After all, Klauber would be giving her $100-a-week. She was encouraged by a girlfriend, who was doing publicity work for Bonstelle, to change her mind. According to sister Edith, Ann insisted that Bonstelle, "cover up her hair and find out whether or not she could act." "The request was fulfilled with a vengeance," said Edith.[8] Ann's first assignment was that of a black maid. "Miss Bonstelle made me marvelously happy," Ann would recall. "I'd have to wear a black wig, and *that* meant that I was being given a part because I was an *actress,* and not because of my hair."[9] Ann made her own costumes, often going without sufficient food to buy fabric. The sacrifices paid off. It was under Bonstelle that Ann learned the ABC's of her trade, and the importance of taking on "fifth business" parts. Miss Bonstelle, a respected stage manager and actress, boosted the career of Katharine Cornell, and was an early influence upon William Powell, Melvyn Douglas and Frank Morgan – actors who would eventually co-star with Ann on screen.

In the fall, Ann returned to New York City for the October opening of *Like a King* at the 39th Street Theatre. She found lodging in a theatrical boarding house on West 88th Street. Fellow thespian Monroe Owsley, a fellow tenant who was studying at Columbia, encouraged Ann's pursuit of the stage. He was her frequent escort about town. Years later the pair would co-star as brother and sister in the film *Holiday* (1930). Since the out-of-town success of *Like a King* held so much promise, it came as a shock when, panned by critics, it failed to impress on Broadway. The madcap play, by John Hunter Booth, lasted 16 performances. Ann played the part of Phyllis Weston, the sweetheart of James Gleason, who returns home penniless from the "big city." Gleason gives the impression he is really a great success and has returned to modernize the sleepy old town and make it "snappy." *New York Times* critic Alexander Woollcott found the story "a shameless and stereotyped assault on your sensibilities," but felt the actors excelled in achieving "a good deal of innocent merriment." Woollcott noted the "uncommon skill and adroitness of comedian James Gleason," and that producer Klauber "has done well in selecting the comely and interesting Ann Harding ... who has indisputable credentials for the stage."[10] The *New York Herald* was compelled to critique Ann's "golden hair banded like sibyl about her head."[11]

Before Ann could register disappointment at the play's sudden demise, she accepted a secondary role in *The Lonely Heart*. Initially, she had her doubts about the part, which required her to scream and be hopelessly in love. "I'm sorry, but I can't scream," she told the director. "I'm not the screaming type, and I wouldn't know how to produce a scream. Besides, this girl is madly in love. I've never been in love, and I couldn't project something I know nothing about."[12] Still, the director had faith in her. Edward Sheldon's play, originally written for John Barrymore in 1914, had never been produced. In 1916, at age 29, Sheldon, whose acclaimed plays had a sincere sense of social justice, was assaulted by a crippling disease that would eventually take his sight and leave him paralyzed from the neck down. In November 1921, rehearsals were underway for *The Lonely Heart* with Basil Sydney in the lead. Sadly, the production folded after one week. Ann referred to *The Lonely Heart* as "a very beautiful play ... which closed in Baltimore without being given a real chance."[13] She still considered herself to be, in her words, "an appallingly bad actress."[14] Much to her surprise, Ann was then offered a starring role. After glancing through the play, Ann promptly handed it back to the producer. The complexity of the character she was to portray overwhelmed her. "I'm afraid I'm not ready to carry eighty-five sides of anything so that it would be interesting," she said.[15] He found her attitude incomprehensible, but Ann knew her limitations. Jasper Deeter had instilled in her the idea that "greatness" as an actor could never be attained through mimicry. Ann needed more experience. She made a sensible move and returned to stock.

For the winter season of 1922, Ann headed to Bonstelle's company in Providence, Rhode Island. Ben Lyon, a juvenile lead, was on board. He was featured with Ann, the company's newly appointed ingénue. Lyon was quite a cut-up. Once, after a haranguing from Bonstelle, the irrepressible Lyon took the middle-aged and very proper Bonstelle over his knee and paddled her! "She should not only have fired me," remembered Lyon, "she should have had me arrested."[16] Bonstelle, fortunately, was a good sport. Ten years after the fact, in 1931, Lyon was asked to interview Ann about their early stage experiences together. Ann conspired inwardly to embarrass Ben on this occasion. Without a clue to her intent, Lyon drove to her mountain-top home, feeling rather carefree, and putting aside the fact that Ann was a no-nonsense kind of gal. "Well, Ann," he began, "it has been ten years since we were so bright and hopeful, back in Miss Bonstelle's stock company in Providence. You were an ingénue and I was a juvenile." Shaking her head, Ann interrupted, "Bennie, *that's* no way to start an interview … it makes us look like a couple of doddering old people … like a reference to something that happened in ancient Egypt, or positively no later than the Civil War. And, Bennie, even if I have graduated into playing great ladies, *you* are still a juvenile. You'll always be just a mischievous boy."[17] Lyon watched Ann puff her cigarette, and smile. Looking into her pale blue eyes, he felt absolutely stumped, as if he hadn't grown mentally since he was five. "I was tempted to slay her," wrote Lyon, "and bury her somewhere in her mountain."[18] Ann broke the ice with a titter, "Do you remember how we all were supposed to make speeches at the end of the season in Providence, and how you made yours first, and what a hand the audience gave you? Bennie, have you ever forgiven me for the mean trick I played on you?" Lyon winced at the painful memory of Ann, the *next* speaker, telling the gaping audience that she had prepared a speech that she would not deliver. "Mr. Lyon," she had said rather indignantly, "had an adjoining dressing room. The partitions were very thin. I rehearsed my speech aloud, not dreaming that Mr. Lyon, *a gentleman*, would hold his ear against the wall. What I am trying to convey to you, friends, is that you have already heard *my speech*."[19]

The antics of 19-year-old Ann Harding had come to the fore once again. Embarrassed, Lyon desperately tried to shift gears. While with Bonstelle, he and Ann had shared their dreams of success, and helped each other with their lines. Lyon had been impressed with Ann's skill in creating costumes. "You made lovely things," he remembered. "You always looked stunning." Lyon looked very sweetly at her and confessed, "You look as lovely as ever."[20] Ann was having none of this. Interrupting him again, she replied rather gravely, "You tell me that I'm lovely, but do you realize, that in all the time we worked together back east you never once tried to make love to me."[21] Ann looked at him like a woman scorned. "Why, Ann," Lyon reasoned. "I was always, in a way, afraid of you. I still am. Other fellows were too. You were always a little queen. Everyone always felt there was something downright noble about you. You commanded respect. You wore your hair wrapped around your head and the college boys were all mad about you. You knocked 'em over. There wasn't an actor in the company who didn't love you, who didn't adore you, but you were so intelligent ... well, I guess we were afraid that if we'd ever said, 'Ann, I love you,' you'd have laughed and we'd have crept away and kicked ourselves. Don't you understand?"[22] "No, I don't at all," Ann laughed, "and I think the truth was that I was too plain for you. You said that I was so noble that I frightened men. Now, would a noblewoman knock college boys over – even figuratively? But I have to hand it to you, Ben, you *are* chivalrous. Your explanation is a gem."[23] The embarrassed Lyon momentarily, on paper, gave up on the interview. He focused on his own impressions of his formidable, former leading lady, stating:

> Ann Harding is a remarkable person. She has a direct mind. She detests fuzzy-edged thinking. She tries to simplify whatever she does. She wants to conserve her energy, and does. Slender, and apparently very delicate, she has immense force, power and conviction. She is unsentimental, cool, awfully honest, and stubborn. She has an alarming sense of humor. And she's recklessly brave.[24]

Lyon illustrated Ann's bravery by retelling the story of a frightfully cold, clear Providence morning, when Ben, Ann, the play's director, and two chaps from Brown University went horseback riding. Ann felt sorry for the college youngster who selected a fiery mare and swapped horses with him. She had been hesitant about riding horses on ice, but went along anyway. The fiery mare refused to canter, flew ahead, skidded, and threw Ann head first upon a large protruding rock. After gashing her left eye, she fainted dead away. Ben carried her to a farmhouse and telephoned for a doctor. Luckily, Major Benjamin Butler, one of the best surgeons in the country, arrived. "Was I born under a lucky star?" asked Ann with amazement when Ben recalled the incident. The Harding-Lyon duo opened the following night in *The Tiger Woman*. "I thought I'd be hideous for the rest of my life," recalled Ann, "and probably lose my sight. Part of my head stuck out like a gourd." Lyon remembered that to everyone's disbelief, Ann, in excruciating pain, played the ingénue role with her misshapen head. She had taken adhesive tape and covered the gash with surgeons' silk. Using crayons, she drew an eye over the patch, put a hat down over the eye, and played her part perfectly. "Game?" asked Lyon. "I'll say she's game!"[25]

The winter season was filled with many roles for Ann. She and Lyon worked in such plays as *Little Women* (Ann played Amy), *Mis' Nelly of N'Orleans* (Ann played the Creole, Melanie Cardanne), and Booth Tarkington's *Seventeen*. During the summer of 1922, Ann trouped with Bonstelle's Detroit company, this time as leading lady. She filled the vacancy left by Katharine Cornell. Ann was cast as Peter in James M. Barrie's *Peter Pan*, and received lead parts in *The Bird of Paradise* and *The Man Who Came Back*. Ann retained vivid memories of her lead in *The Bird of Paradise*. "It was the largest part I'd ever had," she recalled in the fall of 1949. "It called for a Hawaiian accent, something I'd never even heard. I had to learn two songs, singing them and playing the ukulele. And, I had to dance the hula! All that in one day. You can understand why Hawaii holds no special charms for me."[26] *The Bird of Paradise* detailed the doomed cross-cultural romance of a white American male, and a native Hawaiian girl Luana (Ann). By the play's end, Luana readies herself to leap into a volcano! Ann penned a brief autobiographical sketch for *The New York Times,* paying tribute to Bonstelle as "a deciding influence" in her career.[27] However, Bonstelle's "influence" on Ann was definitely overshadowed by that of Jasper Deeter. Theater historian Grace Cohen told this author, "Jessie was always upset that Ann attributed everything to Jasper and not her."[28] Perhaps, it was payback for having Ann do the hula.

The demands placed on Ann's physical health were enormous. Sister Edith noted, "[Ann] was so underpaid that she could not possibly afford to buy the numerous gowns required from week to week, so she sat up until three or four o'clock in the morning sewing and learning lines. Every week found her still sewing frantically during the Monday rehearsal for that night's opening. That year in stock broke down her unbelievably magnificent constitution. Finally she completely lost her voice – there was nothing left but a croak."[29] Ann opted to get coaching from Samuel Kayzer, whose expertise in elocution and voice placement worked wonders. Ann's spirits revived at a poetry-reading open competition at Walter Hampden's theatre. "Afterwards, I had one of the biggest thrills of my life," Ann recalled later. "David Warfield complimented me. And on top of that, W.H. Sothern and Julia Marlowe took me to lunch—and sent me orchids later in the day."[30] Warfield was a highly respected and dedicated Broadway actor—one of the few to become a millionaire. The acting team of

Marlowe and Sothern, who were married, were known as the premier Shakespearean actors of their day.

In the summer of 1923, during her training with Kayzer, director John Cromwell chose Ann for a major role in his new production, *Tarnish*. Ann liked the idea of being involved in this project, which had five equally strong parts. She wouldn't have to be the "star." After rehearsal, the play went out on the road for the usual two-week tryout. Afterwards, she was fired. The producers thought she tossed off her lines deftly, but

(c. 1922-23) Refusing leads on Broadway, Ann decided to work with the Bonstelle stock company in Rhode Island.

superficially, and failed to reach the hearts of the audience. They felt Ann had lost that breathtaking quality that she had exhibited as Madeline in *Inheritors*. Some thought otherwise. Author Violet Dare commented the following year, "I saw [*Tarnish*] in Stamford, Connecticut, with a party of blasé theatre-goers, and every one of us caught up our programs after her first entrance to see who the lovely blonde girl was. She gave an excellent performance, so excellent that I can't see yet just why it was that she was informed that she was not to play the role when it opened in New York."[31] "In the bewilderment of defeat," said sister Edith, "Ann went to Deeter to find out why she had failed. She found him living with his sister in Rose Valley, Pennsylvania."[32]

Jasper Deeter was intent on organizing a true repertory theater company – a group of actors who could meet the challenge of learning multiple parts, while performing in a different play every night. He felt this would enrich the individual and ennoble the theatrical arts. For Deeter, acting and theater was a way of life. He secured rights to the Guild Hall, an old grist-mill that had been a community center. The owner of the building, L. Stauffer Oliver and his wife Margaret Scott Oliver, were staunch and enthusiastic supports of Deeter's ideas. Their daughter, Peggy Oliver Shays, was encouraged by Ann and Deeter in her own career. When interviewed in 2006, Peggy gave her appraisal on Deeter.

> The most important thing I learned from Jasper Deeter, which he instilled in every actor, was that you must *be* that person. You could have all the acting technique in the world, and the audience might think they were watching a "great" performance, but that's all it would be. Deeter said you could fake any emotion – love, joy, hate, fear, but you couldn't fake *honesty.* If you weren't truly *being* the person you were portraying, you would be depriving the audience of the very reason they went to the theatre – to become completely involved in the life of another for the space of a few hours. And the magic would be lost.[33]

Guild Hall was eventually rechristened "Hedgerow." The legend goes that Ann answered the door one day to find a sheriff's agent on the threshold. The theater's income was at a low-ebb, and creditors had complained. When Ann's charm and persuasion failed to deter the officer from doing his duty, she begged that if he threw the company out, they would have to play under the hedgerows. "Deeter, on hand by that time, grabbed Miss Harding's arm and said: 'Annie … that's our name from now on. The Hedgerow.'"[34] (Other reports say Dorothy Kite, one of the seven original actors, came up with the name.) Rose Valley had a tradition of attracting artists and social renegades who felt an affinity for the natural world. Starting in 1901, the architect William Price, a socialist activist, along with other kindred luminaries arrived in Rose Valley determined to create a utopian Arts and Crafts commune. Over the years, they were joined by weavers, potters, painters, musicians, and actors – all who relished the idea of living life artfully. The famous wood-craftsman Wharton Esherick, an organic vegetarian and nudist, joined in Deeter's exuberant theatrical venture, to design, build, and paint stage sets. He also kept the aging mill in safe repair. Esherick had connected with Hedgerow through his wife, a student of natural cures. She was a friend of Dr. Ruth Deeter, Jasper's sister, who ran a natural cure sanatorium in Rose Valley. Ruth appeared on Hedgerow's stage in productions such as Susan Glaspell's excellent *Trifles* (which Ann would do for TV's *Alfred Hitchcock Presents* in 1961).

Rose Valley was ideally tempered for Deeter's avant-garde group of thespians. Initially, two one-act plays were presented on March 3, 1923: Susan Glaspell's *Close the Book* and Ernest Palmer's *That Way*. The following month was Hedgerow's first presentation of George Bernard Shaw's *Candida*. The theatre's popularity was gaining momentum when Ann arrived that summer. She became focused on unlearning the many tricks and unworthy shortcuts to an effect that she had picked up during her time with Bonstelle, and elsewhere. Deeter called together his skeleton troupe to put on *Inheritors*. Ann's Hedgerow debut was on June 23, 1923. The play brought Ann back securely to the original feeling of her remarkable performance at Provincetown Playhouse.

Weeks later, as the fall colors deepened in the heavily wooded areas surrounding Rose Valley, Ann was rehearsing the role of "Dinah" in A. A. Milne's *Mr. Pim Passes By*. Milne, known primarily for *Winnie the Pooh*, was a successful playwright. The quintessentially British drawing room comedy gave Ann a juicy part with clever lines. The day prior to the performance, Ann received a telegram. She was to open cold in *Tarnish* the following week. After the curtain came down on *Mr. Pim*, Ann packed her bags, headed for New York, and toward a major turning point in her career.

Gilbert Emery, who penned *Tarnish*, believed in Ann, and demanded her return. He refused to sanction any other actress for the part. Ann's unforgettable summer at Hedgerow was rich in the kind of growth and transformation she needed as an actress. The critics would rhapsodize over her performance in the Emery play. "Ann Harding is the actress to whom the wise men carried their literary frankincense and myrrh," raved *Time*. After mentioning Ann's "overpowering charm," the reviewer referred to the rest of the cast, stating, "Their performances pale before the brilliancy and beauty of Miss Harding."[35] *The New York Times* gave another glowing report, calling Ann, "a rare combination of winsome girlishness, unforced sincerity and poignantly emotional power."[36]

Tarnish, produced and staged by John Cromwell, had only ragged respect for the male of the species, seeing them as hopelessly "tarnished." Ann's character, young Tishie, attempts to retrieve her family's savings after her alcoholic father gifted all of it, in the form of a check, to a prostitute named Nettie Dark. During their encounter, Tishie's fiancé (Tom Powers), a former customer of Nettie's, shows up. Powers was the one bright spot in Tishie's cluster of woes. She is brokenhearted. One review reported that the ensuing clash between Tishie and her competition "burned and penetrated." "There are two ways for a girl to get a fur coat," argues Nettie, "and, one of them is to buy it." After this insightful encounter, Ann's character discards her naive illusions about life, and allows her "hero" to return. "Men are a bad lot," Tishie concludes at a tense moment. "The thing to do is to find one that cleans easy." Master Acting Teacher and stage manager Richard Boleslavsky said that Emery had decided to throw out 2½ pages of dialogue between Ann and Tom Powers. "Ann Harding," said Boleslavsky, "could bring herself and the audience to tears much better by simply listening silently than by answering every speech of Powers with another speech of the same importance."[37] Boleslavsky, who would later direct Ann in *Taming of the Shrew*, felt that Emery had chosen wisely. Percy Hammond, of the *New York Tribune*, praised *Tarnish*, saying, "Miss Ann Harding as the maiden in distress proves herself to be another of the several brilliant young actresses who have burgeoned of late."[38] The overall effect, according to the *Daily News* critic Burns Mantle: "simple, direct, and honest." The news of Harding's brilliant performance spread like wildfire.

Amid all the praise, the tumult and shouting on opening night, came forth Deeter. He grabbed Ann by the shoulders and shook her. His eyes penetrated deep into hers. "The town may be crazy about you," he glared, "but you gave them a damn sight less than *I* expected."[39] All the praises suddenly meant nothing. Ann felt she had misfired. Her sister could see an upside in Deeter's remark. "She was ridiculously well cast," stated Edith. "Her faults happened to be virtues in that particular role. But she had needed the brake of Deeter's criticism and the next performance was such an improvement upon the first that Ann ceased to worry."[40]

News of Ann's success reached John Barrymore, who was playing in *Hamlet* at the Manhattan Opera House. He confided to drama critic William F. McDermott that he was eager to find a leading lady to act with him in a repertory of good plays. "I want a permanent leading woman," emphasized Barrymore, "such as my father had … somebody of real stature who can play a variety of great roles with distinction. I have looked them all over and I can find nobody. There is only one I haven't seen and I am inclined to guess she might do from what I hear of her. She is young and hasn't had much experience. She's had only one real role on Broadway, in a piece called *Tarnish*. Her name is Ann Harding. Do you know anything about her?"[41] McDermott quipped that before he could answer, Barrymore was swallowed up by Hollywood.

Ann Harding's first real Broadway success was a play that considered the plight of a naïve young girl, and the philosophies of a prostitute. As predicted, Ann had officially "arrived" at the inevitable destination of her father's imagined "Hell." And she felt perfectly at home.

(Endnotes)

1   James Robert Parish, "The RKO Gals," Rainbow Books, N.J., 1974, pg 14
2   Kyle Crichton, "Directed by Simon Legree," *Colliers*, 6/13/36
3   Kyle Crichton, "Directed by …"
4   Ann Fletcher, "Closed Shop? Max Gorelik and the Provincetown," *Eugene O'Neill Review*, vol. 28, 2006
5   Gladys Hall, "The Hot Spot," *Motion Picture*, 12/30
6   Gladys Hall, "The Hot Spot"
7   Ann Harding, "When I Was an Army Girl," *Los Angeles Times*, 5/5/31
8   Edith Gatley Nash, "My Sister, Ann Harding," *Photoplay*, April 1933
9   Lous Sobol, "Down Memory Lane with Ann Harding," New York paper, 1/20/1934, Hedgerow Theatre Collection, UC Berkeley, Bancroft Library
10   Alexander Woollcott, review of *Like a King, New York Times*, 10/4/21

11   James Robert Parish, "The RKO Gals," Rainbow Books, N.J., c. 1974, pg 15

12   Margaret Reid, "Blond-But Not Light," *Picture Play*, May 1930

13   Ann Harding, "Ann Harding," *New York Times*, 10/7/23

14   Margaret Reid, "Blond-But Not Light," *Picture Play*, May 1930

15   Edith Gatley Nash, "My Sister ..."

16   Ann Harding, "My Interview with Ben Lyon," *Screen Play*, September 1931

17   Ben Lyon, "My Friend Ann Harding," *Screen Play*, September 1931

18   Ben Lyon, "My Friend ..."

19   Ben Lyon, "My Friend ..."

20   Ann Harding, "My Interview ..."

21   Ann Harding, "My Interview ..."

22   Ann Harding, "My Interview ..."

23   Ann Harding, "My Interview ..."

24   Ben Lyon, "My Friend ..."

25   Ben Lyon, "My Friend .."

26   Tex McCrary and Jinx Falkenburg, "New York Close Up," *Oakland Tribune*, 11/1/49

27   Ann Harding, "Ann Harding," *New York Times*, 10/7/23

28   Correspondence with Grace Cohen, 6/25/2008

29   Edith Gatley Nash, "My Sister ..."

30   Louis Sobol, "Down Memory Lane with Ann Harding," New York paper, 1/20/34, Hedgerow Theatre Collection, UC Berkeley, Bancroft Library

31   Violet Dare, "Ann Harding," *Manitoba Free Press*, 5/3/24

32   Edith Gatley Nash, "My Sister ..."

33   MFE, "Interview with Peggy Shays, Writer, Mother, Businesswoman, Actress," *http://Biblewise.com*, March 2006 (Shays is the mother of Connecticut Congressman Chris Shays)

34   "Hedgerow Theatre Was Named By Ann Harding, Once Member of Company, Now In Movies," news article from The Hedgerow Theatre Collection, UC Berkeley, Bancroft Library

35   Review of *Tarnish*, *Time Magazine*, 10/15/23

36   Review of *Tarnsih*, *New York Times*, 10/2/23

37   Richard Boleslavsky, *Acting: The First Six Lessons*, Theatre Arts Books, c. 1978, pg 89

38   Percy Hammond's review of *Tarnish*, *Ogden Standard Examiner*, 10/7/23

39   Edith Gatley Nash, "My Sister ..."

40   Edith Gatlry Nash, "My Sister ..."

41   William F. McDermott, "If He Had Met," *Lethbridge Herald*, 2/10/37

Publicity shot for *Stolen Fruit* (1925).

4

Valentino vs. Art

Ann was considered to be reclusive while residing in New York. Deeter's influence reinforced her own objections to being looked upon as a "celebrity." She lived simply, walked to work, and dressed inconspicuously. Columnists regarded her as newsworthy, and were curious about her private life. Even so, Ann wasn't much interested in what anyone thought. "When I began on the stage," she recalled, "I used to go around to the casting offices *as is*. I never was bothered by any monkey business, for I was concerned in selling only my ability as an actress. I let it be understood that if I wasn't liked in a purely professional way, I was ready to go back to punching a typewriter. I don't care to tinker with nature, so I never bobbed or bleached my hair. Personally, I never liked short skirts, so I never wore them. As a result, I was more or less of a mystery, the strange exception to the rule of how an actress should look. What everybody else is doing doesn't interest me. I'm always going against traffic, as it were. Not, mind you, because I want to stand out as an individualist or to attract attention. I hate to be stared at or to be conspicuous. It is just an innate desire to be myself."[1]

Ann lived quietly in her own small apartment, the location of which nobody seemed to know. It was near the Belmont Theatre, where *Tarnish* played for its eight-month run. The play closed in May 1924, and was considered an unqualified success. The film version was released that August, with May McAvoy playing *Tishie*, and Ronald Colman sporting the tarnished hue. Scenarist Frances Marion had tamed it down a tad for the screen. During the play's run, Ann's popularity gave her a close brush with film fame. She had the opportunity to play opposite *the* idol of the silent screen: Rudolph Valentino. Previously, Ben Lyon, who had started a career with First National Pictures, put in a good word for Ann. "[She] didn't even know it," recalled Ben. "And do you know what they said, the big oafs? 'Her hair's too light and her eyes are too pale.'"[2] This didn't stop Valentino. He and his wife, Natacha Rambova, went backstage after a performance of *Tarnish* to inquire as to whether Ann had ever considered a film career. Looking back, Ann was incredulous at her own response to their offer.

> Then and there I committed the *faux pas* of my life. I told Valentino that I was not particularly interested in pictures, and certainly would not appear in silly stories which offended my intelligence, nor do anything which shocked my sense of propriety—and you have no idea how easily I was shocked in those days! Valentino, with good-natured tolerance, asked me to name some story that would illustrate what I meant by "silly and shocking." Since I very rarely went to see pictures [a switch from her youthful days at East Orange High] and my superiority to them was purely theoretical, I was at a loss. But I remembered a story that I had read and considered very inane. It had subsequently been made into a

picture, so I thought it would serve my purpose. "*The Sheik*," I told Valentino, and promptly almost fainted, for as soon as the words had quitted my mouth I realized that I was talking to the sheik himself. But both Rudolph and his wife laughed, and took what they were pleased to consider my frankness as a vast joke.

Valentino arranged to have me make a screen test. He himself made me up for the ordeal. But his make-up didn't look as well on me as it did on him, so the test was a failure. However, he seemed convinced that I had screen possibilities so he arranged for another test. This time Natacha Rambova made me up, spending a great deal of time and patience in experimenting with different cosmetics so that the effect would be the best obtainable. The second test was a great success, and Valentino, who then intended forming his own company, discussed a contract with me at some length. Everyone seemed settled. Then Rudolph was tied up in litigation which kept him off the screen for many months. So my proposed debut opposite him did not materialize. However, I have always cherished a warm memory of the kindness which Mr. and Mrs. Valentino showed to a very young and terribly opinionated actress.[3]

Valentino's aborted project, *The Scarlet Power,* was the film in question. Based on the 14th-century story of El Cid, Valentino would have played a Moorish nobleman and warrior who falls in love with a Moorish princess (the role intended for Harding). This pet project was written by Natacha Rambova (under the *nom de plume* Justus Layne). In December 1924, the film, beset with problems, was sacrificed along with the trim van dyke beard Valentino grew especially for the role. The project failed once again in early 1925, after being re-titled, *The Hooded Falcon*. By that time, Ann, in her pursuit of "dramatic art," had enjoyed another summer at Hedgerow, and experienced her second flop on Broadway.

Ann's Hedgerow experience in the summer of 1924 offered opportunities "to die for." She played the forceful and autoerotic Hilda in Ibsen's *The Master Builder* and three roles in George Bernard Shaw works: the title role in *Candida*, Lady Cecily in *Captain Brassbound's Conversion*, and Lina, the death-defying Polish acrobat, in *Misalliance*. Playing Shaw's archetypical, ideal women, who often retain their financial, intellectual, and physical independence, enhanced Ann's world view. Philadelphia critics that attended *Candida* "praised her performance highly."[4] She had nothing but praises for Deeter's tutelage. "Nothing will ever dull my gratitude to him for the things he taught me," Ann stated.[5]

After being rejuvenated at Hedgerow, Ann returned to Broadway in the fall of 1924. She tackled the role of a lawyer whose very first client, unbeknownst to her, is her long-lost father. The play's original title was *The Horse Thief*. Despite a successful tryout at Chicago's Sam Harris Theatre in April, the play underwent a number of rewrites. Re-titled *Thoroughbreds*, it opened in New York at the Vanderbilt Theatre in September. Author James Robert Parish refers to the production as a "folksy play that only a Will Rogers could have saved." Instead of Rogers, who was still with the Ziegfeld Follies, there was the dour-faced George Marion. After seeing the play, Heywood Broun, of the legendary Algonquin Round Table, referred to Marion as "Massah X" (a pun on *Madame X*, a favorite vehicle of Sarah Bernhardt). While Bernhardt's character was addicted to cocaine and killed a man, Marion was simply a compulsive horse thief. Both characters received the requisite indictment for their respective crimes. Coincidentally, they also had offspring, who miraculously showed up to represent them in court. *Madame X* had critics and audiences weeping hysterically, but "Massah X" was met with a dry eye. Broun, drama critic for the *New York World*, commented, "Throughout the action of *Thoroughbreds* I had an uneasy feeling of having been in this place before ... I didn't think very much of the experience in the first place. Only, it was rather worse this time ... Ann Harding for instance, began with a most carefully prepared drawl and then chucked it over before the end of the first act. It made no difference. *Thoroughbreds* needs a good deal more than dialect."[6] *Time* magazine wailed, "Ann Harding, the blondest actress in the world, forgot her Southern accent after the opening minutes, and gave a generally mechanical performance which disappointed those who witnessed her brilliant playing in *Tarnish*."[7] One critic wagged that the play gave good reason to legalize birth control. After all, Marion met his parental obligations by horse-thievery. Audiences were led to believe that the proceeds of his "trade" had put Ann through law school! On a more positive note, *The New York Times* labeled Ann a "human thoroughbred." Another critic stated, "Ann Harding deserves grateful mention. Indeed her work as the heroine of *Thoroughbreds* is the best of her interesting career."[8] The overall impression was, however, that for Ann, *Thoroughbreds* was a setback. According to her sister, Ann knew she would be panned. Still, it is understandable why Ann chose the role of Sue Wynn. For someone who could "talk horses for days," the play seemed a shoo-in for her. *Thoroughbreds'* heart-warming reunion between long-lost papa and daughter must have rung an emotional bell for Ann as well. Ann's next theatrical step was detailed rather touchingly by her sister Edith.

> As a person, [Ann] had never known an established home as most people know it. The nomadic wanderings of an Army family preclude that precious taking of root. But, as an actress, "Hedgerow" implies to Ann all that the other means to those who have known a home. Whenever she was hurt, bewildered or lost in this world of the theater, there was just one haven, one clear solution to the puzzle—Hedgerow. So, the night that the play closed she was all packed up, her suitcase was stowed into her dilapidated roadster and after the performance she set out at midnight for Philadelphia and Hedgerow, leaving no forwarding address behind her.[9]

In 1962, Ann reflected back on her midnight drive to Hedgerow, traveling in her sluggish "tenth-hand Buick roadster." "I always named my cars," Ann said, "and I named that one 'Hedgehog.' That was because it couldn't be a road hog, not at that speed. I was crossing the Jersey meadows when suddenly I came upon a detour sign and a man signaling me to stop. Well, I wasn't stopping at night for anybody. So I zigzagged around him and kept going. I don't know who he was, but he fired a gun at me. Luckily, he was a bad shot and only winged the window. It's hard to make a getaway at 38 mph."[10]

Hedgerow's winter season of 1924-25, offered Ann a lead in the premiere of Barry Conners' *The Dreamers*. Jeanne Eagles claimed the part was better than her role in the mega-hit, *Rain. Dreamers*, staged in

October and November, co-starred Ann and Deeter in what were referred to as "highly emotional roles." Ann also repeated her leads in *The
Master Builder* and *Inheritors*. Her only extravagance that winter was an
occasional concert. Taking an early train into Philadelphia from Rose
Valley, she would prop herself on the steps of the Academy of Music and wait patiently until the box office opened. She was usually the
first in line. The fifty-cent seat placed her under the balcony roof where
she lost herself momentarily under the grand gestures of Leopold Stokowski casting his spell upon the audience with the help of his Philadelphia Symphony Orchestra. By spring, Ann was completely broke.
The pittance of the communally shared salary that Hedgerow offered
didn't go far. As she would never allow herself to borrow money, Ann
ventured bravely back to Broadway with only a bag of hopes.

Arriving in New York, Ann ran into the colorful and highly successful stage manager Al Woods. The cigar-chomping showman, who
called everybody "Sweetheart," had made a fortune promoting Julian
Eltinge, a female impersonator. In honor of Eltinge's nationwide success, Woods built and dedicated the elaborate Eltinge Theatre on 42nd
Street. It was at the Eltinge that Ann would reinstate her reputation as
an actress of real merit. Woods' stage productions leaned toward the lurid melodrama that had given him his start. He told Ann that he might
be able to find her something and to come see him. The vagueness of
his offer didn't give much assurance, so Ann told him where she could
be reached and headed back "home" to Hedgerow. Within two weeks

Ann's role as the school mistress in *The Stolen Fruit* (1925) lasted 96 performances at Broadway's Eltinge Theatre.(Courtesy of Wisconsin Center for Film and Theater Research)

Woods sent her a wire, "I told you to show up," he emphasized. "Come and see me." The skeleton crew at Hedgerow frantically scraped up enough funds for Ann's train ticket. When she arrived at Woods' office, he greeted her by reaching across his large walnut desk and handing her three plays. She looked them over, wanted no part of them, and told him exactly what she thought. The affable Al suggested Ann visit his rival, the old-time producer Henry W. Savage, also known as "Colonel Savage." Ann went along with the idea. Savage's office was just down the street. She found Savage in conference with his business manager Lou Wiswell and actor-director Rollo Lloyd. That same afternoon, they handed Ann the script to *The School Mistress*, a translation of an Italian play by Dario Niccodemi. The following day, she read for them. "At the end of the reading," recalled Edith, "those three old-timers of the theater were unashamedly dissolved in tears. Rollo and Mr. Wiswell considered the matter closed."[11] Savage, not wanting to appear too anxious, rudely stated, "Hmm, yes, well, as a matter of fact, Miss Harding, I had thought of a brunette in the part." Rollo groaned. In a chilly tone, Ann replied, "I am obviously a blonde, Colonel Savage, and I understand you have a marked aversion to wigs. May I ask what prompted you to waste so much of your time on me?" Savage rose from his chair, indicating the end of the interview. He told her to leave her name and address with his secretary. Ann was not used to such discourtesy, and countered, "If you are interested in looking farther a-field for the casting of the part, Colonel Savage, I see no reason for cluttering up your files with my name and address."[12] She turned and walked out.

Feeling tears of humiliation welling up, Ann returned to Woods' office and told him of her encounter with the Colonel. Woods bellowed, "Why the son-of-a-bitch!" Looking warmly at Ann he softened. "Here, sweetheart, read these – I'll star you in any one you like." Once again, the amiable Woods offered a few manuscripts for Ann's consideration. As she turned to leave, Woods handed her another script, just for fun. It was *The Green Hat*, which was to star Katharine Cornell. After looking over Woods' suggestions, Ann found the "starring" roles depressing. She returned to his office, and held out *The Green Hat*. "This is the one that's going to run," she insisted. "I don't want to be starred. Kit's a grand actress—I'd be very happy to support her, and the part of Venice is just my size."[13] In a matter of minutes, Ann was on board with Cornell and Leslie Howard.

Rehearsals for *The Green Hat's* road-debut in Detroit began immediately. Ann's money concerns were over. Expecting a hefty $150-a-week check, she was shocked the following week to discover that the sum was $300. When Ann picked up her next pay envelope, she found that her salary had mushroomed to $400 a week. This was followed by an unexpected visit from Al Woods, who offered her a contract. Ann signed on the spot, but, as the ink dried, she wondered what he meant when he muttered, "Now I'll fix that so-and-so." The mystery would unravel in a few days.

Ann's role as the bewildered and generous Venice in *The Green Hat* was well-received in Detroit and Chicago. The *Chicago-Herald Examiner's* opinion was respectful. "Ann Harding's Venice," stated the review, "is just as it ought to be, pictorially and sympathetically."[14] The play, which brought British playwright Michael Arlen fame and fortune, is a curiously unhappy one, all about the self-absorbed "lost generation" in postwar London society. Cornell's character, Iris, loses her husband, Fenwick, to suicide on their wedding night. It is explained that he jumped out of a window, because he "had picked up some beastly woman … and caught about the foulest disease a man can have."[15] Amid all the despair, we are introduced to Napier (Leslie Howard), Iris' true love. The second act takes place ten years later wherein Ann's character, Venice Pollen, is about to be married to Napier. Iris, whose life has plunged into one big orgy, unexpectedly appears on the scene. Of course, Napier is still smitten with her. As the story progresses they plan to run away together, until Napier discovers Venice is pregnant. Iris resolves their dilemma by driving off madly in her motor car. The sound of a crash and a flash of light reveal her fate. Oddly enough, audiences and critics found Arlen's cynical, restless, and futile world frequently touching. However, it was the superb acting that kept *The Green Hat* securely in place. (In the 1928 film version, *A Woman of Affairs*, thievery was substituted for syphilis. The team of Greta Garbo and John Gilbert filled in for Katharine Cornell and Leslie Howard. Ann's role was delicately played by Dorothy Sebastian.)

The Green Hat opened in September for a successful run on Broadway, but without Ann. So well-received was her portrayal in the pre-Broadway performances of *The Green Hat,* that Colonel Savage came pleading for her to play in *The School Mistress.* Savage had been unable to cast the lead and admitted that Ann was the one for the part. This is what had prompted Woods to sign Ann to a contract. It enabled him to "fix that so-and-so" Savage, forcing "the Colonel" to give Woods half the show's profit for Ann's services. These turn of events explain the Savage-Woods partnership, which many thought strange. Prior to the New York opening in the fall, Ann went on to tour in *The School Mistress.* In mid-July the tour wrapped up in Atlantic City. With time on her hands, Ann decided to retreat to Hedgerow, where she tackled the role of Ruth in O'Neill's *Beyond the Horizon.* In August, Mrs. Gatley came to Rose Valley to spend a weekend at Strath Haven Inn, and to see Ann's performance in the August 29 revival of *Captain Brassbound's Conversion*. From there Ann returned to New York to prepare for the opening of *The School Mistress*, which had been re-titled *Stolen Fruit*.

"*Stolen Fruit*," wrote Edith, "established [Ann] once and for all as star material. The press hailed her as the new Bernhardt, another Duse; but she refused to be starred, preferring to impress audiences by her performance rather than by seeing her name … over the marquee."[16] "*Stolen Fruit*, presented at the Eltinge Theatre," stated one review, "is a tense and gripping play with shades of poignancy that are penetratingly interpreted by the excellent cast. Ann Harding, as the school teacher who searches among her pupils for her illegitimate child who she was told at its birth had died, does some of the best acting New York has seen this season."[17] Dario Niccodemi's play, which had been staged in every province of Italy, tells the story of Marie Millais (Ann's character) being forced to leave France at the age of sixteen after giving birth to a daughter. She returns eight years later, supporting herself as a school mistress, and attempting to find the grave of her child who she presumes to be dead. The townspeople are suspicious of Marie's reclusive behavior. She doesn't attend church, disappears each evening, and doesn't make friends. They request that the town mayor ask her to leave. When confronted, Marie unburdens her soul to the mayor. "I walk for miles to the graveyard at Maurois," says Marie, explaining her nocturnal departures. "There I kneel at the unmarked grave of a little girl who may not even be mine. But does that matter? Under the ground they're all alike, aren't they, they all belong to me?" The mayor is completely sympathetic and investigates her story. At the finis, the mystery is resolved. The daughter is very much alive and reunited with her mother. Not all critics considered Harding another Bernhardt. *Time* magazine noted, "Ann Harding seems to have bad luck with plays. She was offered the lead in this play … It was a great chance; she took it, and lost. … She gives a genuinely attractive performance, which seems to suggest that with severely competent direction she would be a very fine actress. … The play is rather obvious and only twice deeply interesting."[18] Regardless, *Stolen Fruit* ran for three months before going out on the road.

In December 1925, Susan Glaspell was acclaimed as the "American George Bernard Shaw" after the London premier of *Inheritors.* She was "set above O'Neill in both achievement and future promise."[19] That same month, while completing her third month in *Stolen Fruit,* Ann joined Estelle Winwood and Rollo Peters for nine matinee performances at the Klaw Theatre in Shakespeare's *Taming of the Shrew.* She was cast as the energetic Bianca. The *New York Sun* declared, "For looks and honeyed ways, of course, there was none like Ann Harding."[20] Included in the cast were Jessie Ralph, Walter Abel and Allyn Joslyn. It was unusual for Ann to go outside her self-imposed confinement of *serious* drama. To partake in the Bard's robust comedy was indeed a refreshing exception. She was afforded the opportunity to work under the direction of the highly-esteemed Richard Boleslavsky. In 1922, Boleslavsky had defected when the Moscow Arts Theater visited America. At the end of the 1923-24 Moscow tour, Maria Ouspenskaya defected, and joined Boleslavsky. Together, they co-founded the American Laboratory Theatre, which evolved into the Actors Studio. The team of Boleslavsky-Ouspenskaya taught what became known as "Method" acting, based on the teachings of Stanislavski.

An onslaught of gloom hit Broadway in March 1926, and Ann was offered the lead in yet another serious drama. The cheerless lineup included Evreinov's *The Chief Thing*, Strindberg's *Easter*, the story of a family on the brink of ruin, and *Devils*, a lamentable tale of religious mania. *Schweiger*, premiering at the Mansfield Theatre on March 23, was a depressing chronicle of infanticide by German playwright Franz Werfel. The play told of a neurotic watchmaker who, in a spasm of mental delirium, had once killed a school boy. When his deed is revealed, years later, the distraught man's wife, Anna Schweiger, played by Ann, decides to abort their unborn child. Filled with homicidal impulses, Mr. Schweiger, played by the talented Jacob Ben-Ami, does any future victims a favor by jumping out of a window and committing suicide. Werfel's biographer claims the play intended Herr Schwieger to be "a true Expressionist hero and a near saint."[21] Why Ann chose this particular vehicle is a good question. Could it have been the devastatingly handsome leading man, Ben-Ami? The highly respected Russian actor had fire and imagination. Like Ann, Ben-Ami was repelled by commercial productions, and had focused mainly in Jewish Art Theatre. To Ann, working with his talent fit her theatrical ideal. Drama critic Percy Hammond, whose obliterating wit graced the *New York Tribune*, summed up *Schweiger's* case: "It is all very brooding and cadaverous and, so far as I could peer into it, very dull. Even the blonde and sunlit Miss Ann Harding in her impersonation of the bride of the melancholy horologist was eclipsed."[22] *Time* magazine found playwright Franz Werfel's *Schweiger* to be "airless," but was impressed with the performers. "Ann Harding," stated the review, "the excessively blond young woman … is becoming a better and better actress. Mr. Ben-Ami is, of course, one of the most magnificently accomplished performers of our theatre. It is unpleasant to ponder how difficult an evening *Schweiger* would have been without these two."[23]

Ann's hair continued to be critiqued as part of her performances. In fact, Ann's honeyed tresses where a popular topic of conversation, and considered newsworthy. "The debutantes of New York are bobbed, almost to a flapper," stated columnist Betsy Schuyler, "but the most unusual and gorgeously blonde hair on Broadway belongs to Ann Harding. She apparently secures her locks at some central point on the back of the head, then brings the ends over her forehead in a swirl effect quite too lovely for words. No one would ever want to see her bobbed."[24] And, no one ever did. Ann grew to accept her hair as both a striking asset and a peculiar obstacle.

In April 1926, *Schweiger's* sudden demise after thirty-one performances was buried along with several other stray sensations from the Continent, such as the aforementioned Nichols Evreinov play *The Chief Thing*. The Russian play reminded audiences that life is "theatrical and illusory" by having actors leap across the footlights at the finish and into "real life." By this time, Ann desperately needed to face the realities of her own "real life." She had worked steadily for five years, with no vacations, and no rest. It would have behooved her to pay more attention to Jessie Bonstelle, who emphasized how important it was for actors to maintain their vitality. This, according to Bonstelle, was the key to magnetism on stage. She insisted on players keeping their "body-machines in perfect running order … and knowing how to open their consciousness to receive their share of the tremendous power of the universe."[25] Ann made the mistake of trying to generate the power herself, rather than "tap into it" as Bonstelle suggested. Her sister Edith observed, "[Ann] had reached such a point of utter weariness that it became an effort to eat, impossible to carry on a conversation, unthinkable to start work on another play. But, she accepted an offer to take over the old Garrick Theater in Detroit, and run a stock company there for the summer season."[26]

Detroit had a way of adopting Bonstelle players and claiming them as their own. They had done this with Ann, and she was aware of her huge following. She had last played at the Garrick in Rachel Crother's *Mary the Third* in August 1924. At that time *The Detroit News* featured an article titled "She Returns Victorious," which said that local audiences regarded Ann with "parental pride," following her Broadway success in *Tarnish*.[27] For her new venture in 1926, Ann persuaded a co-star from *Stolen Fruit*, Rollo Peters, to join the Detroit company. Despite Ann's depleted state, Detroit enjoyed an exceptional season of summer stock. In full charge of her troupe, Ann acted as producer, casting director, and business manager.[28] She repeated her starring role in *Tarnish*, added to her repertoire such classics as the comedy *Bluebeard's Eighth Wife* and Philip Barry's *In a Garden*. Barry would later write the high-comedy classic *Holiday*, for which Ann received her only Oscar nomination. As the final two weeks of the season approached, Ann celebrated her twenty-fourth birthday. Peters was called to New York, and Ann found herself with no leading man. "Ann was very, very tired by that time," said Edith. "When the manager of the theater told her, 'There's a guy who has just closed here in *White Cargo* – looks like a good leading man,' she just said wearily, 'All right, sign him up.'"[29] Unbeknownst to Ann, fate had intervened. Her expedient decision would force her to take pause and reckon with realities outside of the theatre.

(Endnotes)

1   Ben Maddox, "Discovering Hollywood *Real* Sophisticate-Ann Harding!" *Screenland*, November 1931

2   Ann Harding, "My Interview with Ben Lyon," *Screen Play*, September 1931

3   "Ann Harding Almost Acted with Valentino," *Los Angeles Times*, 8/23/31

4   Article on Hedgerow referring to Ann's performance in *Candida* the previous summer, 1/23/25, Hedgerow Theatre Collection, UC Berkeley, Bancroft Library

5   James Robert Parish, *The RKO Gals*, Rainbow Books, c.1974, pg 15

6   Heywood Brown, review of *Thoroughbreds, Wisconsin State Journal*, 9/14/24

7   Review of *Thoroughbreds, Time*, 9/22/24

8   Review of *Thoroughbreds, Charleston Gazette*, 9/21/24

9   Edith Gatley Nash, "My Sister Ann Harding, Part III" *Photoplay*, May 1933

10   "My First Car," *Oakland Tribune*, 10/14/62

11   Edith Gatley Nash, "My Sister ..."

12   Edith Gatley Nash, "My Sister ..."

13   Edith Gatley Nash, "My Sister ..."

14   Ashton Stevens review of *The Green Hat,* from *Katharine* Cornell, "I Wanted to be an Actress," Spargo Press, 2007 pg 207

15   Ethan Mordden, *All that Glittered*, MacMillan, pg 45-46

16   Edith Gatley Nash, "My Sister ..."

17   Lucy Jeanne Price review of *Stolen Fruit, Fayetteville Daily Democrat*, 10/24/25

18   Review of *Stolen Fruit, Time* 10/10/25

19   Barbara Ozieblo, *Susan Glaspell: A Critical Biography*, University of North Carolina Pr. c. 2000, pg 180

20   James Robert Parish, "RKO Gals," Rainbow Books, c. 1974, pg 17

21   Hans Wagener, *Understanding Franz Werfel*, University of South Carolina Pr., c. 1993, pg 53

22   Percy Hammond, eview of *Schweiger, New York Tribune*, 4/4/26

23   Review of *Schweiger, Time*, 4/5/26

24   Betsy Schuyler, "Ann Harding Says 'Bob' Still Holds Its Popular Place," *Charleston Daily Mail*, 10/24/25

25   Jessie Bonsette, "Charm Can Be Taught Says Noted Dramatist," *Vidette-Messenger*, 2/5/29

26   Edith Gatley Nash, "My Sister ..."

27   R.J. Mclauchlin, "She Returns Victorious," *The Detroit News*, 8/2/1924

28   James Robert Parish, *RKO Gals*, Rainbow Books, c. 1974, pg 17

29   Edith Gatley Nash, "My Sister ..."

(c. 1926) At 25, Ann's unrequited love for a Detroit judge
was assuaged by a real romance with her new leading man.

5

The New Leading Man

Ann discovered that her theatrical adventure was proving to be a lonely one. She found herself longing for some kind of companionship. In the summer of 1922, Ann had made the acquaintance of Frank Murphy, who served as a judge in the Detroit Recorder's Court. Murphy came from a long line of Irish idealists, and had great tolerance for all humanity. He was educated at Ann Arbor, Harvard, and Trinity College in Dublin. He had turned down a tempting offer from one of the largest Detroit automobile corporations, in order to accept his judgeship at a modest salary. On the other hand, the glitter and excitement of the theater appealed to the tall, good-looking Murphy, and Ann became especially important to him. Murphy's biographer puts it plainly, "Murphy met the stunningly beautiful Ann Harding in 1922, when the flaxen-haired and cameo-faced actress was performing at the Bonstelle Theatre. He kindled a spark in her that flamed from time to time over the years, and she saw in him a heroic quality and idealism that was lacking in other men she knew."[1] In 1926, as Ann supervised Detroit's Garrick Theatre's summer season, the torch Ann carried for Murphy was rekindled.

Since September 1925, Murphy had presided over the racially-charged murder trials of African-American doctor Ossian Sweet. Clarence Darrow, fresh from the famous "Scopes Trial," represented Sweet after being approached by the NAACP. The historical significance of the trial's outcome was important not only for the black community, but as a stepping-stone in a career that would place Murphy as Mayor of Detroit, Governor of Michigan, and the 56th US Attorney General. Ann championed the defense in the Sweet Trials, and followed the story in all its detail. She showed up for the proceedings whenever she could fit it into her hectic schedule.

The trouble for the highly respected Dr. Sweet began when he purchased a home in a strictly white Detroit neighborhood in May 1925. His reluctance to move in was underscored by the fact that Detroit had well over 25,000 members in the Ku Klux Klan. Angry mobs had forced other black families to abandon their newly purchased homes in the area. On September 8, after asking for police protection, Sweet and his wife made their courageous move. Just in case officers ignored threats to his family, Sweet had purchased guns and ammunition. He had to acknowledge the fact that during the previous two years, Detroit police had murdered fifty-five blacks in cold blood. Within a few hours of settling in, the Sweet home was pelted with a hailstorm of rocks. A mob outside shouted threats. As things intensified, the police looked the other way. A shot rang out into an estimated crowd of 1,000. A man was killed. The gunfire came from within the Sweet residence. In the aftermath, unaware that anyone had died, Dr. Sweet, his wife Gladys, two brothers, and the other seven occupants, were arrested and tried for first-degree murder.

Thirty-five-year-old Frank Murphy assigned *himself* to preside over the proceedings. "Every judge on this bench is afraid," stated Murphy about the case, "They think it's dynamite. [The other judges] don't realize this is the opportunity of a lifetime to demonstrate sincere liberalism and judicial integrity at a time when liberalism is coming into its own."[2] Murphy set the tone for the trial by the weight of his presence and solid character. The proceedings were devoid of any pandemonium. Before the case went to jury, Clarence Darrow remarked: "My clients are charged with murder, but they are really charged with being black."[3] When a verdict could not be reached, Judge Murphy declared a mistrial, and released all defendants on bail. Following his decision, Murphy received letters upbraiding him on a daily basis, and warning him that his open-mindedness might damage his political future. Following the mistrial, Dr. Sweet's house was set on fire.

In April-May, 1926, as Ann arrived in Detroit to line up productions at the Garrick, the defense in the Sweet case elected to hold trial for Henry Sweet. Henry was Ossian's younger brother, a twenty-two year-old college student, who admitted to having fired the gun. Again, he was represented by Clarence Darrow. On May 11, Ann was present for Darrow's closing summations. Murphy's biographer notes, "Ann Harding was given a front seat so that she could see her favorite judge in action."[4] Murphy's strong, low voice carried to the farthest corner of the crowded courtroom. Defense attorneys and prosecutors readily nodded their heads when Murphy stated why a motion was "denied," or an "objection sustained."[5] The soundness of his rulings was never questioned. Murphy's fairness, according to trial reporter Marcet Haldeman-Julius, was "unimpeachable." "Next to Darrow," stated Haldeman-Julius, "[Murphy] was easily the most forceful and interesting character in the courtroom."[6]

Ann listened to Darrow's seven-hour closing argument, which became a landmark in the Civil Rights movement. In his risky and brilliant speech, Darrow, an agnostic, stated that he wasn't going to "slobber" over the victim who had departed to his "Jim Crow Heaven." The man was nothing but a "conspirator in as foul a conspiracy as was ever hatched in a community." The police officers involved were as useless as "bumps on a log."[7] Darrow refuted the idea that it was a murder case. The violence the mob had intended for the Sweet family, Darrow emphasized, was an assault on the constitution and laws of the nation. "Did they shoot too quick?" asked Darrow, addressing the use of guns and ammunition. "Tell me just how long a man needs wait for a mob?" Darrow's sarcasm had bite. The courtroom, filled mostly with blacks and a young woman with corn-colored hair, sat riveted by his every word. "Instead of being here under indictment for murder," declared Darrow, "[the Sweets] should be honored for the brave stand they made, for their rights and ours ... they fought not only for themselves, but for every man who wishes to be free."[8] Darrow's final remarks were spoken eloquently:

> I do not believe in the law of hate. ... I believe in
> the law of love ... you can do nothing with hatred.
> ... I believe the life of the Negro race has been a life
> of tragedy, of injustice, of oppression. The law has
> made him equal, but man has not. ... the hopes and
> fears of a race are in your keeping. ... Not one of
> their color sits on this jury. ... Their eyes are fixed
> on you ... their hopes hang on your verdict. ... I ask
> you, in the name of progress and of the human race,
> to return a verdict of not guilty in this case![9]

Henry Sweet was acquitted. Deliberation took less than four hours. Darrow's biographer, Phyllis Vine, reported the May 13 decision as an "electric moment," saying, "As the last juror declared 'Not guilty,' Ann Harding, the actress, leaped out of her chair and threw her arms around

Darrow ... women [were] sobbing convulsively and tears [ran] down the cheeks of men."[10] Judge Murphy confided to a friend that listening to Darrow was the greatest experience of his life. Murphy stated to the Sweet family, "I believe it is a just and reasonable verdict, and may God bless you."[11] The Sweet Trials made the judge a hero in the eyes of Detroit's black community, and deepened Ann's admiration for Murphy. Witnessing the brilliance of Darrow's defense, and absorbing the content of his message, made a lasting impression on Ann. He influenced her worldview, and her decision, several years later, to join the NAACP.[12]

Ann's correspondence with Murphy, from 1922-1936, is held in the Frank Murphy Papers at the Michigan Historical Collections in Ann Arbor. The attraction between the two was an emotional one, and Murphy's physical appearance undoubtedly appealed to Ann. Marcet Haldeman-Julius describes Murphy as slender, having a "splendid physique," thick curly auburn hair, and contemplative blue eyes. Murphy's biographer noted that Ann never fully understood Murphy, "and she discovered, as other women did, that love and marriage were not among his favorite subjects of conversation. She sometimes found solace in her feeling for Murphy, but he seems to have caused her more pain than pleasure, and one of his friends remembered her as 'the weeping blond.'"[13] Ann finally conceded in a letter she wrote to Murphy in 1932, that "all he wanted from the opposite sex was 'surfaces—pleasant ones,' and that he was unlikely ever to commit himself fully to a mere woman."[14] Murphy's biographer, Sidney Fine, felt that Ann eventually was shrewd enough to sense the truth about Murphy. When researching his 1975 three-volume biography on Murphy, Fine discovered a letter from 1940, written to Murphy congratulating him on his nomination to the Supreme Court. The correspondent, Abe Garfinkel, implied that he and Murphy had been lovers in 1933, during Murphy's governor-general post in the Philippines. "Garfinkel wrote that he felt that Murphy had belonged to him ever since. ... Garfinkel expressed admiration for Murphy and regret about a break up apparently caused by a jealous Murphy."[15] When Murphy was in the Supreme Court, FDR prodded him to marry. Reluctantly, Murphy proposed to one of his many female admirers, announced his engagement, and ended up in the hospital with chest pains. After postponing the wedding several times, the woman finally gave up on him. Joyce Murdoch and Deb Price, in their study, *Courting Justice*, suggest that Murphy's homosexuality was always "hiding in plain sight." For more than 40 years, Edward G. Kemp was Frank Murphy's devoted, trusted companion. "From college until Murphy's death, the pair found creative ways to work and live together."[16] Kemp was Murphy's law partner and advisor until Murphy's death in 1949.

While in Detroit, Ann's unrequited love for Murphy was put on hold, temporarily. She had a theatre to run and a new play about to open on Broadway. She also became a charter member of New York's Institute of the Woman's Theatre, geared to establish a woman's voice in theatre management. Nonetheless, cupid's determined arrow had targeted Ann. One evening, while she was enjoying a quiet dinner with friends, she received a phone call from the manager of the Garrick, asking her to come over and meet the prospective leading man. Ann didn't want to be bothered. "If he looks all right and doesn't want too much money," replied Ann, "you have my okay right now. I've seen all the actors I can stand for this year!"[17] The manager indicated that the actor was demanding a large salary, and he needed Ann to help make the decision. So, she grudgingly left the table and drove over to the Garrick. The interview lasted two hours. Ann forgot all about the outrageously high salary, and the actor, Harry Bannister, forgot that he had been determined to return to New York. He got the job, and he got the girl. In a typical Harding fashion, she explained, "You might safely lay our courtship to propinquity. We worked together, played love scenes on the stage every night, rehearsed together every afternoon and always walked to and from the theater together."[18] The result of all this "togetherness," or "propinquity," was propelled by the mutual attraction they felt during that first interview. One must hand it to her. Ann knew of what she spoke. In a 1950 project at MIT, psychologists diagramed the "Propinquity Effect": the tendency for people to form friendships or romantic relationships with those whom they encounter often. This "discovery" was simply a variation on what Ann had observed years before.

In spite of their newly-found companionship, Ann had had her fill of propinquity with Bannister the second her season at the Garrick was over. She headed home again to Hedgerow to repeat her role as Lina in Shaw's *Misalliance*. With a surge of renewed confidence, Ann then headed to New York, already a few days late for rehearsals in the new Al Woods production, *A Woman Disputed*. After Guthrie McClintock backed out of staging the piece, Crane Wilbur took over. A Brooklyn tryout grossed over $18,000, and the following week in Newark, $17,000. Such grosses for a brand-new play were unheard of. "Of course, New York fools the best of us," said Wilbur at the time, "but [the play] certainly has a tremendous popular appeal."[19] *A Woman Disputed*, opening September 28 at Broadway's Forrest Theatre, starred

Ann played a French prostitute in the World War drama *The Woman Disputed* (1926). Louis Calhern played her Yankee sweetheart. (Courtesy of Wisconsin Center for Film and Theater Research)

Ann, Lowell Sherman, and Louis Calhern. Ann outdid herself in the edgy role of a patriotic French prostitute during the World War. As the story progresses, Ann's character, Marie Ange, along with a few other oppressed civilians, attempts to flee the Prussian regime. They are caught. Marie is offered the choice of execution, or saving all their lives by giving herself over to the lusts of Captain von Hartmann (Lowell Sherman). She gives. *Time* magazine sarcastically summed up the plot as "How Ann Harding Won the World War." The review assured readers that Ann's character was subsequently rewarded with the true love of her Yankee sweetheart (Calhern) *after* he learns the reason for her "sacrifice." Before his execution, the villain of the piece, von Hartmann, is rewarded with a long-delayed post-coital puff on a cigarette. Audiences of 1926 ate this stuff up. *Time* felt that Sherman and Harding "helped to make a preposterous plot pleasantly endurable."[20] The *New York Post* reserved its praise strictly for Ann, saying, "There was passion and fire in her, a tartness and tautness that were worthy of better, infinitely better things."[21] The *New York Times* echoed the *Post* review saying, "Ann Harding gave ... a sincere, forthright and vibrant portrayal. She brought to a role a rich voice, ash-blond beauty and histrionic expertness, and carried off the honors of the evening."[22]

Backstage, Ann embodied Marie Ange's tough edges well before the curtain rose. A reporter for *The New York Times*, Samuel Hoffenstein, ventured to her dressing room shortly before Ann was to go on. She was surrounded by several male admirers. Hoffenstein noted that Ann was made up as the "wicked woman" in Act One. He cautiously asked her to what she contributed her success. "To my ability to act," Ann answered, "and to the astuteness of managers in giving me a chance to do it." Hoffenstein implied that her response to his question would not be much help to the young women who have ambitions to go on stage. "It is not intended to be a help," she huffed. "Where did you get the notion that it is anybody's business or pleasure to help anybody else in any particular?" At this point, Ann's young, and now "thoroughly alarmed" admirers, "withdrew in a body." Hoffenstein bravely ventured into what Ann felt to be an interrogation. "You look hard as is called for in the script, Miss Harding," he jested, "but you don't go on for ten or fifteen minutes." This comment was met with complete silence. He repeated his request for her advice to aspiring actresses determined to go on stage. "Tell them not to go," answered Ann. "In the first place, some of them have good figures and that is liable to cut salaries in the case of actresses who can only act. In the second place, they clutter up the waiting rooms of the managers' offices so that an established actress has no place to sit down." Riling her further, Hoffenstein wondered aloud, "What do you think of while Marie-Ange is eating her heart out?" "Officially, I eat my heart out, too," she answered. "Would you have me be insincere? I believe that the true artist suffers with his victims. I am sure that Izaak Walton used to wake up nights, while he was writing 'The Complete Angler,' with an imaginary fishhook in his mouth. Otherwise, his trout would not be true to life. … But privately, and not for publication, while Marie-Ange is eating her heart out, I sometimes wonder where the fellows who play soldiers in war scenes will be ten years from now. Do you think some of them will be generals down at the old Manhattan Opera House? But never mind. Don't misunderstand me. … I suffer more than Marie-Ange. … I could eat her heart out for her with one hand tied behind my back."[23]

Hoffenstein concluded the interview with a simple question: "Do you think acting is art?" Ann had had enough. "Supposing show business isn't exactly drama," she said impatiently. "Supposing acting is a by-product of nervous exhaustion. Do you have to find a name for *everything*? And, if you do, what have you? Here we all are, as the Yale boys say, and devil take the hindmost. If Al Jolson makes you laugh, do you have to go home and compare him to Jonathan Swift? If Ann Harding makes you cry—God forbid—do you have to go home and look up the files of the American Mercury [Magazine] to see if you cried for art or Al Woods? It makes me think of people who say, 'What can [Al] see in that girl?' What if he does? I think he's lucky, even if she isn't art. In a couple of hundred years, we'll all look like the Main Street of Carthage and they'll have new definitions for everything. ... And *every single one of them is art*. Go on out now. It's my cue."[24] *A Woman Disputed* ran for a respectable eleven weeks.

Harry Bannister arrived in New York soon after Ann began rehearsals for *A Woman Disputed*. He had been cast in a minor role as a police inspector in George M. Cohan's *Yellow*. According to his 1942 WWII draft registration, Bannister was born in Holland, Michigan, on September 29, 1888. Following in his sister's footsteps, he had toured with stock companies as early as 1907, and made his Broadway debut in *The Passing Show of 1921*. Writer Adela Rogers St. Johns described Bannister as "a handsome, vain actor of the old-fashioned scenery-chewing school."[25] By age 38, Bannister had never given a performance that equaled the acclaim of Ann's in *Tarnish*. *Yellow* was his fourth Broadway production. Critics found the play "muddled," and failed to comment on Bannister's contribution, taking note of newcomer Spencer Tracy.

While their plays ran their courses, Ann and Harry found themselves caught in a whirlwind courtship. The 6'1", medium-build actor, affectionately referred to the 5' 2" Ann as "little feller." It wasn't long before the whirlwind picked "little feller" and Harry up, and after a four-day engagement, placed them directly upon the steps of the Little Church Around the Corner. The chapel was New York City's spiritual refuge for the acting community. On October 21, 1926, the ceremony was performed at 2:30 p.m., the rector Dr. Randolph Ray presiding. Ann's sister Edith, now Mrs. Robert Nash, was matron of honor. Ann's co-star from *A Woman Disputed*, Louis Calhern, was best man. Her producer, Al Woods, was also present. However, the quiet wedding Ann and Harry had envisioned mushroomed into something else. Not more than a dozen people had been invited. "An early edition of the afternoon papers spread the news on the front page," recalled Edith. "When we got to the church, the street was blocked, special traffic officers had

Harry Bannister. The 38-year-old "scenery-chewing" actor became Ann's husband in 1926. The couple predicted their marriage wouldn't last.

been summoned, the sidewalks were jammed, the yard was filled with the overflow from the church."[26] After the service Ann realized the pews were filled with old friends who had come to wish her well. Some she hadn't seen since her high-school days at Bryn Mawr and East Orange High. The most touching reunion occurred when a tall figure approached in the familiar O.D. (Olive Drab) uniform. Edith recalled:

It was Colonel George Vidmer, a friend of father's, who told Ann that the only quarrel he had ever had with George Gatley was over his attitude regarding her going on the stage – that he thought the Army should be represented at this wedding and that he had come in from Long Island to pay his respects. The tears were hard to control at this time, but she squeezed his hand in appreciation, in lieu of the words which were somehow choked up in her throat. Father had not even replied to her letter telling him of her approaching marriage.[27]

When the Reverend Ray retired as rector of The Little Church Around the Corner in 1958, he wrote an article titled "My Most Beautiful Bride." It was all about Ann. Of the 65,000 brides he had married, it was Ann Harding he especially remembered.

That all brides are beautiful is an old, old truth, but if I may be permitted a certain partiality, I would say Ann was the most beautiful of all. Her spun-silver hair was so ethereally blonde, her features so perfect, her eyes such a shining and heavenly blue! She was really like an angel. In view of such heavenly qualities, it is amusing to recall the very earthly snag that almost stopped the wedding. … Ann's mother failed to appear. It created a real situation. Only Ann's maid was reassuring. Knowing of the mother's absent-mindedness, she felt she had simply forgotten about it. And so she had. She had started for the church on schedule, then been distracted by the Fifth Avenue stores. The joy of shopping drove other matters from her mind – yes, even her daughter's wedding.[28]

Bessie Gatley finally showed up, a half-hour late, after she recalled where she was supposed to be. As both Ann and Harry were appearing in Broadway shows, they had selected a matinee-less day for the ceremony. A few hours later they went their separate ways for evening performances. A honeymoon was out of the question.

After the Broadway run of *A Woman Disputed,* Ann worked incessantly, taking the play out on the road. Physicians told her to rest, or face a nervous exhaustion. She refused. Very few of Ann's friends knew how serious her health crisis was. "To the eternal credit of the doctors," said Edith, "let it be said that they each and every one told her the same story—that the only thing for her to do was not to go to the theater at all—that if she insisted upon being such a fool, they would wash their hands of her."[29]

The New Year, 1927, found Ann driving herself without mercy. During a Chicago matinee performance, she ended up collapsing on stage. The curtain was held for 45 minutes while Ann was treated by what Edith described as, an "incompetent doctor." Trouper that she was, Ann revived, and in a semi-conscious condition, she was dressed and thrust upon stage. Her indomitable will helped her to complete the performance. The doctor unwisely permitted her to return to the theatre that evening. "As she reached for her make-up," recalled Edith, "she quite suddenly went out of her head. It was the only real case of hysterics she has ever had in her life. She sent for the stage manager and told him that there was a girl upstairs, playing a bit, who knew Ann's lines—she was a good little actress and could be depended upon to step right into the show." The management point-blank refused, telling Ann they would refund the $3,000 the sold-out house had netted. Ann would have to reimburse the theatre for the loss. Ann went ballistic. She grabbed items from her dressing table and threw them against the walls. She told the managers they could "Go to hell!" and ordered them out of her dressing room. After her tirade, *A Woman Disputed* quickly folded. Mary Newcomb, who took over Ann's role, failed to establish herself as a successful substitute.

Once home in New York, Ann's system failed to rally. She was carried off to a hospital where she was persuaded that rest was imperative. Like a good little soldier, Ann listened to the orders of her physician, Dr. Louise Quinn, and packed herself off to a heavenly resort in the Catskills to recuperate. In February 1927, newspapers reported that she had been sent to a sanatorium at Ossining, New York.[30] During the first weeks of her recovery, Ann would burst into tears at the very mention of stepping on to *any* stage—ever! Her sister noted that it was months before this feeling wore off. It wasn't until the fall that Ann felt like reporting to Al Woods, and fulfilling her contract obligation. *The Trial of Mary Dugan* would be her last great stage success before moving on to Hollywood.

A few years later, after Ann and Harry settled into their magnificent hilltop home in the San Bernardino Mountains, she looked back. "My memories of the theater are not pleasant," she admitted. "Hard work, constant struggle and study, stuffy hotels, cold, ill health. Though not actively discontented then, I felt no firm ground. Crudity and impermanence surrounded me, and too many cross currents of vague dissatisfactions. Life holds much more out here."[31] A marriage plagued with frequent separations did not erase the feeling of impermanence. "When we were married," Ann stated, "we did not expect it to last. We were lonely, both concerned with getting stage jobs in New York, and were swell friends. So we began by realizing that most marriages are not successful. Most lovers delude themselves into thinking they are different from every other couple, that no love was ever as wonderful as theirs. We assumed that we weren't any different from anyone else. Said, 'This will probably bust up in a couple years.'"[32] As it would turn out, Ann and Harry's "bust up" was merely postponed. And, like most "every other couple," the intervening step of motherhood merely prolonged the inevitable.

(Endnotes)

1   Sidney Fine, *Frank Murphy, Vol.2*, University of Chicago Pr., c.1975, pg 89
2   Douglas Linder, *The Sweet Trials: An Account*, c. 2000, www.law.umck.edu
3   Douglas Linder, *The Sweet Trials: An Account*, c. 2000, www.law.umck.edu
4   Sidney Fine, *Frank Murphy, Vol. 2*, University of Chicago Pr., c 1975, pg 165
5   Marcet Haldeman-Julius, *Clarence Darrow's Two Greatest Trials*, Haldeman-Julius co. 1927
6   Marcet Haldeman-Julis, *Clarence Darrow's ...*
7   Douglas Linder, *The Sweet Trials ...*
8   Douglas Linder, *The Sweet Trials ...*
9   Douglas Linder, *The Sweet Trials ...*
10 Phyllis Vine, *One Man's Castle: Clarence Darrow in Defense of the American Dream*, Harper-Collins, c. 2005, pg 260
11 Sidney Fine, *Frank Murphy Vol.2*, University of Chicago Pr., c. 1975, pg 166
12 National Press Release, "Ann Harding Joins NAACP," May 18, 1934, NAACP Branch Files (January – June 1934)
13 Sidney Fine, *Frank Murphy Vol. 2*, University of Chicago Pr., c. 1975, pg 89
14 Sidney Fine, *Frank Murphy Vol.2*, University of Chicago Pr., c. 1975, pg 256
15 Joyce Murdoch, Deb Price, *Courting Justice: Gay Men and Lesbian V. the Supreme Court*, Basic Books, c. 2002, pg 19
16 Joyce Murdoch, Deb Price, *Courting Justice ...* pg. 19
17 Edith Gatley Nash, "My Sister ..."
18 Alice L. Tildesley, "Propinquity – First Aid to Cupid," *Oakland Tribune*, 5/11/30
19 "Wilbur at Work," *Oakland Tribune*, 10/6/26
20 Review of *A Woman Disputed*, *Time*, 10/11/1926
21 James Robert Parish, *RKO Gals*, Rainbow Books, c. 1974, pg 18
22 Review of *A Woman Disputed. The New York Times*, 9/29/1926
23 Samuel Hoffenstien, "Miss Harding Says a Word or Two," *New York Times*, 10/17/26
24 Samuel Hoffenstein, "Miss Harding ..."
25 Gene Ringgold, "Ann Harding," *Films in Review*, March 1972, pg 134
26 Edith Nash Gatley, "My Sister ..."
27 Edith Nash Gatley, "My Sister ..."
28 Dr. J. H. Randolph Ray, "My Most Beautiful Bride," *Parade Magazine, Cedar Rapids Gazette*, 6/8/1958
29 Edith Nash Gatley, "My Sister ..."
30 *Chester Times*, 2/12/27
31 Myrtle Gebhart, "The Happiest Woman in Hollywood," *Picture Play*, 3/31
32 Ben Maddox, "Discovering Hollywood's *Real* Sophisticate-Ann Harding!" *Screenland*, November 1931

Ann taking the witness stand for the acclaimed Broadway production
The Trial of Mary Dugan (1927). With Rex Cherryman

6
On Trial –
Mary Dugan & Motherhood

Ann acknowledged that one of the reasons she was drawn to Harry was his ability to laugh at things. "I have never seen a situation from which he couldn't extract some ray of humor," she said. "My own play spirit had been slowly dying from too much work and insufficient companionship. But when I married I learned, with Harry, to laugh at the little things. And this was no small effort at first."[1] For the latter part of 1927, Ann and Harry resided exclusively in New York. During rehearsals for *The Trial of Mary Dugan*, Ann was bolstered by her husband's wit and companionship, thus avoiding another physical-mental breakdown. In the months ahead, however, there would be more on trial than Miss Dugan.

Before the opening of *Mary Dugan*, Ann had a run-in with Al Woods. It started in Al's office while Ann was reading the script for the three-act courtroom drama. The first act built up into a frenzy, then culminated with a life-size nude portrait of Mary Dugan (Ann's character) being brought onto the stage. "What are you going to do here, Al, instead of the photograph?" she asked him quietly. "Why, sweetheart, that's the best first act curtain I've staged in ten years," replied Al. "Now don't worry." Ann maintained an icy silence. Al could see storm clouds gathering in her heavenly blue eyes. "I'm not asking you to pose for it," he reassured her. "I got that all fixed – got something to show you." Al buzzed his secretary, who came in staggering under a seven-foot likeness of Ann. "See, sweetheart," smiled Al. "I got a *Follies* girl to pose for it!" Ann gaped at the tasteless photo. The girl's head was turned to one side with counterfeit blonde Harding hair superimposed upon it. "For all intents and purposes," recalled Ann's sister, "it was a life-size study of Ann Harding in the nude!"[2] When Ann realized she wasn't dreaming, she sputtered, "Al Woods! *I* know I didn't pose for it, but the people out front could never be convinced of the fact. Take it out of here—tear it up—burn it!" Woods was on the verge of crying. He pleaded with her. Using mixed logic, he told her he wasn't interested in hiring an actress who *wouldn't* be offended by the photo. Directly after leaving Al's office, Ann appealed to Actors Equity Association. They insisted the photo *was* part of the play, and refused to help her. Ann told them, in no uncertain terms, that she was ready to go back to pounding a typewriter for a living. Finally, a compromise was reached by draping the Follies girl in something appropriate for the boudoir. Ann would pay the price later on for this "change of scenery."

Depriving audiences of contemplating Ann Harding wearing only a smile made no difference at the box office. Bayard Veiller's *The Trial of Mary Dugan* opened September 19, 1927, and caused a sensation. The play was a fresh, effective slant on sensational trials. Broadway's National Theatre was boldly dressed as New York's State Supreme Court. The audience was the jury. Actors in police uniforms patrolled the lobby. "Scrubwomen" dusted the props on stage during intermission. In Act One, Ann, as Follies beauty Mary Dugan, was ushered on stage, accused of murdering her sugar daddy, a prominent millionaire banker. The trial was on. The National Theatre's walls trembled as battling attorneys pried open confessions of innocence, shame and guilt. The audience was startled when Mary confessed she lived with a married man, and tittered after the District Attorney growled at her: "You mean to say that you lived with him because he gave you a Rolls-Royce?" "Yes," Mary stiffened. "A girl gets kind of used to luxury."

As the final curtain fell, the audience not only knew what verdict to render, but understood the motives of Mary Dugan. Ann's character, like her stage father before her, "Massah X" from *Thoroughbreds,* turned vice into virtue. Her love affairs with multiple men enabled her to put her younger brother, Jimmy Dugan (Rex Cherryman), through law school. It is Cherryman who comes to his sister's rescue. He replaces Mary's fumbling excuse of a lawyer, who, it turns out, is the real murderer bent on framing Mary Dugan. *Time* found the play moved "more swiftly than the law with all its ruthless directness. Its plot has the fascinating features of a front page murder story."[3] *The New York Times* found the play to be "pieced together with superb theatrical skill. … when the jury clapped eyes upon the winsome person of Ann Harding, with golden locks, tearful eyes, and one of the truest, bluest personalities ever seen inside a smelly court room, every man in the audience immediately had the verdict at the tip of his tongue … Miss Harding in the rather negative part of Mary Dugan sniffed and sobbed in a mellow voice with complete verisimilitude."[4] *Mary Dugan* was a smash hit and ran two seasons for a legendary 437 performances.

Although Ann was repelled by having a nude likeness of her on stage, she had no problem at all embracing the character of Mary

Dugan. She bluntly told Hollywood reporter Ben Maddox a couple of years later, "I have no sense of morals. What is sin? Drinking and promiscuous love affairs? I suppose such actions would qualify. Well, if I felt like leading a wild life I would. But doing wrong just isn't fun for me because it's contrary to common sense! Leading a fast life automatically reacts against one. So why court obvious disaster? I belong to no established church. Heaven and Hell, in my way of reasoning, are just the morning after. I could never get any fun out of doing something which would make me sick or remorseful the next day!"[5]

Harry Bannister's play, *Revelry*, which opened shortly before *Mary Dugan,* pointed a crooked finger at the Warren G. Harding administration. The play was blasted by Atkinson's *The New York Times* review. He said the production's "scissors and paste-pot structure ... brings none of the magic of the theatre into the sordid tale it unfolds." Bannister's contribution was lumped together with what Atkinson labeled as, "an average troupe of players with various degrees of skill and incompetence."[6] The play closed after a few weeks. Bannister then had his hopes set for the lead in a dramatization of Sinclair Lewis' evangelical-themed *Elmer Gantry.* Bayard Veiller, who had penned *Mary Dugan,* spent six months translating the sensational 1927 novel for the stage. The book had been banned in Boston, and denounced from pulpits nationwide. Much to Bannister's disappointment, Veiller destroyed the manuscript, returned his $2,000 advance royalties, and explained that any production of the novel would offend "too many people, especially clergymen [and] increase hostility toward the theatre."[7] The following year, Patrick Kearney's stage adaptation included such pernicious touches as Gantry seducing a deacon's daughter, and upon being corralled into marrying her, praying, "Show me some way out of this marriage, for Christ's sake, Amen." This version of *Gantry* premiered on Broadway, but *without* Bannister. (*Gantry's* most acclaimed version would be on film, and would garner Burt Lancaster an Oscar in 1961.)

The Bannisters mixed socially with other promising talent such as Kay Francis (who had just played in the Al Woods production *Crime*). The couple joined Kay and actor McKay Morris (whom Ann had toured with in *The School Mistress*) for dinner soon after the opening of *Mary Dugan*. On Ann and Harry's first anniversary Kay invited them over for cocktails.[8] For New Year's 1928, Ann and Harry took a break from the stage to enjoy a belated honeymoon through the Canal Zone. On January 16, they arrived back in New York from their nine-day cruise aboard the *S.S. Ancon*. The famous steamer had been the first ship to transit the Panama Canal in 1914. Refreshed from their voyage, Ann continued her success with *Mary Dugan*. She reaped an income that winter that enabled Harry to invest in a summer stock company at Pittsburgh's Nixon Theatre. During Ann's five-week summer vacation, she joined her husband in Pittsburgh, to give birth to their "joint production" - a daughter.

Jane Bannister was born July 24, 1928, in a Pittsburgh hospital. A week later, in a weakened condition, Ann was back on stage rehearsing the old Jane Cowl role for Harry's production of *Smilin' Through*. Intent on her husband having a profitable run at the Nixon, Ann attempted another role in James Montgomery's comedy *Nothing But the Truth*. While rehearsing in a wheelchair, she collapsed. Bannister was without a star. His high hopes for the Nixon Theatre engagement proved disappointing.

At the end of August, Ann became a "gold digger" once more, and joined the Chicago company of *Mary Dugan*. Baby Jane went with her. While the *Trial of Mary Dugan* repeated its Broadway success, Ann confessed that motherhood was her best role ever. In December, she offered an interview to Walter T. Brown, an editor of the Associated Press, while holding five-month-old Jane in her arms. Ann adjusted the nipple on a bottle of milk, Jane squirmed impatiently, and Brown listened. "Harry and I are working as hard as we do," rationalized Ann, "the sooner to have a small home with a yard around it for this little lady."[9] Between acts, Brown observed that Ann was immediately at Jane's side. "The fun of motherhood is being with her, and doing things for her," Ann added. As for seeking new stage opportunities, she balked. Ann's tune was changing. She glanced down at Jane, and smiled, "Oh, I haven't an ambition to do this or that role. The stage is not everything. *This* is the greatest role." After lapsing into momentary baby talk with Jane, Ann expressed interest in directing plays that Bannister might produce. "In that way," enthused Ann, "we three could be together all the time. My home is going to be my first interest, but I would like to do directing, too. I think a woman with energy and strength can have dual interests, but always the home first."[10] At one point, Ann traveled with infant Jane from Chicago to New York, stopped off there for a week, and then went to Philadelphia, then back to Chicago. One columnist commented, "The matter of keeping milk bottles sanitary, and all the difficulties of traveling with a tiny baby, did not frighten the cool, courageous Ann."[11]

Harry's luck turned when he was offered a lead in the New York Theatre Guild's touring production of Eugene O'Neill's experimental, banned-in-Boston play, *Strange Interlude*. Bannister's engagement began at New York's John Golden Theatre on December 17, 1928. Stopping at twelve major cities en route to the Pacific Coast, every performance was sold out. Bannister took on the role of Edmund "Ned" Darrell, a doctor, who impregnates his patient, Nina Leeds, to avoid the possibility of her having a mentally disabled child. The calculating Nina had aborted her first baby upon discovering that her husband's family had a history of insanity. During their "procedure" Nina and the doctor had fallen in love. *The New York Times* critic J. Brooks Atkinson compared the play's tormented themes to a bucket that drops "to the bottom of a black well." He also felt that the touring company did not hold up to the original cast, finding Bannister, "forceful without catching the prescience of Mr. O'Neill's mood."[12]

According to Ann's sister Edith, as the cast headed to California after a New York run, "Ann arranged the cancellation of her contract with Woods, [and] after making a final appearance in *Mary Dugan* in Newark, bundled Jane and the nurse, the crib and the carriage onto a train heading for Los Angeles."[13] Ann anticipated a long rest, and avoided relocating to one of the more obvious areas like Beverly Hills, where acquaintances from New York had taken up residence. She focused on the heart of the San Fernando Valley, twenty minutes northwest of the Hollywood hubbub. Locating a cozy cottage to rent on Sun Swept Drive, in the suburbs of Van Nuys, Ann felt right at home. The place had a yard, surrounded by a vine-covered wall, where Jane could lie in her carriage under real orange trees. Harry arrived in Los Angeles in March 1929 for the opening of *Strange Interlude* at the Biltmore Theatre.

Edith had left out one important detail. Film historian Gene Ringgold claims that Woods took revenge on Ann's vetoing the nude photo for *Mary Dugan*. Ann was first in line for the lead role as Nina Leeds in the Broadway premier of Eugene O'Neill's *Strange Interlude*. Woods refused to release her from her contract. It is a fact that O'Neill had specifically suggested Ann for the role. In a letter dated April 4, 1927, O'Neill noted that Ann Harding, as Nina, "would look it better than anyone."[14] After Woods' refusal, the coveted role of Nina was handed over to the legendary Lynn Fontanne. O'Neill revealed his full power as a dramatist in *Strange Interlude*, and won the Pulitzer Prize for Drama. "Ann's disappointment was keen," stated Ringgold. However, in one of her typically ambiguous responses to the press regarding the matter, Ann mused, "I had no idea Mr. O'Neill was particularly aware of my existence."[15] By the time Harry's tour reached the west coast, Ann was contentedly focused on hearth and home. *Strange Interlude's* engagement at the Biltmore, with Judith Anderson in the lead role, was well-received. The house was packed for every performance, and moved over to the Music Box for an extended stay. The *Los Angeles Times* felt the cumulative effect of the play had great power. However, the *Times* felt that the principals were secondary to O'Neill's authorship, and that Bannister fell short of being "consistently good."[16]

Harry enjoyed coming home nights to the place Ann had found. They were able to share in little Jane's triumphs: her first words, first steps, and all the little tricks that keep parents bragging. "But why live in Van Nuys?" people would ask. Aside from the aforementioned reasons, Ann considered the advice of her friend, actress Pauline Garon, who was one of the dozen original guests at Ann and Harry's wedding. When Garon, recently divorced from Lowell Sherman, heard that Ann and Harry were headed west, she warned them ahead of time to keep a low profile. Ann recalled, "Pauline said to us, 'Keep this happiness of yours a deep, deep secret. Never let anyone know, because there is nothing in the world that Hollywood resents so much or punishes so inexorably as a happy marriage. They simply won't have it. They will destroy it as surely as you let them find out!'"[17] Lowell Sherman, Ann's co-star from *A Woman Disputed*, blamed Garon's parents for their divorce. She blamed Hollywood. In the meantime, thanks to her advice, peace and happiness hovered over the Bannister-Harding home.

The California climate was invigorating and healing for Ann. She was not anxious to return to the stage, and was unwavering in her devotion to Jane. Ann would soon discover that film work was much more accommodating to motherhood than the stage had been. Even so, a couple of years later when the going got rough, Ann still rallied for Jane's sake. One deeply impressed by this mother-daughter relationship was Oscar-winning scenarist Adela Rogers St. Johns. After a trying day at the studio, St. Johns followed Ann home one evening to rework some dialogue from Philip Barry's *Animal Kingdom*. Ann looked almost sick from nervous exhaustion. St. Johns watched in amazement at Ann's transformation upon seeing Jane, who was three at the time.

> When we went into Jane's bedroom … [Ann] threw off every trace of that fatigue. It was an effort, but plainly she wasn't going to let Jane see a worn-out, white-faced mother. From somewhere within herself she conjured up life and joy and color. I watched them as they romped and laughed and I was vitally conscious of … a woman who works as hard or harder than any man and who is also a mother. I saw Ann put her baby to bed and kneel down and listen to the little prayers that children have said to mothers for centuries. And I remember that as I looked at Jane I wondered if she was praying to a God

Upon arriving in Los Angeles, Ann and daughter Jane enjoy
the California sunshine. (1929) (Courtesy of Wisconsin
Center for Film and Theater Research)

she didn't as yet quite realize, or only to her gentle
mother, who had been the companion and joy of
her whole existence. And I remember thinking that
it didn't matter much for perhaps they were one.[18]

Ann's own philosophy on motherhood wasn't of the old school. She
came to her own conclusions on the subject, saying, "I think mothers shouldn't take themselves so seriously. After all, mother love is
planted in us before we are born … it's no credit to us that we love our
children. If we deserve it perhaps they will love us back, but they owe
us nothing just because we love them. We haven't done anything special when we have cared for them in their helplessness. Now that I'm a

mother myself, I can say the things I've thought for years yet couldn't mention …. One of them is that mothers aren't naturally wiser than other people; they don't discover through the physical act of bringing forth a baby exactly what is best for that infant … People who have studied children are quite likely to know better than mothers who haven't."[19] As far as sidestepping motherhood for the sake of a career, Ann put it bluntly, "It is silly to talk about choosing between the two when the obvious solution is to have both."[20] Ann scoffed at the furor over men and women working shoulder to shoulder. "Certainly we aren't the first generation to do it," she argued, pointing to the pioneer women who worked in the fields, assisted in the plowing, hoeing and harvesting.[21] "I've never heard any complaint leveled against *them* for these activities," she added. Ann felt the discontented, unsuccessful wives were women of too much leisure, and emphasized that "busy women [do not have] time to magnify petty slights."[22]

Despite her philosophies, Ann had to admit that her break from work was a godsend. Little Jane was becoming huskier, happier, and pinker. Ann's vitality returned, and she acknowledged that her new surroundings had something to do with it. She exclaimed to one visitor, "Grass! Real trees – not props! A sky without smoke over it! Roses in January! Neighbors, if there were any, would probably think me mad. I go to pieces every morning at the sight of flowers growing and goldfish in a pool. And it isn't a park! I can walk on the grass and pick flowers without trembling before signs warning me not to. Years of living in hotels and twentieth-floor apartments have made me a fool for nature."[23] She and Harry took into consideration the potential Southern California might afford them. The following year, Ann told a reporter, "No one even knew I was in town. For two months we were in bliss, marred by no worries on my part about my work. I was just a regular housewife, taking care of the baby and cooking. It was a delightful, if long, delayed, honeymoon."[24]

After Bannister's nine-week west coast run of *Strange Interlude*, Judith Anderson departed, and the company was without a female lead. The play was scheduled to head back east. "The Guild had offered Nina to me," said Ann. "I was going to continue on the road, working with Harry, which was grand."[25] But, instead of impressing the few measly million inhabitants of Chicago as Nina Leeds, Ann Harding decided to make yet another complete about turn. She opted to abandon the stage and mesmerize the world ... on celluloid.

(Endnotes)

1   Ann Harding, "How I Make My Husband Happy," *San Mateo Times*, 6/17/31
2   Edith Nash Gatley, "My Sister ..."
3   Review of *Trial of Mary Dugan*, *Time*, 10/3/27
4   J. Brooks Atkinson, review of *Trial of Mary Dugan*, *New York Times*, 9/20/1927
5   Ben Maddox, "Discovering Hollywood's *Real* Sophisticate-Ann Harding!" *Screenland*, November, 1931
6   J. Brooks Atkinson, review of *Revelry*, *New York Times*, 9/13/27
7   "'Gantry Will Not Appear on Stage," *Gettysburg Times*, 10/29/1927
8   Kay Francis Diary, October 21, 1927, Wesleyan Cinema Archives
9   Walter T. Brown, "Stage 'Mary Dugan' Believes Motherhood Greatest Role," *Gazette and Bulletin(PA)*, 12/21/1928
10   Walter T. Brown, "Stage ..."
11   Elza Schallert, "Are The Stars Good Parents?" *Picture Play*, May 1930
12   J. Brooks Atkinson, review of *Strange Interlude*, *New York Times*, 12/18/1928
13   Edith Nash Gatley, "My Sister ..."
14   Doris Alexander, "Eugene O'Neill's Creative Struggle," Pennsylvania State University Pr., c 1992, pg 124 (Earlier that year, O'Neill had also mentioned Ann for the role of Pompeia in his rarely produced play *Lazarus Laughed*)
15   Gene Ringgold, "Ann Harding," *Films in Review*, March 1972
16   Edwin Schallert, review of *Strange Interlude*, *Los Angeles Times*, 3/5/1929
17   "Hollywood's Forbidden Sins," *Picture Play*, February 1934
18   Adela Rogers St. Johns, "The Harding-Bannister ..."
19   Alice L. Tildesley, "How Shall Women Escape Boredom?" *Oakland Tribune*, 6/14/31
20   "Ann Harding Speaks," *Lincoln Star*, 5/31/31
21   Duane Hennessy, " Hollywood Film Shop," *Mexia Weekly Herald*, 8/4/31
22   Alice L. Tildesley, "The Woman of 1930-Success or Failure?" *Galveston Daily News*, 12/29/30
23   Margaret Reid, "Blond – But Not Light," *Picture Play*, May 1930
24   "Ann Harding Honeymoon Postponed Three Years," *Oakland Tribune*, 11/16/30
25   Margaret Reid, "Blond – But Not Light," *Picture Play*, May 1930

7
Hollywood Bound

When Ann and Harry arrived in California, film studios were luring talent from Broadway. Some of Al Woods' former players, such as Sylvia Sidney, Kay Francis, Leslie Howard, Joan Blondell, Clark Gable and Claudette Colbert, were becoming locked exclusively into filmmaking. As a self-appointed spokesperson for her fellow stage actors, Ann felt called upon at one point to explain the phenomenon of Broadway talent being gobbled up by Hollywood. She penned an article for *Theatre Magazine* cleverly titled "Broadway, You'll Find, Runs West." Her perceptions were on target. Ann claimed to have met so many familiar faces from her stage days in Hollywood that she caught herself "absent-mindedly searching for a subway kiosk." In the summer of 1930, while filming *Holiday*, Ann, and her co-star Mary Astor, took a break together one afternoon. Ann recalled,

> I had to apply my brakes to avoid a head-on with
> June Collyer and Dorothy Burgess, like us pilgrims
> from Broadway. … In the space of the first fifteen
> minutes we met Ruth Chatterton, Basil Rathbone,
> Claudette Colbert and Helen Twelvetrees – all driv-
> ing. Out on Sunset Boulevard we passed—or were

passed by—Jack Barrymore and Walter Pidgeon.
We saw George Arliss and Raymond Hackett in
Beverly Hills. And then, from a side street, which
he had no right to do, there came Dennis King in a
speedy roadster. He waved cheerfully and went on.
"The king," Mary observed, "can do no wrong." ...
It is impossible to go anywhere now without running into a Broadway face. ... stage folk are not here
long before California weather and California real
estate enter into their thoughts and their conversations. The weather is first and then, if there has been
a contract signed, that is where the real estate comes
in. And, how it comes![1]

In the summer of 1929, before "the contract" and "the real estate"
came into the picture, the Bannisters were focused on the theater, and
their Chicago engagement of *Strange Interlude*. Although Ann was
enthusiastic about playing opposite Harry on stage, she later admitted she didn't miss anything by *not* playing Nina Leeds. "I'm glad I
didn't," stated Ann. "It was an awful ordeal for the actors. Toward
the end of the run Pauline Lord [the original Nina in the Guild tour]
would give her long speech and then sigh, 'Thank God, that's over.'"[2]

Frank Reicher, a fellow actor who had left Broadway for Hollywood, became the link between Ann and film stardom. Having kept
a low profile for several months, Ann finally decided it was time to
mingle and venture outside of her comfy shell in Van Nuys. "We
wanted to see a studio," Ann explained, "and our friend Frank Reicher
took us through Pathé studio. After lunch he suggested that we have a
test made. We refused, as we had refused a couple of previous suggestions from other companies [Fox, Paramount, MGM]."[3] Pathé, with

its crowing-cock trademark, was an American offshoot of a French film company that had invented the newsreel, among other cinematic innovations. By 1929, Pathé, whose top star was Constance Bennett, was struggling to compete with the larger studios. Their string of action features went by the wayside in favor of more sophisticated fare. Ann was the epitome of a cosmopolitan leading lady. Reicher was anxious to see how she looked and sounded on film, and kept nudging her. Finally, Ann complied, although she was more concerned about Reicher losing his job. "It would be a lark," she told him, "but I know a screen test costs a studio a great deal of money, and I don't want you to be responsible for having made one of me, since I have no intention of doing picture work." As a sort of jest, Ann and Harry filmed a low comedy scene, despite Reicher's plea for something more serious. Even so, Pathé was impressed with what they saw, and kept making offers until Ann could not afford to refuse. In truth, she held out until they also offered Harry a contract. The couple agreed they would sink or swim together in this new racket.[4]

Reicher had been assigned as dialogue director for the film version of the scintillating 1927 Philip Barry stage hit *Paris Bound*, which asked audiences to believe that a young married couple could remain spiritually committed while philandering with others. Reicher asked Ann how she would like to play the leading role. She was impressed that Pathé would produce such an "intelligent" play. "It's such a grand part," Ann gushed, "that I can hardly think of anyone else having it. I loved the character. She has intelligence; she thinks straight and recognizes her mistakes."[5] The influence of Jasper Deeter was also behind Ann's decision to tackle the role. He had cautioned her never to utter a line in a part until she believed in the character and identified herself with its personality.[6]

Ann's screen debut in *Paris Bound* (1929) co-starred
Fredric March. (Pathé) (Courtesy of Photofest)

In *Paris Bound*, Ann's character (Mary) consents to remain faithful to her fiancé, Jim (Fredric March) ... in spirit. On their wedding
day, we see a tipsy ex-girlfriend of Jim's, Noel (Carmelita Geraghty),
proposition him. He resists temptation. Four years later, Mary decides *not* to accompany Jim to Europe on business. "I have a notion
that married people need a holiday from each other once and awhile,"
Mary explains to him. She stays home with their child. While on the
Continent, Jim frequently succumbs to Noel's previous offer. Upon
finding out this bit of news, Mary turns conventional and tells her father-in-law, "I'm not doing any sharing. I'm going to divorce." Re-en-
ter Richard (Leslie Fenton), a ballet composer, who has long carried
a torch for Mary. He claims that he cannot finish his "masterpiece"
until they consummate their love. Mary's compassion for Richard's

dilemma melts into a passionate kiss. When Jim arrives home, Mary attempts to tell him of her plans for divorce, but is reminded instead of the spiritual vow they had made: "Nothing in any world can affect us!" She realizes that what happened to Jim could happen to her ... could happen to any couple.

Edward H. Griffith, director of *Paris Bound*, was impressed with Ann's dauntless and disciplined personality on the set. Before production began, Ann seriously sprained her finger. Her physician designed a removable splint for her to wear during filming. Cast members in Ann's bridal scene had been warned to avoid *any* contact with her hand. After Griffith called "Action!" he looked on in horror as someone grabbed Ann's hand with considerable force. "Miss Harding almost fainted with pain *after* the scene was finished," recalled Griffith, "but not a soul on the set knew that anything had happened until I had called 'Cut.' She went through with the smiles and animation demanded of her, spoke her lines as beautifully as always and gave no indication of her own suffering. To do that demands that one be a great woman as well as a great actress. She has inherited some of [her father's] soldier qualities."[7]

Paris Bound's premier on August 3, 1929, proved that Ann's discipline paid off, and that the camera adored her hair and eyes. The dynamic teaming of Harding and March brought a naturalness to the screen. Although it suffered from the static camerawork of early sound films, *Paris Bound* was, according to *Time* magazine, "an immediate and brilliant success."[8] Film critic Chester Bahn thought *Paris Bound* the finest picture "since the screen found its voice." He continued, "Ann Harding makes a splendid impression ... She is an actress of ability. Her work throughout has the sterling mark of sincerity. ... Miss Harding and Mr. March play a climactic moment that is purest gold."[9]

Mordaunt Hall of *The New York Times* felt *Paris Bound* maintained the theme and tenor of the play. He agreed with Ann's consensus of her role. "Her actions and cutting off of parts of words," Hall wrote, "are very natural. ... It is in fact a joyous relief to study the work of an actress in a motion picture who is so modulated in her talking and whose performance throughout is so different from other players."[10] In a typical ploy for 1929, ads for the film promised audiences, "You'll gasp at every spoken word!" Pathé began to promote Harding as "the girl with the sex appeal voice." Director Griffith joined in the hype to say, "Any man who heard her voice over the microphone would want to see her in person."[11] Along with her coiffure, the quality of Ann's voice was invariably mentioned in reviews. At the apex of her film career one critic christened Ann as having "The Voice of Temple Gongs."[12]

During the filming of *Paris Bound*, MGM released *The Trial of Mary Dugan*, the talkie debut of Norma Shearer. If MGM had known that the play's original star was available and living in Los Angeles County, it would have made no difference. Shearer had signed on for the lead as Mary Dugan in late 1928. Besides, she was the wife of MGM's top producer, Irving Thalberg. Prized roles fell into Norma's lap, and she rarely disappointed. Critics hailed Shearer's voice and performance a triumphant success. When asked a few years later if she would like to do a remake of *Mary Dugan*, Ann was emphatic. "Oh no!" she shook her head, "I just hated that play—although it had such a long run on Broadway. To sit there, in that courtroom, my character exposed, inch by inch, was real torture. In fact, I used to faint at the end of the show night after night. I loathed it."[13] As it turned out, Ann's own decision to align herself with Pathé was a smart move.

Harry and Ann's first Hollywood social outing was a buffet supper at the Hollywood home of their friend from Broadway, Kay Francis. The September 7, 1929, affair included the Fredric Marches, Charles MacArthur and Helen Hayes, Paul Lukas, Sally Eilers, and directors King Vidor, John Cromwell, and Edward Sutherland.[14] Ann's first interview for filmland's classiest magazine, *Photoplay*, was with Marquis Busby, a critic for the *Los Angeles Times* and one-time lover of director Edmund Goulding.[15] Busby enjoyed Ann's friendly spirit and "gorgeous" sense of humor. He had waited patiently from 7:30 pm until

Ann and Harry in *Her Private Affair* (1929). (Pathé)

midnight in order to capture a twenty-minute chat with Ann between takes on the set of *Her Private Affair*. Harry, her leading man, was nearby, sitting for portraits, and popping in at one point to present her with a popcorn ball wrapped in bright red paper. Busby thought the confection looked unappetizing, but thought Ann exquisite. After Scene 20, Retake 2, Busby noted that Ann put aside acting immediately. She patted the head of an assistant and cooed in her million-dollar voice, "Tell me you love me." All the assistant could manage was a sheepish grin. Ann perched herself atop a suitcase near Busby and looked around to ask, "Can I bum a cigarette from someone?" Another assistant came forward. "Oh, there you are!" Ann smiled. Turning to Busby she said, "We smoke the same brand. He's such a comfort." She mentioned how much she loved the west coast, the joys of motherhood, and how sweet Harry was. Minutes later, Viennese director Paul Stein pages Ann for an emotional wrestle with the film's heavy, Lawford Davidson. The dramatic plot, according to Busby, was rather obvious. "Well, do I get the letters," Ann's character asks, "or must I pay cash on delivery?" "You needn't make me out quite the blackmailer," replies Davidson. After a struggle, Ann pulls the trigger of a revolver, which emits smoke after an ineffectual "pop." Busby thought it just the kind of plot Al Woods would love. Ann rejoined Busby, and talked about Harry's passion for aviation. After *Strange Interlude* had closed in Salt Lake City, Harry, now a licensed pilot, had flown to Los Angeles. Interrupting her again, director Stein called her back to the set. Ann excused herself, and apologized, "I must shoot that nice villain again." Busby commented that he "almost forgave her entirely" for the badly interrupted interview, which she didn't seem to take very seriously.[16]

"The Voice of Temple Gongs" could not save the overwrought melodramatics of *Her Private Affair*. Ann's woebegone tremor rang a death knell throughout the film's 61 minutes. Paul Stein, who had directed Constance Bennett in her successful talkie-debut, was of no help. Neither was Ann's former costar from the stage, Rollo Lloyd, who served as dialog director. Released on the heels of *Paris Bound*, audiences were drawn to it expecting more cinematic caviar with Ann Harding. James Robert Parish refers to the film as an offering of "re-hashed beef stew."[17] As Vera Kessler, Ann plays a wife recently recon-ciled with her husband, a prominent Viennese judge (Bannister). She is being blackmailed for her flirtation with a notorious gigolo. The scuffle between Vera, her tormentor, and the revolver ended in his demise. Ann's best moment comes at a society nightspot. Guilt-rid-den that her paramour's servant was arrested for a crime she commit-ted, Vera loses control when a rumor surfaces that a society woman committed the murder. Guests down tubs of champagne while at-tempting to zero in on who the woman might be. Having her fill of "the bubbly" and the topic at hand, Vera exclaims, "Just think! That woman may be anywhere. Anywhere at all. Why, she may even be here!" Her friends look at her incredulously. "Vera, you're acting so strangely!" On the verge of hysterics, Vera wails, "Well, why not? If, as you say, she's a woman of prominence in society, then what could be more natural than that she should be here, tonight? I can almost see her. People come up to her. They greet her. Why, at this very mo-ment she may be discussing the murder!!" Ann is wonderfully over the top. It's the film's most interesting, if bizarre moment.

Bannister, as Judge Kessler, presides over the murder case. As an actor, Bannister lacked animation. His voice was a steady, deep, monotone. His profile sported an unusually-shaped, bulbous nose. There were moments in *Her Private Affair* when Ann herself seemed unsure of her performance. As an acting team, Ann and Harry lacked fire. The Lunts they were not. Surprisingly, the film did well at the box office. *The New York Times* felt that Ann easily led her co-players with a sensitive portrayal. "The more crucial moments," stated the review, "smack too much of improbable coincidence, but primarily because of Miss Harding's charm, the film eventually shapes itself into a well-rounded study of extortion and its consequences."[18] The *Los Angeles Times* was more on target, saying, "After it is all over ... one has the sense of having gone through an unnecessarily exhausting experience."[19] One wonders why Ann, who had approval of her scripts, would select *Her Private Affair*. Adapted from Russian playwright Leo Urvantzov's neurotic drama, *The Right to Kill*, the play had failed at Broadway's Garrick Theatre after 16 performances. Ann was less than enthusiastic about Urvantzov and his ilk, saying, "I'm so impatient with the Russian authors because they try to probe so deeply. I think they see difficulties and tragedies where none exist. They disturb me, and as I want serenity, I refuse nowadays to read them. I think they breathe bad air, these Russians. They need sunlight."[20]

On screen, Ann and Harry may have been a bust, but on the home front, things couldn't have been better. Ann pointed out, "It's the sophisticated thing to speak sarcastically of marriage, to deplore children and to talk slightingly of one's husband. I refuse to be dishonest for the sake of being orthodox. I'm happy and I don't care who knows it."[21] After three years of marriage, Ann wasn't pontificating about the glories of marital bliss. However, reporters portrayed her as the self-satisfied housewife type. "I don't know why they do it!" she laughed. "Certainly I don't harp on the happy home theme. I give them all kinds of leads, but somehow every interview comes out in the same mold. All this funny Victorian gush has been shoveled on me!"[22] "Naturally, my happiness is built on my marriage, child, and home. Sacrifice? *Please!* I loathe that word. It implies a denial of one's own wishes ... Service? A craven term, a false humility. Just call it finding one's contentment in others."[23]

While she barely escaped being behind bars in *Her Private Affair*, Ann's next role landed her in prison and into the arms of Ronald Colman. She had the good fortune to be loaned out to producer Samuel Goldwyn for his production of Blair Niles' *Condemned to Devil's Island*. Niles, who also ventured into unheard-of territory in her gay-themed *Strange Brother*, was reportedly the only woman to set foot inside the infamous French penal colony. The international sensation caused by her book led to prison reforms. Her work was in good hands. Goldwyn used only the best Hollywood had to offer. The beautifully lit and inventive photography of George Barnes and Gregg Toland was a vast improvement over other sound films being made. Visually, *Condemned* is stunning to look at. And the long hours of rehearsal Goldwyn insisted upon paid off. Colman is excellent as a suave thief named Michel, who brings his charm to the grisly penal colony. Ann, looking angelic in her grim surroundings, is effective as the lonely, unhappy and terrorized wife of Vidal, the warden (Dudley Digges). The plot is far from complex. Michel's good manners and aristocratic air place him in the warden's house as a servant. Going beyond the call

Condemned (1929). A suave Ronald Colman woos an angelic
Ann in the Samuel Goldwyn production. (United Artists)

of duty, he finds himself giving his heart to the warden's abused wife.
Michel has the temerity to point out to her, "We are *both* prisoners."
After a steady diet of Michel's sweet attentions, Madame Vidal tells
her belching, pompous, uncouth excuse-of-a-husband, "I loathe the
sight of you!" The warden puts two-and-two together. Michel ends
up in solitary and the wife is sent home to France. Mordaunt Hall
for *The New York Times* found the first half "gripping and very real,"
but conceded that Colman's prison escape through a swamp, and
eventual capture, too melodramatic. The "climatic" scenes indeed
slow down the film's momentum. Many approved of director Wesley
Ruggles' bravura style, while others felt the film needed less charm

and more realism. The *Times* review stated, "Miss Harding is lovely as Mme. Vidal. Her voice is deep but her interpretation is charming. Miss Harding senses the importance and strength of restraint. In one scene she somewhat unnecessarily displays her wealth of hair, but that was probably insisted upon by the producer."[24] (Wearing a nightgown for the scene in question, Ann had logically let down her hair.) Colman received an Oscar nomination for his combined work in *Condemned* and his first sound feature, *Bulldog Drummond.* (He lost to George Arliss in *Disraeli.*)

Upon signing on for *Condemned* (which was shot in both silent and sound versions), Ann had anticipated adventure. She was in for a surprise. "When I heard I was to play in the story of a gay ne'er-do-well who was convicted to the French prison on Devil's Island in the South Atlantic," Ann told one correspondent, "I looked forward to some interesting location trips. I thought we might go down to the ocean front, at least. Every scene of the picture was shot right on the United Artists' lot. We had our own private ocean, our own special ship … I was particularly amazed when, instead of pulling the ship away from the dock, we pulled the dock away from the ship."[25] Ann's major gripe during the production centered on the fact that Pathé was getting $5,000 a week from Sam Goldwyn for her services; she did not share in this little "bonus."

Ann had only praises for her charismatic co-star, Colman, which she expressed for a nationwide broadcast at the film's premier on December 5, 1929. The gala cinema society affair was held at Grauman's Chinese Theatre. On-the-scene columnist Myra Nye reported, "Ann Harding's modest little speech of appreciation of Ronald Colman made before the microphone in the foyer; the real excellence of the picture … all made for an outstanding pleasure even for habitual first-nighters."[26] Ann Harding was now a full-fledged movie star. And, she was amazed by the quantity of fan mail. "They come by the mailbag-full," she marveled, "from all parts of the world. Many ... from college boys, and they all get a desire to talk at length about their ideals. That may be because I have long hair."[27]

In the fall of 1929, Howard Hughes tested Ann as a replacement for Greta Nissen in his production *Hell's Angels*. He rejected Ann, along with Carole Lombard, June Collyer, and Dorothy Mackaill. Ann's buddy from Jessie Bonstelle's troupe, Ben Lyon, introduced Jean Harlow to Hughes. In spite of her lack of experience, Harlow had the "assets" Hughes was looking for. In January 1930 it was announced that Ann and Harry would co-star in Charlotte Bronte's *Jane Eyre*. "I want to make a picture in which I make the action," Ann enthused. "A dramatic picture, based on *Jane Eyre* is my next. It's a grand story. You know that marvelous scene where the wedding is stopped in the middle?"[28] After weeks of preparation, the project came to a halt. In April, after Ann withdrew from a proposed all-star production titled *Beyond Victory*, RKO was arranging to borrow her to play opposite Richard Dix in *Cimarron*. This would have been a smart move, as the film would win Best Picture in 1931, plus six other nominations, including a best actress nod for Irene Dunne. As it turned out, Ann got her own Academy Award nomination for her next project, an adaptation of Philip Barry's *Holiday*.

Film critic Mick LaSalle alludes to Ann's unadorned acting style in 1930's *Holiday* as a refreshing cinematic plunge. In it, Ann's character is in love with the fiancé of her sister (Mary Astor). "[Ann] has many close-ups in which she faces a man she adores," notes LaSalle, "[She] can't say the one thing she wants to say. Looking at Harding, is like looking into clear, deep water. Nothing stands in the way. No stylization, no attitude, no posing. In fact, little about her technique could date her as a thirties actress."[29] It had been on a dare from actress Laura Hope Crews, who was filling in as editorial adviser for Pathé, that Ann took on the lead character of Linda. Initially, Ann felt it was not her type of story. Crews bet Ann $50 that *Holiday* would prove her biggest success yet. Ann accepted and, fortunately, she lost.[30] Philip Barry, who had also penned *Paris Bound*, was important in establishing Ann's screen image as an intelligent, well-bred woman whose aloofness set her apart from the others. Her patrician looks conveyed refined passions. She had unique beliefs and attitudes about love and life.

In *Holiday*, watching Ann Harding one gets the surreal impression of an actress breathing color into a black-and-white film. She absolutely steals the thunder from the entire cast, and in the process manages to strengthen the players' essential connections to each other. Critics conceded that Ann's Linda, the warm, independent, blonde with a cool million, was a portrayal of unusual merit. Mary Astor played Julia, a materialistic,

Holiday (1930) (l-r) Robert Ames, Hedda Hopper, Edward Everett Horton, Ann. (Pathé)

status-conscious woman, who is pitted against her free-thinking, discontented, and compassionate sister. Ann's friend from Broadway, Monroe Owsley, played the sisters' booze-loving brother, Ned, who didn't have the nerve to rebel against family traditions he found repellent. Owsley had played the role for thirty-eight weeks on the New York stage. Their father (realistically played by character actor William Holden) is capable of dominating everyone in his family, except Linda.

Upon meeting her sister's fiancé, Johnny Case (Robert Ames), Linda warns him, "Money is our God here!" In jest, she chastises him for not being in the Social Register. "What!" she exclaims, "You

Ann received her only Academy Award nomination for *Holiday*.
Robert Ames co-starred. (Pathé)

mean to say your mother wasn't even a Whosit?" Her down-to-earth attitude about life sums up her palatial surroundings in one sentence, "Oh! If only I could get warm in this barn." Johnny surprises everyone by declaring he wants a lengthy "holiday" from the business world, while he is young enough to enjoy it. While Julia is hesitant about his plan, Linda sympathizes with him, steals his heart, and eventually runs away with him. Before this happens, Linda stands up to her father, his control issues, and his reverence for riches. "You thought I'd come around, didn't you?" she tells him, defiantly. "Not me!" The father argues, "If you're not happy here, why don't you go away?" It is exactly what she needs to hear. Linda's resolve to leave home is fired anew when Johnny kisses her. She gazes at him. Her eyes hold an incredible display of heart as she tenderly admits, "I wish you weren't so attractive." Julia simply shrugs her shoulders at these events. It isn't long before Linda recognizes the truth of her sister's feelings. She grabs a hold of Julia, exclaiming, "You don't love him! It's written all over you! You're *relieved* he's gone!" Julia readily admits, "I'm so relieved I could sing with it." Finally, Linda cuts loose, packs her bags, and heads off to join Johnny on his voyage abroad.

The New York Times offered, "From what was generally regarded as a good play, the film producers have managed to make a good picture. The role of Linda is filled by Ann Harding, who goes about it more than capably. ... She is graceful, she has the boyish manner suggested by the role."[31] NEA correspondent Dan Thomas enthused, "Ann Harding, in our opinion, gives by far the best performance yet recorded by a camera—which is saying quite a lot in view of the fact that she always has been considered above the average."[32] Los Angeles critic Eleanor Barnes observed, "... a haunting wistfulness that Miss Harding has exclusive copyright on, makes Linda intensely human and understandable."[33] Raves about Ann's performance simply wouldn't stop. Harrison Carroll praised, "In *Holiday* she gives a performance so sensitive, so true, so simple that I am completely won over."[34] Harrison had originally balked at the idea of Harding playing the part of Linda. He thought her screen persona too placid. A couple of weeks after his review in the *Los Angeles Evening Herald*, he explained, "I still do not believe that she physically was the type for Linda. But she has penetrated the soul of that ... courageous girl, and through the medium of her sensitive art she has illumined it for all of us to see. Out of all the plays and pictures I have seen, no actress is, for me, more completely associated with a part."[35]

Holiday's director, Edward H. Griffith, was further intrigued by Ann's unvarying quality as actress and individual. "I would say Miss Harding's most outstanding characteristic is her serene restraint," declared Griffith. "This rare gift is not an artificially cultivated one. Miss Harding's economy of movement and expression is part of her mental as well as of her physical self. I've frequently observed her sitting in a group at the edge of the set, between scenes. She was always curiously still. Here was no restless, neurotic woman, swinging her foot or twitching her hands, but a delightfully quiescent one. At the same time she is vivid and luminous, differing from her less serene sisters as does a candle burning steadily in still air, from one that flickers in the breeze."[36]

A few months before *Holiday* began filming, Mary Astor's husband, director Kenneth Hawks, lost his life in a mid-air collision while filming *Such Men are Dangerous*. Astor, extremely bitter about her husband dying for, as she put it, "one lousy scene in a movie," had been living in a listless daze of alcohol and work. She collapsed on a Paramount set, and was later diagnosed with "incipient tuberculosis."[37] Rest, sun, and a change of diet revived her spirit by the time she signed on to work with Ann. The two women found companionship and support in a friendship which helped them weather many storms in the years ahead. Astor was adept at pointing out the reality of most Hollywood "friendships." "We were friends (or enemies)," she stated, "of everybody else in the business. We were worse name-droppers than people who dropped our names. Another actor was a 'best friend,' 'know him very well,' 'died in my arms,' 'gave him his first break in that picture of mine.' That is *if* the actor had more than three figures in his weekly check, *if* he'd just received an award or plumy assignment ... *if* he gave huge parties. Sometimes we did make real friends. Such a one was Ann Harding."[38] Astor elaborated on what made Ann special for her.

> Ann was an actress rather than a star – and there *is* a difference. Her name ahead of the title, which technically made her a star of the picture did not affect or enlarge her status on the set. She was one of the first who disregarded the old star-system behavior of special treatment, special chairs, *Miss* Harding, etc. I had seen her in two of her successes on Broadway, *Tarnish* in 1923 and *The Trial of Mary Dugan* in 1928. To both she brought a new, realistic quality. In the picture she went easy on makeup: no beaded eyelashes, no heavily rouged mouth. She had beautiful skin and used practically no greasepaint and she had gorgeous, natural silver-blonde hair. She was thoroughly a member of the company, hard-working, no nonsense. These very qualities made me like her because I felt so uncomfortable with so much of

the phony nonsense that seemed to go with being an actress. With me it was a passive irritation; I felt it but didn't scratch. She did. She said, "I don't want to look like an actress, I want to look like a person." And she did and she was—a person.[39]

Astor felt "lucky" to be working in the Philip Barry project, which she found stimulating, because she found herself asking, "*Who* am I playing?" rather than, "What do I do?"[40] Years later, Astor pointed out the limitations of early sound equipment that plagued *Holiday*. For instance, it was impossible to overlap conversation. "There had to be time for the sound man to switch off one mike and switch on another," said Astor. "If the action started with you standing beside a table and then included a move to a chair by the fireplace, you could speak into a mike at the table, but you couldn't talk on the way over; you'd have to wait until you sat down—where there was another mike in the fireplace! ... I don't really know why *Holiday* was a good picture ... I'm sure there was some razor-sharp editing to pull it all together."[41]

Watching the film today, the limitations of sound equipment are obvious. "At first," said Ann, "I had a hard time getting my voice on the right level and keeping it there. A sound track is a funny thing."[42] Ann mentioned one difficulty that was resolvable in filming the Barry play. "The theme itself is slight," she pointed out, "with practically no action value. The play's whole importance depends on the dialogue and the various psychological moods. And it is through the lines alone that the story is told. We had long debates, line by line. I hated to see one of them go. Some scenes ... had to be sacrificed for the sake of continuity. Linda, my part, proved difficult too. She is really an outsider, but what a grand person. She stands on the edge of it all and forces her way into the plot by sheer personality. In the first script Linda was practically nothing, but by fighting for a line here and there she has been built up to her true importance."[43]

It is a crime that cinema aficionados associate *Holiday*, not with Ann Harding, but with Katharine Hepburn in George Cukor's 1938 remake. Labeled as "box-office poison" at the time, Hepburn managed to tone down her usual pretense and mannerisms. The role was a breakthrough for her. Ann's "fighting for lines," building her part up, and her "serene restraint" as an actress, holds its own against Hepburn. On screen, Hepburn is off in her own world ... shining, of course, but self-contained. Harding's vulnerability contributes immensely to the cohesive ensemble spirit in the 1930 version, and, unlike Hepburn, she establishes rapport with her co-stars first, and her audience second. Harding is unique, but, *natural*, and immersed in her relationship with the other players. Her sisterly bond with Astor had depth, whereas Hepburn and Doris Nolan (as Julia) were coolly distant. After witnessing the two film versions, one notices that Harding *was* Linda, while Hepburn, although vibrant and interesting to watch, was *playing* Linda. Harding's departure from her family was a momentous breakthrough, whereas Hepburn's highly confident take on the role should have had her out of her father's mansion *years* before. Granted, as Johnny Case, Robert Ames had the body language of a sad sack. Cary Grant, on the other hand, takes Johnny and breathes life into him. He exemplifies, with a few somersaults, the carefree spirit ready for his "holiday." This is partly due to Donald Ogden Stewart's rejuvenated script with its dashes of screwball comedy, which appealed to contemporary audiences. Regrettably, the 1930 version is available only through private collectors, and the

**Ann and Mary Astor played sisters in *Holiday*. Astor said,
"Ann was an actress rather than a star – and there is a difference." (Pathé)**

prints are at best mediocre. Fortunately for Hepburn, author Barry
was charmed by her take on the role in 1938. Afterwards, he specifically wrote *The Philadelphia Story* for her, which revived her career on
Broadway and in Hollywood.

On Ann's 28th birthday, the premier for *Holiday* at Carthay Circle
Theatre was replete with the usual Hollywood ballyhoo. Emerging
from her limousine, a slim, graceful Ann, wearing a dress of pale yellow
chiffon embroidered with black lace, stood in front of the radio mike, a
battery of cameras, and an on-rush of young autograph seekers calling
her name. "Oh, my dears," she pleaded, "please wait until I come back."
Of course, there was no coming back. The evening moved forward.
After the screening, Harry Bannister, acting as master of ceremonies,

introduced the cast. A smiling, radiant Ann came on stage and stole the show with a kiss for Harry. Society columnist Myra Nye thought Ann provided "a strong contrast to the disillusioning gaucheries of those 'in person' whose expert ease in the picture had just been witnessed." Nye thought Ann's carriage was "pre-eminently graceful."[44] A birthday celebration followed the premier at George Olsen's supper club. The horse-shoe shaped table was graced with wildflower arrangements – the centerpiece being a huge birthday cake. Aside from cast members, those invited included Joan Crawford, Kay Hammond, Bebe Daniels, Patsy Ruth Miller, Ben Lyon, Douglas Fairbanks Jr., Robert Montgomery, and Ann's sister and her husband Robert Nash.

Before production on *Holiday* began, Ann had registered complaints about the low- quality scripts being offered her. She was also not entirely satisfied with her performances. Pathé, interpreted Ann's dissatisfaction as wanting more money, and raised her $2,000 a week to $6,000. She was bewildered by the offer. Writer Gene Ringgold stated that Ann simply, "resigned herself to nursing her bruised ego in an atmosphere more luxuriant than anything she had ever known."[45] For awhile, Ann accepted the inevitable and decided to suffer in style. "I earn more in a week than my father, General Gatley, earns in a year," she stated. In a sense, Ann owed her father *something* for disowning her. The uncanny similarity of the father in *Holiday* to her own had fueled her performance ... especially, the confrontation scene between father and daughter. When he suggests she leave home, she resolves to go out on her own—echoes of George Grant Gatley and daughter Dorothy. When *Holiday* premiered, General Gatley himself was suffering. During the summer of 1930, he had checked into the Presidio's Letterman Hospital in San Francisco. It would be a permanent stay. But that wasn't all. The tough-as-nails, hard-nosed army man was asking for Ann.

(Endnotes)

1   Ann Harding, "Broadway, You'll Find, Runs West," *Theatre Arts*, October 1930
2   Marquis Busby, "That Sex Appeal Voice," *Photoplay*, October 1929 (The *Oakland Tribune* did announce that Ann had taken over the role of Nina from Pauline Lord, in Wood Soanes April 7, 1929 column; *Notable Names in American Theatre* credits Ann with the role of Nina in a March 1929 tour)
3   Margaret Reid, "Blond-But Not Light," *Picture Play*, May 1930
4   Jack Grant, "The Star Who Amazed Hollywood," *Motion Picture*, July 1931
5   Alma Whitaker, "Luck Pursues Ann Harding," *Los Angeles Times*, 8/25/29
6   Alma Whitaker, "Luck ..."
7   "Ann Harding Star in *Paris Bound*," *The Daily News (PA)*, 10/2/29
8   *Time Magazine*, 10/12/31
9   Chester B. Bahn, review of *Paris Bound*, *Syracuse Herald*, 9/22/29
10   Mordaunt Hall, review of *Paris Bound*, *New York Times*, 9/21/29
11   G.D. Seymour, "Talkies as Aid to 'It'," *Charleston Gazette*, 6/2/29
12   From review of *Double Harness*, *Photoplay*, September 1933
13   Lynne Myddleton, "The Ann Harding the World Never Sees," *Film Pictorial*, 12/12/36
14   Myra Nye, "Society in Cinemaland," *Los Angeles Times*, 9/8/29
15   Andre Soares, "Edmund Goulding: Q&A with Biographer Matthew Kennedy," *Alternate Film Guide*. 2008 www.altfg.com
16   Marquis Busby, "That Sex Appeal ..."
17   James Robert Parish, *The RKO Gals*, Rainbow Books, c. 1974, pg 20
18   Review of *Her Private Affair*, *New York Times*, 1/11/30
19   Muriel Babcock, review for *Her Private Affair*, *Los Angeles Times*, 12/6/29
20   Ben Lyon, "My Friend Ann Harding," *Screen Play*, September 1931
21   Stephen Anders, "It's No Crime to be Happy," *Hollywood*, November 1931
22   Ben Maddox, "Discovering Hollywood's Real Sophisticate-Ann Harding!" *Screenland*, November 1931
23   Myrtle Gebhart, "The Happiest Woman in Hollywood," *Picture Play*, March 1931
24   Mordaunt Hall, review of *Condemned*, *New York Times*, 11/4/29
25   Muriel Babcock, "Films Satisfy Yearnings," *Los Angeles Times*, 12/1/29
26   Myra Nye, "Society in Cinemaland, " *Los Angeles Times*, 12/8/29
27   Cedric Belfrage, "She Doesn't Play," *Motion Picture*, July 1930
28   "The Girl on the Cover," *Photoplay*, June 1930
29   Mick LaSalle, *Complicated Women*, St. Martin's Press, N.Y., c. 2000, pgs.81-82
30   Hubbard Keavy, "Screen Life in Hollywood," *Galveston News*, 12/8/30
31   Review of *Holiday*, *New York Times*,7/3/30 and 7/13/30
32   Dan Thomas, review of *Holiday*, *Newark Advocate*, 8/16/30
33   Eleanor Barnes, review of *Holiday*, *Illustrated Daily News*, 8/8/30
34   Harrison Carroll, review of *Holiday*, *Los Angeles Evening Herald*, 8/8/30

35   Harrison Carroll, "Pathé Film is Fine Product of Talkie Art," *Los Angeles Evening Herald*, 8/23/30

36   "Silence Made Eloquent by Serene Star," *Los Angeles Examiner*, 12/14/30

37   Mary Astor, *Mary Astor My Life*, Dell, c. 1959, pgs. 167-169

38   Mary Astor, *Mary Astor, A Life on Film*, Dell, c. 1967, pg 81

39   Mary Astor, *Mary Astor, A Life on* ... pg 84

40   Mary Astor, *Mary Astor, A Life on* ... pg 86

41   Mary Astor, *Mary Astor, A Life on* ... pgs 83-84

42   Marquis Busby, "That Sex Appeal ..."

43   Elena Boland, "Ann Harding Displays Viking Quality," *Los Angeles Times*, 8/3/30

44   Myra Nye, "Society of Cinemaland," *Los Angeles Times*, 10/10/30

45   Gene Ringgold, "Ann Harding," *Films in Review*, March 1972 pg 136

8

Reconciliation

One year after the release of *Paris Bound*, Ann Harding, Pathe's most spectacular star, whose voice, looks and talent had proved irresistible to film audiences, was among the ten top money-making stars of the cinema.[1] *Los Angeles Times* critic, Edward Schallert, referred to Ann as the new Queen of Hollywood, out-topping Garbo and Shearer.[2] *Holiday*, in its fourth week at Carthay Circle Theater (where it would stay for two months), was playing to capacity houses. As if to cement her achievement, Ann was invited to imprint her hands, footprints (made in high heels), and signature in the forecourt of Grauman's elaborate Chinese Theatre on Hollywood Boulevard. This honor was reserved only for the biggest stars. The tradition began in 1927, with the imprints of Mary Pickford and Douglas Fairbanks Sr. Ann's tinted gray square included her inscription, "Whatever Success I Have, You Make Possible."[3] While arc lights crisscrossed the skies of Hollywood, sound cameras were on hand to record the event. A large crowd of fans and Hollywood elite had gathered for the festivity. Harry Bannister stood by, while cement artist Jean W. Klossner, whose concrete formula was guarded until his death, was there to assist. It was August 30, 1930. Ann was filled with anticipation and hope, but *not* about the ceremony, her career, or the new home she and Harry had built. Something far more important was in the offing ... a reconciliation with her father.

Since the falling out between himself and his daughter, George Grant Gatley had continued his command at various army posts: Camp Lewis on the Pacific Coast in the state of Washington (1922-1924), and Fort McDowell on San Francisco Bay's Angel Island, where he was stationed from August 1924 to 1929. During his command at Fort McDowell, an average of 22,000 men a year left for, or returned from, overseas posts. Fort McDowell was handling more men than any other army post in the nation. In 1930, soon after receiving his new assignment to command the 15th Field Artillery at Fort Sam Houston, Texas, Gatley was advised to return to San Francisco for treatment at Letterman General Hospital. News reports at that time did not offer the specifics of Gatley's illness, other than it was a "dread disease." He was down for the first time in a lifetime of fighting. While the general battled his final foe, Bessie Gatley was in constant attendance at his bedside. Upon recognizing the inevitable, he asked to see his daughter, Dorothy. This came as a shock to those who knew him. According to the *San Antonio Light,* during his recent post at Fort Sam Houston, Gatley was still forbidding the use of his name with that of Ann Harding.[4]

Ann, naturally, was beside herself with joy, sorrow, and apprehension. At last she had the opportunity to melt the rift between herself and the man whose profound influence had colored her character and gave her strength as an individual. She arrived in San Francisco September 10, 1930, the day of her father's sixty-second birthday. Ann entered Gatley's hospital room, and the two looked at each other. Without saying a word, and fighting back tears, they embraced. According to Ann, he kept her in his arms and held her close for a long, long time. "I was his baby-child again," Ann said, "crying out my long-locked sentiments. Moreover, he admitted that he had become proud of me! That must have been quite a difficult beau-geste for the hardened soldier-officer."[5] Ann, and her sister Edith, who had accompanied her from Los Angeles, spent a few days with their father. The years of rancor simply melted away. Upon returning to Los Angeles, Ann was still in a state of disbelief. She realized that she had never lost respect for her father, and was eager to point out his finer qualities. "There were times I longed to be his little girl again," she admitted.[6] "Well, it's over now. It's all right now. At last. I think he understands. I have told him that I love him. I do. I have a tremendous admiration for the grand old battle-axe type of man. There were giants in those days. *He was one of them.* I know that he has always loved me. ... I feel that we have one another now."[7] Ann didn't elaborate on her father's health. She emphasized the emotional healing that took place. "He's the bravest thing I ever saw," said Ann. "He is taking his illness like the soldier he is and all during the time I was there he kept everyone around him screaming with laughter by his brilliant wit. I wouldn't take anything for that reconciliation. It was the one thing I needed to make my life complete."[8]

Before he passed on, General Gatley would have the privilege of seeing what he once referred to as his daughter's "painted face" on screen. Ann made arrangements to send him a print of *The Girl of the Golden West,* a creaking melodrama about a California mining camp.[9] It was perfect fodder for the "grand old battle-axe type of

The "lost" *Girl of the Golden West* (1930). Ann tried to save James Rennie, as well as the antiquated scenario. (First National)

man." The David Belasco play (1905) had been filmed twice before. First National Pictures borrowed Ann for a sixteen-day shoot, which was actually completed *before* Ann began *Holiday,* but not released until later. The role of the gun-toting, swaggering Minnie, who owns the Polka Saloon and who falls in love with an outlaw, seemed quite a stretch for the genteel Ann Harding. As Pathe had offered Harry

nothing since his dismal debut in *Her Private Affair,* one of the deciding factors for Ann in signing on for *The Girl of the Golden West* was
her insistence that Harry be offered the second male lead as the sinister sheriff. Stage actor and husband of Dorothy Gish, James Rennie,
who could have passed as Bannister's double, vocally and physically,
took the romantic lead. "I hope *The Girl of the Golden West* will be
a success," Rennie stated. "You know, it really is the papa of all the
western melodramas and, I still think the best."[10] Indeed, even Gia-
como Puccini had used the Belasco tale as fodder for an Italian opera.
During filming, Ann and Rennie did the best they could to make it
all work. Unfortunately, Bannister felt as if he had to make up for
his back-door entry into the feature, and was a complete nuisance on
the set. He arrogantly began to lecture director John Francis Dillon
on how to do his job. Ann did what she could to placate Dillon and
maintain her harmonious relationship with Harry.[11] The surmount-
ing on-set friction resulted in the film's mixed critical reception.

Today, *The Girl of the Golden West* is the only "lost" Harding film.
Perhaps it is just as well. *Box-office* magazine found its appeal "questionable."[12] *Variety* observed that the film duplicated the stage dialogue, thus
calling attention to the story's inherent artificiality.[13] *Oakland Tribune*
critic Wood Soanes, said Ann was the only reason to see the film. "Miss
Harding has a sort of ethereal beauty that fitted the character of the
angelic saloon keeper perfectly and she has sufficient command of the
dramatic technique to carry her through the physical interpretation."[14]
Muriel Babcock for The *Los Angeles Times* was amazed at how Harding
could transform the tired bones of pure hokum and make it into something worthwhile. "The presence in the cast of that refreshingly human
actress, Miss Ann Harding," wrote Babcock, "served to imbue it with a

rare and poignant charm. Because of her, *The Girl of the Golden West* should take on, in the eyes of its old-time admirers, a new delight. If *The Girl of the Golden West* is a good picture it is because of Ann Harding."[15] Comments on Bannister's performance were far from enthusiastic. The barbed tongue of Elizabeth Yeaman told readers of the *Hollywood Citizen News* that if it weren't for Ann Harding, "You would laugh at the exaggerated villainy of Harry Bannister … he has dutifully given a literal translation of an antedated characterization."[16] In spite of Ann's fine efforts with backwoods English, some reviews stated that she ran the full gamut of dramatic emotions. Norbert Lusk for the *Los Angeles Times* thought the film verged "perilously near a parody on old-time western pictures. Miss Harding … does not succeed in making the heroine a credible figure. … Rennie is spiritless and un-magnetic."[17] Popular columnist Robbin Coons, who witnessed the first cut of the film in July, put it bluntly, saying, "The whole thing is so 'meller' as to verge on burlesque."[18] In September, upon hearing the film stood up as a good talkie, Coons attributed the transformation to clever editing. "The day of 'cutting' miracles is not past!" he mused.[19] Ann had anticipated biting sarcasm for *The Girl* … from what she called "smart-cracking, pseudo-intelligent" critics. She hoped film studios would continue to provide them with "much needed hokum," dastardly villains, and something "to snicker at." "Otherwise," Ann smirked, "they may lose their individuality entirely."[20]

After Pathe nixed plans for Ann and Harry to film something titled *The Greater Love,* Ann fulfilled her own prophecy to provide more hokum for the screen. She signed on for an old chestnut at Fox Studios. In No-

In the Academy Award-nominated (Best Picture) *East Lynne* (1931). (Fox)

vember 1930, she began work on the 14th film adaptation of Mrs. Henry Woods' 1861 Victorian best seller, *East Lynne*. Harry became a regular, uninvited visitor to the set. Director Frank Lloyd was not charmed by Bannister's generous offering of unsolicited advice on how *East Lynne* should be filmed. Lloyd found Bannister stubborn and defiant. He had no choice but to ban him from the sound stage. Fox officials asked Ann to ensure that Harry would stay away from the studio.[21] Ann was deeply concerned about her husband's career, but had decided it was essential to stay focused on the integrity of her own. In so doing, she brought a genuine and heart-felt tenderness to *East Lynne* that kept it afloat.

After witnessing her in *The Girl of the Golden West*, some thought Ann was sealing her doom as an old-fashioned heroine. Upon completing *East Lynne*, she was asked if the cloying melodrama weighed her down. Ann took offense. "It isn't that at all," she vigorously denied. "Of course, it has one of the original seven plots. But it deals with men and women and babies, doesn't it? We tried to project men and women of 1931 into that mellow period of sentiment. And I think we did a good, honest job of it."[22] Co-star Clive Brook upped the ante on the film's importance, saying "What *Uncle Tom's Cabin* did for slavery in the United States, *East Lynne* did for woman's struggle for equal rights and her righteous place in the sun of a man's world."[23] Brook felt the story exposed the plight of women as spectators and victims of man-made laws. Ann discovered Brook to be charming and "easy to play with," but called him a "dog" for beating her at her own game—"which is to underplay," Ann stated, "and make the other guy work."[24] She also found that she was energized by the integrity of the script. "The scene where Lady Isabel tells everybody off," said Ann, "we retook over and over again. But the more I played the scene, the more I enjoyed it. It lifted me right up. If there had been one fusty, false note in it—as any actor—I would have been tired out. But I wasn't. I was thrilled."[25] *East Lynne* allowed Ann to display her effective and pleasant mezzo-soprano while singing Irish composer Michael Balfe's "You'll Remember Me," from *The Bohemian Girl.* Richard Fall, who completed the incidental music for the film, mentioned that Ann, "extracted more beauty of heart and soul from this lovely melody than any opera prima-donna whom I have heard sing it."[26]

The plot of *East Lynne* centered on Lady Isabel Carlyle (Ann), whose youth and ebullience are stifled by the controlling machinations of her sister-in-law Cornelia (tellingly played by Cecilia Loftus). After three years of marriage, Lady Isabel is banished from her home by her neglectful husband Robert Carlyle (Conrad Nagel). He and his sister suspect her of infidelity with aristocrat William Levison (Clive Brook). Although she is innocent, Isabel is forced to leave her child behind. "The law is on my side," her husband tells her. "You've forfeited all rights to motherhood. There isn't a court in England that will believe your story." (Ann told Jasper Deeter that, as an actor, Nagel was an "impossible stick." "He's just like his part," said Ann).[27] Isabel, having had her fill of humiliation, takes the opportunity to rip into her husband and his formidable sister. (It is this scene that Ann found to be so straightforward, truthful, and energizing.) "How can I expect you to believe me after you've listened to *her*?" she argues. "It has always been her word against mine, her wishes against mine, her orders against mine." Cornelia counters, "How can you say that? I never interfered." Not losing a beat, Isabel argues, "You did! You interfered with every move I made, every breath I drew. You drove off my friends. You ruined my home. You've dominated me and my child. You crushed every impulse. Destroyed every bit of romance. You've made my home a prison! Well, you're not going to drive me out, because I'm going. Do you understand? I'm leaving on my own free will!"

After boarding passage to Calais, Isabel accidentally meets up with Levison on deck. He makes promises of gaiety in Paris and Vienna. She looks out into the mists and sea that surround them. "Fog," she mutters softly. "Fog getting into our lives. Our hearts. Our souls." Once in Paris, their interlude, and the film itself, loses momentum. With the outbreak of the Franco-Prussian War, a bombardment occurs, resulting in Levison's death and injury to Isabel's eyes. She suffers nobly while going blind. The real stretch comes when Isabel returns to *East Lynne* for one last glimpse of her child. During their reunion, the strain of weeping hastens her blindness. *Time Magazine* wrote the film's epitaph saying, "Someone in the Fox script department has detected that *East Lynne* is more than a dramatic critic's joke. [The film] is not worth the talent that has gone into it. … Silliest sequence: the end in which Ann Harding, about to go blind, goes home for a last look at her child before walking over a cliff."[28] The *Los Angeles Times* mused, "The picture falls down [literally] in its ending." However, the *Times* conceded that Ann's Lady Isabel was "luminous," and that the picture was "a marvel of transcription … tasteful, restrained and moving."[29]

Many were impressed with the new twists on the original story. Los Angeles film critic Harrison Carroll, commented, "*East Lynne* easily might have become an orgy of sentimentality. Instead, it is an unexaggerated, believable story of tragedy undeserved. Ann Harding … is a heroine of rare courage and spiritual beauty. Director Frank Lloyd has keyed his situations down to a low pitch. As a natural result the entire cast leans towards underplaying rather than flamboyant

As an actor, Ann found co-star Conrad Nagel to be "an impossible stick—just like his part." (Fox)

melodrama."[30] In New York City, where the film was held over, *The New York Times* credited Ann's performance and Frank Lloyd's direction for the film's success. "When Miss Harding appears," stated the review, "she captures one's full attention ... the play does not seems so very old as it is done here. ... Lloyd's direction of this costly production is vastly superior to anything he has done in several years."[31] Seen today, Ann's performance comes close to maneuvering *East Lynne* into an honest and timely piece of cinema.

Although the United States was in an economic crisis, Fox Studio didn't spare a dime on *East Lynne*. Depression audiences who could spare the change, witnessed the ornate wedding scene, an elaborate ball, and the Parisian sequences which employed many hungry actors. At the time *East Lynne* was released, unemployment had risen to 15.9 percent. To the 3,718 extras hired to provide atmosphere in *East Lynne*, it was a godsend. As one news article put it, "And that is the reason, people, why so many folk in Hollywood are eating today."[32] Ann's own pocket money was not wanting either. The $25,000 bonus that Fox gave Pathe for her services was, this time, handed directly over to Ann.[33] *East Lynne* was a gigantic hit, and garnered an Academy Award Nomination for Best Picture of 1931. The announcement for the annual ceremonies proved to be a double blessing for Ann, as she was nominated in the Best Actress category for *Holiday*.

George Grant Gatley died on Friday, January 9, 1931, at the age of 62. Aside from acknowledging his fine military record and command of the 67th Field Artillery Brigade of the Rainbow Division in the World War, news reports stated he was descended from a long line of "seafaring folk." A full military funeral was held the following Monday, and interment was at the Presidio San Francisco National Cemetery. Ann asked for a cordon of military police to be strategically placed about the cemetery. She knew that crowds would appear—not out of respect for her father—but to see Ann Harding, the movie star. When Bay Area newspapers thoughtlessly accused her of being "high hat," she had to fight back the tears. "I just wanted the body of my daddy to be laid to rest surrounded only by those who cared," stated Ann.[34]

Bessie Gatley was left out of the news loop as far as involvement with her daughters. She was rarely mentioned at all. One exception was the time Bessie telegrammed Ann regarding an inherited family estate in Virginia. As a descendent of Captain James Vermillion, Bessie found herself with 350 acres in the heart of rich tobacco country. In her eyes, the plantation had been mismanaged. Vermillion had forbidden the planting of tobacco, believing it offensive to women. Bessie asked Ann to fly back east and meet with her. Ann immediately complied with her mother's wishes and boarded a Maddux Transcontinental flight. Together, they decided that the income of the plantation could easily be tripled by raising tobacco.[35] Profits from this venture, along with a pittance from her war widow's pension, afforded Bessie some financial comfort. Before long, she had the added comfort of a new husband. On June 19, 1933, at age 57, she married a Bay Area cellist named Charles Frisbie. Frisbie was the antithesis of old General Gatley, and younger, much younger. The talented cellist was 39, seventeen years Bessie's junior. (In the *Los Angeles Times* column "Intention to Marry," Bessie and Charles fudged on their ages, giving them, respectively, as 48 and 43).[36] Frisbie, whose talent occasionally brought him to the Los Angeles area to perform on NBC radio, is best described by his former pupil, Sherrill Roberts. I contacted Ms. Roberts in 2008. She fondly recalled,

> I remember hearing that Charles had been married
> to Ann Harding's mother. He was a profoundly good
> influence in my young life. Charles had a wonderful
> calmness … and a deep appreciation of the spirit of
> music. He had an inquiring mind, and was interested
> in all sorts of things and ideas. He also had a quirky
> sense of humor. Sometimes during my lessons when
> I was frustrated, Charles would announce that we
> needed to count the cats to make sure all four of
> them were still in the house. So we would look in
> all the rooms, count all the legs, and divide by four.

Sometimes we would count the legs and tails, and
divide by five. Then we would return to the lesson,
refreshed. Can you see why I adored him, and still
do 50 years later? And why to this day I make my
cello studio a refuge for all my students?[37]

Sherrill became a student of Frisbie in 1957, three years after Bessie
passed away. Ann never made a point of talking about her mother's
new marriage. She focused solely on her father's legacy. After Gatley
died, there were numerous "official" occasions for Ann to pay homage
to the late general. The year following his death, Ann was honored by
veteran's of the Rainbow Division at their annual "Rainbow Ball" held
at Shrine Auditorium. Against a colorful military background and
with all the pomp and ceremony of dress parade, Ann took the arm of
Brigadier-General Howard to lead the grand march, after which she
was given the title "Colonel Harding of the Rainbow."[38] "Colonel Harding" earned her stripes on the soundstages of Hollywood as well, with
her self-discipline and poise. "I have almost too much discipline," Ann
laughed. "I regard obedience to those in command of my pictures as a
matter of course. I call them 'Sir,' the salute of one's officers to which I
am accustomed. They look bewildered at first, but I think they like it!"[39]

In early 1931, Ann's "obedience" to those in charge at the studio
was peppered with a lot of "No, Sirs!" She was not exactly acquiescent
when it came to script approval. She was decisive in her arguments. Although her screen characters might struggle, she insisted they must be
devoid of weakness. Numerous stories she thought unbelievable were
shelved. Ann was on the verge of taking the lead from Ina Claire in
Rebound, and held up production before deciding it too similar to *Holiday*. She and director Edward Griffith locked horns on many points of

the film's production. Ann insisted that her battles with producers and director's were patiently fought. "Ridiculously patient," Ann analyzed herself. "A fault, not a virtue. I'll stand for too much. *Never* do I attempt to reform people; I've no missionary spirit at all. I bear with something distasteful, until I no longer can endure it; on a sudden decision, I step out, cutting the association abruptly – and forever."[40] Ann referred to Harry as her "business manager," saying he fought tooth-and-nail on her behalf. "He thinks of me so much—too much," Ann offered. The truth was, that Harry the actor, was going nowhere. For awhile, he obsessed about changing the shape of his nose. Perhaps a plastic surgeon could save his foundering career.[41] Out of what some considered pity, Ann insisted Harry be allowed to walk unnoticed through crowd scenes on each of her films, as sort of a good luck charm.

In 1931, Joseph Kennedy, who had controlling interest in Pathe, sold out to RKO. RKO-Pathe became a new complex. Before long, Ann's four-room bungalow, along with that of Pathe's other top female star, Constance Bennett, would be relocated from Culver City to Hollywood. In the process, Ann's staunch supporter, Pathe president E.B. Derr, was forced to resign. The new production chief, Charles R. Rogers, offered Ann a new 65-page contract with a sizeable salary increase in the Spring of 1931. Ann was hesitant. "My first contract was a simple three-paragraph affair," she stated. "It said simply that I was to get so much for nine months work a year. It also provided that I had a word in selecting my stories."[42] Ann balked at the inclusion of a morality clause. "I must lead a decent life," she scoffed. "The new contract … has clauses saying that I must work in any picture that my employer wants me to; that I could be suspended for this or that; it was terrifying. But, oh, it offered me so much more money."[43] All six of Ann's film releases did well at the box-office, and she knew it. The contract remained in dispute and unsettled. "I prefer to remain comparatively poor, but happy," Ann told her employer.[44] The film colony was held in rapt attention at Ann's maverick attitude during her contractual struggle. One thing that definitely ignited a spark in her battle was her return to Hedgerow on April 21. It was the company's eighth anniversary. More than 200 playgoers taxed the capacity of the little theatre when Ann gave a repeat performance of Glaspell's *Inheritors*. A remarkable performance and standing ovation highlighted her and Harry's vacation to Rose Valley. One review stated her dramatic fervor and intelligence had the "persuasion of a hypnotist."[45] Ann reiterated that she returned to Hedgerow in order to realize her mistakes.

Louella Parsons had jumped the gun in February, saying Ann had *signed* the three-year contract. In truth, Ann wanted some changes made, not in salary, but in terms. "I have to do everything and can't do anything," she complained. "I can't make pictures for any studio except Pathe but I must make any picture they want to put me into and I must do this and I must do that … I do want something to say about my pictures … I know as well if not better than anyone else what I can do best."[46] On June 1, Louella got back on track from an "inside source" regarding Ann's new three-year contract. "Ann Harding has held out for her rights," tooted Ms. Parsons. "Why shouldn't she? She is one of the biggest bets in pictures today. I learned that Miss Harding will get $260,000 for the first year; $300,000 for the second and $400,000 for the last year."[47] It turned out that it wasn't Harry, but

lawyer Ralph Blum, husband of Ann's good friend, actress Carmel Myers, who stood up for Ann in resolving her battle with Pathe.

Her contract signed, Ann's next film at RKO-Pathe, was based on the
English bestseller, *A Little Flat in the Temple*, by Pamela Wynne. Scenarist
Horace Jackson, who was nominated for an Academy Award for *Holiday*,
was also on board. Filming began the first week of June 1931. Harry managed to wheedle his way onto the set of this one, too. Several weeks after
filming started, a reporter sat on the sidelines for a couple of hours watching Ann and co-star Leslie Howard attempt to play a love scene. The two
stood very close to each other. Ann looked into Howard's eyes. She was
hinting to him that she loved him. Howard stood stiff as a board, his arms
hanging down to the side. Ann doubled up on her supply of sex appeal,
but the English actor simply wouldn't respond. Exasperated at his gall,
and outright lack of response, Ann stepped back and struck a pose like a

With Leslie Howard in *Devotion* (1931). (RKO-Pathé)

tough shop girl. "Good God!" she exclaimed. "Ain't yuh gunna do nut-hin?"[48] Reporter Stephen Anders said that everyone had a good laugh. Howard relaxed and warmed up a bit, but Bannister's presence on the set was counterproductive. Anders stated that when Ann realized that Harry had returned to the set, she rushed up to him as though she hadn't seen him for years. It had been all of a half hour. "Let's go away off somewhere together," she sighed. "To Alaska!"

Ann and Harry's romance was now held together by their mutual passion for aviation. Her disillusionment with his career, and his inter-ference in her own acting assignments was assuaged by Harry's enthu-siasm for flying, and for that matter, her own. "Flying is a blessed release to me," said Ann. "Up in the clouds, away from whatever troubles me, I see how small we all are and how little our troubles count in the eternal majesty of creation. I come back feeling that my woes aren't half as big as I had thought. I know that few people have the joy of a plane, but per-haps a walk out away from people would do the same."[49] Ann and Harry spent hours fantasizing about the trips they could take. En route to Ann's Hedgerow engagement in April, the couple had taken the train to Detroit to purchase a new custom built, six-passenger cabin Bellanca monoplane. Upon their return to Hollywood in May, the Bannisters had completed a 4,000 mile air trip. In August, Ann landed the family plane for the first time with a co-pilot. "The ship really runs itself," she demurred. Al-though daughter Jane was there to greet her parents at the airport, she was left out of these ventures. Ann was hesitant to take Jane up, for fear the noise might frighten her. In the fall of 1931, Ann and Harry joined an air cavalcade of forty-five planes routed to Lower California for the first Na-tional Aeronautical Association meeting on foreign soil. The event was followed by a banquet at the hotel in Playa Ensenada.[50]

A Little Flat in the Temple, re-titled *Devotion*, was completed on Ann's 29th birthday. Directed with proper English spirit by Robert Milton, the film, while considered "pleasing entertainment" by *The New York Times*, netted a $40,000 loss for RKO-Pathe. Some fans weren't enthralled seeing a courageous and bright woman like Ann Harding play a frustrated wallflower. Nonetheless, she was a wallflower with *je ne sais quoi*. After falling for a young barrister, David Trent (Howard), Shirley Mortimer (Ann) finds an inventive way out of her shell. To be near him, she dons a masquerade and places herself in his employ as governess to his small son. Her disguise consists of a brown wig, spectacles, middle-aged frocks, and a convincing cockney accent. The whole point for the audience is to remain in suspense until she's found out. Prolonged interventions, as well as a few oddball characters, delay the inevitable. The most bizarre cast member in this Cinderella-meets-Mrs. Doubtfire-story, is Harrington (Robert Williams), an artist, for whom Trent won an acquittal. We are led to believe Harrington was justified in killing his wife, because she was a dipsomaniac, and slashed one of his prized paintings! When Trent's own "supposed dead wife" shows up, Shirley's disguise is finally pierced. In spite of what critic Mollie Merrick referred to as a "hackneyed and quite unbelievable tale," the team of Howard and Harding charmed audiences. "These two gave us moments that are almost unparalleled in celluloid for tempo and genuine emotion," wrote Merrick.[51] Reporter Chester Bahn echoed Merrick, saying, "You are watching real persons handle real situations. Ann Harding, whose beauty is of that flawless type which defies description, does not rely upon her face; Ann acts. Leslie Howard does not portray manly, gentlemanly charm. He lives."[52] Harrison Carroll found *Devotion* riddled with unrealities, and lacking dramatic unity. "What does call for unqualified praise," he admitted, "is the acting of Ann Harding, Leslie Howard and a large and uniformly excellent cast. Favored with high quality photography, the luminous beauty of the star is caught as never before. Her voice, of course, remains one of the most thrilling of the screen. As for Howard, at last he finds something worthy of his talents. The result is a finely-drawn characterization, on par with that of the star. They are perfect teammates."[53] As mature actors, skilled at their trade, Harding and Howard turn *Devotion* into a cinematic miracle, albeit a minor one.

Leslie Howard confessed that he felt Ann was "the finest contribution the stage has yet made to talking pictures." He recalled their teaming in 1925 for *The Green Hat.* "We became friends," Howard said, "I grew to like her as a person quite as much as I admired her as an actress. Ann is such fun. Her wit is a delightful blend of gentle satire and pure fun. She has a nice intelligence, eager and quick and utterly devoid of mental shams. When I came to Hollywood a few months ago I renewed acquaintance with her, and found that her ascent to the premier ranks of present-day actresses had not changed Ann one whit."[54] Ann enjoyed working with Howard, felt he was a genius, and was in high spirits at the film's premier at Carthay Circle Theatre. She spent the entire intermission chatting with boys and girls who had broken through police lines to mingle with the stars. At curtain call, co-star Robert Williams gave everyone a good chuckle when he announced, "It has been wonderful making this picture with Miss Bennett." Williams' intentional *faus pax* alluded to Ann's major competition at RKO, Constance Bennett.

Ann's admiration for Leslie Howard helped convince director Tay Garnett that Howard was the perfect choice for her next project, based on Harry Hervey's novel, *Prestige*. Hervey, who was becoming much the rage, had recently sold to Paramount *Shanghai Express* for Marlene Dietrich, and was working on a screen adaptation of *The Cheat* for Tallulah Bankhead. At this point, Ann felt confident enough about *Prestige* to cable Howard in London to return to Hollywood for the male lead. Howard cabled back from France, "All too tempting. I wish I could suggest you come here to the Riviera." Ann shrugged, "That boy has the right idea."[55] Howard was resting up before returning to New York, and rehearsals for Phillip Barry's *The Animal Kingdom*. Howard thought the $5,000 weekly salary that RKO had paid him for *Devotion,* "sheer lunacy." "No actor is worth that much money!" he scoffed.[56] It wasn't long before Ann had second thoughts about *Prestige,* and felt her own inclination to return to Broadway. In late August, she was contacted by Eugene O'Neill. He wanted her for the lead in *Mourning Becomes Electra.* She made immediate negotiations with RKO-Pathe to be released and start rehearsals with the Theatre Guild. RKO and David O. Selznick would not allow it. They felt Ann's absence from the screen would diminish her worth to the studio. The role of Lavinia Mannon was handed over to Alice Brady. *Mourning Becomes Electra* ran from October 1931 to March 1932. Years later, Ann was still fuming over the missed opportunity. "I did everything but blow up the entire lot to convince the obtuse gentlemen in command of my fate that it would greatly *enhance* my value to them to release me for *Electra*. Unable to make them see the light, I tried to break my contract but that proved hopeless as well. It is a major tragedy of my professional life that I was deprived of that great opportunity."[57] In the aftermath of this disappointment, Ann agreed to appear in a local engagement of *Smilin' Through* for producer Henry Duffy. The sets had been designed, and rehearsals set to go when RKO put their foot down again.[58] Ann felt the short engagement at Hollywood's own El Capitan Theater, and a role with which she was familiar, would have put no strain on her film career.

Delays on *Prestige* offered the Bannisters time for a vacation to New York. As it turned out, Ann went alone. After a year of doing "nothing," Harry was actually working on a film assignment. Ann registered at the Warwick Hotel, and immediately checked out after newshounds discovered her whereabouts. She stayed with friends instead. Reportedly, Ann said that reviews of her films "meant nothing to her."[59] Louella Parsons, taking offense, laid down the law for Ann, saying that she was ill-advised to make such a statement. "Reviews," scolded Parsons, "mean everything to her and every other star."[60] Ann paid no attention. After a short visit to Connecticut, she flew home, via Detroit, arriving in Los Angeles on October 12.

Shortly before Ann's return, it was announced by the Academy of Motion-Picture Arts and Sciences that she had been nominated in the Best Actress category for 1930-31. Competing with her were: Marie Dressler for *Min and Bill*, Irene Dunne for *Cimarron*, Marlene Dietrich for *Morocco*, and Norma Shearer for *A Free Soul*. *East Lynne* was up for best picture, along with *Cimarron*, *The Front Page*, *Skippy*, and *Trader Horn*. The awards were to be handed out at the Academy's annual banquet on November 10. Hubbard Keavy reported that while the general consensus in Hollywood favored Lionel Barrymore for best actor in *A Free Soul*, there was some division of opinion on the selection of best actress. "There is a definite leaning, however," reported Keavy, "toward Ann Harding, whose name is in the list for *Holiday*, and Marie Dressler is an unofficial close second for *Min and Bill*." Film critic Chester Bahn didn't find Shearer's performance distinctive, as it adhered to the Shearer formula of "Soiled Doves." The rough slapstick of Dressler marred her performance, according to Bahn, while Dietrich "possibly intrigued, but that was all." His personal choices were Ann Harding and Irene Dunne, who, he felt gave the category's most "honest, intelligent and sensitive delineations." "Alas," Bahn stated, "that may cost them the award on Tuesday night."[61] He was right. One must also consider that it had been well over a year since *Holiday* was released and fresh in audiences minds ... an important factor in Ann losing.

Over 2,000 attended the Academy's brilliant affair at the Biltmore Hotel. The evening started off with a long-winded speech by the Vice President of the United States, Charles Curtis, in which he compared the Academy Award to the Nobel Peace Prize! While *East Lynne* lost out to *Cimarron*, the 13 ½ inch gold-plated statuette (yet to be christened "Oscar") was awarded to Marie Dressler for best actress. Norma Shearer, the previous year's winner, handed over the prize, calling Dressler an "old fire horse ... the grandest trouper of them all!" Dressler offered a humorous and brief acceptance speech. "I feel so important tonight," she smiled, "that I think Mrs. Gann should give me her seat." Dolly Gann, the Vice-President's sister, was seated alongside her brother, as guest of honor. In the roar and applause that followed, Mrs. Gann, got up and rendered Dressler her chair. The levity was underscored by the fact that Gann had recently won a "seating" etiquette controversy between herself and Washington D.C. icon Alice Roosevelt Longworth.[62] Ann was the only one among the ten "best acting" nominees who was conspicuous due to her absence.[63]

Ann's own affection for Dressler was evidenced after the veteran actress passed away in 1934. In the hours following Dressler's death, Ann wrote a memorial, contacted a national radio program, and offered to read it. Dressed in black, she approached the microphone and praised Dressler as an individual and for her talent as an actress. Ann closed with a reading of the Twenty-third Psalm. Columnist Jack Grant, visiting one of the studios during the broadcast, said many were moved to tears by Harding's heart-felt sentiments. He acknowledged that such a tribute was something that "only an Ann Harding would think of."[64]

Prestige (1931) With Melvyn Douglas. "*Prestige* almost killed mine," Ann complained. (RKO-Pathé)

In place of Leslie Howard for *Prestige*, Melvyn Douglas was borrowed from producer Samuel Goldwyn. By the time shooting began at RKO, it was no secret that Ann violently opposed the concept of *Prestige* and wanted out of it. After reading the script, she avoided story conferences. When director Tay Garnett, and scenarist Rollo Lloyd, came up to her house to confer on *Prestige* she persuaded them to join her guests Robert Montgomery and Robert Williams for a tennis match instead. Ann relaxed in the pool. Against her pleading and begging, *Prestige* finally went into production. In late November, to avoid suspension, Ann found herself aboard a train en route to the Florida Everglades for location shooting. While passing through Salt Lake City, Ann posed for photographers with director Tay Garnett. "The west coast of Florida," Ann explained to the crowds, "with its palm trees and jungles and lagoons, makes an ideal location for a picture with an Asiatic tropical setting."[65] Garnett said he expected ten days of location shooting near Venice. When the company arrived in Jacksonville, Florida, Ann, suffering from a dislocated shoulder, disembarked to seek a physician.[66] Hearing the news, Harry boarded a plane for Jacksonville, along with Ann's physician Dr. William C. Branch. The three of them ended up motoring from Jacksonville to Sarasota, with Ann at the wheel, arriving three hours late for a public luncheon in her honor. A "brake problem" was their excuse. Ann was no slacker when it came to driving, and known for her punctuality. In Hollywood, she had ended up in traffic court after racking up several speeding tickets for thundering around in her red Packard straight-eight roadster without a operator's license.[67] The truth was, that Ann *herself* had insisted on stopping the car en route to Sarasota. Apparently, Bannister and Branch were embroiled in a dispute, and Ann wouldn't budge until it was resolved.[68] Three hours late, meant three hours sitting in the car.

On December 11, Ann completed her jungle scenes and sailed to Havana to join Harry. For a few days she reminisced and visited scenes from her childhood. This getaway failed to cheer her up. Upon her return home, Ann was in a gloomy mood. Still, she volunteered overtime to work out scenes with Melvyn Douglas, and took tests with minor players so they might get the "feel" of the action in *Prestige*. Not completely devoid of humor, Ann would imitate the chief electrician's sharp whistle that warned when the lights were too hot. This immediately stopped production. The bewildered man looked confused for several days until he caught Ann with both fingers in her mouth, doing the whistling.

Ann informed reporter Harrison Carroll that she expected to be "finished" with the film industry in two years. For one thing, Ann was unhappy with the "trick" wording of contracts. She had been under the impression that she could turn down roles and take a voluntary suspension of salary. Ann hadn't been aware that by refusing a picture, the studio had the right to suspend her. Ann's next project, titled *Westward Passage*, was not to her liking, but she told Carroll she wasn't going to make any trouble.[69] She said her only hope was the keen story-sense of her new boss David O. Selznick. (RKO-Pathe had merged with RKO-Radio during the production of *Prestige*). Reporter Elizabeth Yeaman zeroed in on the real problem with Ann Harding projects: Ann herself. "There are two sides to her complaint," wrote Yeaman, "Several directors will tell you that this blonde star is vacillating in regard to stories. She will read a story and approve of it.

Writers will be set to work on it, and by the time they have finished the script ... she will suddenly decide she doesn't want the story. These reversals of decision cost studios a great deal of money and right now the economy is the rule."[70] Even so, in the case of *Prestige*, Ann's instincts were on target. The film had a net loss of $175,000.[71]

Prestige promoted the idea that colonialism in French Indochina had become a burden for the "prestigious" white race. While this premise is being presented, Lucien Andriot's camerawork zooms in and out, as if visual activity could compensate for the drivel serving as dialogue. Ann's character, Therese Du Flos, has been thoroughly schooled in the belief of the white man's superiority by her father, Colonel Du Flos. As she is about to join Andre (Melvyn Douglas), her fiancé, in a remote jungle outpost, Du Flos advises his daughter, "Take to him your race for a wedding gift. The prestige of the white man. That is the only weapon you two will have!" After a stopover in Saigon, Therese finds herself floating downstream in a small boat. With jaws wide open, crocodiles along the river bank provide an ominous welcome to Lao Bao, a Malayan penal colony. From this point on, *Prestige* is unable to escape its incredible lack of authenticity. Therese finds Andre soaked with sweat and alcohol, his spirits broken. After she helps him to "buck up," a native priest presides over their wedding. Andre, looking heavenward, prays to the white man's God to sanction their union. Things intensify in this stifling atmosphere when Andre's superior officer, Captain Baudoin (Adolphe Menjou), drops by for one obvious reason: to prey on Therese. The Captain scoffs at Therese's house servant Nham (the talented black actor/musician, Clarence Muse), saying he looks "a bit pale," and jests that crocodiles in the area prefer "dark meat." Nahm is *Prestige's* only real hero. He comes to Therese's defense by killing Captain Baudoin, and ends up a prisoner himself. The lurid, racist scenario frequently exploits the strikingly blonde Harding against the dark-skinned natives. The climax consists of a prison riot in which, horror of horrors, dozens of inmates show depraved lust for her white flesh. Andre, in an alcoholic daze, literally whips them back into their place. *Prestige* insisted that native peoples are fearful of whites, and hopelessly superstitious.

After shooting the film was complete, Ann, horrified at what she saw in the screening room, begged to buy the negative of *Prestige* and have it destroyed. It caused a definite rift between her and director Garnett. "I have never seen a sadder lad than Tay Garnett was over *Prestige*," pouted Louella Parsons. "He felt that the picture was given bad advance publicity after Ann Harding asked to buy the print. He was so upset that Patsy Ruth Miller, his well known spouse, marched him off to New York."[72] While licking his wounds, Garnett was coaxed back to Hollywood by Darryl Zanuck. Garnett's next film, *One Way Passage*, with Kay Francis and William Powell, was one of the director's best.

Initially, Ann may have enlisted for *Prestige* because of its military setting – a "call of duty," as it were, to play the daughter of a colonel. Only one scene in *Prestige* reflected a semblance of reality. When Therese attempts to tell the stern Colonel Du Flos that she loves him, he refuses to listen. "There are so many things I want to say to you," she pleas. "Things I've been storing up for years. Aren't you going to let me forget just for five minutes that I'm a soldier's daughter?" The old army man begrudges her a kiss. The *Los Angeles Times* thought *Prestige* a "pretentious failure," and "a severe blow to the popularity of Ann Harding."[73] The *Los Angeles Record* hit the nail on the head by saying, "Ann Harding—what blasphemy to put her into a picture like this!"[74] Enough said.

In the debris left behind from Ann Harding's battle over *Prestige* she felt that her career was in shambles. "*Prestige,*" she said wryly, "almost killed mine."[75] Nonetheless, General Gatley's daughter insisted she had everything under control. "I have my husband, and Jane," Ann offered proudly. "I'm planning my life as my father, an efficient army officer, would have planned a campaign, calmly, sanely, strategically. And there you are."[76] After the premier of *Prestige,* Harry flew Ann to Palm Springs for a therapeutic purge. It would take another year before Ann found her niche, her legacy, as a film actress. And, before *that* would happen, her calm, and "strategically" planned private world crumbled and collapsed around her.

Ann attempted to adopt a new friend while on the set of *Prestige.* (RKO-Pathé)

(Endnotes)

1   Gene Ringgold, "Ann Harding," *Films in Review*, March 1972 pg 137

2   Edward Schallert, "Crowned Heads Lie Uneasy Yet …," *Los Angeles Times*, 5/17/31

3   Stacey Endres and Robert Cushman, *Hollywood at Your Feet*, Pomegranate Press Ltd., (LA), c. 1992 pg 83

4   "Star, Parent Now Friends," *San Antonio Light*, 9/20/1930

5   Ann Harding, "When I Was an Army Girl," *Los Angeles Times*, 4/5/31

6   Ann Harding, "When I Was an Army Girl," *Los Angeles Times*, 4/5/31

7   Gladys Hall, "The Hot Spot," *Motion Picture*, December 1930

8   Cal York, "Stars and Studios," *Photoplay*, December 1930

9   Gladys Hall, "The Hot Spot," *Motion Picture*, December 1930

10   "Actor Sets Sail Under Own Colors," *Los Angeles Times*, 10/9/30

11   Gene Ringgold, "Ann Harding," *Films in Review*, March, 1972, pg 137

12   Review of *Girl of the Golden West, Box-office*, 11/11/30
13   Review of *Girl of the Golden West, Variety*, 10/29/30
14   Wood Soanes, review of *Girl of the Golden West, Oakland Tribune*, 11/15/30
15   Muriel Babcock, review of *Girl of the Golden West, Los Angeles Times*, 9/15/30
16   Elizabeth Yeaman, review of *Girl of the Golden West, Hollywood Daily Citizen*, 9/13/30
17   Norbert Lusk, review of *Girl of the Golden West, Los Angeles Times*, 11/2/30
18   Robbin Coons, review of *Girl of the Golden West, Lincoln Star*, 7/10/30
19   Robbin Coons, "East Lynne is Being Filmed by Two Firms," *Oakland Tribune*, 9/27/30
20   "Wisecracking Critics Pasee, Actress Says," *Los Angeles Times*, 9/14/30
21   James Robert Parish, *The RKO Gals*, Rainbow Books, c. 1974, pg 23
22   W.E. Oliver, "Star Puts Her Baby Above Career," *Los Angeles Evening Herald*, 1/31/31
23   "*East Lynne* Aid to Women," *Woodland Daily Democrat (CA)*, 4/22/31
24   Letter from Ann to Jasper Deeter, c. 1931. Howard Gotlieb Archival Research Center, Boston University
25   W.E. Oliver, "Star Puts Her Baby Above Career," *Los Angeles Evening Herald*, 1/31/31
26   "Fine Singing Voice Gift of Lovely Ann Harding," *News-Palladium (MI)*, 3/14/31
27   Letter from Ann to Jasper Deeter, c. 1931. Howard Gotlieb Archival Research Center, Boston University
28   Review for *East Lynne, Time Magazine*, 3/2/31
29   Philip K. Scheuer, review for *East Lynne, Los Angeles Times*, 2/5/31
30   Harrison Carroll, review of *East Lynne, Los Angeles Evening Herald*, 2/4/31
31   Mordaunt Hall, review for *East Lynne, New York Times*, 2/21/31
32   a.p.l., "The Talkie Ticker," *Suburbanite Economist (Ill)*, 1/20/31
33   Chester B. Bahn, "Interchange of Players in Disfavor," *Syracuse Herald*, 11/9/31
34   *The New Movie Magazine*, April 1931
35   "Tradition Goes Up in Smoke as Women Puff," news article, 6/30/30
36   "Intention to Marry," *Los Angeles Times*, 6/9/33
37   Sherill Roberts, emails dated: 5/3/2008, 5/5/2008
38   "Colonelcy Will Be Given Tonight to Ann Harding," *Los Angeles Times*, 5/8/32
39   Myrtle Gebhart, "The Happiest Woman in Hollywood," *Picture Play*, March 1931
40   Myrtle Gebhart, "The Happiest ..."
41   Louella Parsons column, *Fresno Bee*, 8/13/31
42   Jack Grant, "The Star Who Amazed Hollywood," *Motion Picture*, July 1931
43   Muriel Babcock, "Ann Harding – 'I Didn't Sign, But I May," *Los Angeles Times*, 3/22/31
44   Jack Grant, "The Star Who Amazed Hollywood," *Motion Picture*, July 1931
45   "Ann Harding Returns to Rose Valley to Lead Cast in Play," *Chester Times*, 4/22/31
46   "Ann Holds Out on Pathe Deal," *Reno Evening Gazette*, 4/18/31
47   Louella Parsons, "Ann Harding Signed; Gets $260,000 First Year," *Fresno Bee*, 8/13/31
48   "Speaking Confidentially," *Hollywood*, November 1931
49   Alice L. Tildesley, "10 Ways to Snap out of the 'Blues'," *Oakland Tribune*, 1/31/32
50   "Crowd Booked for Air Journey to Ensenada," *Los Angeles Times*, 11/18/31
51   Mollie Merrick, review of *Devotion, Kansas City Star*, 9/17/31
52   Chester B. Bahn, review of *Devotion, Syracuse Herald*, 9/27/31
53   Harrison Carroll, review of *Devotion, Los Angeles Evening Herald*, 9/16/31
54   "Admiration Mutual in This Case," *Los Angeles Times*, 9/13/31
55   Harrison Carroll column, *Los Angeles Evening Herald*, 9/21/31
56   Gene Ringgold, "Ann Harding," *Films in Review*, March, 1972 pg 139
57   James Robert Parish, *The RKO Gals*, Rainbow Books, c. 1974, pg 25
58   Harrison Carroll, "Behind the Scenes in Hollywood," *San Mateo Times*, 9/24/31
59   Louella Parsons column, *Modesto News Herald*, 10/17/31

60   Louella Parsons column, *Modesto News Herald*, 10/17/31
61   Chester Bahn, "Hollywood Will Name Outstanding Cinema Players Tuesday," *Syracuse Herald*, 11/8/31
62   "Dolly Gann Yields Seat at Banquet to Marie Dressler," *Appleton Post-Crescent*, 11/11/31
63   Hubbard Keavy, "Screen Life in Hollywood," *San Antonio Express*, 11/22/31
64   Jack Grant column, *Movie Classic*, October 1931
65   "Ann Harding on Way to Florida," *Salt Lake Tribune*, 11/30/31
66   "Actress Injuries Mystify," *Los Angeles Times*, 12/4/31
67   "Ann Harding to Face Judge on Traffic Counts," *San Antonio Light*, 6/4/30
68   Report from *Hollywood Citizen News*, 12/7/31
69   Harrison Carroll, "Behind the Scenes in Hollywood," *San Mateo Times*, 1/15/32
70   Elizabeth Yeaman column, *Los Angeles Record*, 1/5/32
71   Report from the files of Rick Jewell, author of *The RKO Story*, contacted by author on 11/2/2008
72   Louella Parsons column, *Modesto News-Herald*, 2/24/32
73   Philip K. Scheuer, review of *Prestige, Los Angeles Times*, 3/7/32 and comment by critic Norbert Lusk, 2/14/32
74   Review of *Prestige, Los Angeles Record*, 3/5/32
75   Gene Ringgold, "Ann Harding," *Films in Review*, March 1972 pg 138
76   Ben Lyon, "My Friend Ann Harding," *Screen Play*, September 1931

Ann, Jane and Harry happily perched while building
their new mountain-top home. (1930)
(Courtesy of Wisconsin Center for Film and Theater Research)

9

Intermission

The languor of California's mild winters, coupled with new careers, had induced Ann and Harry to buy a hill. Their decision began as a lark one evening early in 1930. They had turned off Outpost Road onto the twisting, corkscrew known as Mulholland Drive. Up they went, toward the Santa Monica Mountains. The car stayed in second gear until they reached a rocky, wind-blown plateau. Ann got out of the car, walked over to the plateau's edge, and sat down. Views of the San Fernando Valley, the jeweled seaboard of the Pacific, and a silver-capped Mount Baldy, surrounded her. She looked off toward the twinkling lights of Hollywood, turned to Harry, and saw that he was also filled with the beauty of it. "This is it, darling," Ann sighed.[1] The following day they found the owner, and paid cash for the property. Energized and determined to do as much as possible on their own, they began clearing the ground. Ann, in knickers and boots, piled the brush. She felt the whole experience and team effort to be "fine and earthy." Bannister began designing a house with staunch beams, fine walls, and quiet luxury. They paid upfront for all materials and expenses, and, upon completion, liked to boast, "It's the only house without a mortgage in Southern California!" Ann and Harry created one of the more spectacular celebrity homes. A solid rock wall rose up to anchor the white walls, red roof and dark wood balconies of the Bannisters' new residence at 7430 Pyramid Drive. Ann and Harry had removed themselves from the outside world. They preferred it that way. Undaunted by the winds, and looking *down* to watch birds fly, Ann referred to herself as happily "perched."[2] She relished the security, and feeling of permanence. "As for being a homebody," she said, "I suppose my husband, Mr. Bannister, and I are *that* above anything. Since we came to live up here, we can't be dragged away from our home."[3] Witnessing the line of baby washing outside the kitchen entrance, visitors knew what Ann meant when she said the screen as opposed to the stage allowed her to live like a human being. Almost.

Like many stars with children, the reality of occasional kidnap threats necessitated that the Bannisters have a gated driveway. Using the latest technology, when they arrived home at night, Ann and Harry simply pressed a button for the lights to turn on, and the garage door to open. A turntable in the garage pointed the car to any angle desired. Offering no protection, their police guard dog, "Menace," greeted them (and strangers alike), with a friendly and enthusiastic round of hand licking. Inside, the large living room was both grand and cozy. A large stone fireplace with a deep davenport nearby emphasized the feeling of home. It was a place where "Whoopee," Ann's scotch terrier, could occupy the couch, and not be reprimanded. The dog, and his feline companion, "Satan," had run of the house and romped over everything and everybody. A total of sixteen rooms, and half as many baths (Ann's was green and lavender), completed the interior. In Ann and Harry's bedroom (twin beds), there was a hidden staircase that led to the tile roof, where another set of beds was placed directly under the stars. As Ann and Harry shared an interest in astronomy, this observatory-bedroom was perfect for keeping charts of the skies. It also was handy during heat waves.

When asked what she and Harry called their castle-on-the-hill, Ann laughed, "You'd never guess. We call it 'Janie's House.'" They had tried for months to come up with a name. Then, out of the mouth of babes, Jane settled the matter during an afternoon drive, with a simple request: "I want to go home to Janie's house."[4] Jane's nursery, overflowing with dolls, had its own private balcony. "Making early provision for any *Juliet* tendencies she may develop," Ann mused.[5] Modernistic interpretations of Mother Goose characters, whom Jane affectionately kissed goodnight, paraded along the walls. Ann was happy with Jane's nurse—a priority in her commitment to a film career. "If I hadn't the assurance that [Jane] was being properly cared for," Ann confirmed, "I would drop my career in an instant and devote my time to her—a job which I consider more important than anything else."[6] When columnist Grace Kingsley visited the Bannister home, she made the mistake of saying she couldn't see how Ann could possibly find time for both Jane and a career. Ann silently left the room, then returned with Jane in hand. Ann looked Kingsley dead-on and asked, "Does she look neglected?"[7]

Ann felt that the existence of Jane made the love she and Harry felt for one another deeper and steadier. "She is the living proof of its existence," said Ann. "She has never heard a minute's unpleasantness in our household. And by a minute I mean just exactly that—sixty seconds."[8] On workdays, Jane was brought into her parents' bedroom for a family morning romp. Ann usually arrived home from the studio just in time to tuck Jane into bed, and tell her a goodnight story. Sometimes they would rush up to the roof to watch the stars. On days off, the threesome would have a morning swim followed by breakfast. Jane, who could swim by the age of three, had her own shallow pool adjoining the large one of her parents. She also had a grassy garden to play in. On rare snowy winter mornings, Ann would be outside making a snowman for her little girl.

Jane referred to Ann as "my very deeeear mother," but she wasn't about to be an accomplice to Ann's occasional tricks and subterfuge with RKO. On one such occasion, Ann was upset about losing some of her lines in *Devotion*, so, she called in sick. Director Robert Milton, out of concern, showed up at Ann's doorstep to inquire about her health. Ann quickly grabbed a bed jacket. Milton entered the room where he found Ann coughing as no dying person ever managed to cough before. Impressed to no end, he looked at Jane, who was standing nearby, and apologized, "So sorry your mummy's sick." Jane nonchalantly replied,

Pyramid Place. Ann and Harry's castle-in-the-clouds was purchased in 1990 by talk-show host Arsenio Hall ($3.5 million). "Arsenio never walked through it before buying," a source told the *Chicago Sun-Times*. "He just rode over in a helicopter." After bulldozing the property, Hall has left it barren.

"Oh, she isn't sick. She's only acting."[9] Ann said she sank back into a "state of coma," but did regain her precious lines of dialogue.

Although Ann had nixed the idea of Jane playing a bit part in *East Lynne* (fearing the bright studio lights might harm her eyes), she said she wouldn't be at all disappointed if Jane took up the profession as an adult. Jane was fond of some of her mother's co-stars, especially Robert Williams, who had played the eccentric artist in *Devotion*. Williams admitted his love affair with little Jane, who called him regularly to inquire about his health. After not seeing each other for several weeks, Williams made a point of telling the curly-headed little girl, in loving terms, how much he had missed her. Jane laid a tender hand on his knee, and said feelingly, "Bobby!" On another occasion, Jane interrupted Williams while he was expressing his devotion to her. In her own, adorable, precocious way, Jane cautioned, "Don't tease me, Bobby."[10] (Williams, who had also co-starred on stage with Ann in *The Trial of Mary Dugan*, died in November of 1931, following a long overdue appendix operation.)

Occasionally, Jane accompanied her parents on social outings. That is, if the hosting household had children. She refused to go inside of Carmel Myers' beach house, upon finding out there were no other little girls inside to play with. Jane had better luck at the home of Nils Asther. Eight months after Asther and his wife Vivian Duncan had a baby girl, Ann and Harry took Jane to meet the newborn. Asther lived just down the hill from them. While Jane and baby Evelyn indulged in baby talk, Ann and Harry mingled with the other guests, such as the Lewis Stones and Charles Bickford. After a buffet luncheon, there was light entertainment. Tenor Jose Mojica thrilled, Ramon Novarro serenaded, and Vivian did a few of her own numbers. Before the baby's bedtime, onlookers were delighted to see Ramon Novarro and Ann

Harding dance a tango … *this* was a baby shower, Hollywood-style.[11] (The following year, Nils and Vivian would divorce.)

The Bannisters didn't have to leave Janie's House for entertainment. Harry built Ann her own little theatre for putting on plays and showing films. A tunnel connected the theatre and tennis court (which was on top of the theatre) to the main house. Ann's quieter moments were spent playing the piano, listening to Beethoven, reading *The New Yorker* cover-to-cover, or delving into works of Irish novelist Donn Byrne. But, most of all, there was gardening. Tanned and rosy, Ann loved to work outdoors, and tramped around in knickers and a shirt. Projects around their home were endless. "The beauty of it," said Ann, "is that we can always be doing something in the way of planting, terracing, and so forth. How can we ever be bored with this place?"[12] To prove her point, Ann took up delphinium culture, tending and experimenting with them. Her own delphinium specimen won first prize at a local flower show. She respected the natural environment that surrounded her. "I came across a section of tangled, rough beauty—ferns and wildflowers," Ann commented. "I determined to care for it, and let it develop, adding nothing unless it is necessary to fill in a vacant spot or two, in which case I shall select simple plants in conformity. In life, we should cultivate the qualities native to us."[13] Ann found the garden to be a tonic when she was 'keyed up' following a ten-hour stretch at the studio. "Something about the warm, damp earth relaxes me," she explained. "I love the feel of it in my hands and the fragrance of the growing things around me. Usually my small daughter helps with her tiny spade and we giggle and gurgle until my husband comes out to discover the cause of the commotion, and he, too succumbs to the lure of the soil."[14]

The Bannisters rarely entertained more than four people at once, and avoided screenland's social whoopee. "Speaking for myself," said Ann, "a thoroughly dull time is one spent at a cocktail party—most parties, to be frank, or artificial entertainment of any kind … are not for me."[15] Several months after arriving in California, she and Harry attended their first Hollywood party. They felt completely out of place. The room was filled with husbandless wives and wifeless husbands. "People looked at us with the expression usually reserved for the inspection of some odd freak," Ann remarked. "A married couple at a party together? Heavens!"[16] According to Ann, the consensus in Hollywood was that couples were supposed to enjoy each other *less* after marriage.

London-born journalist Cedric Belfrage (founder of the left-wing *National Guardian*) found Ann to be "a thoroughly happy woman." Despite this fact, he referred to her as "his latest passion" (he had five wives). "I am a Bolshevik," wrote Belfrage, "and 'happy' people are to me like red rags to a bull." Ann thoroughly engaged the "Bolshevik," while telling him of her own concerns. She and Harry had been warned about the "necessity" of attending certain parties, which she considered to be political moves, in order to maintain one's film career. "I just can't go in for this business of mixing up careerist politics with one's private life," she told Belfrage. "I could never entertain people I loathed just to get work out of them."[17] Ann preferred the more spontaneous type of dinner invitations, like the time she asked the crinkled old stone mason, who worked on their home, to stay for dinner. He was hesitant and apologized that his manners may not be up to snuff. "Never mind manners," Ann insisted. Her butler, a square-jawed Swede named Gus, eyed the visitor with an unwelcoming glare. Gus was the perfect specimen of dignity, and was always horrified if Ann or Harry even poured themselves a drink of water. On this occasion, Gus served the Bannisters, but had to be called back after every course to serve the old mason. When the meal was over, Ann walked into the kitchen and quietly told Gus, "You're through. I can't tolerate snobs in my home."[18] Gus was replaced with a more democratic Chinese houseboy.[19] One could always count on Ann's being direct, and never "beating around the bush." And, Harry? Guests were surprised by his boorish behavior. "Well, I'm sleepy. Goodnight, everybody," was a typical exit line for Mr. Bannister. While guests rolled their eyes, Ann would explain, "Harry works so hard. He says life is too short not to do as you like whenever it's possible. He's so honest."[20]

When columnist Harrison Carroll visited Ann at home, he referred to the location as "aloof," but found Ann to be "brisk like a breeze." He mentioned her restless energy, strong opinions and lack of pretense.[21] Ann proclaimed herself a "rank individualist," and had formidable opinions on a lot of things, particularly happiness. "I think unhappiness is a crime," she liked to point out. "In fact, only stupid people are unhappy—except for brief intervals when real grief overtakes even the happiest. If they weren't stupid, they wouldn't be unhappy, because they'd find a way out, or they'd put their minds to thinking how to get the utmost joy out of life as it stood, until luck changed. The trouble with our generation of women is that they accept other people's conclusions on what is enjoyable, what is relaxation, what is smart, and so on. ... My idea of real fun is work. Work that I love. You can't be happy if you are doing work you loathe."[22] Ann thought of the thousands of young women doing shorthand and typing, gritting their teeth and hating their jobs. "It makes me furious!" she declared.

Ann's real fury was reserved for her numerous and unpleasant experiences at beauty salons. It only took one look, one instant, for Ann to pick up on "attitude." "As a rule," she lamented, "[they] regard me and my locks with dismay. 'All that hair! What a mess! And what a funny color! And why doesn't she have it cut?' If that girl *really* cared about her job, she'd enjoy working with something new."[23] Another gripe of Ann's was the trend toward pessimism ... individuals who were proud of being unhappy. "It's the stylish manner among intellectuals," she stated with her usual outspoken charm. "A frown places you among the higher reaches of Menckenites, and a smile sports you as a Babbitt." Popular journalist H.L. Mencken targeted many of America's sacred cows, but his wit was crisp, and like Ann, Mencken's opinions had bite. Ann was the antithesis of a Sinclair Lewis social-climbing "Babbitt" (from his timely novel). She was hardly a conformist, or materialist, and stated very clearly, "Money is only a medium of exchange."[24] De-

spite the fact that Ann related some of her pet peeves to Harrison Carroll, he felt she came across as one of the most positive personalities in Hollywood.

Ann contended that she lived solely in the present and never proclaimed affiliation with any particular doctrine. Her philosophy of life was simple, and direct. Devoid of any deep-seated yearnings, she saw herself living

Ann lets down her famous hair.

each day to the fullest. "I have no physical, mental or spiritual problems to solve," stated Ann. "And, I don't bother my head over religious questions. I let my conscience be my guide, because I haven't tried to decide whether there is a future life or not. My worrying over the question won't solve it or help me in any way. So I let it alone. If there is a future life, it is there. If there isn't, I'm not going to worry about that, either."[25]

Columnists complained that the Ann Harding seen in films was not to be recognized on the street. "I'd like to gather up all those old funny dresses she insists on wearing," wrote one critic. "She came into Hollywood Stationery late yesterday afternoon, in a formless-looking grey coat, carried an old-fashioned bead bag … her black hat might have been a skull cap, for all the distinctiveness it possessed— and , lo and behold, from beneath her coat protruded another one of her dollar-day bargain dresses!"[26] When her career took off, Ann only had five dresses on her closet hangers. She had no time or inter-est for glamour, and preferred to convert her earnings into govern-ment bonds. She was more interested in *where* she was going than what she was going to wear. "If clothes are clean, comfortable … they suit me," she said. "The greatest advantage to having money is that it enables you to look like the devil if you want to do so. Only the poor and the climbing have to dress up to impress."[27] After one fash-ion critic sneered at Ann's "shabby coat," Ann offered a hopeless sigh. "That's the only French model I ever owned," she said, "and it cost me $750."[28] Ann did make a point to wear gowns especially designed for her when attending a premier. On such occasions she enjoyed accessorizing with amber, yellow diamonds, and antique gold. She simply stated that she refused to make clothes, and jewels a "fetish."

Ann's face, free of make-up, had a natural, rosy glow. Her pale eyebrows and lashes took close scrutiny to reveal themselves at all. Without cosmetics, only the loosely coiled, corn-colored hair gave passersby a clue as to who she was. One interviewer scheduled an appointment, and failed to recognize her at all. He waited an hour and a half in front of a theatre, then left in disgust, failing, as one report stated, "to associate the shabbily dressed woman standing only a few steps away as the beautiful celebrity with whom he had an appointment."[29] Louella Parsons, who liked giving Ann a bad time, smugly observed that Ann looked less an actress than any other star. "Miss Harding," Parsons barbed, "doesn't care a hang for clothes. To meet her on the street you would mistake her for a housewife on a marketing expedition."[30] Adela Rogers St. Johns, a champion of Ann, was also blunt in her assessment, claiming, "[Ann] was the worst dressed woman I ever saw in my life!" St. Johns tellingly commented on Ann's propensity to dote on Harry in public. "She used to sit around at parties and smile at her husband," said St. Johns. "Apparently she had no mind of her own at all."[31] Ann wasn't being singled out entirely. Katharine Hepburn and Dietrich received plenty of flak for wearing men's pants in public. They were unconventional. Ann was looked upon as just plain untidy and badly groomed. She balked at all the attention made of her disinterest in glamour and her insistence on not playing the star. Her reaction left no second-guessing as to how she felt about it. Ann penned her own rebuttal, saying,

> People often express surprise that I do not look
> like an actress off-screen. Sometimes I suspect that
> they are rather disappointed to discover that I dress

plainly, that I wear practically no make-up, and that
I lead a very normal, quiet life. It seems to be the
popular conception that an actress must live, in
private life, the roles she portrays in her professional
life. Personally, I have never been able to figure out
any reason why an actress should look like an actress
off-stage or off-screen any more than a nurse should
look like a nurse outside of a hospital. To me, acting
is a profession and should be treated as such. ... I
believe that the actress who wears her profession
on her sleeve, as it were, outside of her work, is, as a
rule, merely dramatizing herself. When she acts off-
stage as well as on, she is wasting her talent. It is like
using nectar to quench a casual thirst.[32]

"*Be yourself!*" was Ann's motto. She felt that if people didn't like
you *as is*, what difference did it make in the end? "You can find someone who does!" she insisted. "I don't tread on anyone's toes, and I
don't crave to dictate morals, manners, and customs. I expect to be
free from such supervision myself."[33] Even so, Ann made an occasional off-the-cuff remark about actresses who played the glamour
game and dramatized outside of their profession. She was amused
by the idea of Pola Negri riding a rollercoaster, and couldn't imagine
Marlene Dietrich being truly "excited" about anything.[34]

There were a few film stars that accepted Ann on her own terms. She
considered them her friends. Joan Crawford, a fellow San Antonio
native, was among them. "I cherish Ann's companionship more than
that of any person I have ever known," Joan confided to columnist Ben

Maddox. "Just to be with her makes one happy, forces one to realize how insignificant all the petty things which annoy us are. She is so supremely happy and radiant. All you have to do is look into her eyes to find what a beautiful soul she has. There isn't an ounce of falseness or pretense in her. Ann Harding is my idea of the perfect woman, as well as the perfect actress!"[35] This was indeed an unusual comment from a star-driven icon like Crawford. She and her husband, Doug Fairbanks Jr., were both champions of Ann and were always seen at her premiers. Ann and Joan were often accompanied by Kay Hammond (a costar from *Her Private Affair*) on shopping expeditions. The trio also lunched together at the Embassy Club, but mostly visited at each other's homes for swimming, tennis, backgammon, or just to sit around and talk. In Crawford's 1962 autobiography, *A Portrait of Joan*, she mentioned that during her four-year marriage to Fairbanks Jr., evenings at home were spent with their "closer friends," Ann and Harry Bannister.[36] Mary Astor bonded even more intimately with Ann. Even so, Ann admitted that she understood men's minds and interests better than the petty concerns that preoccupied most women.

As an actress, Ann also had her famous admirers. Ethel Barrymore was one of them. So was Marion Davies. Lillian Gish, who had seen Ann on the stage and wasn't inclined to rave about anyone, opted that Ann was one of the screen's finest emotional actresses.[37] Barbara Stanwyck was at the forefront of Ann's champions. "I don't go to many pictures," said Stanwyck, "and there are only a few actors who can *get* me sufficiently to make me lose myself in the story. Ann Harding is one of them. Miss Harding is so entirely natural at all times that she makes me believe in her and what she is doing. I have always hoped that my own work showed the same degree of sincerity. When I see an Ann Harding picture nothing but her work and the story interests me. I am really able to lose myself."[38] To Ann's credit, Stanwyck stated there was no need to mention other actresses after talking about Ann Harding.

"Though I invite disaster by saying it," Harrison Carroll wrote, "Ann Harding and Harry Bannister seem to be among the happiest couples in Hollywood. They live on a hilltop above the film colony and apparently enjoy the serenity of domestic peace."[39] Louella Parsons echoed Carroll's sentiment. "I don't know of any two young people who have a

(Above left) Harry, Ann and relief pilot Lee Miles (US Air Race Champion of 1934) return to Los Angeles after a 4,000-mile jaunt. (May 2, 1931)

better time together than Ann Harding and her husband … they are congenial, they are great pals and they are in love with each other."[40] Ann felt the same way, and was not shy about saying so. She deferred to women's rights activist Margaret Sanger's belief that love must be exercised into action for it to grow and develop. Ann and Harry's mutual interests in flying, tennis, hiking, and golf created both comradeship and focal points outside of business and careers. This mutual sense of play allowed them to continue being sweethearts. "This give and take of jokes and light banter which is so characteristic of courtship," said Ann, "helps to keep one's marriage interesting."[41] Ann felt that she and Harry appreciated what they had, appreciated each other, and were willing to say so. "There is an ancient and cynical remark," said Ann, "about there being small use in running for a street car that one already has caught. May God deliver either my husband or me from that frame of mind!"[42] Ann emphasized the importance of being non-invasive, respecting personal rights and space, and not presuming on the good nature of the other. She used the analogy of East Indian ants to drive her point home. "[They] burrow into furniture," Ann stated, "until there is nothing left of the original structure but a hollow shell."[43] Ann maintained that she and Harry had succeeded in holding on to their separate identities. But somehow, amidst all the comforts of a hearth and home that he had helped design and create, Harry was claiming to have *lost* his identity. He was ready to get off the "streetcar." Harry claimed he had *become* a hollow shell, a "Mr. Ann Harding," and wanted out.

(Above right) Ann christens her second private plane (August 14, 1931). She was ready to fly solo in more ways than one.

(Endnotes)

1   Lois Shirley, "The Story of a Magic House," *Photoplay*, October 1930
2   Dick Hunt, "Ann Dampens Her Think-Waves in Pool," *Los Angeles Evening Herald*, 8/2/30
3   W. E. Oliver, "Star Puts Her Baby Above Career," *Los Angeles Evening Herald*, 1/31/31
4   Louella Parsons column, *Los Angeles Examiner*, 3/11/31
5   Myrtle Gebhart, "The Happiest Woman in Hollywood," *Picture Play*, March 1931
6   W.E. Oliver, "Star Puts Her Baby Above Career," *Los Angeles Evening Herald*, 1/31/31
7   Grace Kingsley, "How Stars Bring Up Their Children," *New Movie*, February 1931
8   Ann Harding, "Happiness After Marriage," *Screen Book*, August 1930
9   Sara Hamilton, "Annie, the Moom-Picture Star," *Photoplay*, May 1932
10   Dallas MacDonnell, "Married Actor Gets Involved in Love Affair!" *Hollywood Daily Citizen*, 6/24/31
11   Grace Kingsley, "A Baby Holds Company," *Los Angeles Times*, 11/15/31
12   Alice L. Tildesley, "How Shall Women Escape Boredom?" *Oakland Tribune*, 6/14/31
13   Myrtle Gebhart, "The Happiest Woman in Hollywood," *Picture Play*, March 1931
14   Ann Harding, "Beauty That Really Lasts," *Movie Romances*, November 1931
15   Alice L. Tildesley, "How Shall ..."
16   Ann Harding, "Happiness After Marriage, " *Screen Book*, August 1930
17   Cedric Belflrage, "She Doesn't Play," *Motion Picture*, July 1930
18   Sara Hamilton, "Annie, the Moom- Picture Star," *Photoplay*, May 1932
19   Myrtle Gebhart, "The Happiest Woman in Hollywood," *Picture Play*, March 1931
20   Dorothy Calhoun, "Looking in on Ann and Harry," *Motion Picture*, June 1931
21   Harrison Carroll column, *Los Angeles Evening Herald*, 9/12/31
22   Alice L. Tildesley, "How Shall ..."
23   Alice L. Tildesley, "How Shall ..."
24   Alice L. Tildesley, "How Shall ..."
25   Mary Sharon, "Ann Harding *Isn't* Contented," *Silver Screen*, September 1931
26   Potter B. Brayton, "Up and Down the Boulevard," *Wisconsin State Journal*, 10/5/30
27   Ben Maddox, "Discovering ..."
28   Myrtle Gebhart, "$15,000 a Year For Clothes," *Los Angeles Times*, 6/5/32
29   Mark Dowling and Lynn Norris, "Hollywood Speaking," *Arcadia Tribune*, 4/1/32
30   Louella Parsons column, *Los Angeles Examiner*, 8/12/30
31   Adela Rogers St. Johns, "Has a Movie Mother Any Rights?" *Photoplay*, August 1936
32   Ann Harding, "My Recipe for Success," *Hollywood*, January 1931
33   Ben Maddox, "Discovering Hollywood's Real Sophisticate, Ann Harding!" *Screenland*, November 1931
34   Ann Harding, column she wrote for the *Los Angeles Evening Express*, 9/25/31
35   Ben Maddox, "Discovering Hollywood's Real Sophisticate, Ann Harding!" *Screenland*, November 1931
36   Joan Crawford and Jane Kesner Ardmore, *A Portrait of Joan*, Doubleday, c. 1962, pg. 77
37   Louella Parsons column, *San Antonio Light*, 12/19/29
38   Julia Gwin, "She's a Movie FAN, Too!" *Silver Screen*, January 1934
39   Harrison Carroll, "Behind the Scene in Hollywood," *Sheboygan Press*, 8/9/30
40   Louella Parsons column, *Los Angeles Examiner*, 4/6/31
41   Ann Harding as told to Lillian Genn, "How I Make My Husband Happy," *San Mateo Times*, 6/17/31
42   Ann Harding," Happiness After ..."
43   Ann Harding, "Happiness After ..."

Hollywood's "Happiest Couple." (c. 1931)

10
"Mr. Ann Harding"

Below us lies Hollywood. The city of shattered
marriages and miserable homes. Up here on our
hilltop we are as far from all that unhappy ferment
as though we were on another planet. ... We are,
you see, one. ... Is it any wonder that I am ready
to believe there can be a heaven on earth?[1] – *Ann
Harding* (August 1930)

Ann's lofty assessment of her life with Harry would prove bittersweet,
and hit a brick wall in 1932. In spite of her influence to keep him on
payroll at RKO-Pathé, the studio simply tolerated Bannister's presence. He was the "necessary evil" in keeping their very popular star,
Ann Harding, happy. During interviews, Ann politely mentioned the
"sacrifices" Harry made for her career. On March 21, 1932, Harry secured a release from his contract. He received 80 percent of his annual
salary ($50,000) in the settlement, for doing nothing.[2] Just prior to this
"windfall," he told columnist Elizabeth Yeaman, "I feel sorry for movie
and stage people whose interests are limited to their work. I think it is
the desire for money and more money."[3] Yeaman commented, "Appar-

ently Bannister is unaware of the driving ambition which keeps most players in the harness. Money is not the only lure for an actor or actress." He was dissatisfied with the parts he had been given. Yeaman was blunt in her assessment of Harry's sad story. "It's my guess," argued Yeaman, "that he was dissatisfied with the *lack* of parts assigned to him."[4] There was much more behind his decision to leave the studio than anyone had imagined. Ann and Harry, "Hollywood's Happiest Couple," were preparing to file for divorce. The news fell like a bombshell.

Harry explained to columnist Louella Parsons that he wanted to prove that he had some ability as an actor. "I never had a chance on the screen," he told her. "As the husband of one of the most idolized screen figures, I was forever labeled 'Ann Harding's husband.' I had no opportunity as an individual."[5] Previously, Bannister had inferred to Parsons that the problem may have been his nose. "I thought at the time he was joking," she reported. "I couldn't see anything wrong."[6] Indirectly, Harry was really blaming Ann. "No studio," he emphasized, "would accept me as anything but 'Mr. Ann Harding.'"[7] In the fall of 1931, after eighteen months of being placated with a generous salary, but no acting assignments, Harry flew to San Diego to film RKO's *Suicide Fleet*. In this World War saga, Bannister looked uncomfortable in his attempt to impersonate an ornery naval commander. His dialogue consisted mostly of barking orders (i.e., "Sound the general alarm!") Director Albert Rogell made a point of keeping Bannister's back to the camera. Richard Jewell, in his *RKO Story*, thought the gag-filled script "consistently artificial," and "the naval maneuvers … pure hooey."[8] The *Los Angeles Times*, as an afterthought, stated, "Harry Bannister is momentarily in evidence."[9] The reviews for *Suicide Fleet*, and Bannister's subsequent release, Paramount's *Husband's Holiday*, failed to mention Bannister's "ability" as an actor. The performances of fifth-billed actors (as he was in both films), didn't usually garner mention or appraisal.

For whatever reason, Ann and Harry wrote divorce-announcement letters, using personal stationery, and forwarded them to the press. "The 'Ann Hardings' Frank About Divorce," quipped one typical headline.[10] Their decision came as a jolt to those who knew them, as Harry had recently told of their plans for Ann to quit pictures when her contract expired in 1933. He boasted that they were financially comfortable, were looking forward to travel, relaxation, and touring in a play a few months out of the year. Harry's divorce-letter to the press, which Ann had typed, stated that in order for him to "preserve" her respect and devotion the best solution was divorce. Ann's letter, dated March 21, 1932, was tinged with apologetic tones for having made Harry a martyr to her career. It read:

> We, Harry Bannister and Ann Harding Bannister, are getting a divorce, because, during our three years in the motion picture industry, we have been placed in a position which is untenable.
>
> Due to Harry's constant and generous effort to forward my interests, often at the expense of his own, he is gradually losing his identity, becoming a background for my activities, and looked upon as "Ann Harding's husband."

> We have decided that the only way for Harry to reestablish himself in this profession, is to cut the Gordian knot, to set forth on his own – quite apart from me – and win his way back to the standing he enjoyed in the Theatre, before this unfortunate situation in pictures has a chance to reach us, and destroy the love and respect we have for each other.
>
> We have found courage to preserve the thing we have in the way that seems best to us.
>
> – Ann Harding Bannister.[11]

The divorce was prepared in what appeared to be a congenial spirit. While at a preview of RKO's *Symphony of Six Million*, a few days before their announcement, Ann and Harry asked reporter Jack Grant to come to their home for some "glorious news." That next evening, Grant, a longtime friend and confidant of Ann's, listened for three hours, while she and Harry sat on a divan holding hands. They talked about Harry's release from his contract, and his plan to return to the stage. Grant noticed no difference in their attitudes toward each another, but sensed something was afoot. Harry shared his disappointment about losing his "big opportunity," a minor role, in John Barrymore's *State's Attorney*. After two days' work, he was fired. Elizabeth Yeaman stated in her column that casting Bannister in the role of a heavy "defied common logic."[12] (The fourth-billed part of a gangster-chief went to William "Stage" Boyd.) According to Harry, he pleaded with RKO officials, "Don't do this to me! It's my chance. I've waited for it a long time. You know what it means. People will say I couldn't play the part."[13] RKO told him not to worry; they would issue a statement to the press saying he was too ill to play the part. "Brilliant, wasn't it?" Harry said bitterly.

"I don't mind saying I hit the ceiling! This was too much. I told them that if such news were released, I would personally summon all the reporters in town to my house and tell them it was a lie!"

RKO then offered "rebel" Harry a bit part in one of Ann's films, trying to get him to break his contract. "I'll play extra parts," Harry blasted, "I'll scrub floors if you tell me to! The only way I will release you is for you to buy my contract." Harry felt he had won the battle. Before Jack Grant left their home, Ann told him not to print the story right away. "You'd better wait," she said, with a note of concern in her voice. She and Harry stood in the doorway with their arms about each other, and Ann promised there would be a better story in a couple of days. As for losing his big opportunity in *State's Attorney*, Bannister's statement to reporter Hubbard Keavy came closer to the truth: "I'd rather be flying my plane or playing golf anyway."[14]

Instead of putting any real effort into his own career, Harry was a spectator of his wife's. He focused on the "toys" afforded by Ann's success. His avocation for flying took precedence over any kind of real work. "Harry Bannister, really prefers to pilot his own plane above everything else," stated *Hollywood Citizen News*, in a typical news story. "Yesterday, he hopped into a two-seated open-cabin plane and joined the search for missing planes. He returned last night, but expects to hop off on the search again today."[15] In April 1932, Welford Beaton commented in the *Hollywood Spectator* that Bannister's "humiliation" over being known as his wife's husband must have been of "very recent date." Ann's contract clause providing Harry $1,000 a week was simply, according to Beaton, for his own private income. "Bannister went gaily on his way," Beaton stated, "indulged his hobby of aviation and continued to draw his $1,000 a week because his wife is a good actress."[16]

Columnists got tired of hearing Ann come to Bannister's defense. Reporter Harry Lang gibed, "You could not step into the Bannister household without hearing stories from Ann of how wonderful Harry was. He had been the architect of the house. He had planned this and that. He was such a wonderful aero-plane pilot. Harry had a little theatre built into the house. ... [he] was going to act there, for their friends, old burlesques of foolish plays that used to tour the countryside. Harry, you see, has played the one-night stands, and they thought those goofy old comedies would amuse their friends. 'I wish I had gone through the kind of theatrical training Harry did,' Ann would say, making that old barnstorming sound wonderful."[17] Adela Rogers St. Johns stated that the consensus in Hollywood was that since Bannister hadn't done well, he spent his time interfering with Ann's career. "It was plain enough," voiced St. Johns, "that the beautiful new home, the charming tennis court and swimming pool, the playground for Jane, all the luxury and beauty with which the child was surrounded must be coming from Ann's salary."[18] If Ann and Harry truly loved one another, why would they sacrifice their home, their joint relationship with little Jane, for something as capricious as an acting career? Or, was Harry's real concern his status as a celebrity? Publisher John R. Quirk pointed out the obvious, saying that in spite of Ann's intention to remove herself and her husband from the ferment and ambition of Hollywood, Harry succumbed to the same noxious air filled with ego and self-importance.[19]

The blinding glare and spotlight of publicity overpowered the modest moon above Ann's dream home and her stairway to the stars. She had wanted to believe in her marriage, and was quick in offering the formula for a happy relationship. Ann admitted that her opinions on the subject lacked the scholarly finish of a Havelock Ellis (the famous sexologist),

or feminist-socialist Ellen Key. Such comments gave hint to her choice
of reading material, but ultimately, Ann felt her marital *experience* carried
enough weight to support her point of view. Sadly, her views, however
genuine, were rooted in fantasy, not reality. She would have to eat her
words. Swallowing them wasn't easy. Ann knew the public's voracious
appetite for details on her divorce could never be satisfied. So, she had
her telephone fixed to make strictly outgoing calls, and announced she
could only be reached by telegram.[20] She also quit offering interviews.
Louella Parsons, outraged by Ann's snub, was told by publisher William
Randolph Hearst, "I am going to refuse to notice her in any Hearst paper.
She isn't any good anyhow … The young lady certainly needs some disci-
plining, and we'll do our best."[21] Parsons warned that if Ann continued to
shoo away the press "like so many flies," she'd live long enough to step off
trains without seeing *any* waiting newspaper delegations.[22]   Ann was not
deterred by such drivel. To her, becoming more reclusive was a necessity.
One columnist aptly summed up her situation, saying, "Ann has locked
herself in her castle and pulled the moat and drawbridge in with her."[23]

"There are more divorces now than ever before," Ann had once stated
matter-of-factly, "but not more unhappy marriages. People are trying, blunderingly perhaps, to cure unhappiness today where formerly
they endured it."[24] With no shoulder to cry on, Ann followed her own
advice and took the cure. While the public digested the news of the
Bannisters' divorce, Ann drove to Palm Springs to reflect on the loss
of her ideal marriage. She confided in no one. Mrs. Gatley had left
for Europe in mid-March, and was not available for comment on her

daughter's decision. Ann's sister, Edith, first heard of the divorce from a reporter. One columnist stated that Ann's friend, Joan Crawford, was "shocked into tears" by the news.

Louella Parsons was suspicious of Ann and Harry's declarations, saying that their letters to the press could not be "entirely accepted on their face value."[25] Ann's reclusiveness suggested that her straightforward explanation of divorce must hold a deeper secret. An editorial from the *Kansas City Star* quoted prominent career women's reactions across the country to Ann's statements to the press:

> "I am sorry that a woman who is such an entertaining screen artist did not have better taste than to try to tell such a shallow story."

> "I read that fairy tale composition and wondered the real reason for the divorce."

> "That story sounds silly, and pretty Ann Harding must think so herself if she takes the trouble to read it."

> "Ann Harding's story is a queer tale. I do not think she has told why she is ready to leave her husband, but she has lost something in the eyes of her public by this play for publicity. I am sorry she undertook to explain at all."[26]

Many of Ann's faithful fans felt betrayed. Her films had glorified true love. How could she push it aside? "Ann was the darling of the Women's Clubs," wrote reporter Helen Louise Walker. "She was probably invited to be guest-speaker at more gatherings of feminine culture-seekers than any other actress in pictures. ... Well, when 'dear' Ann Harding's much-publicized domestic bliss suddenly exploded in their faces—those staid patronesses of the arts were hurt. 'It just goes to show that you never can tell,' they sighed to one another. 'She looks like such a sweet thing—and so *good*. But ... divorce ... oh, *dear!*'"[27] In October 1930, Ann, representing Hollywood, made her radio debut on the "Women's Achievement Broadcast." The program was hosted by Mrs. Thomas G. Winter, who, as public relations director for Will Hays, helped put the screws of film censorship into place. The highlight of the broadcast was Ann's speech on combining "A Career and a Home." A few weeks later, Ann repeated her radio address for 500 attendees at the Van Nuys Women's Club. After her divorce, Ann felt nothing but wrath from such organizations. Prominent among them was the California Daughters of the American Revolution, who had established Ann as their "ideal." As their guest speaker, Ann assured them she would raise the standards of motion pictures, and stand by her old contract, "Which is unique," she explained, "in that I may cut out lines that are objectionable to me."[28] The group assumed that "no divorce" was part of the deal. Surprisingly, Ann empathized with her detractors. It was as if she herself had been insulted by the whole debacle of leaving Harry behind. Looking back later, she stated, "The fan identifies himself with the hero in an hour of high adventure and emotional release. He doesn't enjoy coming out into a sweltering or freezing or otherwise uncomfortable world, to find on the nearest magazine stand that the person whose talent and personality have the blessed power to lead him into a land of dreams is a driveling fool, a fake, or a monster. He feels, somehow, that he himself has been insulted, too.[29]

Some felt Ann had chosen an inopportune time to make the break from Harry. Aside from being in the middle of making a film, she had received an ominous letter with threats of kidnapping. She first learned about it over breakfast coffee, while reading the newspaper. Her secretary, not wanting to alarm anyone, had turned the letter over to the authorities. A taxi driver also reported to police that he was shot in the leg after refusing to guide kidnapers to the Bannister home.[30] Prompted by the fate of the Lindbergh baby (who was still missing at that time), iron bars were put across Jane's balcony window. Ann arranged for Jane's nurse to sleep in the same room.[31] Two guards were assigned to patrol the Bannisters' residence. All visitors (including Ann's sister Edith) were required to halt at the gate, and wait until the guards received permission to admit them. At night, the grounds were illumined by a system of floodlights activated by the slightest warning. Los Angeles Chief of Detectives Joseph Taylor suspected the threats to Jane were the work of a disgruntled former employee, or a prank.[32] These incidents distanced Ann even further from the press. The only comment she would offer was, "Fame and money aren't worth it. I wish I were the most obscure person in the world."[33]

After returning from Palm Springs, Ann reported daily to the set of *Westward Passage* (a project for which she had little enthusiasm), and worked twice as hard dodging reporters asking her to elaborate on the divorce letters. RKO arranged to film ship scenes at Fox studios (using sets from 1931's *Transatlantic*) in hopes of avoiding the persistent newshounds. In spite of the precaution, emotional stress took its toll. Ann wept openly out of the camera's view. Tears ruined her make-up, scene after scene.[34] After several days of this, she finally had a collapse. Her physician, Dr. Branch, put her on sedatives so she could sleep.[35]

Amid the turmoil, Ann managed to keep her appointment with Bay Area film critic Wood Soanes. He avoided the obvious questions, allowing Ann to comment on her film work, and technical difficulties on the set of *Westward Passage,* where the production was limited to the use of one camera. In spite of a severe head cold, and the fact that the filming process required that she repeat the same line over and over for each shift of the camera, Ann eloquently expressed her feelings:

> One of the most deadly things in the theater or on the screen comes when the player grows weary of his lines. As soon as it becomes work to do something, one is inclined to be indifferent. And no matter what you may say, the success of the sound picture depends upon the spontaneity with which the lines are read. In the studio you make a picture with only your director for an audience. By the time you have looked over the criticisms of the critics scattered all over the world, you may have made two other pictures containing the same faults. And it is axiomatic that three bad pictures can ruin the career of the best players. [36]

Ann emphasized to Soanes that she needed the stimulus of the stage not only for variety, but for the reaction of a live audience. Hedgerow was always in the back of her mind, but it would be a year before she returned to the stage in Rose Valley. Ann completed work on *Westward Passage* in April. Or, at least, she thought she did. The end result was such a mess that she was called back again and again for retakes. Producer David Selznick ordered several comedy sequences to "liven up various parts of the yarn."[37] There was one person who felt he benefited from the experience ... a young British actor by the name of Laurence Olivier.

Laurence Olivier would become one of the most revered actors of the 20th century. He felt his first two films in Hollywood died the death of dogs, but that working with Ann gave him an adult confidence on screen for the first time. His biographer, Donald Spoto, wrote that Ann "provided Oliver with a brief lesson in un-temperamental, generous filmmaking collaboration, insisting that his role be expanded and often arguing that close-ups should favor him. Her performance was artless, and Olivier too, became natural and unselfconscious. For the first time, something of his personality was evoked by the camera."[38] Olivier wrote to his family in England that Ann Harding was "angelic" with generosity and kindness to him.[39] Despite Ann's divorce proceedings, she wasn't *all* gloom and doom. When Olivier asked her if she was a natural blonde, Ann is reported to have told him, "Yes. I could prove it to you if I knew you better."[40]

Co-star Laurence Olivier was amazed at Ann's generosity while filming *Westward Passage* (1932). (RKO-Pathé)

The crux of *Westward Passage*, based on Bryn Mawr graduate Margaret Ayer Barnes' novel, centers on the heroine's indecision as to whether she wants the security of a conservative, comfortable life, or a blithe and uncertain one. Oddly enough, it was the first film in which Ann played a divorcee. The initial scenes are ingratiating. Ann (as Olivia) and Olivier (as Nick), a hopeful author, light up the screen as young newlyweds. "Oh! This is heavenly!" Olivia declares upon entering their honeymoon suite at a country inn. Not missing a beat, Nick replies with a wink, "*This...* is the bedroom!" ZaSu Pitts, in a delightful turn as the innkeeper, gets his drift and flutters, "Oh, My!" As the story progresses, we see Nick facing a stack of returned manuscripts, and a marriage for which he is ill-prepared. When Olivia announces she's pregnant, Nick is frank. "No use lying," he tells her over cocktails, "I'm *not* glad." The couples' arguments are anchored in reality and have emotional punch. Divorce is inevitable. *Westward Passage* advances six years with Olivia, her daughter (Bonita Granville) and second husband, Harry (Irving Pichel), vacationing in Europe. Olivia has found stability, and her daughter adores Harry. Who should pop in but Nick. He attempts to rekindle a flame, but Olivia hesitates. "Tisn't such a very good idea to look back," she tells him.

At this juncture, *Westward Passage* loses steam. Selznick experimented with several endings, and the problem for Ann was that the final scenario worked *against* the maturity she had developed for her character. The film's ending is distastefully contrived, as we are led to believe that Olivia would forfeit a stable and loving relationship with Harry for an erratic life with Nick, a coercive and despicable character with all the charm of a stalker. Author Barnes, on the other hand, created Olivia as a woman who fully re-embraces the comfort and solid-

ity of her second marriage. Los Angeles critic Harrison Carroll felt
Westward Passage contained Ann's "least interesting screen characterization."[41] *The New York Times* was generous, saying Robert Milton's
direction for *Westward Passage* was "capital," Harding and Olivier's
performances were "emphatically clever," and the film had "moments
of ingratiating comedy."[42] To her credit, Ann's performance manages
to balance the talented Olivier, who fails to dominate the film with
his emotionally extravagant, yet impressive characterization. *Westward Passage* lost $250,000 for RKO, and Olivier stayed away from
Hollywood for the next seven years. Although he deftly portrayed
the selfish young writer, only Garbo was fascinated by Olivier's portrayal, asking him to play the lead the following year in MGM's *Queen
Christina.* She changed her mind after two weeks of filming, and the
shame-faced Olivier returned home to England.

On March 25, 1932, Harry packed off to Reno to establish the required
six weeks residence for divorce proceedings. He announced his intention to go to New York as he had an offer to resume his stage career.
For reasons of his own, Harry underwent a fitness campaign at May-
berry Dude Ranch in the Sierra Foothills. He coped with his new freedom differently than Ann, and gave a hearty welcome to any publicity
he could get. He took the former quarters of world heavyweight boxer
Jack "I Can Lick Any SOB in the House" Dempsey. Harry also retained
the services of Tillie "Kid" Herman, Dempsey's trainer. Early morning
horseback riding was followed by 8-10 miles of roadwork, running and
shadow-boxing. Newspapers across the country featured Harry and

Tillie trading punches in the ring at Reno Stadium.[43] Harry posed for photographers while he took a break from his rough routine, and milked a cow. Harrison Carroll remarked sarcastically, "All this, of course, is in preparation for his screen and stage comeback."[44] Divorce fans in Reno eagerly waited on the sidelines to witness the biggest divorce-bout since Jack Dempsey parted ways with film star Estelle Taylor in 1931.

Ann flew to Reno on May 6. She was tired, having worked on retakes for *Westward Passage* until three in the morning. A bronzed and athletic-looking Harry greeted her at the airport at noon. He had thoughtfully requested that no close-ups of Ann be taken due to her hectic schedule. As a reward she gave him a kiss on the cheek. They dined privately with Ann's attorney, William Woodburn. Four hours later, she served Harry his summons. Harry's counsel was no less than the lieutenant governor of Nevada, Morley Griswold. The following day, clamoring onlookers jammed the Washoe County courthouse. Taking time out from teaching Bible classes, Judge Thomas "Barney" Moran, ruled that Ann and Harry's hearing would be a "private affair." His Honor, who had granted over 20,000 divorces, relished the idea of marrying a woman to a new husband immediately after granting her a divorce.[45] Alas, Ann had no man waiting. She told her story, as the stout, middle-aged judge tilted his head back and peered at her under his glasses. She charged "cruelty" (a foregone conclusion). It took fifteen minutes in the Moran divorce mill to grind two Bannisters into a Harding and one Bannister. Ann retained their home, and received custody of Jane. Dressed in black and a silver fox fur, Ann emerged from the courthouse with a tear-stained face. She was arm and arm with Harry. After lieutenant governor Griswold escorted Ann to the car, the ex-couple drove to the Heidelberg, a resort noted for its beer, and had what they called a "reverse honeymoon breakfast."[46] It was, Reno agreed, the friendliest divorce the town had ever seen.

Harry drove Ann back to the airport. Her pilot, Fred Kelly, pointed the plane homeward for a three-hour flight through heavy storm clouds. When Ann stepped down from her sea-green Bellanca plane in Los Angeles, she offered no smile to onlookers, simply stating, "Mr. Bannister and I are parting the best of friends."[47] Despite her troubles with Harry, *someone* seemed to be looking out for her. At the end of May, in the presence of 6,000 people at Shrine Auditorium, Ann was designated "Colonel Harding of the Rainbow" by the U.S. Army. In the spirit of her late father, she held her chin high as an honorary Colonel's eagle was pinned on her shoulder.

Harry, piloting his Travelair plane from Reno, arrived in Hollywood and checked into the Beverly-Wilshire Hotel. Contrary to previous announcements, he *now* stated he had no intention of returning to the stage. "I will confine my work to motion pictures," said Harry. "Several offers have been made to me. As yet I have not made a decision on any of them."[48] He planned to set up bachelor quarters at Malibu Beach. In the aftermath of what the press heralded as Ann and Harry's "24-hour love divorce," the judicial machinery in Reno was deemed too liberal and lacking "dignity." Within weeks, new regulations went into effect.[49] The Bannister "love-divorce" became an easy target. The comedy team Wheeler and Woolsey had already spoofed the Nevada divorce mill in *Peach-O-Reno*, where court proceedings were broadcast from radio W-G-I-N, "The Breath of Reno." Bert Wheeler, in drag, played Mrs. Hangover, a professional divorce co-respondent who was "afraid of getting sober." While Ann and Harry made headlines, Robert Woolsey called a press conference crying that he and Bert, too, had to "divorce." Wheeler was "losing his identity" working in tandem.[50]

By July, contrary to what he had previously stated, Harry bade farewell to Hollywood and his "film offers." On July 13, he took off in his sport bi-plane for New York. Ann and Jane were at the airport to bid him goodbye. Also on hand was 18-year-old Nanci Lyon, a "film actress," to whom the 43-year-old Harry was reportedly betrothed. Ann offered the couple her congratulations. Harry was noncommittal about Miss Lyon, and claimed that he was headed for London to fulfill a stage engagement. Miss Lyon, a petite and slender chorus girl from Eddie Cantor's *The Kid from Spain*, told the press, "I am very fond of Harry Bannister. My father, State Senator Charles W. Lyon, and my family completely approve of Harry."[51] As it turned out, Nanci was the little blonde who sat next to Bannister the previous year at Reno's July 4 Max Baer-Paulino Uzkudun fight. Ann was filming *Devotion* at the time, and had turned on the radio to hear an announcer at Reno's Race Track Arena, say that "Ann Harding" had accompanied Harry to the fight.[52] Harry fluffed off the incident telling Ann that there were a lot of blondes attending the event. What he didn't tell her was that Miss Lyon had flown to Reno *with* him![53] Louella Parsons noted that Harry and Nanci had been seen lunching together "again and again."[54]

During Bannister's stay in England, Miss Lyon and her family occupied his Malibu beach house. Although she posed no threat to eclipse Bannister's name, he soon found out there was no escaping his new moniker, "The *Ex*-Mr. Ann Harding." While in England, Bannister denied his engagement to Lyon. He had the temerity to imply that Ann's career was in decline as a result of his departure. As if coming to her rescue, he suggested they may remarry.[55] If anything, it would be Ann coming to rescue Harry from himself. He had a collection agency at his heels, as well as three lawsuits for nonpayment of shrubbery (Beverly Hills), building materials (Michigan), and clothing (New York).[56] To top things off, there never *was* a London stage engagement for Bannister.

After weeks of being "unavailable," the consensus among the press was that Ann Harding needed to change her Garbo-like attitude. Oddly enough, Ann had recently aligned herself with Garbo's manager, Harry Edington. Edington was responsible for Garbo's policy of silence, inaccessibility and seclusion, which coincided with Garbo's own distaste for publicity. Edington called his approach, "inverse publicity."[57] Ann made a point of saying that her aloofness was her *own* idea. "After the divorce," said Ann, "I decided the only thing to do was not to talk about anything."[58] She excused herself from being a public figure, somewhat bitterly. "I am a human being," Ann pointed out, "yet I am not permitted to go places and enjoy myself as other humans do. As a star of motion pictures, I have been mobbed by curious people on the streets. I am afraid now to walk alone on a busy street—the thought makes me shudder. As a result of this peculiar adoration of film stars by the public, I have become more or less a recluse in my home. I sit there at night and think of the many sights and sounds I am missing. I want to be part of the throng, yet circumstance prevents me doing so."[59]

By mid-summer, Ann got rid of her "shudders" long enough to have some fun fooling the public. In July, she wore a bobbed black wig and affected a thick southern drawl while attending the premier of Norma Shearer's *Strange Interlude*. Ann was introduced as Sally Archer of Roanoke, Virginia, to dozens of her friends. Her escort was actor Alexander Kirkland, who played Shearer's on-screen husband. (Bannister had played the lover in the stage version.) Earlier that same evening, Kirkland had taken Ann to the home of director Rouben Mamoulian, who promptly offered "Miss Archer" a screen test. The only friend to pierce through the disguise was Elissa Landi. After Ann gave Landi a knowing wink, Landi kept the discovery to herself.[60] Ann came up with the idea after being detained at a concert, signing autographs in the lobby. She missed the program's first number. Vowing not to let *that* happen again, she bought the wig.

It wasn't long before Ann began to relish her newfound freedom. She took time to relax and go sailing with her good friend Mary Astor (Ann had inherited Mary's seven-room suite at RKO). The now-freelancing Mary had just purchased a new yacht. Ann's "liberation" also included a collection of speeding tickets. When patrol officers pulled her over just south of Santa Maria, she claimed that she was in such "good spirits" that she couldn't help traveling fast.[61] Ann faced a similar charge in Paso Robles for going 65 miles per hour. It wasn't long before she began filing her citations alphabetically by town. After being pulled over in Yerba Linda in September, she jested the only letters left were K, Q, X, and Z.[62] While she dashed around town, writer Ben Maddox referred to Ann as "the personification of today's speed-loving woman."[63] In another incident, Ann was driving her sixteen-cylinder roadster, shooting around and between other cars, and finally pulled over by a "very, very mad copper." "Say, what do you use that head on your shoulders for, anyway?" he demanded. "To make a hundred thousand dollars a year. What do you use yours for?" Ann was reputed to have replied.[64] The National Aeronautic Association was not concerned with Ann's divorcee status or her speeding tickets, but her interest in aeronautics. They invited Ann to speak at the Ambassador Hotel. The highlight of this event was a speech by Amelia Earhart, who had recently completed her transatlantic solo flight.[65]

Aside from Alexander Kirkland, Ann certainly wasn't hurting for escorts. Bramwell Fletcher, a handsome, young blond supporting player in films (*Dracula*), was a frequent beau. The two enjoyed spending time at Lake Arrowhead, and hiking under the pines. In October, Ann surprised everyone when she showed up at Mary Astor's Halloween party looking, as one reporter raved, "too smart for words." While the merrymakers gathered round the big bonfire dressed in outdoor gear, Ann sported a fetching coral tweed suit with a small, saucy hat to match. "Well, I never cared for clothes before in my life," Ann explained to one guest, "but I went to Howard Greer for some garb for a picture [*The Animal Kingdom*], and that got me infatuated with glad rags. I bought every gleeful garment within sight. And then I went home and gathered up all my old clothes and gave them away."[66]

Ann's newfound interest in clothes was undoubtedly nudged by her more serious interest in director Dudley Murphy. Ann and Murphy, a very tall, blond fellow, met in the Spring of 1932 (possibly earlier), just before he made *Sport Parade* at RKO.[67] The 34-year-old Murphy had recently married Josephine "Jo-Jo" Johnson, the 18-year-old daughter of a Fox executive, in Tijuana. This didn't discourage Ann. During that fall, she was seen vacationing around Palm Springs with the avant-garde independent filmmaker. Murphy, one of the first to take black performers seriously, had directed blues singer Bessie Smith in her only film, *St. Louis Blues*, and would direct Paul Robeson in *Em-*

peror Jones. Having studied cinema in Europe, Murphy admittedly had difficulty adjusting to the factory-style moviemaking in Hollywood. Ann was intrigued by Murphy's interest in film as an art, as well as the independent film. Her purchase of the screen rights to Hemingway's *The Sun Also Rises,* and her determination to make the first feature-length Technicolor film, was partially due to Murphy's "visionary" influence. In turn, after motoring around Palm Springs with Ann, Murphy was inspired to purchase a cabin monoplane. His impact on Ann was a lasting one. Bannister would later implicate Murphy in a nasty custody battle in which Ann would face a jail sentence for contempt of court.[68] Yes, life was beginning to look *interesting* again for Ann.

David O. Selznick joined RKO in 1931, as "savior-elect" and head of production. The company was near collapse. Its stock plummeted from a high of 50 to a low of 1 7/8. Fifty films were released. Few made money. The corporation's net loss for 1931 was $5,660,770.[69] Ann quit battling the plummeting studio, but not before putting up one last fight. She conceded that after her outburst regarding *Prestige* she had decided to become "docile" and do whatever RKO wanted.[70] But her next project, director William Wellman's *The Conquerors,* had her playing opposite Richard Dix (as a pioneer in the old west) and Ann could think of nothing less exciting. She summed up the project by saying, "Pine Trees just can't grow from petunia seeds."[71] To get out of it, she offered to tear up her $5,500-per-week contract.[72] "I thought they were paying me more than just a face to photograph and a voice to register," Ann lamented. "But if that's all they will take, that's all I can give them."[73] She no longer held out for veto power over her stories. "Of course [films] must make money," Ann admitted. "But I wanted people to feel that an Ann Harding picture story was something Ann Harding felt. And now that I can't, I feel as if I had let them down."[74] While this was going on, Cecil B. DeMille tried to borrow Ann for the feminine lead in the last of his biblical trilogy, *Sign of the Cross*. The role of the Christian slave girl was eventually assigned to Elissa Landi.[75] By August, Ann grudgingly joined the cast of *The Conquerors* on location in Stockton, along the San Joaquin River, and Sonora. It turned out that she had something in common with co-star Dix, whose own father was disgraced by the idea of having an actor for a son, and refused him the use of the family name (Brimmer). Ann behaved like a lamb under director Wellman. He had been an aviator during the war, and knew how to give orders. [76] Unfortunately, Ann's "Yes sirs!" weren't enough to keep the film's simple storyline from being inflated into epic proportions. In spite of her excellent performance, another Ann Harding film bit the dust at the box office.

The Conquerors echoed 1931's *Cimarron*, which also starred Richard Dix. His bravado as Roger Standish, the pioneer banking tycoon in *The Conquerors*, seems dated, but Ann's more genuine take on the role as his wife (Caroline) holds true, and has backbone. Her most memorable scenes are when she witnesses her son's death in the path of an on-coming train (her unearthly shriek penetrates to the bone), and later in the film, when Standish's banking firm comes near collapse. A depositor enters their home and points a pistol at Standish, who disarms the man and tells Caroline to get the police. She quietly refuses. "I told you to get the police!" he shouts at her. Caroline low-ers her eyelids, looks up, and quietly implores, "And, just cause more misery?" She's the voice of reason. Both men turn to her in disbelief, recognizing the deeper truth of which she speaks. Ann was the catalyst which made the scene work, and it was a testament to her art.

The *Los Angeles Times* praised, "Miss Harding's work is beautiful to watch ... she typifies the role of pioneer wife with an unerring sense of accuracy."[77] *Hollywood Citizen News* reported, "Miss Harding is throughout charming, beautiful and capable. She has not had the opportunity to give so good a performance since *Holiday*." The same review said "Phooey!" to the idea that American bankers would forfeit their own millions for the sake of depositors, and that the film was "far below the standard of *Cimarron*."[78] *Film Daily* thought the film "episodic" in its attempt to cover three generations.[79] Richard Jewell's *The RKO Story* points out "the sluggish ... structure was one problem. Richard Dix's overblown performance another."[80] Dix playing his own grandson during the last reel borders on burlesque. He looks ridiculous. Recurring financial panics in *The Conquerors* underscore the futility of the human ambition for wealth (which, undoubtedly, was *not* writer Howard Estabrook's intention). *The Los Angeles Record* saw this as the film's shortcoming, pointing out the hollowness in "high flown speeches of belief in the future of the country."[81] In *The Conquerors*, America is a place gone mad with greed.

Ann's own take on her performances in *Prestige, Westward Passage,* and *The Conquerors* was less than satisfying. "I was ... greatly disturbed over the quality of my work," Ann commented. "It was vague, indefinite, detached. ... I watched the mask of myself on the screen ... an empty mask that went through meaningless gestures of acting."[82]

The Conquerors (1932) with Richard Dix. (RKO)

Studios often used the ploy of hiring a "lookalike" actor as a threat to keep their top stars in line. MGM hired Rosalind Russell to make Myrna Loy mind her manners. Russell stated that all she got out of the deal was Loy rejects. RKO hired what many considered a human replica of Ann Harding, a young actress named Julie Haydon. After Haydon played Ann's grown daughter in The Conquerors, she waited months for another important role. One morning she bobbed her hair before meeting with an RKO executive. She was greeted by his secretary, who exclaimed, "Why, Miss Haydon, you've had your hair cut and you don't look a bit like Ann Harding anymore. We gave you a contact because you resemble her."[83] Haydon stated it was a real blow to her ego. RKO's ploy probably amused Ann. Fortunately, the next three years would supply her with a number of critically acclaimed roles—roles that she believed in. A new contract that would allow her to make one picture a year independently, or at another studio, gave Ann new zest for motion pictures. Her personal life, however, continued to provide ample fodder for more news headlines.

(Endnotes)

1   Ann Harding, "Happiness After Marriage," *Screenland*, August 1930
2   Harrison Carroll column, *Los Angeles Evening Herald*, 3/23/32
3   Elizabeth Yeaman, "Stage Venture Contemplated by Film Star," *Hollywood Citizen News*, 2/25/32
4   Elizabeth Yeaman column, *Hollywood Citizen News*, 3/21/32
5   Louella Parsons, "Ann Harding Divorce Case," *Los Angeles Examiner*, 5/6/32
6   Louella Parsons column, *Fresno Bee*, 8/13/31
7   Louella Parsons, "Ann Harding Divorce Case," *Los Angeles Examiner*, 5/6/32
8   Richard B. Jewell and Vernon Harbin, *The RKO Story*, Arlington House, c. 1982, pg 43
9   Philip K. Scheuer review of *Suicide Fleet*, *Los Angeles Examiner*, 11/27/31
10   "The 'Ann Hardings' Frank About Divorce," *Kingston Daily Freeman (NY)*, 3/29/32
11   "The Real Reasons for Ann Harding's Divorce!" *Motion Picture*, 6/32
12   Elizabeth Yeaman column, *Hollywood Citizen News*, 2/19/32
13   "The Real Reasons ..."
14   Hubbard Keavy, "Filmdom, Amazed at Ann Harding Divorce," *Florence Morning News (SC)*, 3/30/32
15   Elizabeth Yeaman, *Hollywood Citizen News*, 2/3/32
16   Wellford Beaton, *Hollywood Spectator* story, *Modesto News-Herald* editorial, 4/19/32
17   Harry Lang, "The Story Behind the Harding Headlines," *Movie Mirror*, June 1932
18   Adela Rogers St. Johns, "Has a Movie Mother Any Private Rights?" *Photoplay*, August 1936
19   James R. Quirk, "Close-Ups and Long-Shots," *Photoplay*, May 1932
20   Harrison Carroll column, *Los Angeles Evening Herald Express*, 2/23/32
21   Samantha Barbas, *The First Lady of Hollywood: A Biography of Louella Parsons*, UC Press, c. 2005, pg 143
22   Samantha Barbas, *The First Lady* .... Pg. 143
23   Thomas Reddy, "When Reporters Call, Ann continues to Play Sphinx," 1/1/33
24   Alice L. Tildesley, "The Woman of 1930 – Success or Failure," *Galveston Daily News*, 12/29/29
25   Louella Parsons, "Movie-Go-Round," *Los Angeles Examiner*, 4/3/32
26   "Women Here Refuse Ann Harding's Divorce Reasons," *Kansas City Star*, 3/24/32
27   Helen Louise Walker, "The Studios Know *Your* Secrets by the Favorites You Pick," *Motion Picture*, April 1933
28   Myra Nye column, *Los Angeles Times*, 3/11/31
29   Harry N. Blair, "She Takes It On the Chin," *Picture Play*, April 1935
30   "Star's Child Guarded," *Clearfield Progress (PA)*, 2/20/32
31   Myrtle Gebhart, "Hollywood Protects Itself Against Kidnappers," *Los Angeles Times*, 4/3/32
32   "Letters Warn Miss Harding," *Hollywood Citizen News*, 2/9/32
33   "Screen Gossip," *Hayward Daily Review*, 3/22/32
34   "The Real Reasons ..."
35   Harry Lane, "Hot News," *Movie Mirror*, June 1932
36   Wood Soanes, "Ann Harding Says Stage Alone Gives Stimulation She Requires on Screen," *Oakland Tribune*, 5/15/32
37   Jimmy Starr column, *Los Angeles Evening Herald Express*, 5/5/32
38   Donald Spoto, *Laurence Oliver*, Harper-Collins, N.Y. c1992 pg. 68
39   Anthony Holden, *Laurence Oliver*, Collier, N.Y., c1988
40   Terry Colman, *Olivier*, Henry Holt & Co., N.Y., c2005, pg 50
41   Harrison Carroll review of *Westward Passage*, *Los Angeles Evening Herald Examiner*, 6/13/32
42   Mordaunt Hall review of *Westward Passage*, *New York Times*, 6/4/32
43   "Bannister's 'Idleness' Active – Puts Lot O'Punch in His Reno Loafing," *Los Angeles Times*, 4/22/32
44   Harrison Carroll column, *Los Angeles Evening Herald*, 4/14/32

45   "Over & Under," *Time Magazine*, 5/11/31

46   "Ann Harding Gets Divorce and Flies Here," *Los Angeles Examiner*, 5/8/32

47   "Ann Harding Gets Divorce ..."

48   "Bannister Will Stick to Screen," *Los Angeles Times*, 5/9/32

49   "Reno to Slow Divorce Mills," *Los Angles Times*, 5/30/32

50   Hubbard Keavy, "Screen Life in Hollywood," *Florence Morning News*, 5/29/32

51   "Ann and Daughter Bid Bannister Farewell," *Los Angeles Times*, 7/14/32

52   "No, Folks You're Not Seeing Double," *Los Angeles Times*, 7/31/31

53   "Bannister Denies Pretty Blond His Latest Interest," *Fresno Bee*, 5/14/32

54   Louella Parsons column, *San Antonio Light*, 7/15/32

55   Chester B. Bahn, "Remarriage of Ann and Harry Looms," *Syracuse Herald*, 8/23/32

56   "Bannister's Plane Held on Old Bill," *Los Angeles Times*, 7/19/32

57   Allan Jordan, "The Man Behind Garbo," *Movie Mirror*, June 1932

58   Harrison Carroll column, *Los Angeles Evening Herald Express*, 6/20/32

59   John Scott, "Do Stars Really Shun "Hardships" of Publicity?" *Los Angeles Times*, 12/11/1932

60   Article from *Hollywood Citizen News*, 7/20/32

61   "Ann Harding So Happy She Gets Speed Tickets," *Los Angeles Times*, 6/15/32

62   "New Champion," *Los Angeles Times*, 9/26/32

63   Ben Maddox, "Discovering Hollywood's Real Sophisticate-Ann Harding!" *Screenland*, November 1931

64   "They Done Her Wrong," *Oakland Tribune*, 2/10/35

65   "Public Invited to Hear Amelia," *Los Angeles Times*, 7/6/32

66   Grace Kingsley, "Hobnobbing in Movieland," *Los Angeles Times*, 11/6/32

67   "The Hollywood Roundup," *Hammond Times*, 7/24/35 (During the Harding-Bannister custody case in 1935, attorneys tried questioning Ann on her actions and trips during a two weeks period after her divorce--the implication being that she spent this time with Murphy)

68   Susan B. Delson, *Dudley Murphy, Hollywood Wild Card*, University of Minnesota Press, c. 2006, pg 159

69   Richard B. Jewell, *The RKO Story*, Arlington House, c. 1982, pg 32

70   John Scott, "Do Stars Really shun 'Hardships' of Publicity?" *Los Angeles Times*, 12/11/32

71   Sara Hamilton, "Annie, the *Moom-Picture* Star," *Photoplay*, May 1932

72   "Ann Harding Willing to Tear Up contract of $5,500," *Times Evening Herald*, 6/23/32

73   James Robert Parish, *The RKO Gals*, Rainbow Books, N.J., c. 1974, pg 26

74   Sara Hamilton, "Annie, the *Moom-Picture* Star," *Photoplay*, May 1932

75   Louella Parsons column, *Los Angeles Examiner*, 6/6/32

76   "Ann Subdued," *San Antonio Light*, 7/31/32

77   John Scott, review of *The Conquerors*, *Los Angeles Times*, 11/26/32

78   James Francis Crow, review of *Conquerors*, *Hollywood Citizen News*, 11/8/32

79   Review of *Conquerors*, *Film Daily*, 11/19/32

80   Richard B. Jewell, *The RKO Story*, Arlington House, London, c. 1982, pg 53

81   Review of *The Conquerors*, *Los Angeles Record*, 11/25/32

82   Elza Schallert, "Why I Have Kept Silent for Two Years," c. 1934, Hedgerow Theatre Collection, UC Berkeley, Bancroft Library

83   "Actress Finds She Is Simply 'Threat' Player," *Charleston Gazette*, 4/14/35

The Animal Kingdom (1932) with Leslie Howard. (RKO)

11

Shaw Bites, and Sharks

"For all our big talk, we still belong to the animal kingdom"

—Ann Harding (as Daisy Sage)

On December 29, 1932, lucky New Yorkers were ushered into Radio City Music Hall's opulent "small theatre," the RKO Roxy (seating 3,500). It was the grand opening. The audience gazed toward electric stars twinkling in the ceiling's six-ton chandelier (the world's largest). A crimson-red curtain parted, and censorship czar Will H. Hays walked on stage to declare Radio City's complex the "boldest architectural gesture of all times." By the time the "Roxyettes" finished their machine-age dance donned in glistening metal headgear, the clock had struck 10:30pm. Next in the line-up was the world premier of the Ann Harding-Leslie Howard feature *The Animal Kingdom*. Critics and patrons both agreed the film was well worth the wait. Ann knew she needed another *Holiday*, and it looked as if this was it. She was working again with material based on a Philip Barry play, and in the director's seat was Edward H. Griffith. Critic Maurice Kahn found Griffith's efforts "unusual, fresh, well conceived and equally as well executed." He singled out Ann's performance saying, "Miss Harding is both natural and at ease as the mistress toward whom sympathy properly but ultimately swings."[1] Chester Bahn, for the *Syracuse Herald*, warned that the film's subject matter "may be met with protests." Even so, he felt *The Animal Kingdom's* "spiritual quality" shone above it.[2]

The Animal Kingdom centered on Tom Collier (Howard), a young publisher, who marries Cecilia (Myrna Loy). She persuades him to betray his aesthetic ideals, wanting him to only publish moneymaking "bestsellers." Tom's former lover, Daisy (Harding), expects more of him. While Cecilia triggers Tom's lust, Daisy speaks to his soul. Barry intended the part of Daisy Sage, Ann's role as a young, budding artist, to be an extension of the character she had played in *Holiday*. The film contained the kind of blatant adult themes that Will Hays, in the following months, would suppress. Advertising for the film focused on Daisy's world view: "She did not believe in marriage! Their love was too real, too splendid!" Daisy refers to herself as a "foolish virgin—well, foolish, anyway." She is keenly disappointed when she first learns of Tom's intent to marry Cecilia. He senses this, and rationalizes that his and Daisy's physical relationship had cooled. Daisy agrees, saying, "Well, it's true. That side of it was never so much to us, not in comparison, not after those first crazy months. But I thought that was natural. I was even glad—glad that it was other needs that held us together." Daisy intuits that it is basically sex, not love that Tom wants from Cecilia. "For all our big talk," Daisy tells him, "you know, we still belong to the animal kingdom." Playwright Barry reversed the roles usually assigned to mistress and wife. Writer/critic Mick LaSalle, in *Complicated Women*, his ode to Pre-Code Hollywood, puts it succinctly,

> Daisy and Tom's interaction is exhilarating. When
> he sees her, he becomes buoyant, and they talk about
> painting and books and mutual friends. Yet only
> at the end is he able to see his wife as a mercenary
> stranger and realizes that Daisy, the woman he can
> talk to, the woman with whom he shares interests and
> values, is not just his soul mate but the one he loves.[3]

Leslie Howard created his role in the original Broadway production of *The Animal Kingdom*. Initially, Katharine Hepburn was cast as Daisy. She only lasted two days. Howard was quoted as hating Hepburn's "outrageous posturing," and "insufferable bossiness."[4] He applied pressure to have her removed. Critics praised Ann's take on Daisy. "Miss Harding gives by far the best performance she has turned in since *Holiday*," wrote NEA correspondent Dan Thomas.[5] "Upon Miss Harding," said The *Los Angeles Times*, "the opportunity to return to her earlier, happier forte rests gracefully; she is poignantly real in her devotion to this foolish Tom whom she knows so well, so much better than anyone else."[6] A number of critics put *The Animal Kingdom* on their "10 Best Lists." Film historian Gene Ringgold noted, "*The Animal Kingdom* was one of 32's best and most important films and remains a highlight in the career of everyone associated with it."[7] Myrna Loy also got her lion's share of praise. "When an actress can make you see, believe and understand such an uncompromisingly despicable character," raved *The Los Angeles Record*, "she is a real actress. Miss Loy has done this."[8] Loy had deep admiration for Howard, saying, "Oh, working with Leslie was heaven ... *heaven*. What a strong, brilliant actor, yet how easily he seemed to accomplish it ... That cool, lean exterior belied a passionate nature, which manifested itself on the set. I resisted temptation. ... And don't think he wasn't persuasive."[9] Howard was in hot pursuit of Loy off screen. He wanted to run away with her. Decades later, Loy ran into the deceased Howard's wife, Ruth, in London. "Myrna," she said, "Leslie loved you so much." Loy thought, "Oh, brother, little does she know ...."[10]

When *The Animal Kingdom* came up for rerelease in 1935 and 1937, Will Hays and the Production Code office denied it. The fact that Howard's and Ann's characters had "lived together" for three years was one thing, but Ann uttering the word "virgin" was no longer permissible. Also considered in poor taste was Tom's reference to patronizing a London whorehouse where he had left money on the mantle for services rendered. It is quite obvious to the viewer when Tom is comparing the tempting Cecilia to a manipulative courtesan. He signs a hefty check over to her and places it on the mantle before leaving her for good. At the film's finish, Tom returns to "mistress" Daisy without the benefit of a wedding ceremony, another big no-no. At the Roxy premier, *Time* magazine noted one anecdote that would have given Hays apoplexy had he caught it.[11] Commenting on the cold weather, Tom smoothly suggests, "I think we best bring the brass monkeys in tonight." He was referring to an old colloquialism about brass monkeys freezing their balls off! Hays' training as a Presbyterian deacon had overlooked such "monkey business."

Adela Rogers St. Johns worked long hours with Ann on dialogue issues for *The Animal Kingdom*. She found Ann to be high-strung, and "stubborn as a mule about her own set and established ideas." "But I *knew*," stated St. Johns, "that she was gallant, fair, considerate in argument, and I was intensely grateful for her sweet and gentle humor."[12]

As the liberated artist and mistress in *The Animal Kingdom*. (RKO)

When speaking to the press about her role as Daisy Sage, Ann admitted she learned more about life from the characters she played than through her own personal experiences. For 1933, her assessment was a bold one.

> I spend a greater proportion of my working hours
> being the character in that picture, than I am myself.
> I get to intimately understand another's point of
> view. In *The Animal Kingdom*, as Daisy Sage, I get
> to understand how a good woman can come to live
> with a man out of wedlock. If, I personally happened
> to be a bit intolerant toward a woman who would do
> such a thing, my playing the role of such a woman
> would be bound to change my viewpoint. Having,
> as it were, stepped into the shoes of such a woman I
> learned that circumstances may alter cases—and for
> the time being to think as another thinks.[13]

While in England, Harry justified his visit by purchasing rights to the play *Late One Evening*. He had had no real offer for a London stage role. He was soon back in New York nightclubbing with former vaudeville actress Fay Marbe. His fiancée, Nanci Lyon, would find greener pastures with character actor William Frawley (who would later play Fred Mertz on TV's *I Love Lucy*). *Late One Evening* premiered soon after *Animal Kingdom* was released. According to Walter Winchell, Bannister lost a sizeable bankroll ($40,000) in the misadventure.[14] The play opened January 9, 1933, at Broadway's Plymouth Theatre, and folded after eight performances. News reports stated Bannister "spared nothing in elaborateness" on the "lavishly mounted" production. *The New York Times* felt the play had "nothing vital to give the actors or the audience."[15] *Time* magazine warned playgoers, "There are many plays more suitable to spend your money on."[16] Never one to mince words, Louella Parsons stated the obvious. "Bannister," she huffed, "in spite of his laments of being Mr. Ann Harding, has done nothing to justify his promises to make good."[17]

While Bannister bombed on Broadway, Ann headed back to Hedgerow. Before leaving her routine at RKO, she joked, "I was wondering when I am to have a parole. I've been a model prisoner and, therefore, should have some time off for good behavior."[18] Having sold her apple-green Bellanca monoplane for $25,000, Ann took the train to Philadelphia. Business manager Harry Edington quashed rumors that Ann and Harry were going to remarry, saying, "There is nothing farther from the truth."[19] It was hardly an auspicious moment for Harry to remarry anyone. Arriving at Hedgerow mid-January, Ann wanted rest, the touch of nature, and reassurance from Jasper Deeter. The two co-starred in Shaw's *Misalliance*. Ann also repeated her role in *Inheritors*. She celebrated her return to Hollywood on February 1, by attending a concert of violinist Fritz Kreisler, along with Joan Crawford and a few other friends.

For months it had been announced that Ann would play the daredevil aviatrix in director Dorothy Arzner's *Christopher Strong*. Ann was Arzner's first choice for the role, and the two had conferred on the project. As it turned out, Ann's new rival at RKO, the up-and-coming Katharine Hepburn, played the unconventional "lone eagle" of the air. Canadian writer Joseph Worrell commented to this author, "Hepburn's performance and energy just knocks the film out of kilter for any status quo readings of heterosexual behavior and relationships."[20] He found it difficult to take Hepburn's character (Cynthia) seriously when she shows interest in men (in this case, Colin Clive). With Ann's experience and passion for aviation, her own masculine edge could have come to the fore when playing Cynthia. Her oft-repeated Hedgerow role as Lina, the daredevil acrobat and aviatrix in *Misalliance*, had critics stand up and cheer. Lina was a lightning rod for issues of gender. "The manner in which Miss Harding, garbed in the mannish clothes of an aviatrix, portrayed the man-hater and honor-lover was exceptional," stated one review. "Her deep voice ... aided her in lending the proper atmosphere to her part. [She] was the recipient of much applause."[21] Whether Ann would have offered a more conventional feminine turn to the "unconventional" role of *Christopher Strong* is a good question.

Sinclair Lewis' *Ann Vickers*, bought specifically for Ann, was suddenly handed over to Irene Dunne. Following a flurry of story conferences, Ann and RKO decided on Ethel Barrymore's 1919 Broadway hit, *Declasse*. Upon returning from Hedgerow, Ann began rehearsals with Joel McCrea as her romantic lead and director Edward H. Griffith.

After two days, the studio removed McCrea from the cast. Griffith got weary of the old stumbling blocks associated with Ann's films and also asked to be released. The real problem was the play itself. The idea of a divorced woman being a social outcast had become passé. There were more weeks of story conferences. It was finally decided that Ann would co-star with Kay Francis in Rachel Crothers' *When Ladies Meet*. But, by the time filming began, Kay was out, Myrna Loy was in, and the roles were reversed (Ann would play the wife, not the young author). It was the first of three productions Ann signed on for with MGM. RKO's new production chief, Merian C. Cooper, hoped that MGM's influence would boost Ann's troubled career at the box office. Columnists blamed Ann's temperament for her career problems. But, any belligerence on Ann's part was strictly reserved for story conferences. On the set she was the ultimate in professionalism. Ann's take on her situation was typically philosophical. "I am just standing serenely still," she told reporter Mollie Merrick. "I'm not in rhythm with the universe or in tune with the alphabet, or in step with the spheres. I've just decided it is foolish to get all wrought up over a career."[22] Merrick, glad to get an interview (the first since Ann's divorce), was at a loss for words. She stood and watched, as Ann sped off in her new white roadster with red leather upholstery.

Before starting her new film, Ann took Jane to Smoke Tree Guest Ranch in Palm Springs. Amid 375 acres of pristine desert, Ann relaxed, while Jane, taking a break from kindergarten, explored the grounds while clutching her new grey kitten. Back in Hollywood, Jane made a rare visit to the MGM studio. At 4 ½, she had a tendency to disappear. Crew members discovered her on top of a runway with the electricians. The cast went into a panic. That is, everyone but Ann. She refused to call her daughter down. "Can't that child climb ladders?" she asked. "I did when I was a girl. I'd a lot rather run the chance of her getting a few bruises than of planting fear in her mind."[23] Jane's antics didn't receive half the uproar on the set of *When Ladies Meet* as the visit of the cantankerous George Bernard Shaw. He made Ann Harding cry.

Shaw, the white-whiskered Irish playwright, known for his caustic remarks, visited MGM on March 28. After luncheon, he was escorted by Marion Davies to watch Ann, Myrna, and Robert Montgomery, who were in the middle of doing a comedy scene. After introductions, Shaw walked up to Myrna Loy and questioned the necessity of one of her lines. Loy sensed he was trying to get a rise out of her. "Well, Mr. Shaw," she replied, "that's the line, and that's the way the director wants it. That's the way it goes." He gave her what she considered to be an intimidating smirk. "He apparently did these things deliberately," Loy later recalled, "because after failing to goad me, he tried Ann Harding. Polite and deferential, Ann mentioned that she'd appeared in *Captain Brassbound's Conversion* at the Hedgerow Theatre in Pennsylvania."[24] Ann remarked, "In a few months I'll be playing again your Lady Cecily." Shaw looked perturbed. "And would you mind giving me the name of the manager?" he asked. "I'm sure it must have been a piratical performance." Ann stiffened. Her eyes blazed as she answered back, "Indeed it was not! Hedgerow had permission in writing from your agent."[25] Loy observed, "[Shaw] behaved very badly—berating Ann, threatening legal action, thoroughly demoralizing her—then just walked off the set."[26] Ann bit her lip, and left for her dressing room in tears. Production stopped. Cast and crew looked glum. They liked Ann. The press, however, were delighted by this turn of events. They had a field day. When Ann returned, she told reporters that Shaw's remark was "an uncalled for bit of rudeness to an organization which has sincerely admired him for years." "It cut to the quick," she added.

Many felt Ann should have been more in tune with Shaw's personality, and thought her foolish. He was *known* for rudeness. That same day he had refused to sign an autograph for John Barrymore's young son, telling John he only gave autographs to "old people who had not much longer to live."[27] Barrymore failed to shed a single tear. Coming to Ann's defense was Marie Dressler, who was truly upset about Shaw bringing Ann to tears. "I just wish I had been around when he did that," she barked, "You can tell how old he is by his jokes!"[28] Everyone had groaned when Robert Montgomery enthusiastically suggested he, Ann and Myrna put on white beards before Shaw made his appearance. This might have done the trick, and put the old satyr in his place.

When Ladies Meet (1932) When George Bernard Shaw visited the set, he failed to goad Myrna Loy, but induced Ann to tears as she fled to her dressing room. At far right, Alice Brady brought her giddy humor to the proceedings (on screen). (MGM)

As it turned out, Ann rallied after Shaw's nasty attack. When asked if she would go ahead with plans to appear in his play, she said, "Why not? The misfortune of his having outlived his usefulness in no way affects the value of his earlier and truly brilliant work."[29] Columnist Dallas MacDonnell (future wife of Western sidekick Smiley Burnette) took her hat off to Ann, saying, "We've discovered a new reason for Ann's being our favorite actress. That thrust at G. Bernard Shaw was simply perfect. Ann can say more interesting things in five minutes than the alleged Irish wit can perpetrate during a world tour."[30] With a dash of humor, Jasper Deeter answered reporters' queries with, "We have a special contract for the production of everything George Bernard Shaw ever wrote. But, even if we had no such contract, we would certainly steal his play, so highly do we think of them."[31]

Myrna Loy recalled that the Shaw-Harding confrontation made a lasting impression on her. "That upsetting incident," said Loy, "presented me with my only opportunity to know Ann Harding at all. We'd both done *The Animal Kingdom*, but hadn't worked together. Although, as the title implies, *When Ladies Meet* gave us several scenes together, she remained a very private person, a wonderful actress completely without star temperament, but withdrawn."[32] Loy stated that she, Robert Montgomery and Alice Brady became a "coterie of three," occasionally going to her house or to a restaurant after work. Ann wasn't exactly anti-social, but she ... never joined in. The day the film wrapped, she brought a game on the set—paper, pencils, and instructions for cast and crew to list all 48 states. Ann finished in six minutes, Montgomery in seven, and Myrna in seven-and-a-half. The stars graciously took a backseat to a technician who listed all 48 states and their capitals in eight minutes.[33]

When Ladies Meet offered an unusual twist on the love triangle, as well as a new solution for resolving it. Rachel Crothers' characters were human, and each carried a measure of sympathy. The results were convincing. The story builds to a powerful climax in which Harding (Clare, the wife) and young novelist Loy (Mary, the mistress) meet for the first time. Mary discusses the details in her new novel (which parallel her affair with a married publisher). Clare talks about her husband's philandering. They respect each other's opinions. Mary asks Clare if living with a man out of wedlock is "moral or immoral." Clare senses Mary's struggle with the issue and replies, "If she honestly believes it's right, it's perfectly right, for *her*." She also points out that doing things on the sly costs the girl "her place in the sun." Clare tells Mary that she can't hold a man through her own effort. "He has to have something in *him* that will make him stick," she advises. "Nothing else will pull a man and a woman through the ghastly job of living together." The real jolt comes when they discover they are talking about the same man. It's a riveting scene. Perhaps, due to her own personal battle with Bannister, Ann holds the screen. She gives the film dramatic weight and poignancy, while grounding Mary's airy philosophy. Harding has the stronger, although smaller role, and one can understand why she selected it. Film critic and author Mick LaSalle brought home the essence of *When Ladies Meet*, saying:

> *When Ladies Meet* … remains on the side of the women—both women—while the philandering man is the villain. At the end, Harding loses her love for her husband and leaves him, in large part because she has seen Loy and is horrified at how he has used her. "You're not worth a minute of one anxious hour that either one of us has given you," she tells him. "You'll never cost me another one. Never." When the movie ends, we believe Harding will stick to her guns. [34]

LaSalle points out that after July 1934, when the Production Code went into effect, wives gratefully took back erring husbands. Women who transgressed were punished; ending up in prison or condemned to life-long loneliness. "Such was the Code's version of morality," emphasized LaSalle.[35] Adding levity to the plot of *When Ladies Meet* were Robert Montgomery, as Mary's love-struck boyfriend, and Alice Brady (in her talkie debut) as a gushing scatterbrain. Frank Morgan, although scarcely the type, was excellent as the philandering publisher. *Photoplay* raved, "Ann Harding's quiet, heartbroken denunciation of her husband is a masterpiece, while Myrna Loy never has drawn a character to better advantage."[36] Wood Soanes for the *Oakland Tribune* gave Ann unqualified praise, saying, "It is Miss Harding, to my way of thinking, who is chiefly responsible for blending all of the performances of *When Ladies Meet* into a sincere diverting drama. Her reading of that scene in which the wife relates her domestic problems to her rival, without knowing the girl is a rival, is one of the most affecting episodes the cinema has ever offered."[37]

In the spring of 1933, Bannister made his most surprising (and baffling) career decision to date. He turned his back on the stage, and became a flying war correspondent ... in Shanghai! Jane and Ann bid him farewell at the Burbank Airport on April 11. From San Francisco, he accompanied his plane (boarded on ship) to China. News dispatches from Bannister at the battlefront (China's Great Wall region) were of brief duration, if at all. Within a few weeks Japan and China negotiated an end to the conflict. Bannister negotiated time out for a

round-the-world cruise. Los Angeles socialite Gail Hall Wright was
on the same voyage. When she returned to California, she delighted
lucky listeners with tales of traveling second-class with Harry. After
"roughing it," Harry arrived in New York from Cherbourg on September
16. He recuperated in his luxury penthouse on 52nd Street. Staying
put for awhile, Harry pursued nightclubbing with Mary Garden's
former protégée, soprano Mary McCormic. It wasn't long before
McCormic was trilling that Bannister was her new fiancé. But, first,
she had to divorce the sleek Prince Serge Mdivani of Russia (whom
she had stolen from silent film star Pola Negri). After three years of
marriage, the prima donna had grown tired of supplying her prince
with polo ponies, and he was bitter about being cut off from her bank
account.[38] "I love fiancés," McCormic stated, "and, Harry is such an
adorable one. Gee, I'm nervous! You know, with every divorce I get
more nervous."[39] McCormic told of her and Harry's plan to live on
a farm, in Connecticut, with "cows and potato patches." But, before
McCormic could dig up her first potato, she and Harry had split up.
"We had temperamental difficulties," McCormic explained tearfully.

Ann kept busy playing rounds of golf with Leslie Howard at the
Lakeside Country Club, and lunching with Joel McCrea at the Roosevelt
Hotel. She was readying a book of her poems to be published,
and had finished a biographical fiction yarn about Hollywood.[40] After
filming When Lades Meet, Ann invited Alexander Kirkland to join her
and secretary Maria Lombard for a holiday in Havana. Upon boarding
the plane, Ann was asked if she and Kirkland were eloping. "Oh, my
no!" Ann exclaimed. "Please don't print anything like that." Like rapid
fire, more questions were shot in her direction. "Well, you know Kirkland,
don't you?" a reporter asked. "Know him? Why certainly I do.

But he just decided three hours ago to go on the trip. I am going to Havana on a little vacation to see friends. Marriage is absurd."[41] Louella Parsons dug in her claws to say Kirkland was "much younger" than Ann (both were born in 1902), and the two had been spending a lot of time together in town and at Ann's house "for dinner."[42] However, Parsons knew the *real* scoop on Ann had nothing to do with Kirkland.

The traveling trio met with disaster soon after arriving in Cuba. On May 3, they acquired a small boat with a skipper from the Havana Biltmore Yacht Club. The party sailed off three miles from shore for what was supposed to have been a two-hour pleasure cruise. It turned into a harrowing escape from death. While making a turn, a squall caught the sail and capsized the boat. Ann fell into the shark-infested waters. The skipper, a forty-five-year-old Cuban named Magin Alvarez Piedra, immediately jumped in to save her. It wasn't long before Ann and her shipmates were clinging to the boat's slippery keel while Piedra swam toward shore for help. "We begged him not to go," Ann later claimed. "He insisted. He said he knew the waters well and could make it. He peeled off most of his clothes and started off." To lessen their panic, Ann, Maria (who couldn't swim) and Kirkland tried to joke and sing Cuban songs to pass the time. Then they noticed a dark fin break the water's surface. Then another fin. And another. Kirkland saw Piedra, in the far distance, throw his hands up as he was pulled underwater. "We were frightened to death," reported Ann, "but we had sense enough to realize that the only hope we had was to hang on. To try to swim out in that water meant only one thing. We had seen what happened to Captain [Piedra]."[43] In an attempt to create an S.O.S., Kirkland asked Ann for her pink silk dress. She managed to peel it off. He tied it to an oar and they watched it unfurl in the wind. Ann straddled one end of the boat and Kirkland the other, but the petite Maria, situated between them, could only lie on her stomach and hold on.

As the sun dropped in the western sky, the ominous dark fins, once again, appeared in the water. One was seen circling the boat. Kirkland later confessed he was devising a scheme to hasten the deaths of Ann and Maria. "We were singing songs by that time," he recalled. "We sang all of the songs we had heard in the night club the evening before. Then I started on a song I had heard when I was a little boy in Mexico. *La Paloma*. But I was not thinking about the song. There was an off-shore wind which broke the waves into white-caps and prevented our signals from being seen for any distance. The women were in great pain from the cold. It was perfectly obvious that they could not cling to the hull all night." Upon seeing the fins streaking through the water, Kirkland grabbed the oar tighter. "If one of the brutes attacked either of the girls," he admitted, "I, at the same instant, [would] crack her over the head with all of my strength, and at least she would not know what was happening."[44]

They were in the water for over three hours before their "pink" distress signal was spotted. The sunset was reflecting a bright glare on the water when Englishman J. L. Waggett and George Andrews, third secretary to the United States embassy in Havana, noticed the pink flutter. Thinking it was a cavorting fish, they decided to sail over and investigate. Ann was burned a brighter pink than her dress by the time she was lifted, frigid with cold, into their boat. Maria's shoulders were blistered. Kirkland's legs were scratched and bleeding. As they attempted to locate Piedra's body, Kirkland glanced back at the oar, rocking in the waves, and drew a deep sigh of relief. It struck him odd that the evening before, he and Ann were discussing the fact that neither of them had an active fear of death or injury. "Wasn't it strange," he recalled afterwards, "that we had spent the evening talking about how we felt about danger, and then had a chance to prove it the next day?" After the boat capsized, as soon as their eyes met, he and Ann recalled that conversation. The fatalism of it somehow sustained them.

"An American and an Englishman saved us," said Ann, "and a Cuban died for us. I am sorry about that, and intend to look up his widow. I certainly desire to make provision for her."[45] The following day, Ann sat in her hotel room recovering from shock and sunburn, telling reporters that during her immersion in the shark-infested waters she contemplated her demise. "We hadn't much hope," she admitted. "The fin was going at the swimming man— there was a scream and he was dragged down. I started thinking about my will and didn't see the rescue boat until it was almost on top of us. It was the most frightful experience of my life."[46] To make matters worse, one of Waggett's crewmen leaked it out that Kirkland, and the two women were found "nearly nude." This bit of hot copy had radio wireless operators eagerly sending out news bulletins. U.S. reporters swarmed Havana. As to be expected, they could not resist asking if Ann and Kirkland (both Hedgerow alumni) were engaged. "I've known Ann for ten years," replied the actor, "and the fact she didn't accept me a decade ago shows she has a pretty strong mind as well as a beautiful face and body." Ann agreed that Kirkland had previously proposed. "Formerly, I treated him as a son," Ann stated, "and now I treat him as a brother."[47] Back in Hollywood, Kirkland, who would have a short-lived marriage to stripper Gypsy Rose Lee in the 1940s, made jest of Ann's assessment of their relationship. "I used to think of her as a granddaughter," he told reporters, "but now I look on her as a fourth cousin."[48]

As would be revealed later, the whole purpose of Ann's trip was

for a secret rendezvous with a married screenwriter. The only intimate moment they shared together was the evening following Ann's
disaster. Said writer stayed up with her all night, "rubbing cocoa but-
ter on her severely sunburned back."[49]

Two days after the tragedy, police investigators formally charged
Ann and Kirkland with responsibility for Piedra's death. The Cuban skipper of Waggett's boat asserted that Piedra, who left behind
a widow and seven children, "could not have been such a fool as to
try to swim ashore."[50] Ann was scheduled for arraignment in court.
A judge would decide if there was sufficient evidence to indict her.
While under police surveillance, Ann was forbidden to leave Cuba.[51]
Ann made arrangements for the Piedra family to receive an annuity
for a period of ten years. Her initial gift was reported to have been
$5,000. Ann placed two of Piedra's children in school, paying all their
expenses.[52] Ann's "secret lover" telegraphed his bank in New York.

After her rescue from shark-infested waters, a sun-burned
Ann meets with officials at Havana's Bohemia Club.

The bank drafted a check for $10,000, which was turned over to the Cuban government.[53] Apparently, this is what they were waiting for. A few days later, a Havana judge deemed the death "accidental" and charges were dropped against Ann and her companions.[54] "Inquiry was made," Ann told the Los Angeles press "and we were exonerated and told by members of the American embassy we could leave. There never was any question but [that] his death was an accident."[55]

Ann's nemesis, Louella Parsons, was the only one to tell the inside dope about Ann and her mystery lover. "Ann is very, very interested in a certain writer," Parsons blabbed a week after Ann returned. "He happened, maybe by accident, maybe by design, to be in Havana just when she and her gay little airplane party reached there. Possibly her desire to be with Mr. Writer is because he is known as a very clever young fellow with a great flow of language and a sense of humor."[56] "Mr. Writer," who actually arrived the day *after* the accident, stayed on in Havana for a few days to make sure things remained square between Ann and the Cuban government. Before long, Maria Lombard and Ann parted ways.

Filming on *Double Harness*, several days behind schedule, began immediately upon Ann's return from pleasure trip hell. "This is the first time I ever kept the curtain," Ann stated. "I am sure the studio understands."[57] William Powell, a year prior to his triumphant *Thin Man*, joined Ann to challenge the American concept of morals and marriage. He liked the script and had great respect for Ann's abilities as an actress. John Cromwell, who produced and directed Ann in Broadway's *Tarnish*, turned the 69-minute feature into top-notch adult fare.

In *Double Harness,* Ann's saucy, yet level-headed character (Joan) targets wealthy San Franciscan playboy John Fletcher (Powell). He finds her "coolly virginal, yet exquisitely inviting." He brings her gardenias. Joan serves him cocktails. He asks if she can be trusted. "Can you?" she replies. "In drinking, yes," he answers. She is not surprised when he invites her to his apartment. She welcomes the opportunity. As they embrace in a passionate kiss, Joan feels her corsage being crushed. "My flowers!" she gasps (a clever allusion to her being "deflowered"). After two months of sexual rendezvous, Joan tricks John into marriage by contriving to have her dignified father find them in a compromising situation. As the Production Code was yet to be fully enforced, Joan's generous offering of pre-marital favors was acceptable. After its initial release, the complete version of *Double Harness* was kept out of circulation for over 70 years.

After John and Joan are married, things backfire. John learns of her pretense. Joan, however, has fallen deeply in love and is not at all pleased. "It makes me so mad I could hiss!" she confides to a friend. Joan had taught her selfish little sister (Lucile Browne) that marriage was a business. "At least it's a woman's business," she told her. "And love is an emotion. A man doesn't let emotion interfere with his business, and if more women would learn not to let emotion interfere with theirs, fewer of them would end up in divorce court." By the film's finish Joan makes it her "business" to win John's love honestly. Cromwell's direction is sleek, and offers a smooth mix of comedy and drama. Lucile Browne was impressed with Ann. Browne had felt that to really succeed, an actress must express genius and temperament. Ann changed all that for her. "Ann was a regular person," Browne stated. "She was always on time, always ready for her scenes, always

Double Harness (1933), Ann tricks William Powell into
marriage. Lucile Browne played her sister. (RKO)

pleasant and even-tempered. I'm going to be like Ann!"[58] Left on
the *Double Harness* cutting room floor was Jean Malin, America's fore-
most gay entertainer during the 1930s "pansy craze." His portrayal
of a heavily-rouged dress designer, who tingles upon touching fabric,
was ruled too flamboyant by RKO. He was replaced by Fredric Santly
- at the cost of $1,669.

Los Angeles critic W.E. Oliver found *Double Harness* an "engaging picture with humor, heart and a touch of sourness which gives
it a sense of actual life. ... Ann Harding scores in a role that would

have been vinegar in the hands of a less capable actress."[59]   *Double Harness* was re-assessed sixty years later after it was brought back into circulation and restored.   David Noh, for New York's *Gay City News,* observed, "Ann Harding … possessed a beauty so patrician she made Grace Kelly look like trailer trash.   The way she and William Powell deftly navigate their way through these sexy, martini-and-temptation-laden shoals make this a particularly engaging Pre-Code charmer."[60] San Francisco critic Mick LaSalle thought it well worth seeing.   "It's especially precious," said LaSalle, "because it is one more of a hand-ful of first-rate vehicles for Ann Harding, who was perhaps the best actress of the early 1930s.   Don't believe it?   See her.   Her technique is psychological, extremely modern.   Don't miss her."[61]

In April 1933, Ann announced that she intended to quit pictures and, in her words, "Get an island off somewhere and stay on it."   By June, she was renegotiating her two-year contract for $6,000 a week (matching Norma Shearer at MGM).   Ann and George Arliss were still the only two stars who refused to sign the studio system's moral-ity clause.   Technically, Ann could do as she pleased.   And, she did.   By employing discretion, her affair with the married screenwriter did not jeopardize her status at RKO.   Ann's agent, Harry Edington, also felt it was time to lift the ban on Ann's no-interview policy.   During a time that was distinctly delicate for her, Edington felt it was a case of "the least said the soonest mended."[62]   Fans had moved on to dampening their pillows over other star break-ups like Joan Crawford and Doug-las Fairbanks Jr.   Ann and Harry were old news.

Ann may have put aside her ambition to return to the stage, but she actively participated in "little theatre."   The Pasadena Community Play-house feted her as guest of honor at a fundraising tea in acknowledgement of her efforts to "further the Little Theatre Movement."[63] In July 1933, she coached her friend Carmel Myers in the production *Lion in Her Lap* at the Pasadena Playhouse. Myers benefited from Ann's influence. The *Los Angeles Times* noted that Myers "revealed the charm of subtlety and a delicately elusive quality."[64] Ann was considering playing a role in *The Road to Rome* for the Pasadena group, but RKO said "no."

The film industry trend of placing women in jobs that were considered strictly men's turf continued with Ann's assignment to play a surgeon. The story, titled *Beautiful,* was to pair Ann once again with Joel McCrea, but before filming began in mid-August, Robert Young took the assignment. *Beautiful* became *The Right to Romance.* In the film, Dr. Peggy Simmons, plastic surgeon, is exhausted from overwork, and depressed. It's no wonder. We witness one of Dr. Peggy's middle-aged patients entering the hospital as if it were a salon. Instead of surgical instruments we see applications of rouge, lipstick, paint and powder. So much for all those years of medical school. "Another old tire patched up for a few thousand miles," observes Dr. Peggy's assistant. Fortunately, Ann the actress turns the ridiculous into the sublime in the scene that follows. Dr. Peggy's tender, reassuring moment with the fiancé (Bramwell Fletcher) of a young crash victim brings the story back to reality. Dr. Peggy's surgical skills save the girl's face and self-esteem.

Ann's character struggles with the realization that she has taken no time out from her professional endeavors, for her true self. "Peggy" has moved aside to make way for "Dr. Simmons." She feels she is missing out on something. Could it be love? Exchanging anesthetic for per-

(Above) *The Right to Romance* (1933). Medical researcher
Nils Asther vies for Ann's affections. (RKO)
(Below) Robert Young was Ann's romantic lead in *The Right to Romance*.
Twelve years later, she played his future mother-in-law. (RKO)

fume, Dr. Peggy decides to take a leave of absence in "Havan – no, it's going to be California," she announces (too many sharks in Havana). While traveling incognito along the Pacific coast, Peggy runs into Bobby (Robert Young), and eventually accepts his proposal for what turns out to be a dismal marriage. A climactic plane crash, in which aviator Bobby (no doubt fueled with alcohol) is found in the arms of his former girlfriend, brings resolve. Peggy comes to the realization that she is a grown-up, but her husband is still a boy. Not to worry. Peggy's longtime admirer, a medical researcher (Nils Asther), has been waiting patiently for her. The film was similar in tone to *Double Harness*, but asks for an even greater stretch of the imagination. Still, Ann makes it work. As *The New York Times* stated, "The actual story is scarcely worthy of its talented star. Nevertheless, there is no little fascination aroused by Miss Harding's restrained portrayal."[65] The *Los Angeles Times* concurred. "Miss Harding," stated the review, "plays desperate ladies well. Her charm, her understanding, lend grace to the romantic portions of the film, and one is not disposed to question her proficiency with the scalpel."[66] *Photoplay* rallied to say, "Harding is in top form." But, to some, *The Right to Romance* was seen as a setback for Ann. New York critic Norbert Lusk felt the film impeded "the progress to the position on the screen to which [Harding's] ability entitles her."[67]

Although the "great" roles weren't falling into her lap, Harding's screen presence was a rich and satisfyingly human one. Casting director Max Arnow offered Ann a consolation prize during the release of *The Right to Romance*, placing her among the "10 Brainiest" women in pictures. "They know what they want, they know how to get what they want, and they know what to do with what they wanted when they get it!" Arnow concluded.[68] Joining Ann in the top three were Kay Francis and Helen Hayes. In spite of Arnow's appraisal, Ann's brains and intelligence were not focused on reaching any heights of superstardom. She lost herself in whatever role she was given and respected actors that did the same. "I wonder how often an actor gives so excellent a performance that its excellence is lost in the reality of the illusion he creates," Ann stated. "I'm thinking of Spencer Tracy in *The Power and Glory*. A marvelous performance he gave, so true that I'll wager many people thought they had seen Tom Garner and forgot that Tom Garner was the actor Spencer Tracy."[69] For Ann, it was "the play's the thing." She refused to have her roles "built up." "Many stars," said Ann, "demand tailor-made roles, while in my humble opinion, the roles in a screen play should be proportioned to the situations in the story. A forced situation for the purpose of bolstering up the starring part is bound to weaken the drama. For the same reason that no chain is stronger than its weakest link, no screen play is stronger than its weakest role."[70] Although Leslie Howard requested Ann for the role of the vulgar waitress/hooker, Mildred, in *Of Human Bondage*, Ann and RKO nixed the idea. Howard had signed on under the condition he could do a film with Harding.[71] Katharine Hepburn and Irene Dunne also backed away from the offer, afraid that Mildred would ruin their images.[72] The role that redefined the career of Bette Davis could have easily done the same for Ann. Still, the year of 1934 would bring Ann screen triumphs and solidify her legacy as the screen's "Gallant Lady."

(Endnotes)

1   Maurice Kahn, review of *The Animal Kingdom*, *Syracuse Herald*, 12/25/32
2   Chester B. Bahn, review of *The Animal Kingdom*, *Syracuse Herald*, 1/1/33
3   Mick LaSalle, *Complicated Women*, St. Martin's Press, N.Y. c. 2000, pg 169
4   Anne Edwards, *Katharine Hepburn: A Remarkable Woman*, MacMillan, c. 1985, pg 74
5   Dan Thomas, review for *The Animal Kingdom*, *Los Angeles Record*, 12/3/32
6   Philip K. Scheuer, review for *The Animal Kingdom*, *Los Angeles Times*, 1/2/33
7   Gene Ringgold, "Ann Harding," *Films in Review*, March 1972
8   Relman Morin, review of *The Animal Kingdom*, *Los Angeles Record*, 1/2/33
9   Myrna Loy, *Being and Becoming*, Alfred K. Knopf, N.Y., c. 1988, pps. 76-77
10 Myrna Loy, *Being and Becoming*, Alfred K. Knopf, N.Y. c. 1988, pg 77
11 Review of *The Animal Kingdom*, *Time Magazine*, 1/9/33
12 Adela Rogers St. Johns, "The Harding-Bannister Fight Over Their Daughter" *Photoplay*, August 1936
13 "Animal Kingdom," *Nevada State Journal*, 3/19/33
14 Walter Winchell, "On Broadway," *Wisconsin State Journal*, 1/23/33
15 Brooks Atkinson, review of *Late One Evening*, *New York Times*, 1/10/33
16 Review of *Late One Evening*, *Time*, 1/23/33
17 Louella Parsons column, *Fresno Bee*, 12/11/32
18 Jack Grant, "Will Ann Harding Remarry Harry Bannister?" *Motion Picture*, April 1933
19 News item, *San Mateo Times*, 1/11/33
20 Email from Joseph Worrell, 7/28/2009
21 Review of *Misalliance*, *Inquirer*, 1/10/25
22 Mollie Merrick, "Hollywood in Person," *Hollywood Citizen News*, 2/11/33
23 Harrison Carroll column, *Monessen Daily Independent*, 4/15/33
24 Myrna Loy, *Being and Becoming*, Alfred K. Knopf, N.Y., c1987, pg 82
25 "Shaw's Sarcastic Word Casts Film Star Into Tears," *Charleston Gazette*, 3/29/33
26 Myrna Loy, *Being and Becoming*, Alfred K. Knopf, N.Y., c1987, pg 82
27 "Shaw Arrives, Jokes, Departs," *Los Angeles Times*, 3/29/33
28 "Miss Dressler, Back, Regrets Missing Show," *Los Angeles Times*, 3/31/33
29 "Ann Harding Pays Shaw Back in Kind," *Los Angeles Times*, 3/30/33
30 Dallas MacDonnell, "Roamin' Around Hollywood," *Hollywood Citizen News*, 4/1/33
31 *New York Times* article, 3/30/33
32 Myrna Loy, *Being and Becoming*, Alfred K. Knopf, N.Y., c1987, pg 82
33 Grace Kingsley, "Hobnobbing in Hollywood," *Los Angeles Times*, 4/28/33
34 Mick LaSalle, *Complicated Women*, St. Martin's Press. N.Y. c.2000, pg 170
35 Mick LaSalle, *Complicated Women*, St. Martin's Press, N.Y., c.2000, pg 171
36 Review of *When Ladies Meet*, *Photoplay*, August 1933
37 Wood Soanes, review of *When Ladies Meet*, *Oakland Tribune*, 7/22/33
38 "New M'Cormic Romance Seen," *Los Angeles Times*, 11/6/33
39 "Mary M'Cormic Divorced," *Los Angeles Times*, 11/15/33
40 Robert Grandon, "Telling on Hollywood," *San Antonio Express*, 5/15/33 (This author was unable to locate these publications. Columnist Cal York write in his May 1933 column for *Photoplay*, that Ann's book was nearly ready for publication. York stated, "They say there's little she doesn't expose about this town that has brought her so much unhappiness.")
41 "Cinema Stars on Air Vacation," *Los Angeles Times*, 4/28/33
42 Louella Parsons column, *Los Angeles Examiner*, 5/3/33
43 "Ann Harding is Saved as Boat Upsets at Sea," *Chester Times*, 5/4/33
44 Llewellyn Miller, "The Man Who Planned to Kill Ann Harding," *Hollywood*, September 1933
45 "Movie Actress Describes Her Sea Immersion," *Charleston Gazette*, 5/4/33

46   "Ann Harding is Saved as Boat Upsets At Sea," *Chester Times*, 5/4/33

47   "No Wedding Bells for This Pair," *Middleboro Daily News*, 5/13/33

48   "Kirkland Denies Marriage," *Times(IN)*, 5/15/33

49   Will Fowler, *The Second Handshake*, Lyle Stuart Inc., N.Y., c1980, pg 41

50   "Miss Harding Aids Hero's Kin," *Los Angeles Times*, 5/6/33

51   "Actress in Death Quiz," *Los Angeles Times*, 5/5/33

52   "Ann Harding to Provide for Lost Sailor's Family of Eight," *Syracuse Herald*, 5/7/33

53   Will Fowler, *The Second Handshake*, Lyle Stuart Inc., N.Y. c1980, pg 41

54   "Ann Harding Sailor Death 'Accidental,'" *San Mateo Times*, 5/8/33

55   "Ann Harding Arrives Home," *Los Angeles Times*, 5/12/33

56   Louella Parsons column, *Los Angeles Examiner*, 5/12/33

57   "Ann Harding Arrives Home," *Los Angeles Times*, 5/12/33

58   Alice Tildesley, "New Stars on the Horizon," *Lincoln Star*, 11/3/33

59   W.E. Oliver review of *Double Harness*, *Los Angeles Evening Herald Express*, 7/22/33

60   David Noh, review of *Double Harness*, *Gay City News*, 2007

61   Mick LaSalle, review of *Double Harness*, *SFGate*, 11/23/2007

62   Alma Whitaker, "Keeping Star a 'Hit' Gives Agent Jitters," *Los Angeles Times*, 7/2/33

63   Article *Los Angeles Times*, 11/16/30

64   Review of *Lion in Her Lap*, *Los Angeles Times*, 7/21/33

65   Mordaunt Hall, review of *The Right to Romance*, *New York Times*, 12/15/33

66   Philip K. Scheuer, review of *The Right to Romance*, *Los Angeles Times*, 11/13/33

67   Norbert Lusk, "Ann Harding Handicapped," *Los Angeles Times*, 12/24/33

68   "Young Casting Director Selects Ten He Thinks Rank as Brainiest in Pictures," *Daily Oklahoman*, 12/25/33

69   Robbin Coons, "Hollywood Sights and Sounds," *Kingston Daily Freeman (NY)*, 1/1/34

70   "Star Frowns on Bolstering of Roles in Films," *Syracuse Herald*, 1/28/34

71   Louella Parsons column, *San Mateo Times*, 1/8/34

72   Louella Parsons column, *Fresno Bee*, 1/17/34

Gallant Lady (1934) Fiancé-stealer Ann charms Otto Kruger. (United Artists)

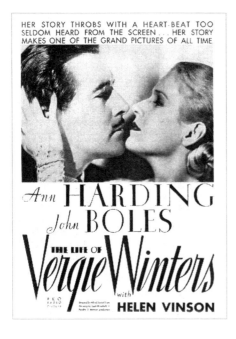

The Life of Vergie Winters
(Courtesy of Joseph Worrell)

12
A Gallant and Rebellious Lady

I'd hate to think I'd go all my life without being married again and having children," Ann remarked in the Spring of 1933.[1] A year later, she got her wish—half of it—a boy and a girl—both illegitimate—both big box-office hits. Ann's legacy as a screen actress began to solidify after being loaned out for a film titled *Gallant Lady*. Considered to be a "woman's picture," or what men in the film trade dismissively (and often unjustly) referred to as a "weeper," *Gallant Lady* represented the kind of role for which Ann would be most remembered. It was filmed at Darryl Zanuck's tiny studio, Twentieth Century Pictures (which was about to merge with Fox). Before its release, *Time* magazine referred to Ann as "the problem child of RKO."[2] Part of the "problem" was being refused other important loan-outs: Universal's undeservedly forgotten *Only Yesterday* and Fox's Oscar-winning *Cavalcade*. Many felt Ann was designed for the role of Jane Marryot (which got a Best Actress nomination nod for Diana Wynyard).[3] When box-office revenues rolled in from *Gallant Lady*, RKO decided they had found a solution for their "problem child." Noting the cash flow from Ann's success, she was offered a second opportunity to have a child out of wedlock in an adaptation of Louis Brom-field's short story *The Life of Vergie Winters*. Women ate these films up. "She crucified her heart at the altar of love!" read the ad for *Gallant Lady*. The real message here was that deception, for women, *especially* unwed mothers, was a necessity. Film archivist Jeanine Basinger, of Wesleyan University, put it this way: "Because of society's restric-tions, women are often forced to live a lie, as polite society would shut them out if they knew the truth."[4] Basinger elaborates,

> I am talking about films that star women like Ruth Chatterton and Helen Twelvetrees and Ann Hard-ing. These noble actresses, patient and burdened by plot, carry on as if it all meant something ... They not only portray heroines, they truly *are* heroines. They elevate unworthy material, and at their best they can actually bring a tear to your eye no matter how ashamed you might be of it.[5]

Because of her success in portraying variations of such roles (sacri-fice being the key ingredient), the word "noble" became synonymous with Ann Harding. The unwed mother story may look ludicrous to-day, but in their time these films had real punch. Contraception for women was illegal. They did not have sexual freedom or equality. Both unwed mother and her child were at risk. And men? They per-petrated the situation. The solutions provided in such films as *Gallant Lady* were usually fantastic. At best, they allowed for compassion and understanding instead of the intolerance and shame fueled by soci-ety and organized religion. *Gallant Lady* is a compelling drama, and certainly worthy of the talents that brought it to the screen. Gilbert Emery, who had rescued Ann's Broadway career by getting her to play in *Tarnish*, wrote *Gallant Lady* specifically for her. He stated that he wished to showcase a talent he had observed and worked with. Zanuck had offered Ann the invitation to choose her own story, and she felt Emery's *Gallant Lady* had potential. "I still have the audacity to think I can spot a good picture story," Ann declared at the time.[6]

Gallant Lady is classic soap opera, but Ann's portrayal of Sally Wyndham trumped the genre. For a startling opener, we see Sally witness her fiancé's death in an airplane mishap. She's not only at a complete loss, she's pregnant. By evening, a dazed Sally ends up on a park bench. A cop, thinking she's a prostitute, scowls, "Hey you! What's the big idea? What makes you think you can get away with hustling' in this park?" To her rescue comes a drunken, disbarred doctor named Dan (Clive Brook), who sees what's going on, and gallantly tells her, "Sorry, I'm late." Dan, the sensitive sort, gets Sally to open up after confessing he had been imprisoned for practicing euthanasia. He wanted to "stop the suffering." Sally divulges she comes from "nice people" who disown unwed mothers-to-be. Before the script has him fade away, Sally's inebriated angel, Dan, sees her through pregnancy, a tearful adoption, and locates a position for her as an interior designer. Predictably, mother and child (Dickie Moore) are reunited a few years later, meeting accidentally in a Paris hotel. Sally, of course, keeps her true identity a secret. It isn't long before she is plotting to win her son's adoptive father (Otto Kruger) away from his pretentious, spiteful young fiancée.

Director Gregory LaCava (*My Man Godfrey*) offered his sensitive touch to *Gallant Lady*, and garnered the film enthusiastic and favorable notices. "*Gallant Lady* looks as if it might be the Ann Harding production that the whole world of picture-goers has been waiting for," raved critic Edwin Schallert. "She looks better on the screen, acts with more

Ann's on-screen benefactor in *Gallant Lady* was euthanasia enthusiast-turned-dipsomaniac, Clive Brook. (United Artists)

of her early positiveness and seems to have renewed the glamour of the personality she flashed in *Holiday* and *East Lynne*. It is curious that she should have had to leave her home studio to accomplish all this."[7] Los Angeles critic Eleanor Barnes zeroed in on Ann's performance, saying, "There is about Ann Harding a certain rare loveliness that the screen emphasizes, which will make a somewhat improbable character seem real when she portrays it. The beauty does not depend upon facial formation nor on her resonant voice, but upon an understanding quality in her eyes."[8] Even Louella Parsons was cooing, "Ann Harding is so charming and so delightfully natural … that she deserves all our choicest superlatives." Parsons commented that Clive Brook's "corking" performance was a refreshing change of pace for the actor. Brook, who was tired of playing husbands on screen, stated, "I suppose I am a little tired of lovemaking. My role in *Gallant Lady* is different, a character part, sumptuously honest to the point where I declare I'm going to get drunk if I want to. I don't get the girl and I'm glad of it."[9] In New York, where *Gallant Lady* broke house records, critic Chester Bahn felt the film lay solidly outside the mother-love, "weeper" category.

> Miss Harding will not make you cry, nor occasion
> you to scoff at sentiment. She plays a glittering role,
> splendidly conceived, nicely modulated, but there
> is no more genuine mother love in it than there was
> in the Dickens orphanage. So spare your handker-
> chiefs, they will not be needed. This must not be
> construed, however, as damning criticism. Miss
> Harding is a clever actress: she sustains throughout
> a fascinating characterization, and makes her Sally a
> highly absorbing person.[10]

Filming *Gallant Lady* had a moment of levity when Ann brought 5-year-old Jane with her taffy-colored curls to the set. For little Dickie Moore, whom Louella Parsons insisted was "the most natural youngster in pictures," it was a case of love at first sight. All Jane did was look at him with adoring eyes, and offer a shy sweet smile. Dickie tumbled—hard. Most all reviews of the film mentioned Moore's contribution. "Dickie Moore, angel child of the screen," stated Los Angeles' *Illustrated Daily News,* "doesn't allow Miss Harding … or any other star to overshadow him."[11]

In spite of the film's success, there was an underlying conspiracy among a select group of New York critics to tailspin Ann's career. Richard Watts, Jr., was among them. He turned the maturity Ann brought to her performances into a negative. Watts called her "spinsterish" in *Double Harness,* and "too determinedly noble for comfort." In *The Right to Romance,* he grumbled about Ann's "smug style," calling her the "most ardently noble of screen heroines."[12] *Time* magazine echoed this sentiment, mentioning Ann's "self-consciously noble character"—a description which was beginning to haunt her. Veteran stage actress Janet Beecher, who played Ann's employer in *Gallant Lady,* was surprised by the press' cool reception when she went out of her way to say how generous and cooperative Ann had been to her. "None of them would print a word of it," reported writer Radie Harris. "Seems as the Fourth Estate (your scribe excepted) have a 'mad' on Miss Harding for refusing to grant interviews."[13] The critics' "we'll-fix-her" attitude contributed greatly to Ann's eventual fall-out in Hollywood.

April 1934. Reporter Dick Mook got his usual warm welcome during his monthly visit to the RKO lot. However, Ann made her "unavailability" obvious, offering Mook nary a nod. Mook watched her and Dorothy Sebastian film a scene on the set of *The Life of Vergie Winters'* millinery shop. When the action stopped, Ann remained aloof. "Miss Harding," wrote Mook, "who likes neither writers nor visitors, is lovely in a little green frock trimmed with dark blue. She has a chair off to one side and there she sits, between shots, knitting—and—knitting—and knitting."[14] Knitting was a popular sport for actresses who preferred concentrating on their work. Warners' star Kay Francis, a good friend of Mook's, wielded needles between takes, but also felt reporters on the set were a nuisance. "What if I went charging into the newspaper office of a columnist when he was trying to make a deadline, proof-reading his copy, or trying to think up an idea?" blasted Francis. "Do you know what would happen? I do. I'd be thrown out on my ear!"[15] She had a point.

Upon its release, Archbishop John T. McNicholas of the Catholic Church and censor king Will Hays waged war on *The Life of Vergie Winters.*[16] Listed among the Catholic Church's films to be boycotted, the film was banned in Chicago and the state of Ohio. Moralists claimed the film justified adultery. After all, it condoned a love that lasted 22 years without the benefit of clergy. Some theatre owners blasted the film's content. A.H. Edwards, who managed an Orpheum Theatre in Pennsylvania, wrote to the *Motion Picture Herald* saying, "One of the rankest, rawest, most salacious, risqué ... pictures that was ever shown in my theatre. I agree with the many worthy organizations who placed this picture on the condemned list ... [the film] will not bring to the theatre that class of decent people which is necessary for success in any small town."[17] *The Lowell Sun*, in Massachusetts, insisted that children were confused as to who the real wife was in *Vergie Winters*. One child was reported to cry out, "But that's not his wife Mama, the other one is his wife." "And that's a sample of the 'wholesome' pictures which are offered to young minds to-

day," huffed the editorial.[18] A filmgoer in Washington, D.C., had a rebuttal. "This is the only country I know of," wrote in J.S. Hook to *Photoplay*, "that believes in bringing the nation's mentality down to the level of a child's."[19] The film barely escaped the film industry's new Production Code Administration (PCA), being released a week prior to its enforcement. Fearing more boycotts, Hollywood moguls felt they had no

Condemned by the Catholic Church, *The Life of Vergie* Winters (1934) contained one of Ann's classic screen portrayals. (RKO)

choice. They *had* to listen. In their minds, box-office revenues came before "art." For the next thirty years it appeared that the Vatican governed what came out of Hollywood. Ann's own opinion on the PCA? "Censorship is silly," she argued. "How would newspapers like censorship? The public stays away from offensive films of its own accord."[20]

The foundation for *The Life of Vergie Winters* is more complex than it is convincing. It's the exceptional acting and directing that make it a go. At the film's outset we witness the funeral procession of John Shadwell, a prominent politician played by John Boles. (Boles had a similar role opposite Irene Dunne in the 1932 hit *Back Street*.) We observe the mournful onlookers, and finally, a shot of Vergie herself (Ann), imprisoned for a crime she did not commit. Flashing back twenty years, we see the story unravel. Vergie's father gets a hefty bankroll for lying to her politically ambitious sweetheart, Shadwell. Mr. Winters tells Shadwell that Vergie is pregnant by another man (Lon Chaney, Jr.). This $10,000 lie eventually wrecks three lives. After the despondent Shadwell marries, he learns the real truth. In a matter of months, Vergie gives birth to Shadwell's illegitimate daughter, which he adopts. They determinedly carry on their love affair over the next two decades. Vergie watches from a distance as another woman raises her child. The kind of town gossip only small minds can muster impinges on Vergie's livelihood. Her millinery store is boycotted by respectable ladies. Madam Claire and her "girls," the only truly decent women in town, keep Vergie in business.

The depth of Vergie's sacrifice is poignantly illustrated in a scene where we see her eight-year-old child Joan (Bonita Granville) enter her shop inquiring about a yellow fan in the store window. During this all-too-brief visit, Vergie offers Joan some yellow hair ribbon.

Gladly accepting, she takes off her hat. While Vergie places the ribbon around her daughter's head to measure, she tenderly inhales the scent of her little girl's blonde locks. "Yellow is very becoming to you," she tells her. (Kleenex, rather than popcorn, becomes a necessity for the audience here.) The dam continues to burst as we move ahead seven years. Vergie prepares her grandmother's lace wedding veil for the girl (now played by Betty Furness). Vergie confesses to Shadwell that his love has placed her "outside the hurt the world can give." She neglected to realize that in her "private world" Shadwell's vindictive wife was capable of murdering him.

Chester Bahn's review for the *Syracuse Herald* assured the ladies "the best cry that they have enjoyed this cinematic season. Miss Harding ... as gallant a lady as was ever risen by a U.S. Army officer ... plays well above type in her delineation of Vergie Winters. The [film] is as much a director's picture as it is the stars. [Alfred] Santell has been painstaking not only in the handling of his players, but in the background and atmosphere. Do not permit the whispers that Miss Harding portrays an unwed mother keep you away. If sex were as tastefully handled in all pictures as it is in *The Life of Vergie Winters* Hollywood would not be confronting the forces of decency."[21] *The Los Angeles Examiner* declared, "Only an Ann Harding with that lovely, frank, open face, with fresh timbered voice ... could make her character so beautifully realistic and so readily understood."[22] Critics marveled at Ann's transformation during imprisonment, and were touched by her bewildered display upon being released. During these final moments, Ann offered a raw vulnerability and the haunting image of someone whose world has been completely shattered. Nothing noble, or gallant here.

The *Los Angeles Times* placed *The Life of Vergie Winters* at the very top of the mother-love category. "Reminiscent of *Back Street, Jennie Gerhardt,* and several other pictures in the same mood, it is definitely superior to them all," stated reviewer Norbert Lusk. "The picture is singularly free of an obvious play for tears. Alfred Santell's direction glosses over flaws of narration and gives every character and every incident authenticity and the dignity of reality. In short, *Vergie Winters,* is an extraordinarily persuasive work. Miss Harding gives her best performance since *East Lynne.*"[23] Lusk noted that each performance in the film could be considered the "best one." While Ann's performance stabilized the film, her insistence that every role be a strong link allowed Bromfield's story to rank as something "superior." Los Angeles critic Edwin Schallert concurred with Lusk, saying although the illicit love angle was a worn-out idea, *The Life of Vergie Winters* was "made of finer stuff" than *Back Street.* Ann's subtle and human portrayal gave a face to the unwed mothers of the world.

After "walking" in the shoes of Vergie Winters, Ann could think of no reason to soften the cruelty that befell her character. "Vergie Winters had a complete love," Ann told writer W. E. Oliver. "She gave up everything for the man she loved. There was nothing brutal about having her go to prison. The man she loved was her whole life. When he was killed the world ended. She was left just a shell. Her life had been those 20 years of devotion in the back room of her dressmaker's shop."[24] Oliver felt Ann wasn't simply preoccupied with a good role. He found her remarks "deep and personal." With a touch of fire in her voice, Ann told him, "Some women say, 'But my business! My profession!' Believe me, that doesn't mean a thing. Devotion to a man is the only real thing in life!" Oliver declared Ann to be a paradox—one of the "most independent" women he knew offering a declaration of one-man love. At the time, Ann was coming to grips with the futility of her own "illicit" love relationship.

Ann rebelled when RKO splattered sexy billboards advertising *The Life of Vergie Winters* around Los Angeles. They showed her wearing a low-cut gown, and reclining provocatively in Boles' lap—something that emerged from the publicity department's collective imagination. Ann stormed into executive offices, eyes blazing, and issued an ultimatum, "Unless every one of those billboards is torn down wherever they are, I'm through with the company. Right now!"[25] She got her wish. Overnight the objectionable posters disappeared.

Feeling the fire of her convictions, Ann's rebellious, "independent" nature was aroused in the fall of 1933, along with a group of other major film actors. They risked their careers to organize the Screen Actors Guild (SAG). The heretofore infant organization gained clout and membership after high-profile players like Ann, James Cagney, and Ed-

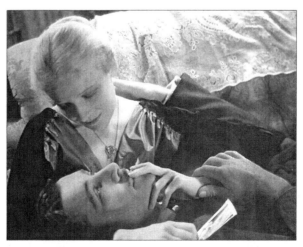

In *The Life of Vergie* Winters, Ann played the
longtime mistress of John Boles. (RKO)

die Cantor joined the ranks. Movie moguls, whose executive salaries were in excess of far larger US corporations, were blaming the *stars* for their financial difficulties. They used this as an excuse for not providing fair working conditions.[26] President Roosevelt ordered an investigation, and it wasn't long before Washington's National Industrial Recovery Act (NIRA) put a ceiling on the salaries of actors, writers, directors … but not studio executives.[27] Their decision became a major concern for SAG, who realized the NIRA ruling (which had actually been written by Hollywood producers) would increase studio control.[28]

Ann announced to SAG members that the plight of screen actors had been brought to the attention of Actors' Equity in New York with "unsatisfactory results." The Academy of Motion Picture Arts and Sciences made an attempt to mediate, but opted to compromise. Eddie Cantor told anyone who would listen that the Academy had "sold the actors down the river." Overnight, hundreds of actors resigned from the Academy, declaring it a "company union." Boris Karloff, known for the flock of shivers he sent down the spine of the nation in *Frankenstein*, recalled the abuse he experienced while filming the role. Working 25 hours straight, in heavy costume and makeup, Karloff was eager to become one of the original SAG members (#9). Along with James Gleason (#7), Karloff was among the original group that founded SAG. Gleason, who had played opposite Ann on stage in *Like a King*, could well have been influential in getting Ann involved with the Guild. She was the first major female star to join the group.[29] Of those originally participating in the SAG "rebellion," only two actors placed in the industry's 15 top-notch salaries. Ann headed the list at $6,000 a week, while James Cagney tallied in at $2,800.

Stars joining in the fight were not concerned with adverse publicity, or patriotic duty. Aside from salary, there were other, equally important concerns. SAG fought unrestricted work hours, demanded time-out for meals and breaks, rebelled against morals clauses, and being told what political affiliations to hold. The Guild's first elected officials were: Eddie Cantor (President), Adolphe Menjou (1st vice-president), Fredric March (2nd vice-president), Ann Harding (3rd vice-president), Groucho Marx (treasurer). At the initial protest meeting held at Hollywood's El Capitan Theater on October 2, 1933, Cantor and Ann were the main speakers. The two caused quite a stir. Afterwards, over 500 actors joined the Guild.

In her speech, Ann declared that "it was time an active organization by Hollywood actors, representative of all players in the local industry, be formed."[30] Eddie Cantor followed up by saying the organization was mainly for the "little fellow." "I don't need a guild," said Cantor, "nor does Ann Harding. ... But to make the organization mean anything, to give it power and worth, it must have the important as well as the less important people in it."[31] The following month, Cantor conferred with President Roosevelt, who listened. FDR suspended NIRA's most objectionable provisions, including salary control. On January 26, 1934, Sol A. Rosenblatt, NRA divisional administrator in charge of motion pictures, visited Ann Harding's home for an official and "secret" investigation. Rosenblatt's meeting with Ann and Guild members focused on the grievances of actor extras, and the enforcement of the studios' oppressive multi-year contract agreements.[32] While in Hollywood, Rosenblatt also warned moviemakers that unless films were "cleaned up," reformers were ready to line up guns "to bang away at the movies."[33] A few days after Rosenblatt's visit, *Variety* linked the appointment of Joseph Breen, as head of censorship and the

PCA, to Rosenblatt's pressure.[34] Breen's brand of Irish-Catholicism would dominate what audiences witnessed on screen for decades.

The budget for SAG was generated from a number of fundraisers. The Guild kicked off their first ball on January 13, 1934, a dinner-dance and vaudeville show. The line-up of the Guild's big-name stars had mushroomed. Master of ceremonies Dick Powell introduced Jeanette MacDonald, the 3 Stooges, and Jimmy Durante. The grand march at the Biltmore's "Sala d'Oro" was led by Ann, after which she and Nils Asther led other dancers to the floor to spin and glide under a bower of flowers. "There's something here that money couldn't buy," summed up one Guild member after watching Bing Crosby, Frank McHugh, and Charles Butterworth, in lavender dresses, imitating the Boswell Sisters.[35] The most extravagant gala was held May 18-20, 1934, a combination circus, rodeo and Mardi Gras. Ann, dressed in a regal white satin empire gown strewn with pearls, was queen of the opening night's festivity attended by 10,000 people. The Los Angeles Times reported that Ann, seated in a horse-drawn carriage, made a "brilliant spectacle" as she toured the circuit of the new Gilmore Stadium. For contrast, President Eddie Cantor, wearing Roman togs and smoking a cigar, caused a panic when the four milk-white horses drawing his chariot attempted to run amok.[36] By the fall of 1934, Ann's rank with SAG moved up a notch to 2nd vice-president, while James Cagney filled her shoes in the 3rd spot. Ann and Robert Montgomery led the grand march at the Guild's Thanksgiving ball held at the Biltmore. Not long after this event Ann began a court battle with Harry. Between filming assignments and fighting for custody of Jane, there wasn't much time for the Guild.

Even with numerous fundraisers, dinner balls, and parades, the

(c. 1934) Ann, second vice-president of Screen Actors Guild, and
Mary Astor are joined by James Cagney, who held a position
just below Ann as SAG's third vice-president.

Guild's real influence took awhile to root. Over the next three years, major studio executives resisted their every move. Producer Irving Thalberg swore he would die before accepting the Screen Actors Guild. He kept his promise. In 1937, the year after his death, SAG threatened to strike on May 10. Studio heads finally accepted defeat and negotiated. For the first time Hollywood actors had a sense of empowerment.[37]

The Depression encouraged many actors to focus on those less fortunate. Black actor and SAG member Clarence Muse, who had worked with Ann in *Prestige*, asked her to contribute her services to his annual "Eastside Christmas Basket" benefit. Ann appeared at the Lincoln Theatre for the December 21, 1932, event, which raised a tidy sum to provide baskets of food for poor black families.[38] Muse was one of the more influential black actors to join SAG, and brought to their attention the dilemma of black actors. He no doubt influenced Ann to join the NAACP in 1934. Ann was also in attendance for the organization's "Anti-Lynch Benefit" in June 1935, aimed at raising $2,500 to sponsor the Costigan-Wagner Anti-Lynching Bill before Congress. Sadly, President Roosevelt refused to speak out in favor of the bill, arguing that white voters in the South would never forgive him, and he might lose the next election.[39] "There are two audiences to confront in America—the black and the white," stated Muse. "The white audience, definitely desires buffoonery, songs, and dances from the black man, while the Negro audience wants to see and hear the real elements of Negro life exemplified."[40]

In lieu of Christmas cards each year, Ann sent money to various relief organizations. In July 1933, she was invited to re-dedicate Pasadena's famous Busch Gardens (of Anheuser-Busch beer fame) where she had filmed scenes for *East Lynne*. (The mansion Fox Studio built was later used as the Wilkes plantation for *Gone With the Wind*.) Due to Prohibition, the Busch estate had been closed for several years. The Gardens' official reopening was attended by 10,000, among them city officials. Ann did the honors, dedicating the grounds for the benefit of the unemployed. She then handed over the key to the Gardens to the President of the Pasadena Civic Relief Organization.

Ann's real priorities rattled the feathered hats attending the annual California Daughters of the American Revolution (DAR) conference in March 1934. The luncheon was sold-out the day it was advertised that Ann Harding was guest speaker. She was a no-show. Once again, she lost their sympathy vote. Columnist Alma Whitaker couldn't believe Ann had turned them down. "It's a poor business to affront the DAR," she scolded.[41] Ann offered no apology.

After many months of planning, Ann was all set to play the pianist in the melodrama *Alien Corn,* a minor Broadway success for Katharine Cornell. When John Boles suddenly dropped out of the film, *Alien Corn* was put on the shelf, permanently. Fresh from directing *Of Human Bondage,* John Cromwell tackled Ann's next project, an adaptation of Charles Morgan's 1932 bestseller, *The Fountain.* Cromwell was deeply committed to bringing Morgan's fine work to the screen, and did so with compelling intensity. The film was subjective, and explored beneath the surface of moods and unexpressed ideas. Censors weren't sure what to make of it, and had difficulty pointing an accusative finger at the sexual tension behind what was essentially a sensational love-triangle.

As pointed out by Los Angeles critic W.E. Oliver, *The Fountain* targeted mature audiences who preferred the more subtle approach of souls in crises. "I have never seen more good performances collected in one picture," said Oliver. "John Cromwell has given the film unhurried direction ... Brooding beauty saturates the film, beauty of the feelings of gentle, civilized folk retaining their decency midst the brutality of war. It will be remembered long for its power and beauty."[42] Oliver praised Cromwell's ability for conveying, on screen, the unusual feeling of thought passing between characters "rather than words." Mordaunt Hall of *The New York Times* felt *The Fountain* offered "much food for thought" and was "by no means a picture to dismiss lightly." "It is beautifully photographed," said Hall, "and has a highly efficient and well-chosen cast. It is an infinitely better vehicle for Miss Harding than several of her previous films."[43] New York's *Syracuse Herald* concurred, "Miss Harding, who can portray poignancy as few Hollywood actresses can, finds a glove-fitting role in Mr. Morgan's Julie."[44] Writer James Robert Parish, in his biographical treatment on Ann, commented that in *The Fountain* "Ann [had] the chance to provide an offshoot to her screen stereotype: the portrait of a sleek and troubled woman who is rather ruthless in pursuing her heart's desire."[45] Indeed, Ann's character is in rebellion of what her life has become. She is straightforward, offering opinions that jar the stuffed-shirt in-laws that surround her. She was never in love with her husband (a marriage her mother arranged), and welcomes the enchantments of passionate, if illicit, love. Ann brings a neurotic edge to an outstanding portrayal. *The Fountain* contains one of Ann Harding's best performances.

Ann takes on the role of a young English woman (Julie) who is married to German officer Rupert von Narwitz (Paul Lukas). She resides on the estate of her stepfather, a baron, in neutral Holland during WWI. Julie finds it difficult to remain neutral when it comes to her feelings for an exiled British flying officer and former acquaintance, Lewis (Brian Aherne). The writer-philosopher, a war

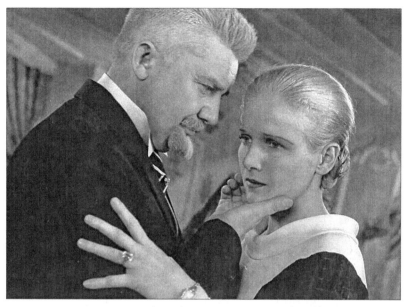

The Fountain (1934) with Jean Hersholt. (RKO)

prisoner, is on parole at the estate. Lewis takes Julie seriously, as an equal, something she deeply appreciates. Julie feels like a prisoner in Holland, herself, and while she respects her husband, she does not love him. Romance enters the scenario the moment Julie discovers Lewis in the library, writing her name repeatedly on a piece of paper. "You'd be any woman's idea of a *perfect* scholar," she smiles softly. He acknowledges her by drawing two hearts connected with an arrow, but regrets he's unable to carve it on a tree. "It's only paper," he says solemnly. "But you're a poet, Lewis," Julie argues. "You should have said to yourself, 'It isn't paper, it's an evergreen.'" "Should I?" he replies, hopefully. In essence, Julie has given him permission to love her. One of the film's most profound scenes takes place in Lewis' cottage. With hands entwined, they acknowledge their need for each other, as well as the obstacles surrounding their love. In their defeat, they discover the beloved "stillness of spirit" Lewis claims to be seeking. "What comfort is there in strength?" Julie's voice throbs. "What peace is there in greatness? What joy is there in courage? Let the strong and the great have their paradise. We don't belong in it." These philosophical interludes fuel their intimacy. *The Fountain* was released the month following the Production Code (July 1934), which no doubt precluded Cromwell from including passionate love-making. Ann wasn't allowed to give Aherne even a peck on the cheek.

The love-triangle in *The Fountain* wasn't seen as "evil" or "sinful." The film was unlike anything Hollywood had attempted. The three leads are transformed by their connectedness. Husband Rupert returns to Holland seriously maimed, only to realize that Julie has fallen for the young Englishman. Rupert's crippling injuries, coupled with Germany's loss, and his recognition of Julie's true affections, encourage him to accept the inevitable and "give up the ghost." After considerable struggle, Lukas does an amazing job of revealing his character's ability to see a "greater truth," humbly let go of his hold on Julie, and life itself. "No one can hurt us but ourselves," he assures Julie, whose torment, he tells her, has been her penance. Rupert admits, "I married you without your love … that was a great wrong." (The only thing that leans toward tedium in these sensitive scenes is the Max Steiner score.) As in the novel, the characters are unable to separate themselves from each other. The friendship between the two men evolves into love and respect. In this way, the main characters lead *each other* into the fertile territory of peace and stillness. They soon realize that it is in having reverence for *all* life that the hidden streams and fountains of enlightenment emerge.

During filming, Los Angeles reporter Edwin Martin was on the set while valiant soldier-husband Rupert comes to grips with the situation between Julie and Lewis. Martin felt the "air of tragedy" was tangible. Director Cromwell sat with chin on his hands, lost, if not in thought, in the present moment. For the scene, Ann's Julie was at the piano pouring her soul into a poignant tune. "There was a stillness about the set that reminded one of a sanctuary," reported Martin, "filled with a dimly religious light, at the altar of which kneels a weary pilgrim [Rupert] asking for aid or understanding or light. The music played on ... there was no other noise save the soft humming of the camera motors ... we watched and awaited. As the scene progressed, Frank Reicher sat with the face of an Indian stoic, Jean Hersholt bit at a long-stemmed pipe, Ralph Forbes leaned over, with his elbows on his knees, and looked into space."[46] Sans dialogue, Lukas was able to communicate Rupert's loss, while accepting "defeat" and understanding.

Ann admitted that *The Fountain* was hardly screen material, but felt it was way out in front as far as helping "the screen to develop its own unique expression." "Maybe we should never have made it," Ann reasoned. "I can give you argument on that, but since we did, we had to do the book and not a Hollywood version of it. Sam Hoffenstein wrote a poet's script and it was shot exactly as written." Ann saw the film's elusive quality as a new contribution to filmmaking. "I expected *The Fountain* would appeal to the higher tastes," she added, "but I had rather a sneaking hope that some of the majority would be interested in it. The letters show maybe I was right after all."[47] The *Los Angeles Times* challenged Ann's assessment on the size of that "majority," saying the cast was "fortunate in having the cadenced lines of the adaptor, Poet Samuel Hoffenstein, to speak. But cadenced lines are not enough. One is required to 'think' *The Fountain*. ... in several stunning individual scenes, one senses the reaching-out ... toward

The Fountain. Director John Cromwell brilliantly guided Brian
Aherne and Ann in this unusual love-triangle. (RKO)

something ... which Morgan tried to express in his novel. In many
respects extraordinary, *The Fountain* will bore those whom it does not
frighten into thinking."[48] Citizens in Greenville, Michigan, weren't
easily frightened. They typified Middle America. "These people
out in the sticks," complained Greenville's theatre owner, "crave excitement!" *The Fountain* failed to draw its rental costs in most mid-
western towns.[49] Box-office tills for the RKO release left a deficit of
$150,000. In cosmopolitan areas like Boston, the film was held over,
and audiences enthusiastic. Director John Cromwell never lost faith
in his film. In 1976, Cromwell's biographer, British writer Kingsley

Canham, praised the film saying, "*The Fountain* is undoubtedly one of Cromwell's most outstanding achievements, and remains one of his favourite films today."[50]

According to the PCA, for a woman, let alone a married woman, to take on a lover demanded hellish consequences. Ann's fate in *The Fountain* managed to escape Joseph Breen's scrutiny and the censor's wrath, but the PCA was tampering with the integrity of many literary classics and plays. Ann's next assignment, *Biography of a Bachelor Girl*, is a case in point. MGM was warned that the numerous love affairs of the female lead were a "dangerous element." As a precaution, the script, by Anita Loos (*Gentlemen Prefer Blondes*), was stripped of the play's crisp and racy edge. After the film's release, the International Federation of Catholic Alumnae was unconvinced of this fact, and voiced their outrage. Less than attentive ears insisted that Ann had uttered the line, "Of course you were always interesting, even fornicationally." Upon review, the line spoken was simply, "You used to be quite a nice boy, even fun occasionally." After *Biography of a Bachelor Girl* opened at Grauman's Chinese Theatre, Philip Scheuer for the *Los Angeles Times* deduced that the film "only pretends to be spicy. Either censor fears or discretion has made its humor guarded."

The premise of *Biography...* is a simple one. Bohemian adventuress-artist Marion Forsythe (Ann) is so notorious, and so impoverished, that while bailiffs denude her studio, a radical editor Richard Kurt (Robert Montgomery) of a popular scandal sheet is able to induce her to "tell all" for $20,000. Hence, the title: *Biography of a Bachelor Girl*. Up-and-coming senator Bunny Nolan (Edward Everett Horton in a typically splendid turn) panics when he gets this news. His career would end in shambles if his scarlet past with Marion was revealed. Bunny trails Marion and Kurt to a mountain retreat (filmed at Lake Arrowhead) to intervene. He needn't have worried. By the film's finish, Marion and Kurt willingly give up publication and give in to love.

As *New York Times* critic Brooks Atkinson said of the play, "*Biography* is not as deep as a well nor as wide as a church door."[51] Atkinson felt playwright S. N. Behrman's ideas remained aimless for over half its length. The same can be said of the film. It isn't until one of the final scenes, where Marion persuades Kurt to soften and open up about his own life, that the viewer begins to care. Unsurprisingly, this dramatic moment (Ann's forte) was also the film's best. In the pivotal role, Ann easily exemplifies playwright Behrman's celebration of tolerance, but there is no presence behind the camera. Griffith's one-dimensional take fails to underscore the spirit behind the play. Behrman's sharp observations and humor regarding prudes, fanatics and political opportunists (a combination that director Frank Capra could easily wrap around his finger), came close to foundering under Griffith's direction. The only successful and truly funny scene takes place in a country store where Marion and Kurt overhear town gossips gasping at the news that Marion had drawn pictures of local boys swimming "without a stitch on." Philip K. Scheuer was blunt in his assessment of the veteran director.

> As with most talkies directed by E.H. Griffith, the
> appeal is almost wholly to the ear; you can putter
> around with your umbrella, your lighter or your
> lipstick as much as you like, and still hear everything.
> There isn't a great deal to see, except some good-
> looking actors; and there is nothing a reviewer can

single out, from start to finish, for special commendation. It's that kind of thing.[52]

Fresh in audiences' minds who had seen the stage play were high-styled performances by Ina Claire (New York) and Alice Brady (Los Angeles). The critics weren't kind to Ann's take on the role. *Time* magazine referred to "Miss Harding's womanly but determined bludgeoning of the role Ina Claire aired on the Manhattan stage."[53] Los Angeles critic Scheuer pointed out, "[Harding] seems scarcely the type … who would be continually forgetting a simple name like 'Kurt.' Claire yes; Brady, yes; but not Harding. Montgomery … hardly suggests the young man of radical leanings."[54] (In scene after scene, Montgomery walks around, arms akimbo, as if attempting to get a grip on his character.) Andre Sennwald of *The New York Times* agreed with the west coast, noting Ann's "difficulty in pretending to be the wise and joyous artist whom Ina Claire interpreted so agreeably on the stage. Unhappily Miss Harding … is not temperamentally of that breed, tending on the contrary to be a coolly intelligent, iron-willed and slightly superior lady who causes the male of the species to shiver with foolish embarrassment under her chill and capable stare."[55] Ouch!

Bay Area critic Wood Soanes appreciated Ann's "finesse and warmth" in *Biography*…, but most felt Ann made a mistake of trying to humanize the part of a vivacious scatterbrain.[56] Ann wasn't exactly the type to play the role of woman who carefully calculated every move in order to stay in the limelight, which was exactly what was expected of her in *Biography* …. In haste, perhaps, Ann had accepted the role only after plans at Warners fell through for her to co-star with Kay Francis and Jean Muir in a biopic of the Bronte sisters.[57]

In spite of its poor reception, the filming of *Biography of a Bachelor Girl* was at least a change from the heavy dramatics of Ann's previous three outings. As usual, sister Edith, who served as Ann's secretary, business manager, and occasional stand-in, was on the set. Over the years Edith had built a portfolio of caricatures of Ann's costars. Robert Montgomery was her latest subject. Montgomery, up to his usual tricks, convinced Ann, this time round, to draw a charcoal moustache on her face, while Griffith kept them waiting for over an hour. Upon his return, a baffled Griffith stared at a mustachioed trio (Ann, Montgomery and Edward Everett Horton). "You see!" said Montgomery glaring back at him. "You've kept us waiting so long we've grown whiskers!" While filming was going on near Lake Arrowhead, Ann dressed herself up in a kid's costume in order to join festivities at the YWCA girls' summer camp near Mt. Baldy. Her niece Dorothy (Edith's daughter, and Ann's namesake) had invited her as a special guest. Ann took part in spelling bees and joined in songs around the campfire.

After production on *Biography...* wrapped up, co-star Horton asked Ann to join him in coaching the Junior Theater Guild's children's production of a comic mystery. She eagerly agreed. Ann had continued her support of the little theatre movement. Between films she frequently ventured to the beautiful seaside resort of Carmel to assist in directing stage plays. She was involved with the staging of three productions in the fall of 1934.[58] Being that Hedgerow was so far away and Ann's work schedule so tight, Carmel's gain was Hedgerow's loss. Ann was unavailable when Hedgerow paid tribute to George Bernard Shaw with a "Shaw Festival Week." They opened with *Candida*, which she had played eleven years previously. Ann told columnist Harrison Carroll at the time, "I shall never be able to repay in full the real debt I owe to the theater, but [and she emphasized this] not the commercial theater. I have been allowed more liberty in the films than on the Broadway stage. It is in the Little Theater that my allegiance lies. It taught me everything I know and I shall always go back to it."[59]

While completing *Biography...*, reporters got wind that Ann was seeing Robert Jackson, former secretary of the Democratic National Committee. Jackson was highly influential in steering the great political machine toward getting FDR nominated. On the rebound from her previous romance (and Cuban nightmare), Ann referred to the Washington, DC, businessman-attorney as "merely a casual acquaintance."[60] Walter Winchell was not convinced. He insisted that Ann was giving everyone the runaround about her new relationship with the 54-year-old wealthy widower. At MGM, Jackson was Ann's frequent luncheon guest. "They were seen together day after day when 'Biography' was being filmed," fumed Winchell. "A casual friend indeed!"[61] Ann insisted Winchell's claim "utterly absurd." Ann explained her "romance" with Jackson as best she could. "It's unfair," Ann told Louella Parsons. "It was embarrassing for poor Robert Jackson, who took me to dinner several times when he was here with Sol Rosenblatt, to read in headlines that he was about to lead me to the

Biography of a Bachelor Girl
(1935). (MGM)

altar."[62]   Aside from conferring with Jackson and Rosenblatt regarding her work with the Screen Actors Guild, it's highly probable that Ann leaned toward Jackson's advice regarding her impending custody battle with ex-husband Bannister.

Ann's status at RKO was in transition. The *Motion Picture Herald* annual poll of "Ten Biggest Money-Making Stars of 1932-33" listed her in 29th place, well above the studio's other divas: Constance Bennett (48th), Irene Dunne (50th), and Katharine Hepburn (58th). Ann outshone Garbo, Dietrich, Colbert, and Kay Francis. Holding at the number one position was the inimitable Marie Dressler.[63] In 1934, Ann held the same position, tying with Garbo. However, Hepburn's new status had soared to 11th place, just below Norma Shearer in the top 10. The writing was on the wall as to who Ann's successor would be. As 1934 turned the corner into 1935, RKO ranked Hepburn as the winner in attracting audiences. She was followed by Fred Astaire. Ann ranked number three, followed by the comedy team of Wheeler and Woolsey. Irene Dunne and Ginger Rogers were fighting for fifth place.[64]

Although Ann had made herself more available to the press, she made the mistake of penning her own article for *Screen Guilds Magazine*. She scoffed at stories that exaggerated her talent as an aviator, acclaimed her ability in fencing, interior decorating, and even chemistry. Ann reasoned, "Fan magazines and actors draw their incomes from the same source. Both would profit by cooperating on a constructive policy for the benefit of the industry as a whole."[65] Columnist Elizabeth Yeaman was outraged by Ann's seeming duplicity, saying that Ann existed on "the other side of the moon." "A resourceful reporter," countered Yeaman, "finding it impossible to extract honey from a pearl, or gold from a block of marble, learns to fabricate something that is acceptable to readers."[66] In December 1934, Bay Area critic Wood Soanes offered what he called an "analytical tear" to Ann's loss of prestige at RKO. He realized that Ann was being shunted aside by Katharine Hepburn. And, it wasn't only the east coast press that had a "mad" on Ann. Soanes' appraisal bears repeating. He believed Ann's downfall began with her "historic proclamation" of intended divorce from Harry, calling it "the most ill-advised piece of literature ever conceived and executed."

> I happened to be in Hollywood the day the story broke. In fact I was talking to [Ann] on the afternoon she had mailed it to the city editors. ... She really felt she had done the right thing. She couldn't understand the antagonism of the reporters whose city editors had tongue-lashed them for not getting the scoop. Even this could have been mended. But Harding had burned her bridges. She was not "at home" to interviewers ... she insisted on doing her work away from prying eyes.
>
> What happened? The gossipers trailed her. Innocent excursions became affairs. The critics lay in wait for her. Fair to middling pictures became twaddle. Whatever she did was distorted—her successes minimized; her failures magnified.[67]

When Soanes was offered another opportunity to interview Ann, he refused, out of professional pride. "I really would have liked to chat with her again," noted Soanes, "because she is a nice girl and she is a good actress, and that's a rare combination." While Soanes was saddened by Ann's struggle at RKO, he felt she was a victim of herself. In spite of her plea in *Screen Guilds Magazine,* Ann had failed on her part of the bargain. She had disregarded the fact that the press depended on scoops provided by the stars themselves. It was their livelihood. Realizing her mistake, Ann held a long, deep breath, wondering what the Fourth Estate would do with her after Harry Bannister revealed he had "sensational evidence' that would ruin her.

(Endnotes)

1   Interview with Harrison Carroll, *Monessen Daily Independent (PA),* 4/15/33
2   Review of *The Right to Romance, Time Magazine,* 12/4/33
3   "Ann Harding May Appear in Film of Lewis Novel," *New York Times,* 2/12/33
4   Jeanine Basinger, *A Woman's View,* Alfred A. Knopf, c. 1993, pg 64
5   Jeanine Basinger, *A Woman's View,* Alfred A. Knopf, c. 1993, pg 393
6   Louis Sobol, "Down Memory Lane wit Ann Harding," New York paper, 1/20/34, Hedgerow Theatre Collection, UC Berkeley, Bancroft Library
7   Edwin Schallert review of *Gallant Lady, Los Angeles Times,* 12/4/33
8   Eleanor Barnes, review of *Gallant Lady, Illustrated Daily News,* 1/27/34
9   Alma Whitaker, "Clive Book to Quit Playing Strong, or Weak, Husbands," *Los Angeles Times,* 1/21/34
10   Chester B. Bahn, review of *Gallant Lady, Syracuse Herald,*
11   Eleanor Barnes review of *Gallant Lady, Illustrated Daily News,* 1/27/34
12   James Robert Parish, *The RKO Gals,* Rainbow Books, c. 1974, pg 29
13   Radie Harris, "Broadway Scoops," *Screen Book,* May 1934
14   S.R. Mook, "Studio News," *Silver Screen,* August 1934
15   Harry Evans, "Okay Francis," *Family Circle,* 8/14/36
16   "Church Demands Movie Cleanup," *Circleville Herald,* 6/25/34
17   A.H. Edwards, "What the Picture Did For Me," *Motion Picture Herald,* 10/6/34
18   Georgiana S. Paquette, "Among Us Girls," *Lowell Sun,* 7/17/34
19   J. S. Hook, letter to *Photoplay,* October, 1934
20   "Film Beauty Selects Hat in Five Minutes," *El Paso Herald Post,* 4/10/35
21   Chester B. Bahn review of *The Life of Vergie Winters, Syracuse Herald,* 6/23/34
22   Muriel Babcock, review of *The Life of Vergie Winters, Los Angeles Examiner,* 7/5/34
23   Norbert Lusk review of *The Life of Vergie Winters, Los Angeles Times,* 6/24/34
24   W.E. Oliver, "Love for One Man Woman's Career, Says Ann Harding," *LA Evening Herald Express,* 7/7/34
25   Jerry Hoffman column, *Los Angeles Examiner,* 7/2/34
26   Tino Balio, *Grand Design: Hollywood as a Modern Business Enterprise, 1930-1939,* Univ. of California Pr., c. 1995, pg 19
27   "Stars Protest NRA Film Code," *Portsmouth Times,* 10/8/33
28   David F. Prindle, *The Politics of Glamour,* University of Wisconsin Pr., c1988, pgs 24-26
29   "Stars Protest NRA Film Code," *Portsmouth Times,* 10/8/33
30   "Actor's Guild to Fight Cut," *Oakland Tribune,* 10/9/33
31   Hubbard Keavy, "Cantor Gives Reasons for Actor's Guild," *Oakland Tribune,* 10/11/33
32   "Code Head Meets With Actor Unit," *Los Angeles Times,* 1/27/34
33   "Hollywood Jittery Over Rosenblatt's Visit," *Los Angeles Times,* 2/4/34

34   Thomas Doherty, *Hollywood's Censor*, Columbia University Pr. (NY), c.2007, pg 62

35   "Hollywood Parades Stars at Ball for Screen Actors," *Charleston Gazette*, 1/15/34

36   "Film Star Frolic Seen by 10,000," *Los Angeles Times*, 5/19/34

37   Ken Orsatti, "The Actor's Road to Empowerment," www.sag.org, 1995

38   Edwin Martin, "Lending a Hand," *Hollywood Citizen News*, 12/15/32

39   www.NAACP.org Costigan-Wagner Bill

40   Clarence Muse, *Screen Guilds' Magazine*, 1934

41   Alma Whitaker, "D.A.R. Sprightly in Piquant Hats," *Los Angeles Times*, 3/18/34

42   W.E. Oliver review of *The Fountain*, *LA Evening Herald Express*, 9/29/34

43   Mordaunt Hall review of *The Fountain*, *New York Times*, 8/31/34

44   Chester B. Bahn review of *The Fountain*, *Syracuse Herald*, 10/19/34

45   James Robert Parish, *The RKO Gals*, Rainbow Books, c. 1974, pg 31

46   Edwin Martin, "Show Goes On," *Hollywood Citizen News*, 7/6/34

47   W.E. Oliver, "Ann Harding to do Colored Versions of Sagas, Fables," *LA Evening Herald Express*, 9/29/34

48   Philip K. Scheuer, review of *The Fountain*, *Los Angeles Times*, 8/12/34

49   "What The Picture Did For Me," *Motion Picture Herald*, 2/2/35

50   Kingsley Canham, "John Cromwell- The Hollywood Professionals, V.5," Tantivy Press (London), c. 1976, pg 72

51   Brooks Atkinson review of the play *Biography*, *New York Times*, 12/13/32

52   Philip K. Scheuer, review of *Biography of a Bachelor Girl*, *Los Angeles Times*, 3/9/35

53   Review of *Biography of a Bachelor Girl*, *Time*, 1/21/35

54   Review of *Biography of a Bachelor Girl*, The *Los Angeles Times*, 3/9/35

55   Andre Sennwald, review of *Biography of a Bachelor Girl*, *New York Times*, 3/2/35

56   Wood Soanes, review of *Biography of a Bachelor Girl*, *Oakland Tribune*, 2/2/35

57   Gene Ringgold, "Ann Harding," *Films in Review*, March 1972, pg 142 (The Bronte sister film *Devotion*, was made in 1943)

58   Read Kendall, "Around and About in Hollywood," *Los Angeles Times*, 10/12/34

59   Harrison Carroll, "Behind the Scenes in Hollywood," *San Mateo Times*, 8/20/34

60   Read Kendall, "Fight Over Child Balks Harding Holiday at Home," *Los Angeles Times*, 12/11/34 (Robert Jackson is not to be confused with Robert H. Jackson, who took over the position of Attorney General from Ann's former beau Frank Murphy).

61   Walter Winchell, "Broadway," *Port Arthur News*, 12/27/34

62   Louella Parsons, "Ann Harding Fears To Dine With Man," *Charleston Gazette*, 4/5/35

63   "Box Office Money-Makers," *Motion Picture Herald*, 1/6/34

64   "Survey Shows Sophisticates Slipping Fast," *Los Angeles Times*, 12/9/34

65   Ann Harding, "Unique and Extraordinary," *Screen Guilds' Magazine*," pg. 3, September 1934

66   Elizabeth Yeaman, "The Other Side of the Moon," pg 8, *Screen Guilds Magazine*, November 1934

67   Wood Soanes, "Curtain Calls," *Oakland Tribune*, 12/13/34

13
Unfit Mother

S he won't get away with it," insisted Harry Bannister, when told that Ann was petitioning for exclusive custody of six-year-old Jane. On Thanksgiving Day, 1934, Ann had taken their daughter to Reno, feeling that divided custody wasn't in Jane's best interest. Appearing tired and worn, Ann told interviewers, "There's very little I can say. I'm not here as an actress; I don't want publicity. I'm just here, as a mother who wants and has to have the right to bring up her child to the best of her judgment and ability."[1] Ann thought it would be a matter of hours before her petition was resolved. Instead, a simple modification of her original divorce decree went on for weeks. Bannister and Ann had conferred earlier in November, but not over custody rights. Ann's lawyer indicated that these "mystery" negotiations "became futile" and had reached a deadlock. Her move for complete custody fueled Bannister's nefarious plan to blackmail her. Although he would later deny it, Ann had received wires and letters from Bannister demanding money ($100,000). He told her that he had certain revelations in his possession that could lead to public scandal. His threats were confirmed by his lawyer, who said that if Bannister was forced to file proceedings, the case could "develop sensational angles."[2]

"I guess Jane and I will have to plan our Christmas here," Ann told reporters who had swarmed the Washoe County Courthouse. "In any event little Jane will have plenty of snow."[3] Sequestered in a cabin thirty miles from Reno, Ann made a vacation out of it and went horseback riding and hiking every day. She felt Nevadans were kind and hospitable— they didn't stare at her, and treated her "like an ordinary person."[4] On January 3, while Jane played in an adjoining law library, climbing up ladders to the book shelves and pushing stick gum through the mail slot, Ann won her battle at a closed hearing. Judge Thomas Moran, who had granted the original divorce, presided. Ann disclosed that Bannister "was not the proper person to have even partial custody."[5] She also alleged that when Jane, accompanied by her governess (who also testified), was on a ten-day visit to Bannister's Malibu beach house, he and his guests behaved in "such a manner as was detrimental to the welfare and well-being of the child."[6] Ann included charges that Bannister threatened to circulate "false and defamatory statements" about her. After Moran's ruling, Ann stated, "Naturally I am very pleased at the court's decision. It was simply, natural justice."[7] For reasons that were unclear, she chose to drive herself and Jane home in a storm that had grounded planes and frightened other motorists into staying put. Averaging 15 miles per hour, she fought snow, sleet and fog for 18 hours before arriving in Los Angeles. Jane withstood the trip with no ill effects, but Ann, her "muscles in knots," was still in bed 48 hours later. This round with Harry had taken its toll.

In truth, Ann's health had been on the decline for months. In October, during retakes on *Biography of a Bachelor Girl*, she had fainted from dehydration caused by the studio's hot Klieg lights. Ann's physician, Dr. Branch, advised her at the time to quit films for the time being and take a trip to Tahiti.[8] Ann declared she was "too tired to pack even a toothbrush to go anywhere."[9] She had completed four major films in seven months, and though her trips to Carmel to direct stage plays were pleasurable, they left no time for relaxation. There was also the constant worry from kidnapping threats. Ann hired a member of Pennsylvania's famous Black Hussars as a personal guard for her and Jane. She also kept a six-shooter in the side pocket of her car, and wasn't shy about showing off her skill with a pistol. She obviously wanted potential kidnappers to know about it. Whitney Hendry, police chief at MGM, was amazed at Ann's ability to score 18 out of a possible 20 hits on the studio's target range.[10]

Upon her return from Reno, Branch's diagnosis of Ann's weakened condition was grim. She finally gave in to his advice.[11] "I am leaving for China, under orders from my physician," Ann told the press, "for a complete rest and change." She booked passage as far as Hong Kong. While making preparations to leave, she spent a day entertaining her niece Dorothy, age 11, and Jane, now 6, taking them shopping and for lunch. When Bannister got wind of Ann's voyage, he panicked. On January 22, he filed a complaint that Ann was not "a fit and proper person to have custody of her daughter."[12] Although he made no specific charges, he was suing to take the child away from her. As he did not want full custody of Jane, he asked the Los Angeles Superior Court to appoint someone else to rear the child. Ann had seen this coming. She fired back at Bannister, saying that he had avoided the recent hearing in Reno. The decision of Judge Moran spoke for itself. Ann referred to the court decree that awarded her sole custody as "a complete refutation of all charges" in Bannister's terse complaint. At long last, Ann and Harry's carefully guarded legend that they had remained "good friends" was shattered.

On the evening of January 25, a motorcycle brigade escorted Ann to the San Francisco Harbor, where she boarded the liner *President Coolidge* for the Far East.[13] She was accompanied by her friend, actress Josephine Whittell (who had played Madam Claire in *Vergie Winters*), and a trained nurse. Ann had intended to take Jane along on the voyage, but decided it was unfair to interrupt her schooling. After arriving in Honolulu, the unexpected happened. Ann stayed put. A certain suave, good-looking, lanky major at Oahu's Fort Schofield had swept Ann off her feet. She had fallen in love. His name was Benjamin Sawbridge. Ann cabled her sister on February 11, saying she felt much improved, and had even learned to operate a surfboard. She would be "up to snuff" in the event she had to return to court.[14] However, when her agent, Harry Edington, cabled back that new contracts were waiting, Ann was unresponsive. She missed the next four boats. She recalled later, "I cabled back: Burn my contract, my house, everything. I'm not coming." Edith answered with a simple message: "Everything in ashes. What now?" "Well," Ann laughed, "I scoured the islands for a topper to that and couldn't find one. So what could I do? I had to come."[15] On March 7, Ann arrived in the Port of Los Angeles at San Pedro, relaxed, tanned, and turning a deaf ear to all requests to comment on her former husband. She resumed work at MGM in *The Flame Within*, with a director she respected, Edmund Goulding. When asked about her rejuvenated spirit, Ann's reply, although it left out her new love interest, spoke volumes.

> That [is] due to the tropical influence of Hawaii,
> and—shall we call it the indifference it seemed to inspire in me toward everything. I felt that I could have returned and Harry Edington, my agent, was cabling and long-distancing, but I ... just wasn't interested.
> I ceased to be Ann Harding and became Dorothy Gatley once again. I went to Fort Schofield, the army

post, near Honolulu, and there Ann Harding, the
motion-picture actress, completely died for the time
being. The officers knew me only as the daughter of
General Gatley, because they had served under him.
There wasn't one word said about pictures. I never
felt for one moment like being on parade ... never
asked for a single autograph—no ballyhoo, no fuss.
... I don't know that it means a thing to the public
for an actress to say that she wants to cease being an
actress every once in a while. It isn't possible in Hollywood. You're on parade. ... The most trivial action
done in public, is thrown on the screen of the world at
large, and magnified, magnified, magnified.

It wasn't that Ann no longer enjoyed the solitude and surroundings
of her own home. "Sometimes I stay there until veritably I could pick
the flowers off the wall," she laughed, "but each and every one of us
must have change. The best recipe of all is actually getting away."[16]
Naturally, she said nothing of Major Sawbridge. Due to renewed
threats from Harry, certain things had to be kept undercover.

Enchanted April was released while Ann was in Hawaii. Although the
film had its quiet charm, it did little to advance her career, or reputation at the box office. The poetic edge of Samuel Hoffenstein, who had
written the screenplay for *The Fountain*, brought a comic touch to this
fantasy about a group of English women who are dissatisfied with their
everyday lives. They connect with each other—and the Mediterranean
castle of their dreams—through a classified ad in a London newspaper.
Ann's character, Lotty, is the catalyst for making their dreams come

true. She is a woman filled with presentiments—she can "see" things happen before they actually become reality. The women soon find their "true selves" while soaking in the atmosphere at San Salvatore near the Italian Riviera. For the sensitive viewer there is something compelling and quite touching in this story. It is witty, human, and doesn't avoid the "ugly" egocentric side of human nature. Ann's Lotty is similar to her character in *Biography...* in that she has great tolerance and sees others in a benevolent light. She rubs off on people. They resist her—consider her absurd, at first. But, they all succumb to her genuine if quirky personality. The film was too small and intimate for audiences in 1935. Americans weren't ready for the simple delights of *Enchanted April* until it was remade in 1992. That version, which had far richer characterizations, garnered three Academy Award nominations. Inspired by Elizabeth von Arnim's bestselling novel, and a play adaptation, the 1935 film, sadly, failed to find an audience. Twelve minutes of *Enchanted April* were deleted after the preview. Double-billed throughout the country, the film was soon forgotten. "Poison to your box office and theatre," a theatre manager in Nebraska reported to the *Motion Picture Herald*.[17] "This picture should be shelved and save Miss Harding what few admirers she has left," reported another manager in Illinois. "It's a shame to ruin a star with such pictures."[18]

Enchanted April (1935) with Frank Morgan. (RKO)

Contrary to the opinions of the nation's theatre managers, *The New York Times* thought *Enchanted April* to be a "gem—handsomely mounted, perfectly directed, and played magnificently by the cast." "*Enchanted April*," said the review, "is at once a wisteria-laden romance and a howling comedy. And it alternates these moods so successfully that the spectator is carried from one to another without being conscious of a bump in transit."[19] The *Los Angeles Examiner* thought Ann did "beautifully by the role," but that the screenplay didn't provide her character sufficient strength. The fact is, none of the characters were allowed sufficient time (66 minutes) to develop and transform. Wood Soanes for the *Oakland Tribune* found Ann's portrayal a major disappointment, saying, "*Enchanted April* is an idyllic romance and Miss Harding, advised of that, promptly went in for her best idyllic manner which took the form of a vacant stare, a sing-song voice, and an otherwise giddy personality. ... Harry Beaumont directed this one ... and need expect no huzzahs for inspired work."[20] *Screen and Radio Weekly* agreed, saying, "*Enchanted April* unquestionably rates as one of Miss Harding's poorest performances. ... For so talented an actress as Miss Harding, such mediocre acting comes as a ... surprise."[21] Although there are moments when she is quite touching, Ann's take on the role leans more toward caricature. When Lotty "sees" that San Salvatore enables people to leave off being ossified and discover the capacity to stretch, Ann's quirkiness diminishes the impact of her keen observation. The less-mannered, natural take on Lotty that Josie Lawrence portrayed in the 1992 remake blossoms on screen.

One curious incident that occurred on the RKO set mirrored the fantasy in the film. While the cameras were rolling for the opening scene, Ann, in front of a make-believe fireplace, suddenly stooped over and thrust her head up the chimney. She reappeared, to the amazement of the cast and crew, holding a dove in her hand. The mystery dove was taken home to Jane for a household pet.

While working on *Enchanted April,* Ann had a major disappointment with RKO. After her plan to film Ernest Hemingway's *The Sun Also Rises* (for which she bought the film rights) was hastened to an early grave by the PCA, Ann placed her bets on Technicolor. *The Sun Also Rises* was originally purchased by RKO in 1932, for a David O. Selznick production starring Leslie Howard as Jake Barnes and Ann as Brett Ashley. (Ann had convinced the studio to use her rather than Constance Bennett.) Unfortunately, Selznick locked horns with censor king Joseph Breen. "It is a story of a nymphomaniac in love with a drunken newspaper man," blasted Breen. "Because of the brazenness with which this lady carries on her sexual indulgences it is my judgment that the [screen] play is quite definitely in violation of the Code."[22] Ann would not give in. She and director Edward H. Griffith tried to get financing for the film. Fox advised them that *The Sun Also Rises* could be released if it toned down the nymphomania of Brett Ashley and the impotence of the hero. Breen once again interfered, demanding a halt to plans for production. Ann had already invested $10,000 in the project, and determinedly bought out Fox's share at another $15,000. She then persuaded Irving Thalberg and MGM to film the Hemingway story. When Breen got wind of this, he had had enough, and lobbied to have the book suppressed on screen forever. Accordingly, the Motion Picture Association made a unanimous resolution that the film "should not be made at all." [23]

Ann put Hemingway on the back burner and put her faith in the possibilities of the new three-strip color film process. She had filmed a color test in the fall of 1933. According to those who witnessed it, the test was a stunning visual experience. "I saw Ann Harding in Technicolor the other day," reported Los Angeles critic Philip K. Scheuer. "She is probably the most perfect of all subjects to date. Under the company's new three-tone process, the tints of the flesh, the light blonde hair, the blue eyes of this actress take on a startling luster."[24] The following year, Ann enthusiastically approached her studio bosses about doing a color feature. "I saw the chance to help this industry take a forward step," Ann said later, "to help save it from the dry rot of pictures made by formula and help to launch it on a glorious new era. I wanted to be one of the pioneers. I went to RKO and offered 'my all'—whatever attraction I may have at the box office, all my enthusiasm, infinite patience with the technical details that might be irksome to the players, and an offer of my services gratis."[25] The studio said they intended to do *The Three Musketeers* as their first color venture. (It was filmed in black and white.) They suggested that Ann could do the second color feature. Her reply wasn't a happy one. "All my vanity, my ego, was badly wounded," Ann confessed. "I said, 'Very well, if that's the way it is—well, that's the way it is. Thanks for your trouble—and I'm out to beat you.'"

In August 1934, Ann called Walter Wanger, a former MGM producer who had become an "independent." Within two days she signed a contract with Wanger to star in *Peacock's Feather*, based on George Hellman's novel. Ann was to play the mistress of Croesus, the world's richest man, whose political enemy is the statesman Aesop of fable fame. With Charles Boyer scheduled to co-star, filming was to begin in December. Ann saw *Peacock's Feather* as the beginning of a new trend, opening a world of fantasy "such as could be done only in colour."[26] "I've always wanted to do myths," she said, "the fables of the Norse, King Arthur and the Greek legends. I always wanted magic to come out of the screen, not merely photography of stage plays. It was time someone did something cock-eyed and beautiful on the screen. I have been laboring five years in this profession and felt it time for me to make a contribution. My bit I hope will be in these colored legends. We've been fussing and fretting for years to get new blood into this rut and now I believe we are on lines which will free the screen to develop its own unique expression."[27]

Ann believed that color would start a new vogue just as *The Jazz Singer* did with sound. As *The Jazz Singer* benefited Jolson, color would reap her considerable prestige and financial harvest.[28] Sadly, Ann and Wanger's plans met a snag when Ann collapsed on the set of *Enchanted April*. Dr. Branch vetoed Ann's plan to appear in an all-color film, saying that if the intense heat of studio lights were doing her injury that a Technicolor film, which requires still greater light, "might prove fatal."[29] The project was postponed. Ann had already made costume and photographic tests for the picture. Movie publicist Harry N. Blair was one of the privileged few who saw these advance color tests for *Peacock's Feather*. "I feel it my duty to prepare her fans for the thrilling surprise which awaits them," raved Blair. "Even Ann, herself, who has never felt that she was any great shakes as a beauty, was moved to remark, incredulously, 'Do I *really* look like that?'"[30] Wanger held off another year before filming his first Technicolor feature, *The Trail of the Lonesome Pine* (1936). For Ann, this disappointment was another reason to let go of Hollywood and move on. She would make but two more films for her studio. On December 11, 1934, filming began on the first feature Technicolor film, *Becky Sharp*, starring Miriam Hopkins. To add insult to injury, the Pioneer production was distributed by none other than RKO. While color did not revolutionize the film industry overnight, Ann's influence in getting the ball rolling has been overlooked. (Wanger's production of *Peacock's Feather* was finally realized in the 1946 Universal release *A Night in Paradise* with Merle Oberon.)

On Ann's return from Honolulu, director Edmund Goulding got her on the radio phone aboard ship. He read to her the script for *The Flame Within*, originally a three-page treatment suggested for Greta Garbo. Garbo wasn't interested, but Ann was intrigued, not so much with the idea of playing a psychiatrist, but with the underlying theme of the piece. Her character surrenders self-interest for fulfillment on a higher level. Goulding's own life struggle was reflected in Harding's role. His biographer, Matthew Kennedy, told this author, "The fact that Eddie was caring for his invalid wife during the production of *The Flame Within*, would suggest it was perhaps the most revealing and personally felt movie of his career."[31] (Mrs. Goulding had died a month prior to filming.) While making *The Flame Within*, Goulding made the decision to keep cameras rolling for longer takes than usual—up to 400 feet, or four minutes of screen time. As a result, his scenes were beautifully sustained by the actors, and had unusual vitality.

On screen we see Ann's calm, clear, professional gaze as Dr. Mary White succumb to romantic attachment for one of her own patients, a young alcoholic named Jack (Louis Hayward). Initially, she was dealing with Jack's suicidal sweetheart Linda (Maureen O'Sullivan), but decided that the real problem was Jack. Mary's skill pays off and

The Flame Within (1935) Ann took over a role intended for Garbo.
Seen here with Henry Stephenson and Herbert Marshall. (MGM)

the young couple marries. Upon returning from their honeymoon, Jack confesses to Mary, the woman who cured him, that he is in love with her. After this rude awakening—a professional wake-up call, Mary realizes she cannot reciprocate her own romantic feelings for Jack, but must die to them. She encourages him to do the same, to be strong—"do the right thing" for his young bride. Such actions, according to Goulding's story, have their own "greater ecstasy." In a climactic moment both Jack and Linda reassure Dr. White that her counsel has succeeded. Jack realizes his own strengths, and Linda finally sees the futility in dramatizing herself. The *Oakland Tribune* noted the film's "feeling of authenticity," and stated, "Miss Harding is well cast, the role lending itself admirably to her constrained style of acting that so often hints at aspirations toward perfectionism."[32]

In *The Flame Within*, Ann's character eschews marriage in order to achieve her potential in the field of psychiatry. Herbert Marshall, her persistent suitor, is someone she can bank on—a steady, loving presence. In the film's final moments, Mary has lost her confidence and self-assurance. Author Mick LaSalle puts his own slant on her dilemma.

> The last minute of [*The Flame Within*] is as chilling as any in American cinema. Harding turns to Marshall and says, "I'm not going on with the work." Marshall asks, "What are you going to do?" And she says, "You tell me." The music soars. They embrace. Their kindly old friend (Henry Stephenson) looks on and beams. Everything about the moment is designed to indicate a happy ending ... except for Harding's performance. Harding plays the moment like she has just had a lobotomy. She plays it as a moment of abject defeat and soul death. Her eyes are vacant. Her mouth is slack. A great actress is doing her best to subvert the moment, but every aspect of the film, from the dialogue to the cutting, is against her. The best she can do is slip out a message, like a captive in a totalitarian land. That message is for us.[33]

LaSalle was referring to the PCA's edict that a woman's place was *not* in the professional world. *The New York Times* commented on the film's strengths as well as the weak ending, saying, "The picture is at its best when Miss Harding is being serenely successful in bringing order into the chaotic lives of two young patients. But when the psychiatrist ... does not know what to do about good old ... Herbert Marshall, who has been waiting for her to give him a definite matrimonial answer, then *The Flame Within* becomes a rather smoky drama, giving off much conversational heat and feeding fitfully on the damp wood of a conventional situation."[34] The *Los Angeles Times* agreed, saying, "Least convincing are the closing moments. The story, one feels, does not end here, except perfunctorily."[35]

Private Worlds (1935), released just prior to *The Flame Within*, was the first major Hollywood feature to venture into the field of psychiatry. In this film, psychiatrist Claudette Colbert dealt with male chauvinism in a mental hospital. The procedures Dr. Colbert and her colleagues use appear dubious. Joel McCrea tells a patient (Bess Flowers) suffering a depressive disorder, "Life's just a bully! When it hits you, you hit right back!" The film is persuasive in introducing the idea that everyone has a "private world"—where the line between sanity and insanity is, at best, opaque. By the finis, Colbert voluntarily steps down a notch in her position, as a concession to her love interest played by Charles Boyer. For the audiences of 1935, the message was clear in both films that any woman seeking fulfillment outside of marriage was asking for trouble.

Ann had barely started *The Flame Within* when Louella Parsons gleefully revealed that one of her scouts in Honolulu reported that a very well-known major at Schofield Barracks had courted Ann while she was in Hawaii. Rumors in "army circles," according to the gossip queen, indicated that the attachment between the two was "really serious."[36] After completing her work at MGM, Ann vacationed at Fort Bliss in Texas. She was the guest of Brigadier General George Vidmer, the West Point classmate of her father, who had attended her 1926 wedding. "Major

Sawbridge was kind enough to escort me on several occasions," Ann told reporters in El Paso, "but that's all there is to it."[37] The International News Service in Honolulu caught hold of Sawbridge. The major was more forthcoming. "I neither deny or affirm the report," he answered, "but any statement Miss Harding wishes to make is all right with me."[38] In May, who should show up in Hollywood, on furlough, but Sawbridge himself. In Honolulu, it was confirmed that Sawbridge had come to propose marriage. Ann was considering giving up her career. Although the couple was seen dining at the Cocoanut Grove at the end of the month, it was ill-timed for the pursuit of romance. Round two with Harry Bannister for Jane's custody had begun. Ann reluctantly conceded, "I am sorry for the humiliation caused the major, but I know now that the marriage can not be. You see, I do not want a second matrimonial fiasco, and things have not worked out as we expected."[39] Louella put in her two cents' worth to say, "Ann … was extremely frank in her admission to me that there might have been a marriage and that when she was in Honolulu she was very favorably impressed with the major who is well read, a West Point graduate, and a charming person."[40]

On May 17, Ann appeared in court denying any pending engagement with Sawbridge. But, more importantly, she refused to provide the requested deposition in answer to Bannister's claim of "unfitness." Adela Rogers St. Johns later commented, "I *know* that Ann Harding would rather have been accused of first degree murder than of being an unfit custodian for Jane."[41] Ann claimed that California had no jurisdiction over the case, as it had already been settled by the Reno court. After her refusal, Bannister dangled a contempt of court action over her head. Also lurking in the shadows was the threat of blackmail. Bannister approached Ann's former Cuban-rendezvous lover, writer Gene Fowler. He had threatened Fowler, who was married, saying he was going to "tell all" unless he received money. No one could have prophesied this fantastic situation.

Gene Fowler had arrived at RKO in the fall of 1931. Author of popular novels such as *The Great Mouthpiece*, his initial assignment was John Barrymore's *State's Attorney* (1932). Upon its completion, Fowler and his family returned to New York's Fire Island, where he immersed himself in designing a new house, as well as his writing. His biographer and friend, H. Allen Smith, wrote that Fowler discovered "something was chewing at him inside … a gnawing sort of thing."[42] Smith explained,

> It seems likely that he told [his wife] Agnes the whole story … The girl this time was a movie actress of almost supernatural charm and beauty, a ravishing blonde leading lady of both films and the Broadway stage. He loved her in the idiot way that Lord Nelson loved Lady Hamilton, and she had gone clean out of her head about him. Then came a fresh summons … RKO wanted him … Panting like a horny boy in a Tennessee Williams drama, he hastened westward, this time alone. Gene and his blonde flew into each other's arms. Breathing heavily. Sheer madness.[43]

Like Ann, Fowler had refused to sign the studio's morality clause when offered a $1,200-a-week writing contract. The tall, trim, well-groomed, forty-two-year-old former newspaperman with an infectious laugh had his reasons. "At my age—and with my liver," Fowler wrote when he returned the contract to RKO, "immorality is a luxury … I like to write about immoral guys and after all, if I'm writing about them I like to get the proper atmosphere."[44] With Ann's recent divorce,

**Ann's passionate affair with rebel (and married) screenwriter
Gene Fowler would only be hinted at in 1930s press releases.**

and Fowler's wife and three children back in New York, the "proper
atmosphere" presented itself and "luxury" in the form of Ann herself
fell into his lap. Years later, Fowler's son, Will, revealed the "sensational
evidence" that Bannister had threatened to disclose. He recalled,

> At this point in time a close reporter friend in-
> formed Fowler that Bannister had seen love letters
> my father had written to [Ann] and that he—Fowl-
> er—was to be named by Bannister as his ex-wife's
> suitor. Pop told his friend that he was aware of
> this, and that Bannister had already contacted him.
> "Bannister was threatening to break up my mar-
> riage and show copies of the letters to my wife," said
> Fowler. "I'll tell my wife *myself*! Then I'm going
> to go out and beat the living hell out of him!" This
> threat reached Bannister's ears. He disappeared.[45]

As soon as Fowler learned that Bannister was going to blackmail him, he met with Myron Selznick, his agent. Fowler told Selznick he was going to "disappear for a while." He took his typewriter aboard an oil tanker bound for New York via the Panama Canal. When Ann got word about Fowler's voyage, she made her hasty plan to meet him in Cuba. A surprised Fowler was greeted by news correspondents in Havana, and the news of Ann's shark nightmare. "Hot-blooded Latins all around her were shrieking for retribution [for the death of the Cuban skipper]," wrote biographer Smith, "and revenge and cash money and things were in a hell of a mess." In Will Fowler's biographical *The Second Handshake*, he mentions his mother being swarmed by reporters when she went to meet her no-show husband at the New York harbor. "'Are you aware of Mr. Fowler's ... friendship with Ann Harding, Mrs. Fowler?' one reporter asked. 'Of course I am,' Mother smiled. 'But I'd like to be on record as saying that I am patient with those who say they are in love with Gene. But I'll be a tiger if they interfere with his talent.'"[46] H. Allen Smith mentions one remark of Agnes' that never went to press. "What's good enough for Mr. Hearst," she said, "is good enough for Fowler."[47] (This is in reference to newspaper baron William Randolph Hearst and his own mistress, film star Marion Davies.)

Once back on Fire Island, Fowler's sabbatical from Hollywood didn't last long. He wasn't over Ann. Agnes told him, "Good God, why don't you pack your bags and go? Don't be sneaky about it. Catch a plane or get on the Century and go on out there. Get her out of your system."[48] Once in Hollywood, Fowler and Ann picked up where they left off. After he and Ann recognized the futility in pursuing their romance, Fowler finally returned home to New York.

A reporter asked why he had "quit the movies." Fowler answered, "I woke up one morning and found my intelligence flying at half mast."[49]

Will Fowler recalled a touching story that occurred shortly after his father's 70th birthday (1960). They both lived in Southern California at the time. Gene telephoned Will and sounded rather distraught. "Get over here right away," he told him. "I've just gone through an emotional experience I haven't quite gotten over yet and I'd like to talk with you." When Will arrived, he found his father sitting at his desk, looking serene, holding a glass of Vat 69 Scotch. His son asked what had happened.

> He explained that he had been down at the Beverly Wilshire Hotel waiting for Thomas Mitchell to show up. "Tommy and I had recently formed the most ex-clusive club in Beverly Hills," he said. "It's the *Beverly Hills Great-grandfather Club*. Mitchell and I are the only members." "For God's sake," I repeated, "what happened?" A sadness came over him. "While wait-ing for Tommy to arrive," he said, "a gentle hand was laid on my shoulder, and I heard a woman's voice say, 'Hello, darling.' I turned around. It was Ann Hard-ing. I stood up, faced her, placed my hands on her shoulders and said, 'but I'm an old man now.'"[50]

Fowler commented to his son on the love letters he had written to Ann, saying, "I'm sorry you never got to read them, Will. They were a thing of beauty; something no one today would ever be capable of composing. They were more than love letters. They were letters, love letters to the world."[51] Fowler felt that the destroyed letters were in-deed a great loss in a world that "so desperately needs love."

In May 1935, Robert Montgomery replaced Eddie Cantor as president of SAG. Cagney took over as first vice-president, and Ann held her post as second vice-president. The new third vice-president, Chester Morris, hosted an afternoon event for the Guild on May 31, which Ann attended. That Memorial Day weekend, Ann, acting in her capacity as honorary colonel, dedicated the Rainbow Memorial Grove at Exposition Park. A four-ton granite boulder and bronze tablet graced the tree-shaded plot while 200 veterans faced east and observed a period of silence in tribute to their departed comrades. A few days later, Major Sawbridge, his mission unaccomplished, left for Hawaii, and Ann took a brief respite in Agua Caliente.

On June 10, Ann carried a petition to the California State Supreme Court, to prevent the Los Angeles Superior Court from hearing Bannister's petition for custody. She stated that Bannister's action was "merely for the purpose of forcing a property settlement" from her.[52] Bannister had obtained one-half of her accumulated earnings in the original divorce settlement. Ann added that she was "willing to pay the amount" allegedly demanded to prevent the case from going into court. Her petition was denied. Soon afterwards, Bannister's lawyer, Michael G. Luddy, confronted Ann in her dressing room at Paramount. After she refused to answer his questions, Luddy once again appealed to the court. Ann followed the advice of her attorney, Gurney Newlin, who objected to the line of questioning. Facing a jail sentence for contempt, Ann had "steadfastly refused to answer questions about her relationship with director Dudley Murphy." Under oath, she had admitted knowing Murphy. When asked if Murphy had been a guest in her home and if she had accompanied him on trips, Ann refused to answer.[53] Typical of headlines for June 24, was that in the *Boston Traveler*: "Ann Harding Faces Jail for Contempt; Keeps Mum on Relations with Director."[54]

Ann's relationship with director Dudley Murphy had reached the tabloids during the summer of 1934. According to his biographer, Susan Delson, gossip columnists linked Murphy with several attractive companions, including Ann. As mentioned, Ann and Murphy had spent time together in 1932. It wasn't long after Ann and Gene Fowler's Cuban rendezvous and break up, that Dudley once again entered the picture. During Murphy's July 1934 divorce, his wife, Jo-Jo, charged that Murphy "stayed out late, and on many occasions did not return home at all."[55] Columnists were cagey in linking Ann and Murphy. Harrison Carroll offered the tidbit, "... Friendliest of the estranged couples are the Dudley Murphys ... She goes about with him half the time ... Ann Harding is THAT proud because her five year old daughter, Jane, saved up her own money to buy Ann two silver candle-sticks on her birthday."[56] Ann's reunion with Murphy was short-lived, not only because of her newfound romance with Major Sawbridge, but the glaring custody issues involving Bannister.

Edith accompanied her sister to court on July 1. Ann remained adamant in her refusal to answer questions about Murphy. When asked about her whereabouts on a particular date, her attorney instructed her not to reply.[57] Ann appealed to the State Supreme Court a second time to stop the Los Angeles Superior Court proceedings. At this point, Gene Fowler stepped in and encouraged Ann to engage attorney Roland "Rich" Woolley. On July 24, Woolley announced a shift in plans. "Miss Harding and I have gone over the matter and feel that it is in her interest to permit the deposition to be taken and the entire matter tried in court."[58] Woolley advised her to "face the issue squarely"—give her testimony, and file a cross-complaint, alleging that *Banniſter* was unfit.

On August 3, Ann arrived at Bannister's attorney's office calm and smiling. "The only trouble with this deposition business," Ann laughed, "is that I'm afraid I'll run out of deposition costumes."[59] A cool picture in a chic straw hat, powder-blue lace jacket and cream-tinted lace skirt, Ann faced five hours of questioning designed to prove her unfit. Her sister Edith sat across the room from her. The nature of the questions was never revealed. Afterwards, Woolley was extremely confident saying, "Miss Harding's name will be cleared once and for all."

On August 7 (Ann's birthday), she scored a minor triumph. She acquired court permission to question Bannister. In this counterattack, it was announced that Roland Woolley would head to New York to interview Sylvia Woolenberg, a "mystery witness." Whatever Woolenberg knew must have carried weight. On September 5, 1935, Bannister, in New York, stated under oath that he had made previous charges against Ann on hearsay, and that she had done nothing improper. After further delays, on October 24, both Ann and Harry appeared in the Los Angeles Superior Court. As Bannister paced the corridor, Ann, flanked by sister Edith and attorney Woolley, entered the building. One reporter commented, "Miss Harding, her gaze as rapt as in some of the scenes that have made her screen mother roles the talk of the nation, walked serenely by [Bannister]."[60] In a surprise move, Harry's lawyers asked permission to withdraw all charges against Ann. They both testified, but did not substantiate each others' accusations. Dressed in black, set off by dull gold accessories and a smartly angled hat, a pale-looking Ann took the stand, and stated briefly, "Jane attends a private school, takes piano, riding, dancing, and swimming lessons—in fact she has everything I can think of. She has a governess that lives with us and also a guard to look after her."[61] Bannister testified while Ann "watched him coldly." When asked if conditions in Ann's home were conducive to Jane's welfare, and whether Ann had ever refused him visitation, Bannister simply replied, "Yes, those statements are true." Lawyers conferred for two hours while the ex-couple, sitting a few feet apart, ignored each other. Judge Lewis Howell Smith ruled that Ann would retain sole custody of their 7-year-old daughter. Although Ann did not press charges against Bannister, she made no concessions. After six months of litigation, she had won round three.[62]

In April 1934, Bannister had had a minor success in New York by reviving the old 1843 P.T. Barnum tearjerker, *The Drunkard*. The play drew capacity crowds and ran for several months. Audiences sat at tables arranged like a beer garden. The price of admission included all the pretzels they could eat, and all the free beer they could tolerate. Patrons munched and guzzled while contemplating the ruinous effects of alcohol being enacted on stage. *The Drunkard* was the beginning of the American Music Hall, housed in an abandoned church on the East Side, last occupied by a congregation of Holy Rollers. *Time* magazine noted that the amount of brew given

July 1, 1935. Ann appeared in Superior Court on a contempt order, accompanied by her sister Edith Nash.

gratis was "lavishly distributed by producer Harry C. Bannister."[63] This venture afforded Bannister the ability to purchase a 76-acre parcel with a sixteen-room house in Warren County, New Jersey. The sale took place not long after *The Drunkard* closed. Bannister contracted to have a $40,000 artificial lake created on the site.[64] During his custody battle with Ann, Bannister had referred to himself as a "gentleman farmer."

Exactly what Ann had on Harry piques one's interest. In the summer of 1936, authorities brought to trial three men accused of attempting to blackmail Bannister, and threatening to make public information "of an immoral nature": Jerome A. Jacobs, a New York lawyer with underground connections, Harry Heckheimer, a former attorney of Bannister's, and Raymond Derringer (formerly a private detective).[65] According to Bannister, the men represented themselves as special investigators employed by Ann. David Slade, counsel for Heckheimer, opened the case by asserting that Bannister was "one of the most disreputable individuals on Broadway—a schemer, a fraud and a cheat."[66] Bannister testified in November 1934 that the men tried to extort $2,000 after threatening to publish "vicious and vile" information about him. When cross-examined as to the content of this "evidence," Bannister replied, "That I had been in a house of ill repute." "And that is false?" the court asked. "Oh," Bannister answered, "I wouldn't say that."[67] When the line of questioning ventured into Bannister's intimate past, he burst out angrily, telling the judge, "I don't see why I should answer these questions!" The attorney for Derringer, John A. Bolles, asked, "Where did you live in 1920?" Bannister nervously toyed with his horn-rimmed spectacles then answered, "I lived with Harry Heckheimer in a Riverside Drive apartment." Bolles continued: "But from 1920 to 1923 did you live with E. Romaine Simmons?"

"No," [answered Bannister]. "Before 1920 did you live with Chamberlin Brown?" "No."[Bannister repeated]. Chamberlain Brown, a well-known Broadway producer and agent, had a line-up of former clientele that included Clark Gable, Tallulah Bankhead, and Barbara Stanwyck.

Defense attorney George Wolf probed Bannister further. "Were you told that the affidavits had to do with your relationship to women?" he asked. "Yes," answered Harry. "Were you told that they had to do with improper relationship with men?" Harry's answer to this surprise question was a simple, "No." Bannister also denied that he had blackmailed Ann for $100,000, by linking her name with writer Gene Fowler.[68] Heckheimer divulged during the trial that Gene Fowler had hired a private detective to check up on Bannister's private life. Bannister had admitted to Heckhheimer that he had learned about Ann and Fowler "from a spy within Miss Harding's family—her sister's husband [Edith's ex-husband, Robert Nash]."[69] It was becoming clear that Harry's verbal attacks and insults toward Ann had been preceded by demands for money, and more money. It was in November 1934, *after* Harry's confrontation with the three men, that he headed to Los Angeles to confront Ann. The two had reached a deadlock in some "mystery" negotiation. At the 1936 trial, it was revealed that Bannister paid the $2,000 to get the affidavits on December 15, 1934, only to find the whole transaction was a "shakedown."[70] Attorney Bolles summed up by saying that, "Bannister knew he was bribing his wife's agent to double-cross her when he paid out the money. ... He paid it out to buy for $2,000 that which his wife had paid $10,000 for and which was her property."[71] Heckheimer, Jacobs and Derringer were convicted and sentenced to Sing-Sing.

The unusual line of questioning in the 1936 case provides a clue as to what Ann had on Harry. After this author contacted theater his-

Attorney Roland "Rich" Wooley guided Ann through messy custody battles for several years. "I'm running out of deposition costumes," Ann airily told reporters before taking the witness stand on August 3, 1935.

torian Gail Cohen, she told me that she knew the real reason Ann divorced Harry. What she had to say threw me for a loop, until I recalled the line of questioning from Harry's 1936 trial. "Paul Valentine told me," said Cohen. "Basically what happened between Ann and Bannister is that she caught him with another guy. I also talked with Melvyn Douglas—he'd been with Jessie Bonstelle's company. So, that's the story."[72] Attorney Bolles, in the 1936 trial, had obviously attempted to link Bannister's supposed "improper relationship to men," with theatrical agent Chamberlain Brown. Brown's personal papers held at the New York Public Library contain his correspondence to young gay servicemen during WWII. The archive notes, "Brown appears to have found stories on these soldiers and sailors in newspapers or muscle magazines and wrote to them, sometimes asking for an autograph, sometimes with the promise of a theatrical career."[73] According to Brown's files, Bannister began his professional association with him in 1921. Another "bachelor connection" of Harry's was RKO casting director Charles Richards. After Harry and Ann separated, Harry shared his Malibu beach house with the thirty-two-year-old former protégé of Cecil B. DeMille. Richards, who never married, would become casting manager for *Gone With the Wind*.

In the summer of 1936, Harry offered writer Adele Whiteley Fletcher his version of what really happened between him and Ann. It began one evening in early 1932, after dinner. Ann had said to him, "Harry, I want to talk to you. Will you step back into the bedroom with me?" Harry followed her down the hall saying, "Mercy, Ann, what an ominous tone. You must be about to fire the cook." Once inside their bedroom, Ann turned to him, declaring, "Harry, I don't love you any more. I haven't been in love with you for months. What do you propose to do?" Bannister told Fletcher that it was the sort of thing one would expect of Ann. "She'd always behaved the way a novelist would have a colonel's daughter behave," said Harry. "She always had been a square shooter."[74] Bannister claimed there had been no unpleasantness or quarrels leading up to Ann's announcement. It was the only part of Harry's rather extensive "exclusive" interview that rang true.

During his world tour in 1933, Bannister had sent his daughter a costume from every country he visited. Jane entertained herself for hours dressing up in them and playing "let's pretend." But, other than his guest stay at Ann's for Christmas 1933, his visitations with Jane were infrequent at best. Jane knew nothing of her mother's difficulties with Bannister. Ann had never told her about their divorce. She thought at age seven, Jane was too young to understand.

The implication of Ann's affairs with two married men verged on causing an uproar in her professional life as well as her private. Front-page headlines involving her "unfitness" may have accounted for the commercial failure of what many consider to be her best film, *Peter Ibbetson*. *Ibbetson* was released in November 1935, after the public had consumed six months' worth of innuendo revolving around Ann Harding. Adela Rogers St. Johns said, "Perhaps in the eyes of a conventional society, [Ann] may have done indiscreet things—she may even have done things condemned by society. A husband was something she didn't want to add to her problems. She has given that little girl love, devotion, careful training, everything that any child could have. If she's an unfit mother—there are no fit mothers ... I think we owe her our understanding."[75] It was in Ann's contract that she be home by seven in order to have an hour with Jane one-on-one. Not all star-mothers were so lucky. "I have not seen my baby awake for three days!" cried Virginia Bruce, whose two-year-old daughter was practically being raised by her parents.[76] Studio demands for long

Ann and Jane (c. 1936)

hours and back-to-back pictures took its toll on less fortunate players. For female stars dependent on their work for economic security, it took more than ordinary courage and the help of a good governess to competently fulfill their role as a mother.

Regardless of whether or not Ann made the best relationship choices, she had the added burden of celebrity. One is reminded of Ann's remark about being in Hollywood, and having her life "thrown on the screen of the world at large, and magnified, magnified, magnified." For Jane's sake, and her own sanity, Ann began searching for a way to flee Harry, the legal battlefield, her Hollywood career, and the tiresome scrutiny of the American public.

(Endnotes)

1   "Actress Fears Child Kidnapping," *Oakland Tribune*, 12/2/34
2   "Ann Harding and Ex-Mate Plan Suits," *Los Angeles Times*, 12/2/34
3   "Fight Over Child Balks Harding Holiday at Home," *Los Angeles Times*, 12/11/34
4   "Ann Harding May Purchase Nevada Home," *Nevada State Journal*, 1/4/35
5   "Ann Harding Wins Battle," *Los Angeles Times*, 1/4/35
6   "Ann Harding May Purchase Nevada Home," *Nevada State Journal*, 1/4//35
7   "Ann Harding Given Exclusive Custody Of Daughter, Jane," *Charleston Gazette*, 1/4/35
8   "Ann Harding, Ill, Ordered to Tahiti for Six Weeks," *Syracuse Herald*, 11/2/34
9   Robbin Coons, "Hollywood Sights and Sounds," *Charleston Gazette*, 4/14/35
10 Harrison Carroll column, *San Mateo Times*, 8/17/34
11 "Ann Harding to Renew Child Custody Battle," *Los Angeles Times*, 1/24/35
12 "Bannister Sues to Take Child From Ann Harding," *Los Angeles Times*, 1/23/35
13 "Ann Harding Off to Honolulu Rest," *Hayward Daily Review*, 1/26/35
14 Read Kendall, "Around and About in Hollywood," *Los Angeles Times*, 2/12/35
15 "Why Ann Came Back," *Kingston Daily*, 4/30/35
16 Edwin Schallert, "Ann Harding Reveals Road to Happiness," *Los Angeles Times*, 5/7/35
17 R.V. Fletcher, report on *Enchanted April*, *Motion Picture Herald*, 3/9/35
18 Wm. A. Clark, report on *Enchanted April*, *Motion Picture Herald*, 5/4/35
19 F.S.N. review of *Enchanted April*, *New York Times*, 3/9/35
20 Wood Soanes, review of *Enchanted April*, *Oakland Tribune*, 2/25/35
21 Whitney Williams review of *Enchanted April*, *Screen and Radio Weekly*, 1/6/35
22 Leonard J. Leff, *Hemingway and His Conspirators*, Rowman and Littlefield, c. 1999 pp 172-173
23 Leonard J. Leff, *Hemingway and His Conspirators*. Rowman and Littlefield, c. 1999 Pg 195
24 Philip K. Scheuer, "A Town Called Hollywood," 12/10/33
25 Robbin Coons, "Ann Harding in Color Film," *Gettysburg Times*, 9/13/34
26 "Contract is Signed by Ann Harding," *The Gleanor*, 8/16/34

27   W.E. Oliver, "Ann Harding To Do Colored Versions of Sagas, Fables," *LA Evening Herald Express*, 9/29/34

28   "Ann Harding Sees 'Peacock Feathers' Starting Color Vogue as 'The Jazz Singer" Did Sound," *Syracuse Herald*, 9/16/34

29   "Rest Ordered for Ann Harding," *New York Times*, 10/20/34

30   Harry N. Blair, "She Takes It On The Chin," *Picture Play*, April 1935

31   Matthew Kennedy to author, 5/7/2008

32   R.O.H., review of *The Flame Within*, *Oakland Tribune*, 6/24/35

33   Mick LaSalle, *Complicated Women*, St. Martin's Pr., N.Y., c.2000, pg 187-188

34   F.S.N., review of *The Flame Within*, *New York Times*, 6/1/35

35   Philip K. Scheuer, review of *The Flame Within*, *Los Angeles Times*, 5/24/35

36   Louella Parsons column, *Fresno Bee*, 3/10/35

37   "Ann Harding Says No Romance Blooms," *San Antonio Light*, 4/11/35

38   Report from *San Antonio Light*, 4/11/35

39   "Major is Sailing Without His Ann," *Charleston Gazette*, 5/17/35

40   "Major Is Sailing Without His Ann," *Charleston Gazette*, 5/17/35

41   Adela Rogers St. Johns, "Has a Movie Mother Any Rights?" *Photoplay*, August 1936

42   H. Allen Smith, *The Life and Legend of Gene Fowler*, William Morrow and Co., N.Y., c. 1977, pg 221

43   H. Allen Smith, *The Life and Legend ...* pg 222

44   Tip Poff, "That Certain Party," *Los Angeles Times*, 12/11/32

45   Will Fowler, *The Second Handshake*, Lyle Stuart, Inc., N.J., c. 1980, pg 39-40

46   Will Fowler, *The Second Handshake*, Lyle Stuart, Inc., N.J., c. 1980, pp41-42

47   H. Allen Smith, *The Life and Legend ...* pg 222

48   H. Allen Smith, *The Life and Legend ...* pg 223

49   H. Allen Smith, "Gene Fowler, Famous for His Exploits, Retires to Write," *Charleston Gazette*, 5/30/33

50   Will Fowler, *The Second ...* pg. 44

51   Will Fowler, *The Second Handshake*, Lyle Stuart, Inc., N.J. c. 1980, pg43-44

52   "Star Charges Kidnap Threat," *Oakland Tribune*, 6/10/35

53   "Ann Harding to Face Citation for Contempt," *Oakland Tribune*, 6/23/35

54   Susan Delson, *Dudley Murphy-Hollywood Wild Card*, University of Minnesota Pr., c. 2006, pg 159

55   Susan Delson, *Dudley Murphy-Hollywood Wild Card*, University of Minnesota Pr., c. 2006, pg 159

56   Harrison Carroll, "Behind the Scenes in Hollywood," *Monessen Daily Independent*, 8/14/34

57   "Ann Harding Balks Query," *Los Angeles Times*, 7/2/35

58   "Ann Harding Shifts Plans," *Los Angeles Times*, 7/24/35

59   "Ann Harding Questioned," *Los Angeles Times*, 8/4/35

60   *Los Angeles Evening Herald Express*, 10/24/35

61   "Ann Harding Wins Battle," *Los Angeles Times*, 10/25/35

62   "The Threat Hanging Over Ann Harding!" *Hollywood*, September 1936

63   Review of *The Drunkard*, *Time*, 4/23/34

64   "Harry Bannister, Actor, Buys Estate Near Belvedere," *New York Times*, 4/22/35

65   Angus McLaren, *Sexual Blackmail*, Harvard University Pr., c. 2002, pg 99

66   "Blackmail Denied," *Fresno Bee*, 8/11/36

67   "Bannister Denies Accusing Wife of Intimacies," *Titusville Herald*, 8/11/36

68   "Bannister Denies That He Attempted to Blackmail Ann Harding," *Winnipeg Free Press*, 8/12/36

69   "Rich Men Mentioned at Bannister Hearing," *Los Angeles Times*, 8/13/36

70   Article from *Detroit Evening Times*, 8/13/36

71   "Bannister Story Called False At Trial," *Reno Evening Gazette*, 8/14/36

72   Conversation with Grace Cohen, 7/14/2008 (Valentine was an actor/dancer/singer and chore-
      ographer who appeared on Broadway and such films as *Out of the Past*)

73   Chamberlain and Lyman Brown Papers, www.nypl.org

74   Adele Whitely Fletcher, "All I Want is to See My Child," *Screen Guide*, August 1936

75   Adela Rogers St. Johns, "Has a Movie Mother Any Rights?" *Photoplay*, August 1936

76   Ruth Rankin, "The Tragedy of Being a Hollywood Mother," *Photoplay*, June 1935

Ann as the Duchess of Towers in the classic
Peter Ibbetson (1935). (Paramount)

14
To Dream—Peter Ibbetson

In spite of sensational headlines surrounding Ann's private life, she
ranked in the top forty (#38) at the box office at the beginning
of 1936.[1] Ann still had the edge over such stellar attractions as Jeanette MacDonald (#43) and Bette Davis (#44). Irene Dunne, who
had relocated to Universal, failed to make the top 50, while Katharine
Hepburn had slipped from #11 to #23. However, things were about
to change for Ann with the release of Paramount's *Peter Ibbetson*. This
prestigious and critically acclaimed film failed to draw audiences and
emerged a box-office casualty. RKO hoped that *The Indestructible
Mrs. Talbot,* which Ann had selected, would boost her marquee value.
Released under the less meaty title *The Lady Consents* (1936), critics
immediately recognized the "Ann Harding formula." In her Los Angeles review, Eleanor Barnes pointed out, "The moment Ann Harding walks on in a scene, there will be nice, polite, unruffled, lady-like
suffering. Suffering done without hysterics. In fact, just suffering."[2]
Hollywood Citizen News complained that the "routine expertness" of
her suffering and "genteel bravado" had become "tiresome."[3] Such

November 1, 1935. Ann sought refuge and romance with a
lanky colonel stationed on Oahu. Accompanying her on the
voyage was pianist Norma Boleslavsky.

typecasting had soured the marquee value of other stars—from Dietrich's exotic creatures to Garbo's sad ones. There was little variation
in the tone, tempo, and themes of the roles Ann selected to play. She
was the first to acknowledge her dilemma. *The Lady Consents*, regardless of critical opinion, was decidedly "upbeat" and made a profit for
RKO. Reporter Edith Dietz visited the set while Ann tackled a scene
filled with humor and amusement. "The change is almost too much
for me," Ann marveled, "I have been pining away for such a long time
my face has the habit of looking sad. It will probably crack."[4] Dietz was highly entertained by the smiling, cordial star, and wrote, "I
wish now I had never talked so much about Ann Harding's coldness,

austerity, solemn dignity." Numerous welcome "changes" were in the works Ann. Her contract with RKO was ending; a fact for which she was grateful. She had decided to freelance and signed with Capitol Films in London. By the summer of 1936, the promise of a new romance would fuel her decision to leave the country.

Upon completing *Peter Ibbetson* in the fall of 1935, Ann had arranged for one final rendezvous with Major Sawbridge. On November 1, Brian Aherne, who had become a dependable friend, bid her adieu at the airport. She flew to San Francisco and boarded the *President Coolidge* for Hawaii. Pianist Norma Boleslavsky (wife of the director) joined her on the voyage. The Boleslavskys had spent many evenings with Ann after her divorce. In her column, gossip queen Louella Parsons offered her unsolicited approval for Ann to marry. "Those of us who love her," purred Parsons, "hope she will say yes to Major Benjamin Sawbridge. He is desperately in love with her. Now that the courts have given her Jane ... there is no reason why she shouldn't live her own life."[5] Arriving in Honolulu, Ann told the press that she was there "to enjoy myself, not to get married." She "smacked" her fist on the desk of her hotel suite when reporters persisted with questions about Sawbridge. "I'll announce my own engagement or marriage," she repeated, "if I'm ever engaged or married." After a nine-day stay on the islands, Ann, dissolved to tears, wept "unreservedly as she bade the major good-bye."[6] Sailing back to the mainland aboard the *S.S. Malolo*, she grappled with her decision to "live her own life" *without* Sawbridge. As a consolation prize, Jasper Deeter paid Ann a visit, which cheered her up immeasurably. Prior to his arrival Ann sent him a telegram saying, "We will whiff our cognac in aging peace and carefree gaiety. The phone is Granite-4884. Hurry home."[7]

Peter Ibbetson, based on George du Maurier's 1891 novel, was a film in which both Ann and Gary Cooper eagerly participated. Their devotion to the project, coupled with the sensitive direction of Henry Hathaway, and exquisite photography of Carl Lang, turned *Peter Ibbetson* into something remarkable. Filmmaker Luis Bunuel, whose films were famous for their surreal imagery, claimed *Peter Ibbetson* was one of the ten greatest films ever made. Andre Breton, French writer and surrealist theorist, referred to the film as "a triumph in surrealist thinking."

In 1932, Paramount bought the rights to the opera based on *Ibbetson* with the intention of casting Jeanette MacDonald in the female lead. When MacDonald was unavailable, they reverted back to the drama.[8] The project was renewed in 1934, with Brian Aherne in the role of Peter. It was Aherne who suggested casting Ann in the film. He knew that Ann was keen on playing the Duchess of Towers, as she tried to buy the screen rights herself. After several postponements, Aherne, and then Robert Donat after him, bowed out of the film. The project was again dropped until Gary Cooper got a hold of the script. Although many felt Cooper would be miscast, he capably softened his earthiness with impeccable understanding of Du Maurier's work. "I have followed the life of the novel from its inception," commented Cooper, "and through the years when it became a play and an opera. Its beauty, delicacy, its fragile web of romance can be accepted only during periods of moral renaissance. The world takes its beauty, such beauty as is in this glorious story, by spells, depending upon the mood of the times."[9] Ann gratefully contracted for her part

Gary Cooper and Ann spend a lifetime meeting in dreams in
the adaptation of du Maurier's 1891 novel. (Paramount)

(and second-billing) in January 1935. Filming began on April 29. As it turned out, Ann was an ideal choice. She thrived in the film's ethereal atmosphere and landscape. The question was, whether or not the world was in the "mood" for a "moral renaissance" starring Gary Cooper and Ann Harding.

In the role of Ibbetson, we see Cooper, an English architect, sustaining an inexplicable sense of emptiness. His blind employer (sensitively played by Donald Meek) cautions Peter not to depend solely on the eyes for vision. Pointing to his heart, he emphasizes, "It will be *there*, Peter." And *there* lies Ibbetson's problem—the loss and separation from his childhood sweetheart, Mary.

Peter takes an assignment in Yorkshire to redesign the stables of the wealthy Duke of Towers (John Halliday). The man's wife, the cool and lovely Duchess of Towers (Ann), also appears to carry a certain emptiness. When Peter challenges her idea for the stable design, she tells him, "You're impertinent." He smiles amicably with the retort, "And I intended to be such a gentleman." Instead of causing him to be dismissed, Peter's determination, tinged with humor, manages to charm the Duchess. The two appear to be engaged in some mystical coincidence upon discovering they have shared the exact same dream one evening. It is over dinner that the climactic moment arrives. The reflective silence is broken by the Duke's query as to when Ibbetson would be leaving. He answers, "Oh, two or three days." "And how long have you been in love with my wife?" the Duke asks. At this point Hathaway creates a tension that could only be cut with a very sharp knife.

The Duchess looks directly at her husband and demands, "Explain yourself!" "I'm not a fool, my dear," he tells her. "You're in love, but that is obvious and not to the point. The point is Mr. Ibbetson, has it gone beyond a kiss, yet?" When Peter remains silent, the Duchess appeals to him, "Why don't you answer? Have we ever so much as touched fingers? Have we ever given such a thing a thought?" It is here that the riddle to their almost surreal bond is resolved. Looking intently at her, Peter replies,

> I've given nothing else a thought. Do you know what you've done for me? You've rid me of a pain in my heart I've carried all my life. She was a little girl and I've carried her in my heart and brain. A little girl in a little garden. We were torn apart. All women have faded before her face until I saw yours… I look at you and don't see her. I see you!

This riveting scene, revealing that the girl and duchess are one and the same, leads to the inevitable clash between the two men, and the Duke's death. Although Ibbetson is incarcerated, the love of Peter and Mary—their "seeing with the heart," transcends prison walls. They continue to meet in dreams. Years pass, and upon Mary's death, a stream of light beckons from beyond the barred window and into Peter's cell. He is coming out of a dream in which Mary suddenly disappeared, leaving behind her gloves. He awakens to the sound of her voice. "We will be together," she assures him, "I'm waiting for you." Peter holds "the gloves" toward the light. As the film fades, we hear the sound of his shackled arm landing on the prison floor—his spirit released by a promise.

The stunning cinematography of Charles Lang emphasized the sensitive edge in Cooper's portrayal, and enhanced Harding's ethereal Nordic beauty. Together they make a striking, otherworldly pair as they roam the landscapes of illusion. The film itself is a testament to the author's query, "Who is to say what is real and what is not real?" Hathaway admitted that the lighting in *Peter Ibbetson* "was mostly Rembrandt." He recalled, "Rembrandt had a faculty of using light to make you look any place he wanted you to look. Charlie Lang and I went through Rembrandt. It had that sort of dark quality in it. It teaches you not to be afraid of the dark. We copied [that] atmosphere ... [using] as little light as possible."[10] Special effects by Gordon Jennings, used shafts of light and slow out-of-focus dissolves to create what Hathaway and Lang envisioned. This camerawork was graciously complemented by Ernest Toc's haunting, Oscar-nominated score.

Cooper had been influential in getting the relatively unknown Hathaway his previous assignment, *The Lives of a Bengal Lancer*, which got the director an Academy Award nomination. The two men would remain loyal friends until Cooper's death. When asked about working with Ann, Hathaway didn't mince words. "She was an absolute bitch," he said. "One time when we were working on a scene, she put on a little tantrum. She went over to her dressing room and I went over and I asked, 'Now what the hell is the matter?' She said, 'Oh my god, working with Cooper—he's such a lovely man—but he's such a—oh, he's so difficult.' I said, 'Look, I want to tell you, I've worked with this man for a long time, and you don't see anything except on film, and this is a very strange quality; this level of quality that this man has, and I would suggest that you watch yourself and not worry about him.'"[11] Hathaway's comment about Harding being a "bitch" could have well been a compliment. "To be a good director," claimed Hathaway, "you've got to be a bastard. I'm a bastard and I know it."[12] Hathaway, patting himself on the back, liked to refer to his fellow bastard-directors such as John Ford, Fritz Lang, and William Wyler.[13] Orson Welles called Hathaway a famous "cruel-to-actors" director. "Real Jekyll-and-Hyde stuff," said Welles. "Sweet, nice man in private life, and turns into this raving maniac on the set. People go off to rest homes afterward."[14]

Hathaway was an odd choice to take the helm of such an un-rugged venture as *Peter Ibbetson.* His background was mostly Zane Grey westerns and action films. Cooper, on the other hand, was a familiar sight in Westerns as well as romantic dramas such as *A Farewell to Arms.* Neither star nor director had theatrical background, and as Hathaway so "cordially" pointed out to Ann, while Cooper didn't have the technique or training Ann was accustomed to, his "quality" registered on screen. And, under Hathaway's direction, it is fascinating to watch Harding's Duchess melt away her patrician dignity with the realization that Cooper is the boy she loved as a child. During her 1936 stay in England, Ann admitted, "The screen is an art that I admire as much [as the stage]—if the right type of story is filmed. Stories of thoughts rather than actions appeal to me. *Peter Ibbetson,* for instance. I adored doing that film with Gary Cooper."[15] Although Ann had once referred to John Halliday (who played the Duke of Towers) as "one of the world's many worst actors," she made no comment on Cooper's acting "technique."[16] Ann felt Cooper to be "rich" in understanding and commented that he had a rare quality for friendship. "Gary *is* humane," said Ann. "He is kind to everyone alike—and friendly to all. One believes in humanity through him."[17] Still, Cooper was something new. Obviously, Ann preferred working with trained professionals. After commenting on *Peter Ibbetson,* she waxed poetic about Leslie Howard, raving, "What a craftsman—he's an absolute challenge, with his perfect timing, and the way he sustains everything and throws the ball right back every time. I think he's the finest actor we have."[18]

While filming *Peter Ibbetson,* Ann kept asking director Henry Hathaway
as to when Cooper was "going to start to act." According to Hathaway,
after watching the dailies, Ann claimed Cooper had
"deliberately stolen scenes" from her.

Peter Ibbetson was not typical fare for American moviegoers. A
love that transcends time and space in the dreams of separated lovers, begged for sensitive, intelligent audiences. While the film was
received enthusiastically in England and Europe, the American imagination proved less flexible and, as one reviewer mentioned, "we fear a
tendency on the part of the audience to snicker up its collective sleeve
at such super natural goings on."[19] *Film Daily* commented, "For class
theaters the picture should do very well, but when it comes to playing
to the real paying public, results do not look too hopeful. The picture
is hardly entertainment for the masses."[20] Although American critics
doubted the mass appeal of the film, they unanimously agreed that
Ann offered superior work. "Ann Harding gives to the picture-go-
ing public the most complete and attractive revelation of her art and

personality that she has ever afforded," raved The *Los Angeles Times*. The review nodded to Cooper's "high achievement," saying, "With great reserve he impersonates this poetic and spirited dreamer. The very ruggedness of Cooper is an asset to the picture."[21] Los Angeles critic Elizabeth Yeaman, who was usually wary of Ann, stated, "Miss Harding undergoes transformation of personality in this picture. Her portrayal of Mary is lacking in most of her stock mannerisms and tragic undertones. Photographically she has never been more beautiful. Her performance is one of the best that she has ever given on the screen. Cooper's own lanky physique and dreamy detachment of personality suit him well for his portrayal of Peter."[22] *New York Times* critic Andre Sennwald, who blasted Ann's performance in *Biography of a Bachelor Girl*, gave all the credit to director Hathaway, saying, "Under Hathaway's management Miss Ann Harding, who has been losing prestige lately, gives her finest performance, while Gary Cooper fits into the picture with unexpected success. Mr. Hathaway skillfully escapes all the lush pitfalls of the plot and gives it a tenderness that is always gallant instead of merely soft."[23]

News correspondent Willa Okker visited Ann's hilltop home soon after *Ibbetson* was completed. She was ushered into the living room before Ann, arriving late from business in town, walked in followed by her fierce-looking police dog. Noting the apprehension on Okker's face, Ann remarked, "Don't be afraid of him. He's an utter fake. We bought him as a watchdog, because he looked so ferocious. But he hasn't an enemy in the world—and no intention of making any." A

sudden tumult of children's voices from outside postponed the interview, and Okker followed Ann to observe several youngsters splashing
in the pool. Jane was attempting to do a handstand underwater. "We
better not let her see us," cautioned Ann. "Jane has been trying for
weeks to stand on her head and she doesn't want me to see it until she
has the feat accomplished." On their way back to the living room, Okker spotted a small, tinted photo of Ann with her head nestled against
the long neck of a white horse. "I'm very fond of that picture—and of
that horse," said Ann. "He belongs to a family I know and they let me
ride him. I only ride occasionally now and do very little jumping. But
there was nothing I wouldn't attempt when I was a child." There was
no stopping Ann's talk of horses and the outdoors. While listening to
her, it dawned on Okker why people misunderstood Ann Harding.
Ann suddenly broke off her discourse and apologized. "I really don't
know what to tell you. In the several years I have been in Hollywood
I have told my life story so many times that I don't know what is good
copy any more or whether I have anything more to give. You'll have
to ask some pointed questions if you want to get material out of me."
Okker replied she didn't have any. She had her story. Ann wasn't the
"stiff, unbending lady" as some had alleged. Her verve and keen interest in what was going on around her made it obvious to Okker that
Ann had taken on the "charming openness which characterized the
wide mountainous region in which she lived."[24]

Not surprisingly, Ann was eager to venture out and away from
her mountain home and the confines of Hollywood. Her plans for
an extended stay in England were settled. A contract with Capitol
Films (Trafalgar Studios) in London had scheduled Ann to film *Camille* with Clive Brook. But, by the end of 1935, MGM was prepar-

ing to star Greta Garbo and Robert Taylor in the Alexander Dumas classic. According to Ann, MGM "got wind" of her project and beat Capitol Films to the draw. "Of course, I was disappointed," recalled Ann, in 1963, "until I saw their film—saw Garbo's exquisite and incomparable performance. I would happily bow out to her any time."[25]

Ann had two more film commitments before she could leave the U.S. Although many protested the Pulitzer Prize awarded the play adaptation of *The Old Maid*, it didn't deter Ann's interest in playing Delia, the malicious, conniving cousin of the dour spinster. Helen Hayes, who never liked how she looked on screen, was offered the title role at $85,000, and turned it down. In November 1935, Irene Dunne was announced as Ann's co-star. Mitchell Leisen was scheduled to direct, but it wasn't long before Ann had a change of heart. She had read P.J. Wolfson's *The Indestructible Mrs. Talbot*, for which RKO negotiated the rights from Paramount. Filming on … *Mrs. Talbot* was completed in 18 days (December 1935)—12 days ahead of schedule. *The Old Maid* was turned over to Warner Brothers and into the capable hands of Bette Davis who acted rings around Miriam Hopkins' Delia. As far as working with Irene Dunne, it would be Ann's sister, Edith, who would do so, becoming Irene's personal secretary for a number of years.

In between takes on *The Lady Consents* Ann quizzed Herbert Marshall on attractive places to stay and visit in England. Marshall admitted he was somewhat out of the loop as he hadn't been home for three years. On screen, Marshall and Ann, as Dr. and Mrs. Michael Talbot, turned the love triangle on its head and gave it a jaunty angle. *The*

Lady Consents is a sprightly, intelligent twist on a familiar theme. As Anne Talbot, Ann offers little resistance when the athletically determined and crisp Gerry (Margaret Lindsay) wins Michael away from her. Initially, when Michael confesses he had kissed Gerry, a.k.a. "The Kansas Cyclone," Anne is amused. "Well," she offers, "did you enjoy it?" They agree it was a "funny" thing for him to do. However, when Michael calls Anne from a restaurant with excuses for not meeting her, she overhears a waiter ask, "Beer for the lady?" Inevitably, Dr. Talbot asks Anne for a divorce (while she is in the middle of a pool game). She graciously concedes ... to a point. "You've given me the swellest seven years a woman ever had," she tells him, "Now beat it ... while I'm still being a lady. It's likely to wear off any minute." Her pent-up emotions are released by her billiard partner-cum-wise old father-in-law Jim (played in excellent form by Edward Ellis). "A few tears would help," he tells her. "I can't," Anne replies, looking as if she would like to. Jim slaps her face. After the initial shock, she breaks down to sob on his shoulder. A nicely-handled scene.

The censors got in the way of P.J. Wolfson's original story, which had the unusual slant of Anne becoming the mistress of her ex-husband. RKO bowed to the PCA and had Anne use money instead of sex to influence Gerry's hold. After the nuptials, Gerry refurbishes the house, prominently displaying her collection of golf and tennis trophy cups. We find Anne, in her new apartment, entertaining her ex-father-in-law and new beau (Walter Abel) with a beer bust. "Did you ever try any of that new canned beer?" Anne asks them. "I could always get 'canned' on the old kind," Jim jests. The scene caused an uproar from the American and Canadian Glass Blowers' Union. They flooded RKO with letters protesting Ann serving beer in cans. There is lots of beer drink-

Teamed with Herbert Marshall for
The Lady Consents (1936). (RKO)

ing in *The Lady Consents* (at least three scenes, and an implied fourth). New York critic Chester Bahn, mused, "And, oh yes, drinking beer. The beer drinking is almost symbolic. It hints at freedom of spirit ... and to the dickens with conventions."[26] Thumbing her nose at censors as well as convention, Ann's ex-wife *does* offer herself to be Dr. Talbot's mistress after his relationship with Gerry sours. "Gerry doesn't matter," Anne tells him, "Let her keep the title. She can be married to you, but *I'll* be your wife." Talbot balks, "Do you realize what that means? I'm not worth it!" Anne gives him an endearing smile, answering, "I *know* that."

Ann's "suffering" in *The Lady Consents* is leavened by dialogue filled with wisecracks and smiles for a refreshing change of pace. In the final confrontation scene Anne refuses to pull punches with Gerry, and threatens to ask for $30,000 in back payment from her original divorce settlement. "That's all he makes in a year!" Gerry cries. "Oh well," Anne suggests, "Maybe you can melt down some of [your] cups." The bright and sophisticated script for *The Lady Consents* was the film's chief delight. The *Illustrated Daily News* noted, "Everyone in the cast jests joyously.

No one says a dull thing to the other, and leading with the quips is Miss Harding."[27]   The Oakland Tribune rallied behind Ann saying, "All those anticipating a good cry over Ann Harding's usual sad plight are doomed to disappointment. She dried her tears, cast off the tragic mask and went gay on her doting admirers in The Lady Consents. Miss Harding's picture ... owes its potency to the manner of playing rather than to the play itself. It is sophisticated, briskly-dialogued and credible drama."[28]   The dynamic of Harding-Marshall-Lindsay crackled on screen. The New York Times stated Lindsay "enacts with great finesse the part of a coldly cerebral girl-athlete with a taste for winning."[29]   Lindsay's fresh independent screen persona was up against a great deal during Hollywood's studio era. In his book, Behind the Screen: How Gays and Lesbians Shaped Hollywood (1910-1969), author William J. Mann said about her, "Hollywood didn't quite know what to do with a glamorous lesbian who refused to play the game."[30]   Lindsay vetoed marriage and lived with her longtime partner Mary McCarty in the Hollywood hills. Many (including Ann) felt that Edward Ellis (the original victim in The Thin Man) playing her crusty, cigar-chewing father-in-law, stole The Lady Consents from the other actors. His death-bed scene, wherein he reunites Ann and Marshall, was such a heart-wringer that cameraman Roy Hunt broke into tears and sobbed for fifteen minutes before he could resume work.

It is not surprising that during the years of Ann's major stardom, reviews invariably overlooked her film wardrobe. Whereas stars like Kay Francis, Norma Shearer, Marlene Dietrich and Joan Crawford had audiences ooh-ing and ahh-ing over their ultra-chic and fantastic costumes, Ann would have none of it. "I suppose," she told one columnist, "since I'm small (5' 2"), I should go in for bizarre effects. Extreme hats. And gowns cut daringly in the wrong places—or the right places, depending on one's point of view. But I simply can't imagine wanting to. It would defeat my whole purpose. You see, I have no desire to startle people into attention, but rather to make them feel easy and comfortable when they are with me."[31] She insisted the same consideration be given her on-screen characters. Reporter Grace Grandville stated that Ann "brought studio makeup men and dress designers to the verge of apoplexy because she wouldn't let them do the regulation things to her face and hair … she shied at wearing the gorgeous clothes they wanted to design for her. She absolutely refused to allow herself to be used as a manikin to show off the weird and wonderful ability of costume designers."[32] Ann's clothes expressed simplicity and the straightforwardness of her personality. Although Ann's beauty was nothing spectacular, and she had no desire to stand out in a crowd, the greatest compliment she could hope for came from one of Hollywood's most influential portrait photographers. RKO's head photographer, Ernest Bachrach, whose camera lens had captured such great beauties as Delores del Rio, commented, "Ann Harding has the most nearly perfect face I have ever photographed."[33]

In February 1936, Ann started work on *The Witness Chair*. In the middle of shooting, she stopped production—she didn't care for the script. Samuel Briskin, the new head of RKO, who considered Ann an "overpriced asset," reminded her that she had selected the story and approved the script.[34] RKO threatened to sue her for $80,000 (the cost of production to date). Ann had no choice but to finish her studio swansong. The film emerged as a rather mournful finis to Ann's reign of major film stardom. *The New York Times* agreed with Ann, saying the "mediocre" film was "less the fault of the players or the director [George Nichols] than of its author, Rita Weiman, and of the persons who devised the screen play.[35] The *Syracuse Herald* review stated, "*The Witness Chair* leaves one slightly cold, despite the heroic attempts of Ann Harding to give it dramatic polish. Miss Harding does exceedingly well in an impossible role."[36] The courtroom drama, told mostly in flashback, revolves around Paul Young (Ann) and her "righteous" murder of her middle-aged, embezzler employer, Mr. Whitaker (Douglass Dumbrille). Paula is fully aware that Whitaker was not only implicating his business partner Jim Trent (Walter Abel - Ann's love interest) for fraud, but running away with Trent's innocent, young daughter. While on screen, Ann's skill pulls the viewer into a story that is undeserving of her talent. She sustains a low pitch, appropriate for her character and perfect for the confines of what is essentially a small film. The hysterics were left to Whitaker's bookkeeper (Margaret Hamilton), who obviously had her own "crush" on the murder victim. The plot leads up to the all-too-familiar moment when the leading lady stands up in court to announce, "You must listen to me! I killed Stanley Whitaker!" Richard B. Jewell, in his *The RKO Story*, found the screenplay "excruciating," adding, "Once a beautiful and magnetic star, Ann Harding left RKO in disgrace following *The Witness Chair*."[37]

It was fortuitous that Ann was already set on leaving Hollywood and redefining her life. In England, she would discover what she always considered to be the real "highlight" of her acting career.

With her work at RKO complete, Colonel Ann Harding of the Rainbow Division made a guest appearance for the Los Angeles Breakfast Club on April 1. The club, a popular meeting place for captains of industry,

Ann's contract with RKO ended
with *The Witness Chair* (1936).
(Courtesy of Photofest)

entertainment heavyweights like Louis B. Mayer, and war heroes, was founded in 1925. National Army Day was coming up, and Ann spoke in defense of a strong Army and Navy program. On the same day, Brigadier General Henry B. Clagett of the U.S. Army Air Corps., offered his views before the Los Angeles Junior Chamber of Commerce. He warned of the nation's inadequate air force and obsolete ships. Ann justified the expense involved in bolstering defense programs and recruiting trained officers. She cautioned, "We can't abolish war by simply saying that we don't want to play Indian with the children next door."[38] Although a strong defense never made for a lasting peace, Clagett and Ann's concern for a more vigorous Army Air Corps. was, in part, confirmed five years later when U.S. bases in Pearl Harbor and the Philippines found themselves inadequately prepared for a Japanese attack.

In the spring of 1936, Ann enjoyed a reunion with two former roommates from her early days in New York. Frank Easton and Monroe Owsley were also boarders on West 88th Street. Easton visited Ann on the set of *The Witness Chair*. They went to her luxurious studio bungalow to chat about the nineteen-year-old Ann who resided in a world of her own, and wasn't much of a mixer. "She ate, lived, and drank

books," recalled Easton, "Her mind was like a steel trap." He felt everyone was "a little bit in awe of her" at the time, yet Ann was "one of the
most sympathetic persons [he'd] ever known." During Easton's visit,
he noted one thing that had not changed. "She's still consumed with a
burning ambition," he observed. Ann, a vision in pale blue chiffon, invited him into the studio lunch room. Between bites of a chicken salad
sandwich she asked, "How's Monroe?" "Fine," Easton nodded. "Those
were thrilling days," Ann reminisced. "I can hardly believe that it was
fourteen years ago. Life was one glorious dream then. With all that's
happened since, happiness, heartache, successes and failures, I've never
let anything disturb that dream. At least, I've tried not to. Of course,
we must accept the good with the bad." Easton asked if the failures
ever discouraged her. She laughed, "Not permanently. My marriage
discouraged me more than anything else ... I suppose it just wasn't to
be." Changing the subject, Ann bubbled over with excitement. "I'm
off to London to do several pictures for Capitol Films. I'm looking forward so much to the trip. It'll be fun working over there–and I'm taking
Jane with me. Life means so much more than just success. I've Jane to
live for and work for. I scarcely know myself. I've taken a new lease of
movie life and feel like making pictures forever."[39]

Easton recalled how crazy Monroe Owsley was about Ann. Men
didn't mean a great deal to her at the time, and according to Easton,
"[Ann] preferred friendship to romance. And, Owsley was that
friend." Constant companions, they went to movies, visited art mu-
seums, attended lectures, or just sat in the parlor and discussed books.
Owsley, of course, played Ann's brother in her first major film hit, *Holiday*. (Many feel that Owsley's performance outclassed Lew Ayres in
the 1938 remake.) Soon after Easton's visit, Ann and Monroe were re-

united on radio in a repeat performance of their roles. NBC's *Chateau Hour* aired *Holiday* on April 25. Ann felt it an honor to be asked to repeat her role in Barry's play, saying, "It is like meeting old friends to be Linda again."[40] It was fortuitous that Ann would reenact the part before leaving for Europe. Life was mirroring the role that catapulted her screen career. Where Linda had left behind a life that had stifled her spirit, Ann was leaving behind the confines of Hollywood and eclipsed stardom. At this point in his own faltering career, the troubled Owsley, who was typecast as drunks and cads, had an uncanny resemblance to his characters. The following year, his life in shambles, Owsley died in a San Mateo sanatorium of acute alcoholism and heart failure at the age of 36.[41] Owsley, who never married, bequeathed all his belongings to a phantom "wife" in his will.[42] Three days after the *Holiday* broadcast, Ann let it be known that *The Witness Chair* would not only be her last picture for RKO, but for Hollywood. [43]

Ann's legacy as being standoffish with reporters would hound her exit as a screen diva. Bay Area columnist Wood Soanes shed no tears at her exile from RKO. Ann's contract had come up for renewal, but the studio was no longer interested. Soanes' heart bled, not for Ann, but for studio publicity agents who had struggled to make excuses for her dismissive attitude toward the press. Soanes mentioned Katharine Hepburn, another publicist's nightmare, following in Ann's departing footsteps. "Hepburn in the throes of temperament has meant no skin off my rather expansive proboscis," wrote Soanes. "The little lady entered Hollywood under a curious delusion of grandeur. Possessed

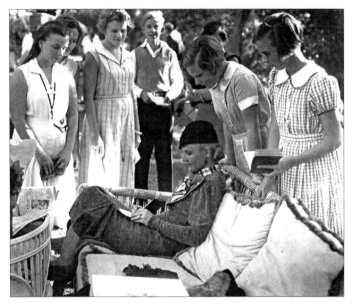

Usually standoffish with the press as well as fans, Ann
takes the time to sign autographs. (c. 1935)

of a certain amount of talent, she seemed to feel it incumbent upon
her to go eccentric in order to attract attention. It was dandy while
she was a box office sensation, just as it was when Miss Harding was
riding the crest of the wave. But the parade appears to have passed
her by."[44] Henry Sutherland of the United Press referred to Ann and
Hepburn as "second rate divinities." "Their sets are closed," he lamented, "They must not be seen, although Hepburn can be heard …
all over the lot. Their stories must be chosen with the greatest care,
chiefly with a view to flattering tender egos. Miss Hepburn [pushed]
newspapermen around railroad stations. Now newspapermen are
not allowed close enough to be pushed. La Harding, never precisely
a torrid temperament, has acquired aloofness as an added charm."[45]
Producer Samuel Briskin was just as eager to see the "freckled" Hep-

burn, amid her own string of box-office flops, disappear from the lot as he was Ann. After the departure of Irene Dunne, Ginger Rogers was RKO's most favored female, albeit, at this point, she was chiefly considered the "other half" of the Astaire-Rogers team.

As Ann prepared to leave for England, the press disclosed that Harry Bannister had married Leah Welt, a forty-two-year-old widow and former resident of Dayton, Ohio.[46] Welt had starred in Harry's production of *The Drunkard*. The news came as a relief. Perhaps now, Harry would leave his ex-wife alone. Ann's spirits soared, not only because of new direction, but the promise of new romance. A talented and highly respected conductor had piqued her interest. As it turned out, Harry *wasn't* all that happy. In a desperate attempt to bar her from leaving the country, he swore out a warrant for Ann's arrest.

(Endnotes)

1   "Shirley Temple Main Attraction at Box Office," *Port Arthur News*, 12/15/35
2   Eleanor Barnes, review of *The Lady Consents, Illustrated Daily News*, 2/6/36
3   James Francis Crow, review of *The Lady Consents, Hollywood Citizen News*, 2/6/36
4   Edith Dietz, "She's Through with Suffering," *Oakland Tribune*, 2/23/36
5   Louella Parsons column, *San Antonio Light*, 11/5/35
6   "Ann Harding Weeps as She Leaves Hawaii," *Oakland Tribune*, 11/17/35 (Sawbridge, who was involved with the African Theater in WWI, would retire in 1946. He died in Tucson, AZ 4/16/74)
7   Western Union telegram, 11/25/35, (Gail Cohen collection)
8   W. Lee Cozad, *Those Magnificent Mountain Movies*, c. 2002, pg 172
9   "Star Sees Role as Moral Indicator," *Los Angeles Evening Herald Express*, 11/13/35
10   Rudy Behlmer, (Polly Platt interview) from *Henry Hathaway*, Scarecrow (London), c. 2001, pp 116-117
11   Rudy Behlmer, (Polly Platt interview) from *Henry Hathaway*, Scarecrow (London) c. 2001, pg 115 Author James Bawden interviewed Hathaway shortly after his 84th birthday for the *Films in Review* article "Henry Hathaway" (March 1984). Hathaway stated that Ann kept wondering when Cooper was going to "start to act." She then accused him of stealing scenes from her after she saw the dailies.
12   www.theyshootpictures.com Henry Hathaway, c. 2002-2009
13   Lyn Haney, *Gregory Peck*, Carroll and Graf Pub., c. 2005, pg 238
14   Orson Welles, Peter Bognanovich, Jonathan Rosenbaum, *This is Orson Welles*, Da Capo Press, NY. C. 1998, pg 222
15   Lynne Myddleton, "The Ann Harding the World Never Sees," *Film Pictorial*, December 12, 1936
16   Reference to John Halliday taken from a letter Ann had written to Jasper Deeter (fall 1928). She made the comment after seeing Halliday a magician in *The Spider*. Howard Gotlieb Archival

Research Center, Boston University

17   Ann Harding, "Charm in Men," *Movie Classic*, October 1935
18   Freda Bruce Lockhart, "Lunch with Ann Harding," *Film Weekly*, November 21, 1936
19   Bildad, review of *Peter Ibbetson*, *Wisconsin State Journal*, 1/30/36
20   Review of *Peter Ibbetson*, *Film Daily*, 10/31/35
21   Edwin Schallert, review of *Peter Ibbetson*, 11/15/35
22   Elizabeth Yeaman, review of *Peter Ibbetson*, *Hollywood Citizen News*, 11/15/35
23   Andre Sennwald, review of *Peter Ibbetson*, *New York Times*, 11/8/35
24   Willa Okker, "The Hollywood Parade," *San Mateo Times*, 10/16/35
25   John Springer, "Great Movie Stars—Where Are they Now?" *Screen Stories*, February 1963
26   Chester B. Bahn review of *The Lady Consents*, *Syracuse Herald*, 2/17/36
27   Eleanor Barnes review of *The Lady Consents*, *Illustrated Daily News*, 2/6/36
28   H.M. Levy review of *The Lady Consents*, *Oakland Tribune*, 2/21/36
29   B.R.C. review of *The Lady Consents*, 2/6/36
30   William J. Mann, *Behind the Screen*, Viking Press, c. 2001, pg 137
31   Ann Harding, "Dress Your Personality," *Charleston Gazette*, 6/19/36
32   Grace Grandville, "The Almost Perfect Face," *Oakland Tribune*, 6/28/36
33   Grace Grandville, "The Almost Perfect Face," *Oakland Tribune*, 6/28/36
34   James Robert Parish, *The RKO Gals* ... pg 34
35   T.M.P. review of *The Witness Chair*, *New York Times*, 4/18/36
36   Chester B. Bahn, review of *The Witness Chair*, *Syracuse Herald*, 5/4/36
37   Richard B. Jewell, *The RKO Story*, Arlington House, (London), c. 1982, pg 95
38   "Air Warning Given Nation," *Los Angeles Times*, 4/2/36
39   Frank Easton, "Her Boarding House Days," *Modern Screen*, June 1936
40   Article, *The Amarillo Globe*, 5/6/36
41   "San Mateo Officials Hide Death of Harlow Friend," *San Mateo Times*, 6/9/37
42   John Hix, "Mystery Will," *Oakland Tribune*, 10/7/37
43   Wood Soanes, "Curtain Calls," *Oakland Tribune*, 4/28/36
44   Wood Soanes, "Curtain Calls," *Oakland Tribune*, 3/11/36
45   Bildad, "Theater News," *Wisconsin State Journal*, 3/5/36
46   Leah M. Welt, passport (4/14/23) – At the time of her marriage to Bannister, it was reported that she was 34 years of age. She was actually 42. Welt's first husband, Ervin M. Welt, died in the World War.

Ann poses for one of her last (and exquisite) glamour shots for RKO. (1936)

15
Candida & The Conductor

A few weeks prior to Ann's departure for England, Los Angeles society was abuzz with the upcoming concert of the world-acclaimed Philadelphia Orchestra under the baton of Leopold Stokowski. Ann, who frequented the symphonies and Hollywood Bowl, invited several friends to join her for the April 28 event. Before the program, scenarist Gene Markey (*Baby Face*) sat down in an empty seat directly in front of her to chat. The two had remained friends since Ann produced his first play, *The Eskimo*, in Detroit. The renowned American conductor Werner Janssen was with Markey, and Ann made a point to invite both men to her home after the concert. By the end of the evening, Ann and Janssen had made an indelible impression on each other.

When Markey and Janssen arrived at Ann's, it was late. Markey, failing to locate his chauffeur, had wanted to go home. Janssen wouldn't hear of it, and insisted they hire a taxi to take them in the direction of Pyramid Place. As if being transported to Valhalla, they got out of the car to hear the strains of Wagner's *Valkyrie* coming from inside Ann's hill-top home. When they entered the living room, they could see Norma Boleslavsky seated at Ann's beautiful ebony Beckwith concert grand piano. Maneuvering through the seated guests and a flood of melody, Ann made her way to greet the late arrivals. As the evening proceeded, Ann was conscious of Janssen's brilliant eyes following every move of his charming hostess. After a private chat together, Ann invited him to play. He sat down graciously, and offered a tender selection by the composer he understood best, Jean Sibelius. Soft music filled the room evoking images of mirrored lakes and long twilights from Sibelius' Finland. The music ended. Ann and her guests sat in silence, spellbound by what they had heard. "I shouldn't have played so long," Janssen apologized. "So long!" Ann exclaimed. "You should play forever!"[1] Janssen never forgot her words.

A few weeks later, Ann left for London. Werner Janssen was in Hollywood completing his score, and first screen assignment, for the Gary Cooper film *The General Died at Dawn*. Paramount thought the time was ripe for better film scores, and Janssen's 600-page effort, in which each character had their own musical motif, was a revelation and would garner him an Academy Award nomination. It is likely Janssen mentioned to Ann that he was sailing for London in August. As it would turn out, Ann's own departure for England was more like an escape from the law.

On March 8, Harry Bannister had made demands that Jane visit him for three weeks on his farm in Stewartsville, New Jersey. He had heard about Ann's proposed six-month stay abroad, but she would not agree to his wish. Jane was in a private school; in fact, she was scheduled to graduate at the end of May from Hammond Hall along with June Lockhart (daughter of actor Gene Lockhart). According to The Los Angeles Times, both girls had written "exceptionally nice poems for the school annual."[2] On March 10, Ann obtained court permission from Judge Lewis Howell Smith to go ahead with plans for her and Jane to leave the country. Ann stated in open court that Bannister was fighting her trip for the sole purpose of demanding more money.[3] A week before their departure, Bannister's attorney filed in Reno to reopen the court battle over control of Jane. Roland "Rich" Woolley, again representing Ann, stated, "The entire matter ... was settled last October. ... The custody of the child was given to Miss Harding."[4] Woolley emphasized that Bannister only made an effort to visit Jane three times from 1932-1935. Woolley confirmed, "From letters and wires in our possession we have every reason to believe that his pursuit of Miss Harding is motivated by ulterior designs only."[5] Ann, in an attempt to take a break from Bannister's latest maneuver, joined Claudette Colbert and Virginia Bruce to see Norway's sensational champion woman figure skater, Sonja Henie, at the Los Angeles Polar Palace. As the press swarmed around, Ann reminded them that she had contracted to film in London the previous year. "This contract was widely publicized," she said, completely exasperated. "There is nothing secret about it."[6] On May 28, in flight from his threats and with Bannister and his attorney in hot pursuit of her, Ann, Jane and her nurse, Katherine Smith, made haste to Quebec to sail on the Empress of Australia. The Canadian port was beyond the usual legal obstacles. To prevent any intervention from Bannister en route, four lawyers traveled with Ann, armed with documentation that would refute any of Bannister's claims.[7]

"Ann Harding Outsmarts Bannister," read the headline on May 30. In a surprise strategy, Ann and Jane boarded the Europe-bound liner Duchess of Atholl, which had departed from Montreal, before Bannister realized what was happening. During their breathtaking escape, Roland Woolley whisked Ann, Jane and her nurse from the Chateau Frontenac Hotel by freight elevator a few minutes before Bannister arrived in the main lobby. From there, they hired a small speed boat and overtook, in midstream, the towering *Duchess of Atholl*. Also accompanying this "flight" was Ann's (and Garbo's) agent, Harry Edington, and his wife, actress Barbara Kent. When Bannister, now graying and sporting dark glasses due to an eye affliction, arrived at the hotel, Ann was still registered as a guest. He wailed to reporters, "Reports that I am trying to balk my wife's plans in order to obtain money are absolutely untrue. I love my daughter and I want her. I believe if I permit her to accompany Miss Harding to England I will lose her forever."[8] (This, from a man who was willing to hire someone else to raise his daughter should Ann lose custody.) Still unconvinced of Ann's "secret" departure, Bannister and a Provincial detective went aboard the *Empress of Australia*, searching frantically for her.

As the *Duchess of Atholl* steamed out of the St. Lawrence River to the open sea, Bannister, angered by being outsmarted, swore out a warrant for Ann's arrest, charging child abduction. The warrant stated that Ann was in violation of the Canadian Criminal Code, which made it an indictable offense, punishable by five years in prison, to take away a child under 14 without the consent of the father or mother. Bannister discussed overtaking the *Duchess of Atholl* by plane and interceding the ship at Father Point, 200 miles away.[9] Ann had had enough. Making herself available to the press, she finally admitted paying Bannister $100,000 for full custody, and that he was "now trying to boost the ante."[10] "Canadian attorneys advised me that Mr. Bannister might wangle several weeks' postponement while the Canadian courts reviewed my documents," said Ann. "There was no question of the ultimate results, but I couldn't afford any delay as my English contract requires that I report in London not later than June 8."[11] Clad in a blue Japanese dressing gown, Ann concluded bitterly, "He has tried to be a nuisance to me everywhere."[12] "It seems that because Mr. Bannister is the father of my daughter I am to be continually harassed and annoyed and that I am to be threatened by him indefinitely. I do not intend to accede to his demands. I do not fear his threats."[13]

From Washington, D.C., Secretary of State Warren Hull contacted the American Embassy in London demanding that they aid and assist Ann Harding "in any move her former husband … may make to gain custody of their daughter in England."[14] Roland Woolley had conferred with Hull on the matter, but this didn't stop Bannister. Provincial authorities dispatched a cable to Great Britain requesting Ann's arrest the moment she disembarked at Southampton. "I am going back to New York," fumed Bannister, "to consult with authorities about the arrest of Miss Harding as a fugitive from justice. She is taking our daughter away from me entirely and plans to establish permanent residence abroad. I claim that's nothing less than kidnapping, and she will have to take the consequences."[15] One news editorial scoffed at Bannister's claim, congratulating Ann for an "abduction" that had been well publicized several months in advance.[16] On June 4, Bannister petitioned the court in Reno to reconsider the last custody decision, which he called "fraudulent."[17]

Reporters in Scotland indicated that Ann "virtually sizzled with indignation" upon her arrival. "Mr. Bannister's attempt to invoke the law against me is an utter farce," she snapped. "I am amazed at the degree of importance apparently given to his futile and untenable efforts to embarrass me."[18] Later that same day, the liner docked in Belfast. She kept her daughter in seclusion, and cried, "Beast!" when one curious male passenger attempted to peer into Jane's locked room. As news-hawks descended upon the *Duchess of Atholl* in Liverpool, Ann thought it best to send Jane ashore separately in disguise. From there, they traveled by train to London, where Ann promptly began to look for a place in the country.

In Hollywood, the film community was assured by Judge Lewis Howell Smith that the British courts would uphold his order granting Ann permission to take Jane to England. "This is probably the first time," said Louella Parsons, "that a case of this sort has arisen in motion picture circles in which an English court must decide on the legality of a Los Angeles judge's ruling." The columnist stated that those close to Ann regretted that she had to resort to subterfuge to get her own daughter out of the country. "We must admit," Parsons rallied, "when the ruse was successful we all felt like cheering."[19] Judge Smith had also ruled that if Bannister in any way interfered with Ann's departure, that all stipulations would be null and void. After Bannister's behavior, the contingency that Ann had to be back in California by December 10 was history. He would have to reach into his own pocket to pay for his expensive array of lawyers from New York, Quebec and England.

On July 15, Bannister did *himself* in when he pressed charges in the aforementioned extortion case. The humiliation from this embarrassment left him seeking seclusion. Bannister's attorney withdrew all motions against Ann on July 24.

Camille was still being considered as a vehicle for Ann when she arrived in England. Richard Boleslavsky, who had directed Ann on stage in *Taming of the Shrew*, was being sought to direct. When production

Noel Coward accompanies Ann to the Theatrical Garden Party held at London's Royal Regents Park. (June 1936)

on Garbo's *Camille* began in July, Trafalgar Studio had to come up with something else for Ann. In the interim, Ann made only one "official" public appearance. Playwright Noel Coward coaxed her to be his guest at the Theatrical Garden Party held at Regents Park. The annual social event was attended by every celebrity, proceeds going to the Actors' Orphanage, of which Coward was president. Ann looked exquisite in a flowing chiffon gown and regal cape of silver fox. Although fans followed her in "mobs," Ann was amazed at the courtesy she received. Soon afterwards, actor Douglass Montgomery included Ann in a private frolic along with her agent Edington, Guthrie McClintic (producer-director and husband of Katharine Cornell), actress Judith Anderson, writer Dwight Taylor, and stage designer Jo Melzeiner. After cocktails at the Lansdowne House in Berkeley Square, the party dined at the famous "society restaurant" Quaglino's. Next up, was the French chanteuse Lucienne Boyer at the Café de Paris. The "bash" ended up at the celebrated 400 Club.

Avoiding further brouhaha, Ann focused on the sixteenth-century mansion she had discovered in the heart of England's wooded countryside. When Jane was not in day-school, the two roamed the surrounding flower-bordered lawns and sat beneath nodding trees edging a small, tranquil lake. They visited neighboring stables to watch the polo ponies. Some evenings Ann went into London to attend one of the West End theatres. When Hedda Hopper showed up on Ann's doorstep—they took off on a long motor tour of English cathedrals. Ann complained that Hedda "walked her legs off."[20]

During these sojourns, what impressed Ann was the English attitude toward celebrities. She found more genuine privacy and rest in England than she could have imagined. She told British columnist Max Breen, "Your people are kind, considerate. I just love the English countryside, but I was terribly afraid it would be the same here as in Los Angeles, where you can't step out of your car without being surrounded by autograph-hunters. But I've driven all round Buckinghamshire, and no one has taken the slightest notice. Even when I *know* I've been recognized, as for instance at the Theatrical Garden Party, people have been courteous and forbearing, and ... and English. Why do you suppose there is such a difference?"[21] Breen simply stated that the English preferred their stars to be a little remote—to keep their "aura of illusion." Pausing for a moment, Ann agreed, "I believe that's it," she said. "We've all experienced the feeling when someone touches us and says in a disappointed tone: 'Oh—you're real after all!'" Contrary to Ann's "melancholy" screen image, Breen observed her talking gaily, with a ready wit and natural humor. He felt *reality* to be one of her greatest assets. "I have never met, in the theatre or the film-studios, anyone who put on fewer airs or made less fuss," Breen stated. "Yet when she enters a crowded restaurant, there is no room for doubt that a star has come in. The general reaction is immediate."[22]

London columnist Lynne Myddleton was also surprised by the "real" Ann. "I liked Ann Harding from the very moment I saw her," wrote Myddleton. "I liked her for taking the trouble to know my name;

for the genuine friendship of her smile; for her complete unaffected-ness. By the time our meal was ended I loved her for her charm, for her courage and her sensitiveness. Here is someone not out to create an impression ... she is too much of a human being for that."[23] Over a meal of smoked salmon, Ann talked of her hopes that Jane would know the happiness of privacy and independence. "If you are independent," Ann said, "you cannot be hurt. If you have privacy—then you have independence! Poor innocent that I was when I first came to Holly-wood." Ann solemnly admitted that she worried, "Often, and *often*." Myddleton noted a look in Ann's clear blue eyes that forbade the ques-tion, "What over?" With a sudden smile Ann flashed back at her, "Oh, I take it out on myself—by playing the piano all night! After which I feel terribly tired physically, but vividly refreshed mentally. Beethoven, Chopin—they seem to do something in me when I'm worried ... But I don't let them do things to other people! I play for myself that is all. My fingers just won't move if I have an audience." While isolated in her thoughts and feelings, Ann selected only the masters to soothe her emotional scars. Both Beethoven and Chopin were essentially lonely men who sought solace in themselves. Ann took a package of cigarettes from the pocket of her mink coat, while Myddleton offered one of her own. Ann shook her head. "I just can't bear any other cigarette but a good American *Spud*." Along with a good chuckle, Ann proposed, "You'll never be able to write 'Ann Harding leaned back in her chair, lei-surely smoking—a *Spud*! It just doesn't do. It is quite unmentionably unglamorous; something to be spoken of only in a whisper!"

Ann began filming that fall. *Love from a Stranger* was based on a 1936 British stage hit by Frank Vosper, who based his play on the Agatha Christie short story *Philomel Cottage*. The film was shot in the new studio erected by producer-director Alexander Korda, a few miles outside London. Over games of pinochle, Ann and scenarist Frances Marion, an *avid* Agatha Christie fan, conferred about the script. Ann prepared herself for what was essentially a melodramatic and gripping thriller—completely different from her usual trend. *Love from a Stranger*, as conceived by Marion's fine script, builds up slowly until the audience realizes they are about to witness a chilling murder. The climax comes as a complete surprise, and offered Ann, the potential victim, a meaty assignment. Ann's co-star, Basil Rathbone, studied for his role as a homicidal maniac by visiting a London insane asylum.[24]

After winning thousands of pounds in a French sweepstakes,

Ann turned the tables on tormentor-husband Basil Rathbone in the British release *Love from a Stranger* (1937). (Released by United Artists)

Carol Howard (Ann), an office worker, quits her job and advertises to rent her flat. She's going to enjoy her fortune and do some traveling. A prospective tenant named Gerald Lovell (Rathbone) catches her off guard with his worldly manner. Although friends suspect she's living in a fool's paradise, Carol is completely charmed. She and Lovell wed, and settle down in a cottage in Kent. This "idyllic" situation darkens with Lovell's storms of rage. He becomes less cunning in concealing his mental "affliction." The oddest things set him off.

While examining a book on unsolved crimes, Carol discovers a photograph of her husband's face under a fringe of whiskers. She learns he had previously married three wealthy women, lured them to cozy country "digs" then murdered them. By the time Lovell, in love with his own brilliance, invites his fourth victim, Carol, to help "tidy up" his darkroom, she's prepared to do some thorough housecleaning of her own. Over dinner, Lovell recalls the strange "ecstasy" he felt as a boy, anticipating whippings from his old school master. As she is unable to escape (Lovell has bolted all the doors), she listens to him rave on, while replenishing his brandy. And, she's getting angrier by the minute. "A woman's weakness is a man's opportunity," a tipsy Lovell crows. "You have exceptional insight into things!" Carol remarks, before her own rage and the power of suggestion manage to "kill" him. Her life depends on what she says. She declares she put poison in his coffee. But, did she? Lovell, you see, has a heart condition.

While the film captures the tone of Agatha Christie's creation, one wishes Lovell's torture had lasted much longer. Adding to the suspense was an excellent, if intermittent, score by England's own Benjamin Britten. He was not happy with how his music was used, and this spirited work would be his only composition for the commercial cinema. Ann's overall impression of England's film industry was not enthusiastic. She found it "unsound." "Production is hand-to-mouth, due to lack of organization and preparation," Ann told the New York press. "The British producers are not prepared to live up to their contracts."[25] She had gone off salary for three months in order for Trafalgar to prepare the script and production.

When released in the US (April 1937) by United Artists, film critic Norbert Lusk found *Love from a Stranger* "the strongest and most adult picture" on Broadway, and "a gripping study of a maniac." "While it is no surprise to find Mr. Rathbone excelling in a realistic role and offering a complete and convincing study of psychopathic insanity," Lusk deduced, "it distinctly is a novelty to find Miss Harding forgetting her superficial mannerisms and playing with compelling authority and simplicity, gaining in strength as the part demands, until finally she holds her own with her co-star in a magnificent climax."[26] The *Los Angeles Examiner* agreed, saying, "The acting of Ann Harding and Basil Rathbone surpasses anything they have done yet on the screen. Miss Harding puts aside her whimsicalities to do some of the finest acting of her career."[27] Rathbone felt that Ann would return to Hollywood "a bigger star than ever."[28]

Time magazine predicted that audiences, accustomed to Ann's "smug" displays of "feminine understanding" on screen, would derive "sadistic satisfaction" from what fate offered her in *Love from a Stranger*. Ann felt the same way. During her screen sabbatical, she said, "Frankly, I was bored with those tear jerking roles. I just took a leave of absence. I knew that if I continued making pictures, I'd forever be cast as the weeping willow."[29] Sam Goldwyn cabled Ann in London, asking if she would be interested in joining John Boles for a remake of the popular tearjerker *Stella Dallas*. She declined. By then, Ann was happily focused on her return to the stage in George Bernard Shaw's *Candida*. *Stella Dallas* was more appropriate for Barbara Stanwyck (*Ladies They Talk About, Baby Face*), who grabbed a hold of the brassy, socially inept character and received an Oscar nomination. As for *Love from a Stranger*, it set a precedent for its genre. A decade later, *Los Angeles Times* critic Edwin Schallert declared that, as a psychological thriller, *Love from a Stranger* was "the daddy of them all."[30] Director Richard Whorf's 1947 remake pales in comparison—its climactic scene, complained *The New York Times*, exploded with "all the thunder of a cap pistol."[31]

Back in Hollywood, Ann's friend, Mary Astor, was making headlines of her own in a courtroom battle far more sensational that anything Ann had experienced. In Astor's attempt to regain custody of her four-year-old daughter, Marylyn, from ex-husband Dr. Richard Thorpe, Astor's diaries, dating from 1929, were being used as evidence. To complicate things, according to Astor, a forgery of her diary was released to the press prior to the introduction of the authentic diary. The "forgery" detailed the sexual appetites of her various lovers, including playwright-director George S. Kaufman. The newspaper version of one Astor entry read: "Ah, desert night—with George's body plunging into mine, naked under the stars …." In Astor's 1959 autobiography, *My Story*, she elaborates on her and Ann's relationship prior to the sizzling headlines. "I told [Ann] something of the situation surrounding my divorce and the diary," wrote Astor. "She is a very vital woman, and a fighter, and she was indignant that I should be forced to submit to such conditions. She had a lawyer whom she praised highly to me, Roland Rich Woolley. She urged me to at least tell Woolley the story and see what he thought of it. ... I yielded to her constant pressure."[32] It was Woolley who suggested that Astor sue for the custody that had been denied her in the original divorce case.

After the trial got underway, the *Oakland Tribune's* headline was typical: "Friends Drop Mary Astor as Case Gets Hot." When Astor looked out over the sea of faces during her trial, her "friends" were somewhere else. Only Ruth Chatterton, seated inside the railing next to her, was present to whisper, "Courage, my dear! Be brave."[33] Chatterton (Astor's co-star in *Dodsworth*) stayed with her until the bitter end. Woolley stated that Ruth should have been a lawyer. The two had many heated discussions in his office. When the judge questioned Astor about her other close friends, Ann's name came up. Astor lamented that, like Ann, she had to buy her way out of her 1933 divorce settlement. "This applies to me," she stated, "and to my best friend Ann Harding. I had to buy Dr. Thorpe's half interest in my Toluca Lake home before I could call it my own."[34] Unfortunately, as Ann was in England, she was unable to testify on Astor's behalf.

After the trial, the judge impounded Astor's diary, which was sealed in a bank vault for sixteen years. It was never made public, and, by court order, a judge was required to witness its burning in 1952.[35] Astor was awarded divided custody of daughter Marylyn. In her autobiography, Astor states quite frankly, "Sexually I was out of control. I was drinking too much, and I was brought up short when I found myself late in the evening thinking someone was 'terribly attractive'— and wondering the next morning, 'Why, why?'"[36]

After Astor's ordeal, Ann wrote her a sympathy letter. Ann told Astor that she would like to stay in England another six months, and implied that she wouldn't mind staying abroad permanently to avoid further entanglements with Bannister.[37] On October 19, Ann filed notice for an additional leave of absence for Jane. Ann indicated that she was still wrapping up her film obligation, and had been offered an opportunity to act on stage. It came as no surprise when Bannister "vigorously opposed" this move. His affidavit was presented in Los Angeles court on November 10. He expected to win. Ann's own affidavit presented by Roland Rich Woolley, ripped Harry Bannister apart. She stated:

> I have always maintained Jane at my own expense.
> She is devoted to me. Her father never seeks to see
> her. He does not communicate with her. He sends
> no presents or good wishes. He takes no interest
> in her education or spiritual upbringing. As far as I
> know he does not devote any time in serious busi-
> ness or matters and earns no money. I struggle for
> my living. He does not keep me.[38]

Judge Lewis Howell Smith made the decision to strike nine-tenths of Bannister's affidavit from the court record. Ann was given until June 10, 1937, to return.[39]

After the completion of *Love from a Stranger,* Ann had no further business in London … except romance. She and Werner Janssen had rekindled their flame. That fall, the couple had arranged to meet at the home of a mutual friend. Their first evening together, Janssen persuaded Ann to play the piano for him. He *liked* what he was listening to. Their meeting was followed by roses, and many telephone calls, as Janssen was conducting the London Symphony Orchestra for the British Broadcasting Company. This explained, in part, why Ann was so keen on prolonging her stay in England.

When an offer came to take the lead in *Candida*, Ann was doubly interested. That is until she was reading novelist Charles Morgan's critical review of Shakespeare's *Antony and Cleopatra* in the *London Times*. Morgan tore foreign actress Eugenie Leontovich to shreds, saying she brought the bard's work to "incomprehensible ruin" with her garbled accent. Ann muttered to herself, "They aren't going to do that to me!"[40] She thought about reviving *Holiday* in its place. The hands of fate stepped in, and Ann found herself face-to-face with Morgan at a dinner party. Morgan, you may recall, was the author of one of Ann's favorite films, *The Fountain*. "What is a British accent?" she boldly asked him. "What is typical? There are six well-educated English men and women sitting around this table, and no two of you speak in the same way!" Morgan may have not had an answer, but he *did* urge Ann to take on Shaw. "You'll be perfect for it," he insisted. With nothing to fear from the *London Times* critic, Ann went into rehearsal.

On November 27, Ann had tea with George Bernard Shaw and Mrs. Shaw, in their flat overlooking the Thames. Afterwards, Ann indicated that Shaw, who had insulted so *many* people, was unable to recall the 1933 incident when he had brought her to tears. "I went, fully expecting to be withered by a barrage of cutting remarks," said Ann. "But nothing of the sort happened. Mr. Shaw was a charming host."[41] The new production of *Candida* would be the first version of the play presented in London since the original (1894). Ann was thrilled at the prospect of working with the playwright. While prepar-

ing for a preliminary run in Blackpool, England, Shaw read the first act
to Ann and cast members and then arranged some of the scenes. He
did this, according to Ann, without "a single wise-crack." "Frankly, Mr.
Shaw is a much better playwright than he is an actor," Ann admitted.
"He was—well, shall we say a little on the overboard side?" Although
Shaw had frequent run-ins with the director, Irene Hentschel, Ann felt
that "inwardly" he was pleased with their "realistic" take on *Candida*.
"Mr. Shaw never admits he's wrong, you know," Ann emphasized. Although Ann had played *Candida* at Hedgerow, the London production
became her most treasured memory.[42] After touring the provinces, the
play had a brilliant and successful opening at London's Globe Theatre
on February 10, 1937. Critics' enthusiasm of Ann's performance went
beyond her wildest dreams. Charles Morgan raved,

> Miss Harding is faultlessly clear; her occasional
> emphasis on a syllable that we should not empha-
> size does no harm to any phrase of Candida's; her
> appearance is more beautiful on the stage than on
> the screen; and, as soon as it was clear that she was
> indeed a stage actress and not merely a film star con-
> descending to the old-fashioned medium of Garrick
> and Irving, the whole audience was with her. The
> result was the best performance of the play, and of
> the part, that I have seen.[43]

Morgan delineates Ann's performance as the wife of the popular, if
pompous, Reverend Morrell, while noting the warmth she brought
to the role. He doubted that Shaw fully intended on the interpretation Ann brought to the role. Morgan felt that Shaw was incapable of
writing with love, and that his large-scale portraits were admired for
their ruthlessness as well as their wit. When Candida tells her hus-

band that she is not deluded by his Sunday sermons and that his congregation follows him only because they are in love with him, Ann,
the actress, wasn't being cynical. She was not out for a cruel attack.
Morgan felt Ann was sacrificing a spectacular effect by being gentle
in the opening act, but admitted, "What Miss Harding is doing is to
prepare the way for her last act, which, when it comes, is magnificent."
The preacher takes his wife's loyalty for granted, as well as her virtue. The fact is, Candida has befriended a young poet, Marchbanks,
who builds castles in the air for her. Upon finding this out, the stiff-
minded and unimaginative preacher asks her to choose between husband and her poet "lover." In the last act, Candida proceeds to show
her impregnable husband that all his success and strength spring
from her. It is her triumph-song. The scene was usually interpreted
to show a woman who enjoys manipulating male puppets. "But Miss
Harding," writes Morgan, "while preserving the comedy, implies the
phrase 'I love you' and so provides Mr. Shaw with his only character
in whom kindness, charity and wisdom shine through the wit." In all
fairness, Shaw, a Fabian socialist, was very much concerned with human rights. He deplored the exploitation of the working class, was a
champion of equal rights for women, and deplored corporal punishment in schools (which was prevalent at the time).

During her record-breaking run in Candida, Ann and Werner filed
their intent to marry at a London registry office. Ann had hoped to
keep the affair private, and was distressed when reporters showed up.
"This all leaked out in New York," Ann told them. "I hoped to keep it
quiet until after my stage appearance in London. I cannot bear a whole
mob of people worrying me about my private affairs. I wanted to be allowed to get on with my job, and I have nothing more to say about Mr.

Ann married conductor Werner Janssen in London, January 17, 1937.

Janssen or myself."[44] Janssen told the United Press, "All I can say is that I am very happy." The two married the following day, January 17, 1937, at Caxton Hall Registry. Ann wore a gray-black frock, waist-length fur cape, and a small black hat. Apologizing for her frequent sneezing during the ceremony, Ann explained, "I've got the flu."[45] The happy couple was joined by actor Clive Brook as best man. Brook and Jane, dressed in yellow, signed as witnesses. "Mummy's married, mummy's married," the eight-year-old announced excitedly, as she hopped and skipped out of the building. Outside the hall, Werner kissed both Ann and Jane, while a crowd gathered around cheering. The happy trio sped away by automobile. Ann enjoyed a 30-hour break from *Candida* before her opening in Brighton, January 19. She was in better humor by then, telling reporters, "I'm so happy. Jane loves her new daddy and he is so fond of her I'm almost jealous."[46] Not everyone in Hollywood was surprised by the news of the marriage. Paramount's musical director, Borris Morros, stated that prior to Ann's departure for England, Janssen frequently took breaks while working on *The General Died at Dawn*, and was usually nowhere around at lunch. Ann's favorite snack spot was right across the street from the studio.[47]

Amid all the excitement, someone had been overlooked ... Janssen's wife. News articles stated simply that Janssen was divorced. They failed to point out that the divorce took place two weeks prior to the London ceremony. Janssen and Ann were in the throes of romance while members of his family in Indianapolis were attending school and enjoying their home in the Ruckle Park area. Elsa Schmidt Janssen and Werner's children, Werner Jr., age 12, and Alice, age 13, were used to Werner Sr.'s absence. He was rarely home, although Elsa accompanied him on his Scandinavian tour in 1935. The couple wed in 1922. The Associated Press contacted Elsa the day before the Harding-Janssen nuptials. Very few papers (I located only one out of hundreds) bothered to relay Elsa's good wishes to her ex-husband: "I wish him the best of luck and still greater success."[48] Mrs. Janssen had been granted $100 monthly support for the two children.[49]

Like Ann, Werner Janssen was ambitious and driven. He could work a two-day stretch without sleep in preparation for a concert. This, in part, explained his gaunt, hollow-cheeked appearance. When Werner was a boy, his father was outraged by the young man's desire to pursue music. When he was in his late teens, the two had words, and there was an unpleasant parting that lasted years. Werner was born June 1, 1899, in Manhattan. His father, a wealthy Hofbrau owner, was counting on Werner to carry on the tradition he had proudly established. Declining his father's offer (and $250,000) Janssen put himself through Dartmouth, receiving his music degree in 1921. He literally

starved while mastering the violin, until he joined Leo Reisman's popular nightclub orchestra. Leaving Reisman, Janssen's compositions for
such Broadway shows as *Ziegfeld Follies of 1925* (wherein he played
the music for Will Rogers' rope act) and Jeanette MacDonald's *Boom
Boom* (1929) became national hits. He admitted averaging three
hours of sleep per night during these years, as he was absorbed in writing his own original compositions combining jazz and classical motif.
In 1929, his acclaimed symphonic poem, *New Year's Eve in New York,*
was presented by the Rochester Philharmonic Orchestra.

Janssen had had his share of run-ins. Broadway's Schubert Brothers had fired him, as had the National Broadcasting Company. A
church in Hanover, New Hampshire, kicked him out after he segued
from sacred music to the pop tune "Where Did You Get That Hat?"
just as an ornately bonneted lady sat down in her pew. Janssen left
the US in 1929.[50] Three years of study in Italy with mentor Ottorino
Respighi yielded Janssen an opportunity with the Royal Orchestra of
Rome. As a guest conductor he then made a splash with Europe's great
orchestras: Budapest, Leningrad, Vienna, Copenhagen, and Paris.
While in Berlin, Janssen was imprisoned for six weeks, and ousted
by Goebbels (the Reich Minister of Propaganda) because of his refusal to remove Mendelssohn's Third Symphony from the program.
After Janssen conducted a concert of Jean Sibelius compositions in
Helsinki (February 1934), the Finn composer enthused: "You may
say that tonight Finland has for the first time discovered my music.
This achievement of Janssen's is the deed of a hero." That November,
as associate conductor (with Arturo Toscanini), Janssen was the first
American-born maestro to lead the New York Philharmonic. *Time*
magazine reported that Janssen "failed to click." On a happier note,

columnist George Ross mentioned an "elderly and especially proud looking gentleman fastening his eyes upon the 'batoneer.'" Werner and Papa Janssen had happily reunited.[51] Janssen rebuffed any criticism. He followed the counsel of Sibelius himself, who, after getting flack that his music wasn't complex enough, told his devotees, "Pay no attention to what critics say. No statue has ever been put up to a critic."[52] Janssen then made the curious if fortuitous decision to score music for Hollywood films.[53] (As a struggling student, he had played at motion picture houses for silent films.) His music for *The General Died at Dawn* (1936) was first of his six Oscar-nominated scores.

After a record-breaking run, Ann cancelled her British contract at the end of March, and turned *Candida* over to Diana Wynyard. As Janssen had received an invitation to conduct the Helsinki Symphony in an all-Sibelius concert, he and Ann decided on a Scandinavian honeymoon. She would finally have an opportunity to see her new husband conduct. This would be Janssen's sixth Sibelius concert for the Finns. For his services to Finnish music, he had already been awarded the country's highest governmental honor: Knight First Class of the Order of the White Rose. Standing room only houses greeted Janssen and Ann. They cheered and cheered his performances. The honeymooners' car was covered with thousands of flowers after each concert. The couple then scheduled a lengthy Scandinavian cruise. As a result, Ann's hair became a shade more golden.

Returning to the US, the newlyweds, along with Jane, and good friend Norma Bolslavsky, arrived in Quebec on April 24. They immediately boarded a train bound for New York. The day before their arrival, Judge Roy of Quebec's Court of Sessions, cleared Ann of Bannister's kidnap charge. "I can't understand what the man was thinking of," said Judge Roy. "He must have known the facts that have been presented and yet he deliberately lied in order that the warrant be sworn out. I cannot see how any man could have such nerve. I officially announce that the motion of Miss Harding's counsel to have the warrant quashed is granted by this court."[54] Ann told the press that she didn't anticipate any further trouble. She was wrong. Bannister was preparing a new custody fight to welcome Ann home.

Arriving in Los Angeles by train, Ann amiably answered questions and greeted the press warmly, even inviting them to breakfast. When asked to talk about how they met, Janssen pleaded, "Must that be told?" Ann, with gracious assurance took his hand. "Sometime it must be told," she smiled. "Let it be of record." Janssen commented that they would be making Hollywood their home. When asked about career plans, he enthused, "Our careers are just beginning. Of course, the climax of my career is Mrs. Janssen ... she is the world to me." Ann felt she was "living in a new world." Janssen blushed while listening to Ann's assessment of him. "You know," she said, "what Mr. Janssen has doesn't come into the world very often. Better judges than I have so stated. I can only realize." It was obvious that Ann had made a transition, and taken respite from her own career, rhapsodizing, "His career is of much more importance than mine."[55] It was a conscientious decision on Ann's part, and she was now committed to enjoy her husband and his musical ambitions.

Ann was impressed by Janssen's limitless energy. He had no interest in his awards, or the past. "If a man writes a thesis for which he gets a medal," said Janssen, "he doesn't talk about [it] ... he goes to work. Why should I talk about the long dead past when I have work to do?"[56] And to work he went. Having a keen interest in radio, and radio acoustics since the late 1920s, Janssen signed for his first broadcast series with the *Chase and Sanborn Hour*. He carefully selected an orchestra of 36 members, a number he felt ideal for the airwaves. He was delighted by NBC's move to bring Toscanini out of retirement, feeling it would go down as being momentous. "The radio is doing its part to advance the cultural side of music," declared Janssen, "and it is to the radio that America may look for its most significant musical progress."[57] Three days before the first broadcast, Ann hosted an informal reception at the Hollywood Knickerbocker introducing her husband to the film capital. She talked about his career, stressing his work with European symphony orchestras. News reports, as an inside joke, referred to the couple as "Ann Harding and her equally famous husband." There would be no threat of Janssen being referred to as "Mr. Ann Harding." Ann made sure of it.

As a highlight to Janssen's premier program, Ann guest starred in a scene from Molnar's *The Guardsman*, which had served as a sparkling vehicle for Broadway legends Lunt and Fontanne. On the same bill was W.C. Fields, who blamed "pernicious dandruff" (instead of alcohol) for his year-long absence from screen and radio. Looking a bit pale, Fields had fainted fifteen minutes before the broadcast. A trouper, he insisted on going on. When asked about Ann, Fields declared, "I know Miss Harding very well. How's your partner, Mr. Laurel?" Host Don Ameche chimed in to remind Fields that Mr. Laurel's partner was a Mr. Hardy. Ann offered no quips of her own, but stunned the audience with her brilliant execution of Molnar's temperamental Viennese actress. She allowed the dialogue to propel the scene from *The Guardsman*, while her actor-husband (Ameche), disguised as a

At a tea held at LA's Knickerbocker Hotel, Ann introduced her new husband to the film colony, May 4, 1937.

Russian guard, attempts to test her fidelity. The question for the audience was, "Did he give himself away?" When the husband accuses his wife of being unfaithful, she scoffs, claiming, despite his disguise, she recognized his kiss. Columnist Paul Damai thought Ann did "marvelously" with the less-than-subtle Ameche. Dressed all in white, she looked particularly beautiful—her eyes glued on Werner during the remainder of the program. Jane sat in the first row, her blonde braids tied with red bows. After the program, and a short session with the cameras, Jane placed her hand affectionately into what one reporter called "the raw-boney one of her lanky new father."[58]

In July, following her sister Edith's marriage to Jack Mackenzie at St. Alban's, Ann made her first professional appearance since leaving England. She recaptured her "weeping willow" mood for director Cecil B. DeMille's *Lux Radio Theatre*. James Stewart co-starred in a presentation of the tragic and tearful *Madame X*. Stewart's natural style and sincerity was a perfect match for Ann, as she enacted the hardboiled woman who murders a man in an attempt to protect the name of her long-lost son. Ruth Chatterton had received an Academy Award nomination for Best Actress for the part in the 1929 film.

The *Los Angeles Times* wailed that the creaky offering was "outdated." "Ann Harding struggled valiantly but futilely against boggy odds," said the review. "James Stewart tried to play the sympathetic son ... but it was no go."[59] Stewart seems to falter in the final moments of the courtroom scene, but judging by the applause, the audience didn't seem to care. A few months later, film audiences again lapped up the "creaky offering" in the MGM remake starring Gladys George (as they would a 1966 Lana Turner version). Ann and Stewart had the usual "guest star" interview with DeMille after the performance. Stewart asked Ann about her English film experience. She wasn't sure *Love with a Stranger* was exactly an "English" production. It had an American producer (Harry Edington), an American director (Rowland V. Lee), and an American cinematographer (Philip Tannura). She switched the subject to Stewart himself. "When I left Hollywood a year ago," she began, "everyone was talking about that amazing young actor who lived with Henry Fonda, owned 30 cats, and played the accordion." To the audience's delight, Stewart hemmed and hawed a few amusing remarks.

On July 20, Janssen made his debut for one of the Hollywood Bowl's "Symphony Under the Stars." Although the season had opened two weeks earlier, the number of arriving celebrities and exploding flashbulbs made it *seem* like an opening. Janssen's reputation, along with ample press coverage of his recent marriage, filled the amphitheatre. *Time* magazine reported, "Ann never took her eyes of the lanky, gloomy-looking young man who conducted all five scores from memory. When, at the end of Sibelius' *Scenes Historiques*, the audience called Janssen back nine times, she looked as pleased as he."[60] Conductor Otto Klemperer was quoted as being "overwhelmed" by Janssen's brilliance.

During the fall, Ann and Werner took a motor trip through New England. It was clear that her priorities were aligned with her husband's. Giving a vivacious smile to reporters, she declared, "I wouldn't even think of talking of future plans now."[61] Any plans, at this point, were all about Janssen. He had received an assignment to conduct the Baltimore Symphony Orchestra's winter season. In December, while conductor Janssen conferred with the Baltimore Orchestra, Ann started apartment hunting. The Baltimore hotel where they were registered was on the black list of the musicians' union, of which Janssen was a member. "Ann was perfectly fine about it," Janssen told the press. "Of course, she belongs to a similar organization in the motion picture field."[62] (Ann was still a SAG officer.) Harry Bannister showed up in Baltimore during this time for what must have been an awkward reunion with Jane. She was accompanied by her nurse and a bodyguard. Bannister had put aside his threats of more custody battles.

Janssen won plaudits from Baltimore's music critics for his debut, and Ann was given equal credit for having "jam packed" the city's old Lyric Theatre. Opening with Mozart's overture from *The Magic Flute*, the program concluded with the final excerpt from Sibelius' First Symphony. Janssen took five curtain calls, while audience members craned their necks toward the darkened box where Ann was seated. Afterwards, he was joined by Ann and his mother, Alice Janssen, in his dressing room.[63]

There were concerns that Janssen was conducting Ann's professional as well as personal life. The couple denied this, saying Harry Edington was still Ann's active manager. The workaholic and self-driven maestro pointed affectionately to Ann, declaring, "She is teaching me to relax."[64]   When Janssen's schedule let up, Ann finally decided to do something of her own: a west coast production of *Candida*. The revival was staged by Phyllis Loughton, who, along with her husband, writer-director George Seaton, had occupied Ann's house while she was in England. Loughton headed Paramount's Dramatic School, and Ann, as a favor, had once addressed her students. In early August 1938, Ann and Loughton started rehearsals at LA's Biltmore Theatre. Vincent Price was approached by producer Homer Curran to play Morrell, but Paul Cavanagh was signed instead. Ann selected 22-year-old Clay Mercer to play the young poet Marchbanks, finding him "ideal."[65] A tryout of the play was held at the San Francisco Curran Theatre. "Miss Harding understands the meaning of the play," praised one review, "and she takes her part beautifully—not spectacularly, but simply through her skill. Miss Harding conveys her tenderness toward her troubled mate and her recognition of his need with a warmth that brings the play to a glowing conclusion."[66]

Bay Area critic John Hobart interviewed Ann for the *San Francisco Chronicle*, noting that her clear blue eyes looked "straight on" at him. "Any actress who thinks she is going to score a spectacular success as *Candida*," Ann told him, "is fooling herself. It is quite wrong, I think, to make a brilliant person out of her—for the sake of showmanship. In fact, it can't be done. For two acts all the part amounts to is practically a walk on. Candida has a most limited imagination; she is kind and sympathetic; but she is not especially clever; she can't even understand Marchbanks' poetry."[67] Ann didn't see *Candida* as a true love-triangle play. Her attitude toward her supposed "lover," the young poet Marchbanks, was "motherly, friendly, solicitous."

Opening October 10, Ann's engagement at the Los Angeles Biltmore Theatre received a great deal of press. She admitted she had stage offers to return to London, and in New York producers were sending her scripts. She declined every bid. "Owing to my husband's engagements in the films," Ann explained, "and in Baltimore with his orchestra other months, I can only undertake a short season and prefer to enjoy that up and down this Coast."[68] On opening night, Joan Crawford, recently christened "box-office poison," wore enough ermine to outfit a royal coronation. She was escorted by Randolph Scott. Others on parade were Mary Astor, Gilbert Emery, director Frank Borzage, Hedy Lamarr, Robert Young, Hedda Hopper, and John Barrymore bellowing, "Where's the men's room?"[69] Los Angeles drama critic James Francis Crow found the throng of celebrities to be a "lamentable" distraction as wandering eyes inside the theatre strayed from the stage to see if that was really "Randolph Scott sitting in the eighth row center with Joan Crawford." Crow decided *Candida* was both "pleasant and pithy," but not strong enough to rival such counter-attractions as Crawford and Scott. His review of Ann's performance was mixed. "Miss Harding is assured and serene, as *Candida* should be," wrote Crow, "and her anger waxes becomingly in the last act when she puts her husband and her lover in their places; but at no time did Miss

(October 1938) Ann appeared in *Candida* at the Los Angeles Biltmore Theatre. Here she reads her own congratulation wires to co-star Paul Cavanagh.

Harding impress me as having attained that mastery of men which is supposed to be, after all, *Candida's* chief characteristic."[70] Crow's review blasted Ann's protégé, Clay Mercer, finding that his "extravagant hysteria" passed credibility. (Mercer's career went no further than becoming a page boy at NBC.) The *Los Angeles Examiner* countered Crow, calling Mercer's performance "capital," and Ann's portrayal "exquisite." "Her controlled power," read the review, "moved the house to waves of applause."[71] "This *Candida* outshines by far the one offered by Katharine Cornell several seasons ago," raved *Los Angeles Times* critic Edwin Schallert. "It is unquestioned that the play points a new way for Miss Harding. It suggests the impression that probably even Shakespeare should be a seasonal experience for her."[72]

At the end of October, Ann finished the last of her scheduled performances for *Candida*. Werner opened his second season with the Baltimore Symphony, with Ann at his side. She stated that she was "tired of reaching for movie plums," and that it would "take an earthquake, or something similar to it" before she would ever make another film.[73] After several slight tremors over the next few years, Ann would finally succumb to the "Lion's Roar" and Louis B. Mayer at MGM.

(Endnotes)

1   Jerome Manfort, "Ann Harding's Romance with Werner Janssen," *Hollywood*, September 1937
2   "Beau Peep Whispers," *Los Angeles Times*, 6/4/36
3   "Ann Harding Victor in Tilt With Ex-Mate," *Hollywood Citizen News*, 3/10/36
4   "Ann Harding In New Fight," *Los Angeles Times*, 5/21/36
5   "The Threat Hanging Over Ann Harding!" *Hollywood*, September 1936
6   "Ann Harding Says Ex-Mate Threatens Her," *Nevada State Journal*, 5/24/36
7   "Ann Harding in Secret Dash to Balk Ex-Mate," *Los Angeles Times*, 5/29/36
8   "Ann Harding in Secret ..."
9   "Ann Harding's Arrest Asked by Bannister," *Los Angeles Evening Herald Express*, 5/30/36
10 "Ann Harding May Face Extradition," *Los Angeles Times*, 5/31/36
11 "Ann Harding Scoffs at Canadian Charges," *Los Angeles Times*, 5/30/36
12 " Bannister Flies to Block Ann Harding Trip Abroad," *Los Angeles Evening Herald Express*, 5/29/36
13 "Ann Harding Charges Bannister Demands More Money," *Nevada State Journal*, 5/25/36
14 "American Envoy Urged to Assist Ann Harding," *Los Angeles Times*, 6/4/36
15 "Harry Bannister Chasing Ann Harding and Daughter," *Los Angeles Examiner*, 5/31/36
16 Editorial, "Ann Harding," *The Daily Gleaner*, (Kingston, Jamaica), 6/6/36
17 "Ann Harding's Child's custody Fight Reopened," *Los Angeles Times*, 6/5/36
18 "Ann Harding in Britain, Irked at Ex-Mate," *Los Angeles Evening Herald Express*, 6/3/36
19 Louella Parsons, "Ann Harding's Custody Fight," *Los Angeles Examiner*, 6/7/36
20 News article, *Los Angeles Times*, 6/17/46
21 Max Breen, "Ann Harding is Fun!" *Picturegoer Weekly*, 11/21/36
22 Max Breen, "Ann Harding is Fun!"
23 Lynne Myddleton, "The Ann Harding the World Never Sees," *Film Pictorial*, 12/12/36
24 Lloyd Pantages, "I Cover Hollywood," *Los Angeles Examiner*, 12/3/36
25 John T. McManus, "Returning Lady of Sorrows," *New York Times*, 5/2/37
26 Norbet Lusk review of *Love From a Stranger*, *Los Angeles Times*, 4/25/37
27 Jerry Lane review of *Love From a Stranger*, *Los Angeles Examiner*, 7/28/37
28 "Basil Rathbone predicts Rosy Future for Ann Harding in England," *Hollywood Citizen News*, 2/2/37
29 Connie Curtis, "The Return of Ann Harding," *Hollywood*, September 1942
30 Edwin Schallert column, *Los Angeles Times*, 6/28/46
31 T.M.P. review of *Love From a Stranger*, *New York Times*, 11/28/47
32 Mary Astor, *My Story*, Doubleday and Co. c. 1959, pps. 189-190
33 "Friends Drop Mary Astor as Case Gets Hot," *Oakland Tribune*, 8/11/36
34 "Hollywood Chatter," *Shoppers News*, 10/8/36
35 Mary Astor, *My Story*, pg 196
36 Mary Astor, *My Story*, pg 197
37 "Ann Harding May Stay in England Permanently," *Los Angeles Times*, 10/14/36
38 "Hurls New Charges at Husband," *Lowell Sun*, 10/20/36
39 "Ann Harding Keeps Child," *Los Angeles Times*, 11/11/36
40 Jessica Ryan, "Frankly Forty," *Movieland*, October 1945
41 John Hobart, "Actress and Sage," *San Francisco Chronicle*, 10/2/38
42 John Springer, "Great Movie Stars—Where are They Now?" *Screen Stories*, February 1963
43 Charles Morgan review of *Candida*, (reprinted for *The New York Times*), 2/28/37
44 Joseph W. Grigg, "Ann Harding Will Marry New York Composer," *Nevada State Journal*, 1/17/37
45 "Ann Harding is Married to Musician," *Daily Mail* (MD), 1/18/37
46 "Play Must Go On" Halts Honeymoon of Ann Harding," *The Evening News* (MI), 1/19/37
47 Robbin Coons, "Hollywood Sights and Sounds," *Billings Gazette*, 2/9/37
48 "Best of Luck," *Kingsport Time (TN)*, 1/17/37
49 "Divorce Granted," *Hammond Times*, 12/31/36

50   Alva Johnston, "American Maestro," *The New Yorker*, 10/20 & 10/27, 1934

51   George Ross, article on Werner Janssen, *Lima News*, 7/13/36

52   Jean Sibelius, Neworldencyclopedia.org

53   "Discord in Los Angeles," *Time*, November 10, 1941

54   "Court Clears Ann Harding of Kidnapping Her Child," *Los Angeles Times*, 4/23/37

55   "Jane Bannister Under Guard," *Los Angeles Times*, 4/26/37

56   Jerome Manfort, "Ann Harding's Romance with Werner Janssen," *Hollywood*, September 1937

57   Richard D. Saunders, "Janssen, Ann Harding Sight Radio Progress," *Hollywood Citizen News*, 5/5/37

58   Betty Klingensmith, "Studio's Stars and Stooges," *Hammond Times*, 5/18/37

59   Dale Armstrong, "Radiopinions," *Los Angeles Times*, 6/20/37

60   "Sibelius for Hollywood," *Time*, 8/2/37

61   "Ann Harding and Mate Back," *Los Angeles Times*, 10/20/37

62   "Symphony Conductor Apartment Hunting," *Evening Times (MD)*, 12/7/37

63   "Ann Harding Aides in Lauding Mate's Music," *Fresno Bee*, 1/10/38

64   John Selby, "Janssen to Wield Baton," *Ogden Standard Examiner*, 1/2/38

65   "Miss Harding Set to Open in *Candida*," *Daily News*, 8/30/38

66   John Hobart review of *Candida*, *San Francisco Chronicle*, 9/26/38

67   John Hobart, "Actress and Sage," *San Francisco Chronicle*, 10/2/38

68   Florence Lawrence, "Ann Harding Prefers California Footlights," *Los Angeles Examiner*, 10/2/38

69   Frank Morris, "Hollywood 's Notables Dazzle Theatergoer," *Winnipeg Free Press*, 10/26/38

70   James Francis Crow review of *Candida*, *Los Angeles Evening Herald Express*, 10/10/38

71   Florence Lawrence review of *Candida*, *Los Angeles Examiner*, 10/11/38

72   Edwin Schallert review of *Candida*, *Los Angeles Times*, 10/11/38

73   "Quits Pictures," *Monessen Daily*, 12/22/1938

Eyes in the Night (1942). (MGM)

16

"There is no play as fine
as a Beethoven symphony"
—Ann Harding – (1942)[1]

As Europe engaged in war, Ann became known primarily as an orchestra conductor's wife and former actress. She had no regrets about abandoning her film career. In Baltimore, she wrote the talks Janssen gave to youthful audiences attending his Young People's Concerts. In Los Angeles, Ann held court backstage, as unofficial hostess, after each of Janssen's performances. When Stravinsky was guest conductor with Janssen, Ann was in her glory, greeting noted musicians and former film acquaintances such as Jerome Kern, Eric Wolfgang Korngold, Frances Marion, Basil Rathbone, Edward G. Robinson, Jean Hersholt, and Walter Wanger. Wanger had used Janssen almost exclusively to score his films (ie., *Winter Carnival, Eternally Yours, House Across the Bay*). "To live constantly in a musical world is more than enough for me," stated Ann.[2] She refused to be interviewed as a film star, but graciously responded to questions asked to Mrs. Werner Janssen, wife of the famous maestro. Ann pointed out the compatibility factor in her marriage:

> The world of the theatre and the world of music are
> closer than any other careers. Their people speak

the same language. Their temperaments are alike. One career speaks volubly to the other.[3]

In November 1939, shortly after the Nazi-Soviet Pact, the Russians attacked Finland, leaving many homeless. In December, Ann and Werner paid the expenses for an all-Sibelius benefit concert chaired by Herbert Hoover, head of the Finnish relief organization. Proceeds went immediately to the Finnish Red Cross. After Janssen resigned as conductor of the Baltimore Symphony, he and Ann were able to offer Sibelius a haven with them should the composer wish to leave the war-torn country.[4] On the home front, Janssen was a champion for the thousands of union musicians across the country. "It's a tragic thing," he pointed out, "Most of them are out of work. There is no telling how many … really good musicians are on the verge of starvation. The trouble seems to lie with the people who are in charge of musical enterprises … a conductor's name doesn't have to end in 'insky.' There are plenty of Americans who are fully as good musically as any eccentric imported from Europe."[5] Musicians were begging Janssen for work, which prompted him in 1940 to form the Janssen Symphony in Los Angeles—45 musicians of soloist caliber. "Forty-five men on their toes," said Janssen, "make better music than 95 half asleep." (Pun intended for the rival Los Angeles Philharmonic.) Janssen's orchestra made a profit, a rare occurrence in the symphonic world. "We don't have lady solicitors making the rounds asking rich folks for donations," said Janssen, "We depend on people who want to hear good music, well played, and we're making money."[6] In 1941, while Janssen made accusations that the LA Philharmonic had stolen his first cellist and two violinists, Ann finally made moves to revive her film career.

Ann had not performed professionally since Orson Welles persuaded her to join his *Mercury Theatre* (*Campbell Playhouse*) on radio, for the dramatic lead in the Nobel Prize-winning play *Craig's Wife* (March 1940). Welles played the hen-pecked husband to Ann's cold, manipulative wife. Ann's clipped, efficient, and determinedly intimidating performance left an indelible chill on the listener. Ann had also done a dramatic sketch on *Rudy Vallee's Variety Hour* (May 1939). The one-act play by Milton Geiger, *Until Tomorrow*, featured a gallant Ann saving a suicidal WWI vet (Vallee). Coincidentally, the following year, Vallee purchased Ann's home on Pyramid Place. (Vallee christened his new home "Silvertip," and he would live there until his death in 1986.)

Columnists reported in January 1940, that Ann was to co-star with Basil Rathbone (as another wife-killer) for Paramount's *Destiny*. It is doubtful that Ann showed any real interest in doing this B-thriller, re-titled *The Mad Doctor*.[7] The role she thought ideal for her screen return was Ma Baxter, from Marjorie Rawlings' Pulitzer-Prize-winning novel, *The Yearling*. In the spring of 1941, Ann tested at MGM to play the stern dirt-farmer's wife whose loving nature is buried under a crusty shell. Spencer Tracy was to play her husband. Filming began in the Florida Everglades, but without Ann. She was frank about her disappointment. At Tracy's request, Anne Revere got the part. However, production came to a halt after three weeks. Despite a $500,000 outlay, rain, heat, insects, and conflict between director Victor Fleming and Tracy, put *The Yearling* on the shelf for several years. Louis B. Mayer, intent on getting Ann to sign a contract, wanted her for *Mrs.*

Miniver (a role Norma Shearer had rejected)—that is, until his pet star, Greer Garson, showed interest. The role earned her an Oscar.[8]

At this point, Ann put Hollywood on the back burner once more as she and Jane accompanied Werner on his South American good-will concert tour. They left on May 9, 1941, aboard a steamer for Rio de Janeiro where two concerts were scheduled with the Brazilian Symphony Orchestra. Janssen conducted symphonies in Sao Paulo, Buenos Aires, Montevideo and Santiago. They returned to Hollywood in July.[9] As usual, Ann had to get court permission to take Jane, age 13, on the trip. Ann was tired of the court procedures involved with their numerous travels. In January 1942, with the help of attorney Roland "Rich" Woolley, Harry Bannister was finally "put to rest." A Los Angeles court decided that Ann could take Jane out of the state without seeking permission. At long last, she had exclusive custody.[10]

Jane had grown to 5' 7" over the previous year, and got away with patting Ann on the head saying, "All right, Mother," whenever she was reprimanded. Ann laughed, "It's difficult to get any discipline when I have to look up, stretch my neck, and try to say in a commanding tone, 'You mustn't do that, Jane.'"[11] Since the sale of her home on Pyramid Place, Ann and Werner had purchased screenwriter Rian James' (*The Witness Chair*) 80-acre ranch in Fallbrook, near Oceanside. It turned into an enjoyable and productive venture. Each week they sent off crops of avocadoes from their orchards and crates of eggs produced by 350 chickens. Two of Rin-Tin-Tin's grandchildren romped around the property. The ranch became more of a weekend retreat when Janssen committed to radio's *Standard Symphony Hour* in Los Angeles. He and Ann bought a two-story home on North Sierra Drive in Beverly Hills. Jane enrolled at Beverly Hills High School. Once again, it seemed like an ideal time for Ann to engage in some acting.

In the spring of 1942, Ann focused on exercise and diet to get in "photogenic condition" for the lead in Warners' *Watch on the Rhine*. Producer Hal Wallis had requested her and it appeared Ann's chances were good.[12] Her co-star from *The Fountain*, Paul Lukas, would repeat his Broadway role in Lillian Helman's anti-fascist play. In London, Ann's friend Diana Wynyard had a great success in the female lead. Days after Ann's test, Bette Davis dropped into Wallis' office, asked about role, and that was the end of it for Ann.[13] In the process, Ann had lost ten pounds—for that she was grateful. "I feel so wonderful," she said. "My family were so good about my dieting and helped me follow my schedule. I went to Terry Hunt's every day, took gymnastics, and massages and really made a business of getting thin. You feel so well, both mentally and physically."[14] Hunt was famous for his Hollywood Health Club, and as Mary Astor was a patron, it is likely she had recommended him. So, it was a slimmer Ann who finally accepted a role in the MGM "B" mystery-thriller titled *Eyes in the Night*. She had no problem playing stepmother to Donna Reed, and claimed she was content slipping into character roles—as she put it, "Before I had to go around holding my face up with my hands."[15] "I've always had a horror of trying to look younger than I am," she admitted. "I'm coming back with an eye toward playing parts that will fit me ... let me be my own age. I didn't care about getting a big role for my comeback. I didn't expect that."[16] "But as far as signing any contract," she stated, "that will depend on the result of my work in *Eyes in the Night*. If I do sign, I'd want it to be with MGM."[17] She saw her return as an experiment. *The New York Times* found the result to be a "tidy and tingling little thriller." The review found Ann, and other supporting players, "adequate to their undemanding roles."[18]

On screen, Ann, retired actress Norma Lawry, finds out that her former beau and co-star Paul Gerente, is romancing her stepdaughter Barbara (Reed). Norma calls him "a rotter," but Barbara refuses to listen. Later, she goes to his apartment to find not only Norma, but Paul's dead body. Concerned about a scandal, Norma begs Barbara, who suspects her of the crime, not to phone the police. "That phony nobility of yours really makes me sick!" Barbara snarls. Neither realizes that said "rotter" was in cahoots with Nazi agents who are after a scientific formula belonging to Norma's husband (Reginald Denny). Tension builds when Norma asks a longtime friend Mac Mclain (Edward Arnold), who is also a detective, to help with her dilemma. What makes the story unique is that Maclain is a blind man, with more insight and "vision" than all the other characters combined. Arnold - delightfully over the top - and his detective dog Friday steal the show. The suspense stays intact, along with a dash of risqué humor. At a crucial moment, Friday is distracted by the large, curly rump of a French poodle, wiggling her canine charms. For an unlikely happy ending, Barbara takes a shine to Maclain. With shades of sexual masochism, she agrees to have him "paddle her canoe" if she doesn't behave. It was Arnold, a fan of author Baynard Kendrick's novel (*The Odor of Violets*), who approached MGM to shoot the story. Director Fred Zinnemann didn't care much for the film, but it proved a surprise hit when revived at a 1986 Berlin Film Festival honoring his career. "The only pleasures were working with the marvelous Ann Harding and with Donna Reed, who was delicate and charming," recalled Zinnemann.[19] He remembered the dilemma of Arnold blowing his lines until the eighth or ninth take, and Friday, after only two takes, running away to hide. "*Eyes of the Night* was something of a nightmare," Zinnemann insisted. "I was determined to do as good a job as possible. It seemed a terribly serious thing at the time … a caption to one of the reviews of it simply read: 'Dog Bites Axis.' That reduced the situation to its proper importance …a good lesson to learn in those days."[20] Zinnemann would direct such classic and Oscar-winning films as *From Here to Eternity* (1953) and *A Man for All Seasons* (1966).

A wave of nostalgia overcame reporter Robbin Coons when he walked onto the MGM set in June of 1942. "Even from far across the stage," said Coons, "you couldn't mistake that voice, low and vibrant, with music in it. Going closer to watch the rehearsal, you could see her sitting up in bed in a blue negligee, her hair streaming far down her shoulders. Nobody else in pictures has hair exactly like it—a soft cascade like white gold. It had to be Ann Harding … one of the best actresses and most beautiful women this town ever saw."[21] When he asked about her reputation of being difficult at RKO, Ann readily agreed, "I was, but only over bad stories." Ann still found contentment in work, but said it was work "with all the old strain of being a star left out!"[22] In *Eyes in the Night*, Ann, looking more mature, was excellent in what was essentially an ensemble piece. Her acting style had ripened—she was obviously a seasoned player, and the most realistic person in the cast. But, for those used to seeing Ann Harding carry a film, her return was a letdown. While she resigned herself to what *was* offered, losing "real parts" such as in *The Yearling* and *Watch on the Rhine*, were understandably major disappointments.

After the completion of *Eyes in the Night*, it was mentioned that Ann would be featured in Metro's all-female cast *Cry "Havoc"*—a war drama set on the Pacific island of Bataan. It was also announced that she was up for the title role of the celebrated female chemist/physicist in MGM's *Madame Curie* (which had been purchased for Garbo). The role went to Greer Garson, who was building a reputation herself for playing women prone to struggle and sacrifice. She had played Ann's role in the 1941 remake of *When Ladies Meet*. After seeing *Random Harvest* and *Mrs. Miniver*, Broadway columnist Dorothy Kilgallen feared Garson would become the "Ann Harding of the 1940s." "You may recall," said Kilgallen, "Miss Harding enjoyed a ... vogue during which she played every chin-up-smile-while-they-torture-you role her studios could unearth for her ... The result was she wept herself out of the public taste."[23] Garson's "vogue" lasted about as long as did Ann's. Nearly all of her post-war films for MGM lost money. As in Ann's case, if Garson's studio had allowed their "gallant lady" an occasional "shady lady" role fans wouldn't have pigeon-holed her so easily.

The animosity between the United States and the Soviet Union was put to the test after Hitler's attack on Russia (June 1941) and Japan's attack on Pearl Harbor. Washington, DC, in developing an alliance with the Soviets (which FDR considered crucial to victory), persuaded Hollywood to create some pro-USSR films. Warner Brothers, a champion of Roosevelt's New Deal, was the first to step in, and opted to tell the story based on the bestselling memoir, *Mission to Moscow*, by former US Ambassador to Russia (1936-38) Joseph E. Davies. Ann tested for the role of the Ambassador's wife. The *real* Mrs. Davies thought her the ideal choice. Due to President Roos-

Mission to Moscow (1943) Ann, in a wardrobe provided by the very character
she was playing (Marjorie Merriweather Post Davies) is flanked by
Russell Hicks, Eleanor Parker and Walter Huston. (Courtesy of
Jenny Paxson and Larry Smith)

evelt's friendship with Davies, the White House had an important
hand in what was seen on screen. FDR and Davies met monthly to
discuss the film's progress.[24] The result was a handsomely-mounted
piece of propaganda.

While on assignment, Davies had gauged the potential of Soviets
joining the fight against the growing threat of the Axis powers. He
seemed unaffected by the arrest of thousands of Russians and foreign-
ers. The US embassy staff threatened to resign after his inaction to
help Americans who had disappeared, or whose passports had been
confiscated. The falsification of history in *Mission to Moscow* covers
up the forced confessions and executions during the Moscow Trials
of 1936-38. Russia's invasion of Finland is explained away as an attempt to protect Finland from the Nazis. While generating favorable

imagery of the US and capitalism, *Mission to Moscow*, dubbed by many as "Submission to Moscow," was difficult for Americans to swallow. In the glorification of Stalin's Russia, Warners lost close to $600,000. The anti-Soviet *New York Sun* called the film, "a two-hour ... editorial." Nevertheless, *Mission to Moscow* served FDR's objective. Davies delivered the film to the Kremlin in May 1943, and Stalin authorized its distribution—the first Hollywood product to be shown in Soviet Russia since the ban on foreign movies began in 1928. Drama critic Clyde Rowen's 1943 review of the film was rational and to the point. He felt *Mission to Moscow* was obvious propaganda, but "acceptable" in its attempt to unite two diverse cultures: the US and Soviet Russia. "Obviously, the facts are distorted," wrote Rowen, "but ... it is an absorbing document, well produced and filled with a sense of magnificence ... not to be dismissed lightly."[25] Historian Todd Bennett pointed out in a 2001 article in the *Journal of American History*, "Neither the film nor Roosevelt's approach was as 'naive' as critics have claimed."[26] Historian Bennett emphasized that *Mission to Moscow* "helped solidify the Grand Alliance at a particularly tenuous moment."[27]

Ann had signed on for what was considered to be a prestige role, receiving a hefty salary of $4,166 per week for six weeks. [28] Loaning Ann a wardrobe of smart suits, gowns and furs, the zestful Mrs. Davies was on the set almost daily. A powerhouse of a woman, Marjorie Merriweather Post Davies (mother of actress Dina Merrill) was a prominent socialite and head of General Foods, Inc. As the wealthiest woman in America, she selected Joseph E. Davies, a corporate lawyer, for her third husband, paying two million dollars to his ex-wife for the privilege. They married in 1935, just before his "mission" to Moscow. (Joseph's assignment came *after* Marjorie's generous contribution to

Roosevelt's re-election campaign.) It was known in Washington, DC, circles that Marjorie was bent on becoming an ambassador's wife.[29]

The voyage to Moscow was actually made in the opulent family yacht, *Sea Cloud*, as opposed to the ocean liner depicted on film. While in Russia, Marjorie thought it best not to flaunt her jewels, but the couple did satisfy their thirst for rare Russian works of art (at nominal prices)—many of which were expropriated from victims of the Stalin regime. Author Dennis J. Dunn, in his *Caught Between Roosevelt & Stalin*, states that the "truckloads of art" given to the ambassador and his wife were a reward for "Davies' favorable reports on the purges."[30] Little about the *real* Marjorie and Joseph Davies (played by Walter Huston) was revealed in *Mission to Moscow*. (At 71, Marjorie's last marriage to Herbert A. May, a top executive of Westinghouse, was short-lived. She learned he preferred members of his own sex. Herbert complained to a friend, "My God, she wants to do it every night!")[31]

"I think there's been a mistake in casting," Ann mused. "Mr. and Mrs. Davies should be playing themselves—they're both charming. But I'm playing the role as Mrs. Davies described it: an ambassador's wife is a background figure. She is pleasant and agreeable, a good hostess and a pleasant guest. I say 'How do you do?' a great many times—I'm trying to use different inflections on it." Ann laughed, "I'm afraid it's a bit part, really. Mr. Huston and I go through the story, observing a lot of fine acting by other people, but we ourselves don't have much to do." In spite of the fact that Mrs. Davies bought her husband's ambassadorship, Ann commented that her influence must be felt, but not seen. "Miss Harding gives a definitely feminine impression of Mrs. Davies," stated The *Los Angeles Times*.[32] "No great dramatics are required from either Huston or Ann," quibbled Hedda

Hopper. "In almost every case the scene belongs not to the stars but to a featured or bit player."[33] Hopper offered her cheeky take on *Mission to Moscow*: "If Joe Stalin doesn't give us everything we want after he sees it, then there's no gratitude in the world."[34] The gossip queen had a point. Max Steiner's score turns reverential when Ambassador Davies and his wife enter the Soviet Union. They marvel at the display of munitions and marching troops in the USSR, and thrill over the breath-taking *pas a deux* at the Russian Ballet (Cyd Charisse as the exquisite prima ballerina). An elaborate State Dinner is held in Davies' honor. On this festive occasion, a dash of humor manages to slip into the dry proceedings as Foreign Minister Litvinov (Oskar Homolka) and Davies discuss how Germany and Japan are devouring the world. During their "talk" we see a close-up of German and Japanese diplomats greedily stuffing their faces at a buffet table.

Amidst a parade of high-profile world dignitaries, Ann's role seems incidental. During one of Davies' "sanitized" industrial tours to see how farm tractors convert into Soviet army tanks, she is finally given a scene of her own. (It was added at the last minute at Mr. and Mrs. Davies' insistence.)[35] The Davies limo pulls up outside a Russian cosmetics factory run by Polina Molotov, a former propaganda commissar, and wife of the Premier. Upon entering the building, Mrs. Davies comments on the display of beauty products, surprised such luxuries were available in the Soviet Union. Madame Molotov replies that "feminine beauty" was not considered a luxury. A factory worker (Virginia Christine – TV's future Mrs. Folger) serves them tea, while Mrs. Davies tells an equally surprised Mrs. Molotov about the responsibility of running her deceased father's corporation. Both women are on equal footing. Molotov had thought American women were merely "ornamental." With all the political hype in *Mission to Moscow*, the most honest evaluation of the "world situation" takes place in the English countryside during Mrs. Davies's conversation with yet another woman, Mrs. Winston Churchill (Doris Lloyd). Over tea, Mrs. Churchill asks her, "Do you ever stop to think ... that men are always trying to make the world better or worse, where most women are content just to live in it?"

Mission to Moscow, along with Ann's next film, *The North Star* (Samuel Goldwyn's pro-Soviet propaganda), were used as "evidence" in the House UnAmerican Activities Committee (HUAC) investigation that began in 1947. As FDR had been involved with *Mission*, Jack Warner got off the hook, but screenwriter Howard Koch, whose credits included such patriotic and popular classics as *Sergeant York* (1941) and *Casablanca* (1942), wasn't as fortunate. Jack Warner had asked him to write propaganda, yet testified before the committee that Koch was a communist sympathizer. Koch was blacklisted— "thrown to the wolves"—to satiate the Committee's penchant for publicity and design to destroy careers.

Lewis Milestone, whose anti-war *All Quiet on the Western Front* (1930) had been universally praised, was signed to direct *The North Star* on a lavish scale. Avoiding the political ponderings of *Mission to Moscow*, the Lillian Hellman screenplay created an idealized version of "North Star," a farm collective on the Ukrainian border. The comrades in this idyllic communal setting are seen as freedom-loving people who take heroic stands against the brutal force of Nazi Germany. Unfortunately, the film wastes precious time establishing the folksy and tuneful life of the Soviets. Critics rightly complained. *The New York Times* commented on the "mixed theatrical forms," saying,

"When the people of the village gather for a sociable evening al fresco, it might even be a scene from *Oklahoma* ... when the bombs suddenly come raining down ... the style of the film abruptly changes to one of vehement reality. The switch is too obvious."[36]

The North Star might have had a different legacy had Hellman's script been scaled down. The most heartfelt moments come from the film's youth, particularly the developing romantic relationship of Anne Baxter (playing Ann's daughter) and Farley Granger (in his film debut). When the two are separated while running guns to the village guerrillas, Granger's character is blinded by a grenade. Their touching reunion has the intimacy audiences identify with and rally behind. The problem with *The North Star* is that it tried to be an epic. Surprisingly, the film garnered six Academy Award nominations (most notably: James Wong Howe, cinematography; Aaron Copland, music score). *Time* magazine appreciated the film's intent, "not primarily as a struggle for Communism, but as a heroic defense by the Russian people of their homes. Only by implication is *The North Star* propaganda."[37] After a brutal re-cut, *The North Star* was re-issued in 1957 as *Armored Attack*. A new narrative turned the story around until it became an anti-Soviet film about the 1956 Russian invasion of Hungary! *C'est la guerre*, Hollywood-style.

The *Los Angeles Times* complimented the actors: "Performances escape criticism from any quarter. All are considered excellent, with emphasis perhaps on Mr. Huston ... and Ann Harding who is said to be 'better than she has ever been.'"[38] This was a very generous assessment of Ann's contribution. If anything sealed Ann Harding's insignificance as a film star it was roles like this. The script affords her little dialogue. When aerial gunners shatter the village, she frantically runs after her youngest daughter, who doesn't understand what is happening. We next see her, in a state of shock, holding the girl's lifeless body. The scenario provides no opportunity for the expression of grief, no dialogue between her and husband (Dean Jagger) as they deal with their tragic loss. Ann's only "real moment" is when she boldly steps forward from a group of villagers to face a Nazi officer's query as to the whereabouts of her husband, the leader of the guerillas. Her voice deepens with resolve, "I cannot answer that question." We next hear her screams from inside the hospital where her arm and leg are purposely broken.   Los Angeles drama critic, and longtime champion of Ann, Edwin Schallert, felt her role wasn't "exactly worthy of her talents and her former stellar status."[39]

By the summer of 1943, Ann had completed her film work, and retreated to the ranch at Fallbrook. The banks of the Santa Maria River ran alongside the property—a perfect place for rest and seclusion, or so she thought. The US army had invaded their hideaway. Thousands of troops were encamped up and down the property line. After checking in on the six new great-grandsons of Rin-Tin-Tin, Ann promptly returned to her home in Beverly Hills.[40] "Suddenly, Camp Pendleton was right beside us," Ann stated. "We could scarcely get into our road for the jeeps. Bugle calls and building noises aren't exactly bird songs. And, gasoline rationing ended our necessary commuting."[41] The Janssens gave up their idyllic ranch life for the duration of the war. As Ann had done her bit on screen to strengthen ties with Russia, Werner put his own career on hold to help the war effort. In September, he announced he was going to work a swing-shift assignment for Douglas Aircraft, at $45 a week. Janssen was giving up thousands of dollars a week through his film, radio, and concerts, to do defense work. "I go to work at 4:15 pm tomorrow," said Janssen, "I'm carrying my lunch, and I'll be through at 12:45 in the morning. They'll have me, until the war is over, and I'll take a great deal of pleasure in thinking that I'll have a small part in building the bombers which are helping make things miserable for Adolf."[42] Janssen admitted that his son, Werner Jr., after completing basic flying training at Fort McClellan, had been the impetus for his own decision. Janssen was assigned to the Douglas materials purchasing department. He didn't give up music entirely, and continued with his Janssen Symphony Orchestra's fall series (October-March) during the war.

On October 1, Ann signed on for a top-billed part in Columbia's B mystery *Nine Girls*. "You naturally never get the choice parts when you free lance," Ann rationalized, "but I don't mind. As a matter of fact, I don't care to have a starring role any more, it absorbs me too much."[43] Ann also tested at Fox for the role of Woodrow Wilson's first wife, Ellen, in the grand biopic *Wilson* (1944). That role went to Ruth Nelson. *Nine Girls* was more demanding than Ann's previous two endeavors, and she delivered. As, Gracie Thornton, an instructor-chaperone of the Gamma Theta sorority, she discovers an unusual way of dealing with a selfish, spiteful girl named Paula (Anita Louise). "I'd like to take that girl apart and find out what makes her tick!" Gracie declares. Using the more expedient route—she murders her instead. That, in a nutshell, is the story, but the script, naturally, doesn't point a finger at Gracie. After all, she is contemplating marriage to Paula's father.

While attempting to frame her "favorite" student (Evelyn Keyes) for the murder, Gracie, pistol in hand, is foiled by the police. Her chilling stare freezes into space … in full recognition of her bitter end. The film, a "sleeper" hit when it was released, was revived at the Los Angeles's 2003 Cinecon event. Kevin Thomas of the *Los Angeles Times* complimented director Leigh Jason's "surprisingly fresh and fun" offering. "The 1944 *Nine Girls*," said Thomas, "attests to Jason's ability to turn a flop play into a lively treat. It's a little too easy to guess whodunit … but the film has such zest and humor that it scarcely matters."[44] Ann gets one line that was made-to-order. When the Olympic-bound "Butch" (Jeff Donnell) turns the radio dial to a classical station, another girl groans, "In heaven's name, what's *that*?" Ann's character gives her a look, then answers, "Well, it *happens* to be Beethoven's Eroica Symphony in E-Flat, Second Movement." During production, director Jason commented, "I have the same advantage in *Nine Girls* as Cukor had in *The Women*. It doesn't take a hero to direct that many women unless you have conflicting comediennes, or too many ingénues who just want to look pretty. Ann Harding, of course, does not conflict with the school girls. She gets her dramatic moments and no one is going to quibble with her."[45] Although *Nine Girls* meanders into comic relief to the point of distraction, today's audience gets a good chuckle when the nasty Paula wrangles a date with another girl's beau over the phone. "Suppose I pick you up and we'll do something gay!" she says cheerily.

Ann returned to the Warner lot in January 1944, for the more popular kind of American "propaganda"—a patriotic wartime comedy called *Janie*. She was reunited with Edward Arnold. They played Mr. and Mrs. Conway, the parents of a freshly-scrubbed and precocious teenager (Joyce Reynolds). Jack Warner had in mind something to compete with MGM's hugely successful *Andy Hardy* series. The picture rightly belongs to newcomer Reynolds, in the title role, but the script lacks the wistful and penetrating style of the Hardy films. *Janie* is blunt in the telling of a sweet and pampered girl who unwittingly supports the war effort by opening the family home to what appears to be a squadron of men from a nearby army base. She does this after Mr. Conway, a news editor, has warned the town about "wolves in uniforms." Amid all the shenanigans, Janie falls for a GI (Robert Hutton), who resembles James Stewart in looks and acting-style. Michael Curtiz, who had directed *Mission to Moscow*, turned the Broadway hit into one of Warners' biggest-grossing films for 1944. Evidently, American audiences were weary of war-themed features and desperate for light-hearted diversion.

When asked about her featherbrained characterization as Mrs. Conway, Ann mentioned that Billie Burke and Spring Byington were the prototypes for the role. "That was the delineation desired," Ann remarked.[46] We get to see her looking regal in a volunteer Army Red Cross Uniform, and chirping to husband Arnold, "We're going to rehearse for disaster and have tea afterwards." After a good start, and a few clever quips, *Janie* rapidly loses steam and credibility. The conniving antics of the youthful cast culminate in a riotous house-party while the parents are away. This rowdy episode, with troops, sorority girls and a military band, goes on and on until a relentless "show-stopping" musical number, "Keep Your Powder Dry," has neighbors calling the cops. While the trumpets blare, the screenplay is blown to smithereens. *The New York Times* aptly summed things up: "We see here a picture in which the comedy is wholly derived from the spectacle of children tearing a house up, to their parents' frozen dismay. ... there certainly isn't any insight in it, nor any sound appreciation of youth."[47] Ann seems lost in a thankless role. A drama critic for the As-

Janie (1944) with Edward Arnold and Robert Benchley. (Warner Brothers)

sociated Press put it plainly, "Ann Harding wastes her talents in a pallid role as the mother."[48] Ann's only good opportunity comes when she's convinced there is a dead sailor on her bedroom chaise lounge. She's distracted from this discovery when another GI pops out of her bathroom to say, "Goodbye!" "It's a dream," she decides, smiling to herself. "I'm ... I'm *sure* it's only a dream." It's a funny moment, but was it worth Ann's time and talent? Apparently, she thought so. She signed on for the sequel the following year: *Janie Gets Married.*

On the set of *Janie,* Ann, again, explained away her career. "I don't want to become an indispensable property," she said. "I like to act in pictures, but I want to be free to put my home life before my career. You can't do that when you're a star. You're too valuable a property of the studio that pays your salary."[49] By the time Warner Brothers got around to filming the *Janie* sequel, Joyce Reynolds had retired to join her husband at Quantico Marine Base. Joan Leslie took the lead.

When this author contacted Ms. Leslie in 2009, she had no specific memories of the film. It was, after all, sixty-five years after the fact. Leslie did have kind words for Ann, however, saying, "Ann Harding was a charming, kind, wise and 'fun' lady and a very fine actress."[50] Ann and Leslie would team once more, in 1955, for TV's *Studio 57*. Agnes Christine Johnson, who had co-written the *Andy Hardy* films, penned *Janie Gets Married*. The result, according to director Vincent Sherman, was "a dismal flop." (Completed in June 1945, the film wasn't released until a year later.) Sherman grudgingly took the director's seat. Years later, he commented, "The excellent cast finally induced me to direct." In truth, the film is several notches better than the original, and provided Ann with a more sizeable and well-written role. Smartly coiffed and gowned, and looking every inch a star, Ann helped keep Sherman in good spirits while he directed her and Barbara Brown (as Janie's mother-in-law). They were about to go into a heated argument over the newlyweds' living room curtains. "I want you to pay close attention to what the other is saying," instructed Sherman. Ann gave him a puzzled look. "You're the director, Mr. Sherman," she replied, "but do you want to set a precedent? It will be the first time in history that two women in an argument ever stopped talking long enough to listen."[51]

Janie Gets Married has a mad mix of in-law interference and love triangles that disrupt the matrimonial bliss of Janie and Dick (Robert Hutton, repeating his role). The highlight of the film was Robert Benchley's dry-wit as Hutton's stepfather. Before the ceremony, Dick's mother insists Van Brunt (Benchley) offer her twenty-two-year-old son, fresh out of the army, a "birds-and-bees" talk. Van Brunt balks, "Those French girls aren't all dressmakers, you know." Not long after the ceremony, Janie's parents witness Dick give a friendly smooch to his army pal, "Spud." (Don't get the wrong impression. "Spud" is a shapely WAC in the form of Dorothy Malone.) Ann's character tries to warn Janie about a husband's roving eye. Instead, she pushes Janie's imagination to the brink by telling her that men are basically polygamists. "You mean they want a lot of wives?" Janie asks. "Oh, no, not wives," Mrs. Conway explains. "That's against the law! But there are times when even the finest men get … well, what you might call a primitive impulse!" Janie is suddenly convinced that "Spud" is inspiring ample "primitive impulse" in husband Dick. Bosley Crowther's *New York Times* review still found Janie to be "an arrested girl." "Her picture is as childish and bromidic," said Crowther, "as was her first reckless juvenile farce. The climax is a slapdash dinner party, at which are served great helpings of soggy farce. … the late Robert Benchley is the one bright and redeeming character."[52]

When columnist Inga Arvad visited the set of *Nine Girls* and asked Ann why Werner's success came before her own, Ann leveled with her, "Because I never read a story as good as a Brahms Symphony." (Ann seemed to alternate between Beethoven and Brahms when making this statement.) A tall dark-haired girl walked up to them smiling sweetly. "This is Janie, my daughter," said Ann. "She always visits me once on each picture." Asked if she also wanted to be an actress, Jane hesitated. Her mother looked a wee bit disturbed by the question. "I don't think so," Jane answered, "but honestly I haven't decided yet." Ann piped up immediately, "She draws awfully well. She is really best at caricatures." In this regard, Jane took after her aunt Edith. Arvad noted that the

Janie Gets Married (1946) with Joan Leslie. (Warner Brothers)
(Courtesy of Photofest)

lines in Ann's face were the kind that came from enjoying life. "She has tiny crows-feet," wrote Arvad, "but of the variety which marks many a gay laughter. Her mouth turns up at the corners and there is no bitterness in her face; just contentment and clear understanding."

During her interview with Arvad, Ann reflected on her feelings about music, and it explained a great deal about her obvious acquiescence to Janssen's career:

> I have always had a great love and desire for music. As a very young actress back east—those were the days when actors had no salaries, but asked for the money they needed at the box office—I didn't seem to want much else except fifty cents and carfare now and then to go to the symphony concerts and operas. I would sit and learn my lines while waiting in the long queue for the cheapest seats. That isn't knowing about music; that is just not being able to live without it.[53]

In 1946, Werner signed on as conductor of the Utah Symphony Orchestra—44 concerts in 16 different Utah cities as a part of the state's Centennial. He had also begun a series of "Musicolor" shorts. For *Toccata and Fugue* (1946), Janssen featured the music of Bach against the background of the towering pinnacles in Utah's Bryce Canyon. Although she demurred when asked about her own understanding of music, Ann *had* acquired great knowledge of it. Always at his side, and because of her appreciation and study of music, Ann admitted, "I seem to have been able to help my husband in many ways."[54] Years had passed since she waited in long lines for "the cheapest seats." Ann now sat in the best the house could offer, as an honored guest. Having declared she was unable to live without music, she found herself literally living *in* it.

(Endnotes)

1   Connie Curtis, "The Return of Ann Harding," *Hollywood*, September 1942
2   Connie Curtis, "The Return of Ann Harding," *Hollywood*, September 1942
3   Louella Parsons, "There's Magic in Musicians for Movie Queens," *San Antonio Light*, 6/28/42
4   "Janssen Planning Benefit for Finns," *Los Angeles Times*, 12/01/39
5   "Conductor Finds Film Hours Long," *Coshocton Tribune*, 11/4/39
6   Frederick C. Othman, "The Fur is Flying Around Werner Janssen," *Corpus Christi Times*, 11/18/41
7   "Destiny Role for John Howard," *Syracuse Herald Journal*, 1/25/40 – also rumored was a 1937
     item saying Ann was being considered to co-star with Warner Baxter in Warners' *Everybody Was
     Nice*; in a September 1938 column, Louella Parsons misinformed that Ann tested for a role in
     Gone With the Wind
8   Gene Ringgold, "Ann Harding," *Films in Review*, March 1972
9   "Symphony conductor Plans Goodwill Trip Thru South America," *Waterloo Daily Courier*, 4/16/41
10   "Ann Harding Wins Child Custody Suit," *Oakland Tribune*, 1/28/42
11   Connie Curtis, "The Return of Ann Harding," *Hollywood*, September 1942
12   Louella Parsons column, *Fresno Bee*, 5/11/42
13   Louella Parsons column, *Lowell Sun*, 5/14/42
14   Louella Parsons, "Ann Harding Still Alluring," *Los Angeles Examiner*, 6/14/42
15   Gladwyn Hill, "Ann Harding's Return to Screen," *St. Petersburg Times*, 6/28/42
16   Connie Curtis, "The Return of Ann Harding," *Hollywood*, September 1942
17   Connie Curtis, "The Return ..."
18   Theodore Strauss review of *Eyes in the Night*, *New York Times*, 10/16/42
19   Fred Zinnemann, *Fred Zinnemann, an Autobiography*, Bloomsbury, c. 1992
20   Neil Sinyard, *Fred Zinnemann*, McFarland, c. 2003, pgs. 22-23
21   Robbin Coons, "Hollywood," *Lebanon Daily (PA)*, 6/18/42
22   Jessica Ryan, "Frankly Forty, "*Movieland*, October 1945
23   Dorothy Kilgallen, "Broadway," *Mansfield News Journal*, 6/16/42
24   Todd Bennett, "Culture, Power, and *Mission to Moscow*: film and Soviet-American Relations dur-
     ing World War II," *The Journal of American History*, Vol. 88. No. 2. pg. 495, September 2001
25   Clyde Rowen, "*Mission to Moscow* Is Great Sales," *Lincoln Sunday Journal and Star*, 6/13/43
26   Todd Bennett, "Culture ..."
27   Todd Bennett, "Culture ..."
28   Thomas Cripps, *Making Movies Black: The Hollywood Message*, Oxford Univ. Pr., c1993, pg. 310
29   Dennis J. Dunn, *Caught Between Roosevelt & Stalin*, University of Kentucky Pr., c. 1998, pg 68
30   Dennis J. Dunn, *Caught Between Roosevelt & Stalin*, University of Kentucky Pr., c. 1998, pg 63
31   Nancy Rubin Stewart, *American Empress: The Life and Times of Marjorie Merriweather Post*, ASJA
     Press, c. 2002, pg 367
32   Edwin Schallert review of *Mission to Moscow*, *Los Angeles Times*, 5/13/43
33   Hedda Hopper, "World-Noted Figurers Stride Through 'Moscow Mission,'" *Los Angeles Times*,
     4/11/43
34   Hedda Hopper, Looking at Hollywood," *Los Angeles Times*, 5/12/43
35   Walter L. Hixson, *The American Experience in WWII: The United States and the Road to the War in
     Europe*, Taylor and Francis, c. 2003, pg 271
36   Bosley Crowther review of *The North Star*, *New York Times*, 11/5/43
37   Review of *The North Star*, *Time*, 11/8/43
38   Norbert Lusk review of *The North Star*, *Los Angeles Times*, 11/9/43
39   Edwin Schallert, "Ann Harding in *North Star*," *Los Angeles Times*, 1/15/43
40   May Mann, "Going Hollywood," *Ogden Standard-Examiner*, 3/15/43
41   Robbin Coons, "Latest Picture Has Ann Harding Enjoying Life," *Kingsport Times (TX)*, 6/6/43
42   "Composer Gets Back at Hitler by War Work," *Portsmouth Herald (NH)*, 9/1/43

43   Inga Arvad, "Hollywood Today," *Kingsport News*, 12/3/43

44   Kevin Thomas review of *Nine Girls*, 8/28/2003

45   "Movie Director Shoots *Nine Girls* Without a Worry," *Daily Kennebec Journal*, 2/14/44

46   "Ann Harding ... Cheerful Future," *Oakland Tribune*, 5/13/45

47   Bosley Crowther review of *Janie*, *New York Times*, 8/5/44

48   Associated Press review of *Janie*, 9/7/44

49   "Hollywood Film Shop," *Vidette Messenger (IN)*, 2/17/44

50   Letter from Joan Leslie, dated June 5, 2009

51   Erskine Johnson, "Hollywood," *Frederick Post (MD)*, 7/14/45

52   Bosley Crowther review of *Janie Gets Married*, *New York Times*, 6/15/46

53   Inga Arvad, "Hollywood Today," *Kingsport News*, 12/3/43

54   Jessica Ryan, "Frankly Forty," *Movieland*, October 1945

17
Re-Enter, Stage Left

"It almost makes me drunk now, hearing an audience laugh!"

—Ann Harding (1949)

Between Werner Janssen's symphonic engagements, Ann finally landed a starring role ... on stage. She selected Tennessee Williams' *The Glass Menagerie.* The melancholy drama won the prestigious New York Drama Critics' Circle Award in 1945. In July 1948, Ann signed with the La Jolla Playhouse (100 miles south of Hollywood), a non-profit, professional theatre founded the previous year by Gregory Peck, Dorothy McGuire and Mel Ferrer. Ann played Amanda Wingfield, the overbearing mother and abandoned wife who lives vicariously through her son (Richard Basehart) and handicapped daughter, Laura (Betsy Blair). Amanda is obsessed with finding a suitor (John Ireland) for the incredibly shy Laura, who is fixated on her collection of glass figurines. Ann's character wavers between hawkish attention to her adult children, and wistful reminiscing about her days as a southern belle with numerous gentlemen callers. The production was considered the "high point" of La Jolla's season.[1] Betsy Blair, who had understudied the part of Laura in the original Broadway production, recalled that Ann, Basehart, and Ireland were "all three wonderful, well-cast actors."[2] Ann especially enjoyed working with Basehart (who had trained at Hedgerow, 1938-42) and felt, as "disciples" of Deeter, they met on common ground. The *Los Angeles Examiner* reported that the "very successful" production was "a decided hit."[3] In the back of her mind, Ann had a desire to return to Broadway. "You always have to come back, torture though it may be," she told legendary publicist Tex McCrary. "You just have to see if you can … ."[4]

Prior to her return to the stage, Ann had taken other lead roles on radio. For the popular *Cavalcade of America,* she played women's rights advocate Abigail Scott Dunaway in *Westward the Women* (1945), and Anna Zenger, the colonial publisher and fighter for "freedom of the press," in *Mother of Freedom* (1946). Her feisty Abigail Dunaway had plenty of attitude and is an absolute delight to listen to—easily the best of her radio performances. The town sheriff tells Abigail she has no right, as a woman, to save her home after her inept husband defaulted on a promissory note. She doesn't take the news sitting down. By the time Abigail makes the stirring declaration, "A government without women in it is only *half* a government," she has brought the message home. Ann was also reunited with Ronald Colman for a *Lux Radio* presentation of A.J. Cronin's *The Keys of the Kingdom.* The story, which had received harsh reviews from the Catholic press, takes place in the interior of China. Colman is an unconventional Catholic priest who doesn't bully his converts into some imagined heaven. Ann, as the staid Reverend Mother, resigns herself to Colman's isolated parish to serve a people she feels are far beneath her. Her formidable presence eventually melts into the same unselfish spirit in which the reverend performs his work. "I was born into arrogance," she apologizes. "From the beginning I knew *yours* was the true humility. I resented your deep, enormous compassion." As the popularity of radio subsided, it would be the stage that offered Ann opportunities to etch performances worthy of her talent, and stretch as an actress.

Between *Janie* and its sequel, Ann had what could have been a disquieting experience—a nightmare come true for most female stars. She played the potential mother-in-law to one of her former leading men, Robert Young. The film was RKO's *Those Endearing Young Charms* (1945). Ann's agent was ready to turn the offer down, but he submitted the script to her, she liked the role, and insisted on playing it. "These old charms are more enduring than those endearing young ones," she joked. "Male stars can continue their romantic careers on the screen for many years, but women seldom can. For every Bette Davis, who achieved early stardom and retained it as she matured gracefully, there are dozens who grasp for eternal screen youth far beyond their time."[5]

Those Endearing Young Charms
(1945). (RKO)

When she walked into RKO for the first time in eight years, there were familiar faces such as soundman Dick Van Hessen and assistant director Nate Slott. The prop man had located the old canvas chair bearing her name and placed it next to the one used by director Lewis Allen. Along with other crew members, Ann was greeted with flowers and an impromptu party. "I must admit this is one of my life's pleasantest surprises," Ann smiled. "Hollywood usually ignores actresses at this in-between age, which makes coming back here a double celebration."[6]

Those Endearing Young Charms was originally a Samuel Goldwyn project, but by the fall of 1944, RKO bought rights to the Edward Chodorov play. Screen tests began the last week in December. The scenario has Ann (third-billed), as Mrs. Brandt, living in New York with her daughter Helen (Laraine Day) and working for the war relief effort. She becomes alarmed when Helen falls for WWII pilot Hank Travis (Robert Young), an obvious womanizer. During a night out on the town, he attempts to persuade both mother and daughter with dancing and alcohol. The drinks keep coming, and before long we see Mrs. Brandt's eyes well up with tears as the orchestra plays the title tune. "Mother, you're crying!" says a concerned Helen. Mrs. Brandt confesses about her long lost love, and apologizes, "I'm behaving like a stupid old woman. I'd better go home." Once sober, she sees through Travis' jaded charm, his lies, and his conniving. When he tries to convince Mrs. Brandt that he loves her daughter, she puts it to him bluntly, "You're in love with a man named Travis!" Helen has her own doubts, but any misgivings either woman has about Travis vanish instantly for no apparent reason. Mrs. Brandt decides her daughter shouldn't carry the burden of "lost love." She urges her to go after Travis before his plane leaves. Anne Jeffreys, who plays a waitress at the Air Base cafeteria and one of Travis' former conquests, comes off with the best line. "It's *your* heart you're breaking," she tells Helen, who then runs to Travis for a farewell smooch. The film was one of the biggest box-office successes of the year with a net profit of $644,000.

The New York Times reviewer Bosley Crowther was dismissive of *Those Endearing Young Charms*, calling it a "silly little film … all romantic cliché in which love and the little lady's virtue overcome the gentleman's dark designs." Crowther noticed the audience was made up of mostly shop-girls released for the Eisenhower parade. They seemed to adore what Crowther labeled, "tickling eyewash."[7] Drama critic Wood Soanes felt the scenario "shrewd" and the acting "natural." "Ann Harding," enthused Soanes, "is what you would expect of an experienced actress in a role that has some meat to it."[8] Although *Time* magazine found Young "systematically caddish," and the film "not remarkably interesting," it pointed to Ann, praising, "Miss Harding's role is superfluous in any strict story sense, but it is the first in a long time that has given her talents any room to move around in, and she makes the most of it."[9]

Jimmy Fidler, the male counterpart to Hedda and Louella, lunched with Ann at RKO. He found her "remarkably happy." "I'm frankly middle-aged and I love it," Ann told him. "I've always wanted to play character parts rather than romantic leads. I'm afraid I have no burning ambition to be a top-flight star again. People with burning ambition seldom find happiness. Their careers become their masters. I'm acting because I like to act."[10] Fidler found a "world of common sense" in Ann's viewpoint. "I've seen so many ex-stars eat out their hearts because they wanted to stage comebacks," he wrote, "most of them … too foolishly proud to accept anything but top billing."

After filming at RKO was complete, Ann and Werner purchased Falcon Lair, the lavish former Beverly Hills residence of silent idol

Rudolph Valentino, for $75,000. Valentino lived in it barely a year before his tragic death. While the Janssens resided there, Rin-Tin-Tin's grandson howled at passersby, but not for long. Several months later they sold it for $100,000. The profit went toward their new showplace in Ventura County –a 100-acre ranch they bought from Western star William "Hopalong Cassidy" Boyd. The down payment was augmented by Ann's sale of the film rights to Hemingway's *The Sun Also Rises* for $50,000. "We're moving to a walnut ranch near Ventura," Ann excitedly told reporter Gene Handshaker. "We can have a cow and chickens and I can raise vegetables!"[11]

Before seventeen-year-old Jane began her senior year at Douglas School in Pebble Beach, Ann laid down the law for the summer of '45. "There's going to be no lying in bed until noon this vacation," she warned. "And, no going to movies every afternoon. You're going to get a job! I don't care what it is, just so it's something that you have to do every day of the week." Ann suggested applying for a position as a telephone operator, or as a department store salesgirl. Jane took none of her mother's suggestions. She studied to be a volunteer nurse's aide, working five days a week at the Los Angeles Good Samaritan Hospital. It was exhausting work. "I could hardly bear to wake her for dinner," said Ann.[12] Jane was so committed to her job that she refused when her mother suggested she take a week off before school started that fall. Attending the all-girl boarding school also turned out to be a good idea. Jane's grades improved dramatically. Ann was convinced it was due to the fact that Jane couldn't carry on three-hour phone conversations with her friends every night. After graduation, Jane attended the University of California in Berkeley, where she would complete her education. By the time Ann was focused on her return to the stage, Jane was living in Hawaii. She had gone there on a vacation, found a wonderful job, and stayed for three years. She roomed with one of her Pi Beta Phi Sorority sisters. When Jane first wired her mother about the opportunity, Ann offered encouragement. "I remembered a vow I had made to the high Heavens when I was 21," said Ann, "that I would never meddle in the life of my children, never! So ... I swallowed my worries and wired back, 'Please write details, but take job. Love Mother.'"[13]

Before putting her Hollywood career on hold for a second time, Ann made two minor films back-to- back: *It Happened on Fifth Avenue* and *Christmas Eve*, both filmed in 1946 and released in 1947. *It Happened on Fifth Avenue* (1947) became a sleeper and was the first film produced under Monogram's high-budgeted unit, Allied Artists. Although the original story was nominated for an Academy Award, the likeable film has a tendency to crawl from one scene to the next. Some have ventured to compare it to Frank Capra's *It's a Wonderful Life*, but *It Happened on Fifth Avenue* doesn't come close to carrying the dramatic weight of Capra's masterpiece. With a budget of more than a million dollars, director Roy Del Ruth created a mostly charming and sentimental film about a hobo philosopher named McKeever (Victor Moore) who spends his annual winter retreats in a boarded-up mansion on New York's Fifth Avenue. Moore's character, a capitalist imposter, waddles across the screen smoking expensive cigars while sharing "his haven" with homeless veterans. The plot begins to boil when Trudy (Gale Storm), the headstrong daughter of the wealthy owner, unexpectedly shows up and keeps her identity a se-

It Happened on Fifth Avenue (1947) with Charlie Ruggles.
(Allied Artists) (Courtesy of Photofest)

cret. She and one of the jobless veterans (Don DeFore) provide the film's romantic interest. Trudy's estranged parents (Ann and Charlie Ruggles), disguised as transients, join the mix, and by the finish are rejuvenated by McKeever's "generosity." The film is half over before Ann arrives, and then retreats to the kitchen. She isn't given much to do other than remind her ex-husband, "You left me and married your money!" Nevertheless, her scenes with Ruggles carry a poignancy and impact that is lacking in the romantic interludes of the younger set. The *New Republic* commented, "Ann Harding's acting gets more real and ... she gets better looking with the years."[14]

The *New York Times* complimented *It Happened on Fifth Avenue* for the "amusing social comment in the temporary reversal of [Moore's and Ruggles'] roles."[15] Following the film's premier at Hollywood's

Grauman's Chinese Theater, *Los Angeles Times* critic Edwin Schallert commented that Ann's work was "sincere, pleasing and efficient," but felt that the "soak the rich" theme may have gone overboard. "A scene where the veterans hurl vegetables at a henchman of the capitalist might evoke some doubt as to its advisability at this juncture."[16] The revitalized HUAC (inactive during the war years) had begun investigating communist infiltration of Hollywood. Perhaps *It Happened on Fifth Avenue* missed the committee's scrutiny, because, as film historian Bruce Elder put it, the film "sings of the generosity of the human spirit, and the feeling of renewal that was in the air in the immediate post-World War II era."[17] It was the favorite film of actor Don DeFore's career.

Roy Del Ruth had definite plans to star Ann in one of the three pictures he was lining up for Allied Artists. A non-specific Hemingway story was mentioned.[18] In September, Ann and Janssen flew to Salt Lake for the premier of his color short, *Toccata and Fugue*. "Viewed from the sky," Ann stated, "Salt Lake is like a big, glittering jewel."[19] Later that fall, she and Werner were honored guests, along with Governor Herbert B. Maw and Mormon President George Albert Smith, at a banquet held at the Hotel Utah. As Utah's new symphony director and his wife, Janssen and Ann were warmly received. The *Salt Lake Tribune* editorial noted, "When Werner Janssen ... was making a speech recently, his wife, Ann Harding of the movies, watched him with rapt attention. Never once did her glance stray from his face. It was a beautiful example of wifely interest and devotion."[20] Ann's "wifely devotion" lasted ten more days before she returned to Los Angeles, where she signed on at Columbia for the unremarkable *Christmas Eve*. Sadly, Roy Del Ruth's Hemingway project for Ann had not materialized.

As if to underscore her desire for character parts, Ann took on the assignment of playing an elderly woman. "Having played *Holiday* with Ann Harding," Hedda Hopper reported, "I couldn't resist going on the set of *Christmas Eve* to see her do the role of a 70-year-old mother. She mothers—by adoption only—George Raft, who plays a night club operator in Rio; George Brent—a confidence man, and Randy Scott—a rodeo star. There also was Reggie Denny … playing a forger. We just don't care what we do with our nice stars in this business, do we?"[21] Producer Benedict Bogeaus had a penchant for casting his films with aging stars the studio system ignored. Ann played an aged recluse, Aunt Matilda (looking closer to ninety than seventy), a curious creature living alone in her Manhattan mansion. She's about to lose her fortune to greedy nephew Phillip (Denny), who wants her committed. Phillip invites a doctor and lawyer to witness Matilda's eccentricities. After she tosses birdseed around her elegant living room, and opens windows to allow a flock of pigeons inside for a feast—they get the idea. Matilda is convinced her three adopted sons, whom she hasn't seen in years, will miraculously rescue her on Christmas Eve from Phillip's nefarious plan. As it turns out, they need rescuing from themselves. George Brent's character survives by cashing fraudulent checks; cowboy Randolph Scott, who has a fondness for firewater, is suspected of stealing babies for a living; and tough guy Raft is a shady gambler who has escaped from the clutches of the FBI. The three male leads parody their screen personas—a fact that would be completely lost on audiences nowadays. Raft's role is amply beefed up by producer Bogeaus, and clashes with the film's spirit. It's as if a mini-noir Raft film has been inserted into the proceedings midway.

Ann's attempt to play the trembling old Matilda was a questionable task, but it appears that she enjoyed herself. In reality, she was younger than all the male cast members. Critic John L. Scott for the *Los Angeles Times* commented, "The bright spot is Aunt Matilda, finely acted by Ann Harding."[22] *The New York Times* agreed, saying she came "closest to the mark" of being convincing. However, Bay Area critic Wood Soanes came closer to the truth. He found the film, "pretty awful," and as far as Aunt Matilda, he warned, "As Miss Harding played the role, the booby hatch was the only place for her; as Raft played a night club operator, Brent a rubber-check writer and Scott a bronco buster, they should have joined her. Denny as the sensible nephew was, to all appearances, the only sane individual in the family group."[23] After this celluloid misfire, Ann stayed away from the screen for nearly four years.

During Ann's sojourns to Salt Lake throughout the winter of 1947-48, she made a point of being there when Edward Arnold joined Janssen's orchestra as narrator for the *Genesis Suite*, a large-scale biblical tableaux with orchestra and chorus. "It's the best way to teach the Bible story," Arnold told reporters for the *Salt Lake Tribune*. Amid the tumult of a heavy rehearsal schedule, Arnold, his wife, Ann and Werner were entertained during every free moment. Ann and Mrs. Arnold were honored guests at a luncheon held at the Hotel Utah. There

Christmas Eve (1947) with George Raft.
(United Artists)

was a pre-concert tea held in the hotel's Empire room, and a supper party after the concert. Before Arnold left town, he and Janssen made an appearance at Auerbach's department store to sign recordings of the *Genesis Suite*. In a 2004 commentary, classical music critic Rob Barnett called Janssen's *Genesis*, "Great fun ... It is very much a case of the Bible according to Heston and Mature."[24] Janssen, accompanied by buses and trucks, spent the rest of the snowy Utah winter bringing Brahms, Mozart and Chopin to coal miners, sheepherders, farmers, and hardened cowboys, many of whom had never heard a symphony orchestra. On alternate weekends the Utah Symphony performed at the Mormon Tabernacle, which held up to 5,000 people.[25] Janssen's contribution to the Utah Symphony was well received and considered a great success, so it came as a surprise when Janssen suddenly accepted directorship of the Portland Oregon Symphony. In April 1947, he telegrammed his resignation to Salt Lake.[26]

In the summer of 1948, after her stage role in *The Glass Menagerie*, Ann took time off to enjoy her husband's second season with the Portland Symphony. Janssen introduced the novel idea of showing color films at his concerts. The musical score was synchronized with footage of waves breaking against the rocky Pacific coastline. The musical accompaniment was a live performance of Mendelssohn's *Fingal's Cave*. Audiences loved the idea, as did the symphony board.[27] At the end of the symphony season (April 1949), Ann prepared for another stage role.

The July 23 issue of *Billboard* magazine announced that Ann Harding's 1949 summer circuit tour in *Yes, My Darling Daughter* was meeting

Seated next to Werner along with members of the Portland Symphony (1949).

"substantial advance activity at the box office."[28] Her fans turned out in droves to see their favorite patrician star "in person." The 1937 play, by Mark Reed, turned out to be a perfect vehicle. Not that being on tour didn't have its challenges. After a month on the road, Ann summed up her feelings about summer stock for the *Fitchburg Centennial*. Sitting at her dressing table, wearing a dress she knitted herself, Ann stated, "It's a pretty strenuous schedule on the road, especially playing with a new cast each week. I don't think I would undertake another summer tour in stock right away. A packaged show ... in which the same supporting players would travel with me would undoubtedly result in a more polished performance. It's amazing how many different types of girls this summer are playing the role of my daughter in *Yes, My Darling Daughter*."[29] Ann felt that the star system was becoming "entrenched" in summer theatre. Reiterating her training from Hedgerow, she stated, "I always believed that the play should be emphasized and not the star. A higher standard of stock production could be maintained if the leading player in one show were given a minor role in the next. The play is the thing."[30] The reporter admired her sincerity, but was not entirely convinced. Kay Francis, Sylvia Sidney, Ruth Chatterton, Constance Bennett, and many of Ann's other contemporaries were doing summer theatre along the east coast. Kay Francis, who was touring in Rachel Crother's *Let Us Be Gay*, offered her objective view on the subject, saying, "It's a great training ground for apprentices when they can work with more experienced actors, whether they are stars nor not."[31] Having a "star attraction" was a welcome shot in the arm for attendance and box-office revenues.

As one wag put it, "*Yes, My Darling Daughter* dealt with the celebrated institution of sex."[32] Ann played a middle-aged professional writer (Ann Murray) who is confronted with her own "liberated" past in Greenwich Village. Initially, Mrs. Murray is outraged when she hears her daughter's plan to spend a weekend with her handsome fiancé. Her daughter brings up the fact that her mother had once been an advocate of free thinking and free love. In fact, in her wild youth, Mrs. Murray was jailed for 30 days. At the end of Act II, Ann put a world of feeling into her line, as she morosely carried out a tray of tea: "God damned sex, anyway!"

During her week at the Ivoryton Playhouse in Connecticut, Ann's performance received positive comment from *The Shore Line Times*: "Ann Harding and Doris Fesette do a mother and daughter act that is equal to anything seen on the Shore Line circuit this season. Those who have eagerly followed Miss Harding's many appearances on the New York stage and pictures will, as usual, be delighted to find that her personal charm and acting skill are as enjoyable as ever." The review complimented the direction of Milton Stiefel (former confidant of the famous theatrical impresario David Belasco), saying the pace and tempo of *Yes, My Darling Daughter* made for "an evening of entertaining hilarity."[33] Ann enjoyed doing a comedy for a change. When producer Richard Aldrich offered her the opportunity to take over Ruth Hussey's role in *Goodbye, My Fancy*, a Broadway comedy with some bite, Ann didn't have to think twice.

Give a college a Science building—then tell the professors what they can say in it. Give them a motion picture machine but tell them what to run on it. That's not generosity. That's an investment—with damned good dividends!"

Agatha Reed in *Goodbye, My Fancy*[34]

Fay Kanin's *Goodbye, My Fancy* was an established hit since its premier in November 1948. Madeleine Carroll was the original star. She left the cast in June 1949, and was replaced by Ruth Hussey. Ann stepped into the role of Congresswoman Agatha Reed during the show's eleventh month at the Martin Beck Theatre. The play provided an interesting reunion for Ann and her co-star from *East Lynne*, Conrad Nagel. Chosen for the *Ten Best Plays of 1948-49*, *Goodbye, My Fancy* challenged women not to back away from life, advocating that an informed citizenry of both sexes was the key to a strong democracy. Academic freedom was in jeopardy at the time. The loyalty oath had been instituted by President Truman in 1947—the same year the HUAC zeroed in on Hollywood. With the recent detonation of the first atomic bomb, author Kanin felt young people had inherited a precarious future. The time was ripe for some healthy debate.

In the play, Agatha Reed, fresh from her "atom bomb" speech on the House floor, visits her old alma mater, a private college for women, to receive an honorary degree and speak to the graduating class. She brings along a documentary film she has narrated about the consequences of war. When the trustees preview the film, it causes an uproar. The college president, Jim Merrill (Nagel), who happens to be Agatha's former professor and lover, acquiesces to the board's view that the film is propaganda, and should not be shown. Agatha tells Merrill, "Is it propaganda to show that the results of another war will be the most devastating the world's ever known?" She then puts a clever spin on the situation by threatening to expose the truth about their former relationship, *unless* the film is shown. Agatha also takes the opportunity to confront Mr. Griswold, Chairman of the Board, about his textile company's war profits. "I made money out of the war," he huffs. "Sure, I did. So did everyone. I'd have been a fool not to." When she asks what he was doing to stop another war, he claims it is beyond his power. "Maybe," says Agatha. "Maybe it's really in the power of your six-hundred-and-twenty-two daughters. But only if they know what war means. If they look at it—if they understand it." Fay Kanin wanted women to think. Not a popular idea at the time. It was fitting that Ann should make her return to Broadway in a vehicle such as *Goodbye, My Fancy*. She had gone full circle. In author Yvonne Shafer's *American Women Playwrights, 1900-1950*, she comments on Ann's taking on Agatha Reed, saying, "Ann Harding made a welcome return from acting in films and the social comment in the role called up memories of her first stage hit in Glaspell's socially significant *Inheritors* in the 1920s."[35]

Back on Broadway. Ann is seen here with Conrad Nagel and
Donald Curtis in *Goodbye, My Fancy* (1949). (Courtesy of Photofest)

Werner freed up his West Coast commitments to be there for Ann's return to Broadway. "I wouldn't have dared go on that opening night of mine," said Ann, "if he hadn't been in the wings to lend me moral support. I tell you I was scared. And quite overcome when I made my first entrance and heard that applause. The people were very kind. They remembered. Fortunately the play calls for me to walk slowly around the set, mulling memories and not saying a word for a minute or so. If I had had to speak as soon as I entered, I don't think I could have done it. I was too chocked [sic] up with memories besides those that a playwright had made up for a character."[36] There was actually more to Ann's challenge than she let on. According to *Newsweek*, Ann "scored a success" after only five rehearsals.[37] She read the play for the first time on October 4; memorized her lines on the train from California; and then slipped in the bathtub her first day in New York, banging her nose. She opened October 17. Ann groaned, "I looked like a welterweight ... the loser, that is."[38] The audience's enthusiasm proved a healing balm. Writer Tex McCrary noted a "special breathless quality" in Ann's voice when she told him, "For so many years, I was typed as a woman who makes people cry—it almost makes me drunk now, hearing an audience laugh!"[39] *Variety* noted, "The house was completely filled, and the audience gave the actress a great, warming hand ... Miss Harding brings a harsh voice and brash quality to her first scenes that are a little disconcerting. She's also a little kittenish, at times ... But, as the play goes on, she gets warmer and softer, and fills the role of a liberal Congresswoman graciously."[40]

Ann was glad to be back, and she wanted to stick around for a while. When the play was scheduled to close on December 3, she willingly waived her salary guarantee, at a sizeable deduction, to keep the play

going for another two weeks.[41] A two-month engagement at Chicago's
Harris Theatre began on December 26. "The handsome Miss Harding,"
stated the *Chicago Tribune*, "is badly made up and not too becomingly
dressed." The review felt that Bramwell Fletcher, who took over for
Nagel, had less charisma and would have "disillusioned" Agatha at first
glance. The new duo failed to "smolder." After getting off to a slow start
at the Harris, the show built to hit proportions and sold out houses.[42] As
Katharine Cornell was scheduled to open there in *That Lady* on January
30, the company moved to the Blackstone Theatre. How this transpired
made headlines. One news article stated: "In a gesture probably unique
in theatre history, Ann Harding, the play's star, Bramwell Fletcher, a featured player, and Jack Potter, the company's manager, got together with
the actors union and worked out an agreement at the eleventh hour,
making it possible for the members of the cast to become partners in the
show, thereby assuring its continuing at the Blackstone."[43]

Author Fay Kanin had many of the same convictions of her main
character, Agatha Reed. Aside from being a writer, Kanin had hosted
the NBC radio program *The Woman's Angle*, which informed women
on current events during WWII. Meaningful academic education for
women was important to Kanin. Not long after Ann's Chicago run in
the play, Kanin and her husband, scenarist Michael Kanin, went on a European holiday. Director William Wyler met the couple in Europe and
began pursuing them to work on a screenplay, that is, until he learned
they had been added to the "secret" blacklist of the HUAC. They had
no idea. "It was ridiculous," said Fay, "but it was very real, and there was
nothing we could do about it."[44] It kept them out of work for two years.[45]

When asked about the major changes she had noticed in the theatre since she left it in 1928, Ann was candid. She observed a change

of economics. If a play did not catch on immediately the financial strain demanded its closing. "The public … can no longer put off buying tickets," she said. "Unless a play is given instant public support nowadays, it is virtually forced to put up a closing notice." There was no time, as she put it, for a play "to catch on."[46] The Chicago production of *Goodbye, My Fancy* closed on February 11, 1950. Shortly afterwards, Ann's co-star from 1925's *The Woman Disputed*, Louis Calhern, contacted her and urged that she reteam with him. Their reunion, he told her, would not take place on stage, but on screen and in Technicolor. It would be another two years before Ann resumed her "return" to the stage.

(Endnotes)

1   *The Burns Mantle Best Plays of 1948-49*, Dodd, Mead, c. 1949, pg 51
2   Betsy Blair, *The Memory of All That*, Alfred A. Knopf, N.Y. c. 2003, pg. 225
3   Edwin Schallert review of *The Glass Menagerie*, *Los Angeles Times*, 6/4/49
4   Tex McCrary, "New York-Close Up," *Oakland Tribune*, 11/1/49
5   "Ann Harding …. Cheerful Future," *Oakland Tribune*, 5/13/45
6   Gene Ringgold, "Ann Harding," *Films in Review*, March 1972
7   Bosley Crowther review of *Those Endearing Young Charms*, *New York Times*, 6/20/45
8   Wood Soanes review of *Those Endearing Young Charms*, *Oakland Tribune*, 8/9/45
9   Review of *Those Endearing Young Charms*, *Time*, 6/25/45
10   Jimmy Fidler, "Fidler in Hollywood," *Nevada State Journal*, 2/3/45
11   Gene Handshaker, "Blond Heroine, Off Screen Six Years, Returns," *Portsmouth Times (OH)*, 3/30/46
12   Jessica Ryan, "Frankly Forty," *Movieland*, October 1945
13   Jinx Falkenburg, "New York Close-Up," *Oakland Tribune*, 11/1/49
14   Review of *It Happened on Fifth Avenue*, *New Republic*, April 1947
15   Bosley Crowther review of *It Happened on Fifth Avenue*, 6/11/47
16   Edwin Schallert review of *It Happened on Fifth Avenue*, 5/17/47
17   Bruce Elder review of *It Happened on Fifth Avenue*, *All Movie Guide*,
18   Edwin Schallert column, *Los Angeles Times*, 9/16/46
19   "Ann Harding Arrives to Join Spouse," *Salt Lake Tribune*, 11/13/46
20   Ham Park, "Senator From Sandpit," *Salt Lake Tribune*, 11/26/46
21   Hedda Hopper, "Troupers Carry On," *Los Angeles Times*, 12/10/46
22   John L. Scott review of *Christmas Eve*, *Los Angeles Times*, 1/1/48
23   Wood Soanes review of *Christmas Eve*, *Oakland Tribune*, 12/4/47
24   Rob Barnett review of *Genesis Suite*, MusicWeb –international.com
25   Larry J. Hall, "Utah Coal Miners Go For Brahms and Heavy Stuff," *Indiana Evening Gazette*, 4/16/47
26   "Utah Symphony's Director Quits, Goes to Portland," *Ogden Standard Examiner*, 4/26/46
27   "Movies Help Symphony," *Indiana Evening Gazette*, 12/28/48

28   *Billboard*, 7/23/49
29   "Famed Chignon," *Fitchburg Centennial*, 8/3/49
30   "Famed Chignon," *Fitchburg Centennial*, 8/3/49
31   John S. Wilson, "The Small, Economy-Size Package," *Theatre Arts*, July 1952
32   "Playhouse to Give 12th Week With Ann Harding in Comedy," *Berkshire Evening Eagle*, 8/11/49
33   Review of *Yes, My Darling Daughter*, *The Shore Line Times*, 8/16/49
34   Fay Kanin, *Goodbye, My Fancy* (Plays by American Women 1930-1960), Applause (NY), c. 1994
35   Yvonne Shafer, *American Women Playwrights, 1900-1950*, Peter Lang Pub., c. 1995, pg 360
36   Jack Gaver, "Ann Harding Returns to Broadway After 21 Years," *Cedar Rapids Gazette*, 10/30/49
37   Article in *Newsweek*, 11/?/49
38   Tex McCrary, "New York – Close Up," *Oakland Tribune*, 11/1/49
39   Tex McCrary, "New York …"
40   Review of *Goodbye, My Fancy*, Variety, 10/19/49
41   "Not 'Good-Bye' to 'My Fancy,'" *New York Times*, 12/1/49
42   "Actors Save Comedy Hit From Closing," *Dixon Evening Telegraph*, 1/31/50
43   "Actors Save Comedy Hit …"
44   Cari Beauchamp, "Woman of the Years-An Interview with Fay Kanin, *Written By*, September 2001
45   Dick Vosburgh, "Obituary: Michael Kanin," *The Independent*, 3/18/93
46   Wood Soanes article, *Oakland Tribune*, 2/1/50

At MGM, Ann mixed with youngsters: Debbie Reynolds (who enjoyed mimicking Ann), Dan Foster, and Rita Moreno.

18
Big Screen—Little Screen

Debbie Reynolds, Ann's co-star in the Technicolor MGM musical *Two Weeks with Love*, recalled, "The whole thing was like going to a party every day."[1] Ann found the set relaxing as well and the tempo upbeat. Dr. Branch, who had prevented Ann from filming her Technicolor debut in 1934, had predicted wrongly. She didn't "expire" from the intense lighting. It had been eight years since she had worked at Metro. At that time, lighting set-ups by film technicians could take hours. "In the old days," said Ann, "players found themselves having to get in and out of moods with distracting lapses of time between. Now there isn't time to revert to normal. Moreover actors now are given less chance of becoming bored with their roles. The entire temper of a company seems improved when necessity keeps a film from dragging."[2] Faster still, was the pace of acting on television. The new decade provided Ann ample opportunity for a variety of challenges in a new medium.

Ann looked striking in color, and was handsomely gowned in *Two Weeks with Love* by Helen Rose (Oscar winner for *The Bad and the Beautiful*). She kept up her evening routine of going to Terry Hunt's exercise salon, dressed in slacks and a sweatshirt. Looking svelte, and capturing the spirit of a wizened mother of four, Ann's contribution to the turn-of-the-century story of a family on vacation in New York's Catskill Mountains was enjoyable. In the opening scene Ann is on double-duty as an actress. While getting her children ready to leave for the holiday, she is equally conscious of the musical arrangement her husband (Louis Calhern) is conducting in the city park just outside their home. She listens through an open window, hoping it's the "shorter" version, so they don't miss their train. She's two places at once and doesn't miss a beat.

Given ample opportunity to sing, Jane Powell, as the eldest daughter, sheds her screen adolescence while being romanced by her suitor, played by the enigmatic Ricardo Montalban. Debbie Reynolds, as the youngest daughter, was a cut-up. A film highlight was the duet featuring Reynolds and Carleton Carpenter, swinging like monkeys from a tree, singing "Abba Dabba Honeymoon." The musical numbers were directed by Busby Berkeley, making a comeback. Reynolds recalled that he would strap himself on a crane and practically disappear. "You could barely see him," said Reynolds. "He'd fall asleep while they were doing the lighting. They'd have to wake him up when they were ready to shoot. ... I had no idea who the great Busby Berkeley was."[3] Debbie had her eighteenth birthday on the set, and it is unlikely she knew much about the "great" Ann Harding either. "I found her fascinating," said Reynolds. "She had a very gentle, ethereal ... manner, with a searching quality to her voice—high and quiet, and breathless at all times. No matter what the scene, she maintained this strange, sweet, whispering sound." Reynolds was a mimic and nothing could stop her. "At the beginning of the day," Reynolds recalled, "I'd come up behind her on the set and say in the identical high, breathless whisper, 'Good morning, Ann.' She'd turn, look at me and repeat innocently, 'Good morning, Debbie.' She didn't realize I was sounding exactly like her. Everybody else on the set did, of course. Finally someone would say, 'Oh, c'mon, Debbie ....' She never got it. Never."[4] Most likely, it would never have dawned on Ann that anyone would do such a thing.

The *Los Angeles Times* rated *Two Weeks with Love* as "first-rate." "Calhern and Miss Harding," said the review, "fling themselves into the youthful activities with the wry charm expected of them."[5]

Faces on the Cutting Room Floor

"The police was just here for Benny," she whispered over the phone in a guarded voice. "Anderson, I told you many times—it would come to this. I told you ...."

"Now mama ...," hesitated Anders Anderson, known by his co-workers as "Cold Man Anderson" on the 12th floor. As night load dispatcher he monitored the electric circuits for Chicago.

"Ya, you always said that," his wife responded. '*Now, mama.*' You shut up now. I told you many times. I said, 'Benny is getting too big for me to handle and he is got bad company.' ... Oh, my boy, my boy! Now it is the police, I tell you—"[6]

This interlude, from Dudley Schnabel's short story *Load*, was a project of director Anthony Mann. *Load* was originally included in the eight-part MGM epic, *It's a Big Country* (1951). Jean Hersholt and Ann played an immigrant couple who learn their eighteen-year-old son, Benny, is to be arrested for robbery and murder. The irony of the piece lies in the fact that Hersholt's character monitors the electric turbine "load" which could not only fry his son in the electric chair, but allow Benny to escape the police should there be a sudden "power failure." Mann preferred dramas that leaned toward classic tragedy—his anguished characters trying to resolve their pain and personal problems (i.e., *Winchester '73, God's Little Acre*). In July 1950, Hersholt reported to MGM for the first time in fourteen years. He had been in many of the most memorable films for the studio. "When MGM sent me the script for *Load*," said Hersholt, "I could not resist ... my role is an actor's dream."[7] Mann opened and closed *Load* with an impressive traveling boom shot. The camera captures a panorama of the city lighted by the power company, before moving down for a close-up of Hersholt's character, the man who controls it. The story departed in the same way. *Load* was deleted from the final print. A few years later, Jean Hersholt bitterly commented, "In *It's a Big Country*, Ann Harding and I co-starred in a sequence, but MGM did not use it at all. I guess there wasn't enough of a message in it."[8] Hersholt's remark was directed at MGM's new president, Dore Schary, who had a penchant for "message pictures." Inside word had it that *Load* was one of Hersholt's finest performances.[9]

At Louis Calhern's request, Ann signed on for the film version of Emmett Lavery's play, *The Magnificent Yankee*. The 89-minute feature was an intimate portrait of Supreme Court Justice Oliver Wendell Holmes and his wife Fanny during their Washington, DC years (1902-32). On Broadway, Dorothy Gish had filled the shoes of Mrs. Holmes. Aside from the fact that Ann was a bigger draw than Gish, Calhern was wary of teaming with his former lover. He and Dorothy had had a romantic liaison that lasted for several years. According to biographer Stuart Oderman, the charming Calhern was a drinker, which complicated the relationship. Gish considered him the love of her life. Although the pair broke up by the time they co-starred in Broadway's *The Magnificent Yankee* (1946),Gish still carried a torch for her leading man.[10]

As they had demonstrated in *Two Weeks With Love*, Ann and Calhern were perfect foils for one another and had obvious chemistry as a team. *The Magnificent Yankee* is uniquely heart-centered cinematic fare. The smooth and tender presentation of Holmes and Fanny's re-

The Magnificent Yankee (1950) with Louis Calhern. (MGM)

lationship makes reference early on to their childless marriage. Fanny's burden becomes explicit when she tearfully remarks, "It isn't fair, Wendell. Why does everything have to end with us? Why couldn't I give you even one son?" Typical of the buoyant spirit of the play, Holmes reassures her, "Fanny, you have the joy of living in you. It's not your fault if we're unable to pass some of that joy along." After this exchange, Clinton, the first of Holmes' many "sons-at-law" appears. Jimmy Lydon portrayed the first of many young law students who fulfilled a year-long assignment as Holmes' clerk. Court Justice Felix Frankfurter, a former law clerk of Holmes, felt the play's surrogate sons were "a bit of dramatic license on Lavery's part."[11] Regardless, Lavery's idea works. When Fanny arranges for nineteen "sons" to show up for Holmes' eightieth birthday, Calhern's reaction is one of the film's highlights.

As Holmes' wife, Ann is his equal when it comes to wisdom and understanding. When he worries about being sixty-one and "making a fool of himself" starting a new career in Washington, Fanny lets him have it in hearts and spades. "Now, top it, Wendell!" she demands. "I won't have you looking backward like that. I won't have you making an old man of yourself! It's never too late for those who love a good fight ... for those who keep looking ahead." Holmes' hearty laughter indicates his "issue" is resolved. "If you'd ever learned to swear," he tells her, "you'd make a pretty good colonel."

Lavery's script wisely distances itself from the reality of politics and world events. It's not the film's purpose. While the "Great Dissenter" of the Supreme Court makes reference to major issues he confronted (e.g., the Sherman Anti-Trust Act), this doesn't detract from the story being told. As the PCA still had a grip on Hollywood,

Holmes ear-curling off-the-bench vocabulary wasn't in the script, nor were his frequent sojourns to the capitol's burlesque houses. But, we do catch him in the act of hiding one of his many racy French novels placed conveniently within reach from his library desk.

At age 63, the real Mrs. Holmes had lost most of her hair by the time she arrived in Washington. MGM wasn't sure how to make up the amply coiffed Ann. They were unable to locate photographs of the older Fanny, nor was there any trace of the diary she kept while residing in the nation's capitol. Ann began a campaign to learn more about Fanny Holmes. "I learned that Mrs. Holmes was a witty, attractive woman," said Ann, "and a great favorite in social circles, but I learned nothing concrete."[12] Even so, Ann matches Calhern's performance to show how love and abiding humor can sustain a relationship indefinitely. At one point, Holmes catches himself babbling on about something and suddenly stops. "Fanny," he asks, "what the devil am I talking about?" With a warm chuckle, she answers, "I'm sure I don't know, Wendell. And, if I did, I wouldn't tell you."

Near the end of Fanny's life, Holmes enters her room carrying the first violets of spring, a book, and a box of chocolates. His affectionate "small talk" is suddenly interrupted when she tells him, "Wendell ... sit down. It's time we looked certain facts in the eye. We've known the best of everything there is. I guess it rather spoils you ... even for a thing called heaven." After making a promise to continue with his position on the Supreme Court after she's gone, he reads to her. She listens contentedly and the viewer realizes she has fully embraced her next step. Jimmy Lydon wrote to this author in 2008. "As to Ann Harding," he recalled, "we all thought of her as a fine actress. I only did one short scene that she was in. She seemed quiet, sweet and reserved."[13]

Ann flew to New York for the splashy premier at Radio City Music Hall. *The New York Times* thought Calhern played with "humor, inspiration and heart." "Mr. Lavery has frankly allowed a good bit of sentimentality to invade and command his script," said the review. "Miss Harding is likewise tasteful and restrained in her performance."[14] Critic Sterling Sorensen said, "Miss Harding ... holds her own in fair competition, in scene after scene. She is the perfect foil for her ebullient husband, bringing him down to earth when his imagination runs away with him, and the film is at its best when they are engaged in mutually pleasant domestic tilts and conflicts."[15] Not everyone was impressed. The *Saturday Review of Literature* liked Calhern, but called the film "The Magnificent Disappointment," accusing MGM of turning one of the country's "intellectual and spiritual giants into a dull-witted midget."[16] The West Coast premier took place on December 20, 1950—in time for Oscar consideration. Edwin Schallert for the *Los Angeles Times* placed *The Magnificent Yankee* as "one of the year's finest screen efforts." "Certainly Calhern should be entitled to maximum Academy consideration for his performance," raved Schallert. "Miss Harding admirably sustains the part through its various transitions ... there are decided demands made upon her for reality in aging in the portrayal. She proves her efficiency ... her passing is movingly carried out in word and action."[17] In February, Schallert offered his "Oscar Forecast." He predicted both Calhern and Ann for the "Best Actor" and "Best Actress" category, but it was Calhern's work that was acknowledged by the Academy with a nomination.[18] (The Oscar went to Jose Ferrer in *Cyrano de Bergerac*). In 1952, Ann and Calhern recreated their roles for *Lux Radio Theatre*.

Before taking another sabbatical (five years) from the "big screen," Ann completed her final picture for MGM. Filming began in January 1951, for *The Bradley Mason Story*, starring Spencer Tracy as a justice-loving lawyer. Ann and Lionel Barrymore were also in the cast.[19] Before things got underway, Tracy was replaced by Walter Pidgeon and Barrymore, due to illness, by Lewis Stone. The story begins with lawyer Dwight Bradley Mason (Pidgeon) eaten up by guilt after unwittingly getting murderer Rudy Wallchek (Keefe Brasselle) off scot-free. Mason decides to go after a crime lord (Edward Franz—playing a member of the city's crime commission) who is behind the whole mess. This he does by killing him. Mason then faces a crossroads—should he take respon-

On the set of *The Unknown Man* (1951) with Walter Pidgeon. (MGM)

sibility for his own crime? As Pidgeon's wife, Ann has little to do other than to watch as her world tumbles around her. She begs her husband to remain silent after Wallchek is convicted for the second murder. "It may not be man's justice," she pleads to Mason, "but it could be God's." In his review of the re-titled film, John Robertson found *The Unknown Man* to be a "wonderfully acted, highly polished movie." "Although improbable," said Robertson, "the story is done with such restraint and honesty that a moviegoer can live every minute of it. ... Ann Harding ... plays Mason's wife with understanding and tact."[20] *The New York Times* was less convinced, calling the film a "not particularly authentic curtsy toward American legal justice." The review found Ann "conventionally restrained," and panned Pidgeon's fine portrayal, by saying, "it's no treat to watch Mr. Pidgeon saunter airily through a supposedly serious probing of a man's conscience."[21]

While on the set, Ann voiced her opinion regarding the strenuous schedule of what she called the "new crop of young players." Between scenes, the studio demanded their new talent to attend diction, French, dance, singing, and piano lessons. "It is almost appalling to me," said Ann, "the things that are required of today's youngsters. When I started in the theater, my one job was to learn to act. Today, this is not enough."[22] MGM was indeed a far cry from Hedgerow. Dawn Addams, who is seen briefly as the girlfriend of Walter and Ann's son (Richard Anderson), concurred with Ann's assessment. Evidently, Addams also spent a lot of time posing provocatively for the camera. A majority of ads for *The Unknown Man* give the impression that Pidgeon was the crime lord and the leggy, full-figured Addams was his sex kitten. Justice and filial devotion were apparently not marketable commodities.

On December 2, 1950, Ann made her television debut on *Don Mc-Neill's TV Club*. After an interview with host McNeill, she offered a dramatic sketch. Several months later she opted to play a "capital

In her "old lady" getup, Ann solves a murder. With Vera Miles,
Glenn Roberts and Douglas Kennedy. *Schlitz Playhouse of Stars*
production of "The Great Lady" (1954).

hostess" in the television film *Washington Lady.* "I guess I'm supposed
to be Evelyn Walsh MacLean," Ann told columnist Erskine Johnson.
MacLean, owner of the infamous Hope Diamond, was a prominent
DC socialite. Ann lamented to the columnist that people were still
wailing that she ought to cut her hair to look more fashionable. "I
know how I'd look," Ann said, "and I'm not cutting my hair for anyone!" Referring to the ends of her long tresses, Ann leaned toward
Johnson, and whispered, "I can just sit on 'em."[23]

Ann's numerous television roles reunited her with former film
costars such as Walter Abel (*Ford Television Theatre*), Louis Hayward
(*Climax!*) and Basil Rathbone (*Kraft Television Theatre*). She usually found herself playing eccentric old ladies, or mother roles. *Lux
Video Theatre,* one of the numerous "live" programs, provided a more

unusual opportunity. The hour-long adaptation of the 1948 MGM drama, *An Act of Murder*, had Ann and Thomas Mitchell as a married couple dealing with the wife's incurable disease. After a climactic automobile wreck in which the wife is killed, Mitchell's character confesses that his intent had been for them both to die in the accident. A thrill-packed trial follows. Columnist Ellis Walker was impressed with Ann's performance, and made a point to interview her during rehearsals for her next project for CBS, "Young Girl in an Apple Tree" (1955). Ellis considered Ann the Grace Kelly of the 1930s. Ann told him she felt television was just as exciting for her as the movie business was 25 years ago. "And that first movie was mighty exciting," Ann admitted. "Do you know I still get mail about *Holiday*?" Ellis talked with one of the assistants on the set, who described Ann enthusiastically: "She's a real old pro. I haven't seen her look at the script all day. She knew it backwards before she set foot in the studio."[24]

Stage 7's half-hour adaptation of the Wells Root story "Young Girl in an Apple Tree" was more typical of Ann's TV work. She played Hallie Adams, the proprietor of a small-town curio shop, who clings to the twenty-year-old memory of her long-lost love Johnny (Regis Toomey), a promising artist. A windfall of $100,000 affords Hallie the opportunity to hire a detective (Whit Bissell) to locate Johnny, which he does. The pair reunite in New York. Johnny doesn't let on that he recognizes her. Instead, he shows Hallie his abstract sculpture titled "A Young Girl in an Apple Tree." She gets the message. It's of her. Johnny admits he had left town in a "haze of hot air," and couldn't go back home. Ann and Toomey work well with the whimsy and heart of Root's story.

The popular *Lux Video Theatre* featured Ann, Ray Danton and Thomas Mitchell in the TV adaptation of "An Act of Murder" (1955).

After completing his appointment with the San Diego Symphony Orchestra (1952-54), Werner Janssen was occupied as music director of the NBC Symphony orchestra in New York. He had taken the plunge into TV himself, producing "Masterpieces in Miniature"—104 films, three minutes each, featuring symphonic music, the world of ballet, and opera. "I'm sure Beethoven will be a relief from puppet shows," said Werner, "when you've had nothing but ham for dinner, a little caviar is good once in a while."[25] While in New York, the Janssens resided at the Savoy-Plaza and remained aloof. "They accept no phone calls," snipped Walter Winchell.[26] As television productions originated on both coasts, Ann was able to take advantage of whatever roles she wanted. Ann's enthusiasm for "live" television eventually cooled down. Movie historian and critic Steven H. Scheuer interviewed Ann in New York in 1956. "I can't see any advantages whatsoever in doing 'live' TV as opposed to film," said Ann. "But please don't get me started on that!" So, Scheuer tried to get her started. A nearby press agent for the show in which she was appearing (*Playwrights '56*) squirmed and turned bright red. The agent chimed in to say, "Miss Harding has some interesting anecdotes. She doesn't believe performers should be starred prematurely." Ann interjected,

"I'm against that. My father was a general. His advice to me was always: 'Don't go off half-cocked!'" There was no stopping Ann now. "The producers can't just make a star," she said indignantly. "An actress perfectly cast in a play may get raves for her performance. But what happens the next time out if she isn't perfectly cast?" Ann talked about her appearance in 1923's *Tarnish*—she got raves, but Jasper Deeter reminded her how lousy she was. Scheuer asked Ann what it was about her current role that appealed to her. She seemed surprised by his question. "It's a *challenge*," answered Ann. "To see if I can play this part which isn't at all like me." She added bitterly, "I'm not sure *what* it's about yet. They're still rewriting it." Asked about her future TV plans after this, Ann answered, "I have no TV commitments. TV comes up like thunder. It's always just one step ahead of doomsday. I have never seen a TV outfit yet that knew what it was doing two weeks ahead of schedule. And 'live' TV is the worst!" Scheurer queried, if "live" TV was so impossible, why did Ann bother? "Why do I do 'live' TV?" she replied. "Because so far it has larger audiences ... and the scripts are sometimes better." Ann glanced down at the script she was rehearsing and admitted, "Not always! But once in a while a good script does come along, so I do it. But I keep wishing it were on film!"[27]

The interview took place during rehearsals for "Center of the Maze" (1956), in which Ann played a liberal-minded clubwoman whose daughter falls for the family gardener. Peter Mark Richman, who I interviewed in 2009, played the gardener. "I have fond memories of working with Ann Harding," said Richman. "I remember her beauty and the care she took with herself (carrying a case of gelatin in small bottles which she mixed with water ... for energy, I suppose). She was of the old school in manner and work habits, and I respected that. She was also strong when she had to be. She didn't like the man who was playing her husband and was responsible for getting him fired. His replacement was more to her liking and quite dignified (to go with her perception of herself). The first guy was sort of a bumpkin, but a good actor. She couldn't see herself as a woman having a bumpkin for a husband. It demeaned her in her eyes."[28]

Tony Award-winning producer Fred Coe (*The Miracle Worker*) had requested Ann for the role. The story's author, Sam Hall, recalled, "It was based on a woman I knew who was a great liberal, a very rich political type whose only child, a daughter, fell in love with a black gardener. And she found out she was not a great liberal at all. The daughter was played by Marjorie Post's daughter, Dina Merrill."[29] Marjorie Post, who Ann portrayed in *Mission to Moscow*, was no longer the Ambassador's wife. The couple had divorced. Needless to say, the 1956 telecast was about a white gardener. Hall was best known, to his chagrin, for the 1960s daytime serial *Dark Shadows*. When I talked to him in 2009, the 88-year-old Hall offered some inside "dope" about the production problems on "Center of the Maze."

> I had written the script specifically for Fred Coe. Fred had a sensational reputation, and he was making a comeback with *Playwrights '56*. I was not involved with the casting. I was pleased when he called and said to me that he had decided on Ann Harding. I had admired her in the movies and thought that she was beautiful and very, very genteel ... which she *was*. Dina Merrill had come back to acting, after being married. Fred had worked with Grace Kelly and Eva Marie Saint, and he was famous for beautiful blondes. The idea of Dina Merrill and Ann Harding as a mother-daughter team ... we thought very good

casting. But, we had a problem with the director, who was Vinnie Donehue. He was a good director, but we really should have gone with Arthur Penn, who was our other choice. But, Arthur Penn and I did not get along, personally. So, I said, "No, no, please, don't give me Arthur."

Rehearsals for "Center of the Maze" were very difficult. It had something to do with Ann Harding. I had lunch with her one day and she told me that she was a general's daughter and that she never for a moment forgot it. She really was rather arbitrary and dictatorial. At one point she wanted us to fire the leading man who played her husband. She wanted us to get George Brent who was now living in Mexico. She had checked with him and he would have gladly come back to New York. She was very taken with him. [Ann and Brent had co-starred on TV two months previously, with obvious success.] We didn't do it, but she exerted a lot of pressure on Fred. I don't know how he got out of it. [The "more dignified" Russell Hicks took over the role.] So, I don't think she was terribly happy during the course of the rehearsals. She was fine in the part. She could act terribly well. And, she worked very well with Dina. She would have probably even been better if the gardener *had* been black. The show could have been much more meaningful than it was. I had great hopes for that show ... it wasn't Ann's fault that they weren't fulfilled.[30]

"Center of the Maze" was Ann's fourth "live" TV show in a row, two of which aired as part of the afternoon anthology series *Matinee Theatre*. These programs, filmed on a single set by a static camera, often suffered from insufficient lighting, and tended to be slow and claustro-phobic. Ann's performance on the program's "Progress Jr. and Minnie Sweeney" (1955), however, garnered critical raves. "Ann Harding, as an almost-over-age school teacher being pressured by proponents of progressive education," said drama critic James Abbe, "did a su-perb job of acting ... in as nearly a perfect dramatic production as television has yet come up with."[31] Television critic Bill Bird stated, "Veteran actress Ann Harding ... has received more fan mail than any other performer who has appeared on *Matinee Theater*."[32] According to Los Angeles columnist Edwin Schallert, Ann was reported to be up for an Emmy Award for her work on *Matinee Theater*.[33] (Ann was *not* nominated, and forty-one-year-old Mary Martin won the award for Best Single Performance by an Actress in *Peter Pan*).

Compared to shows like *The 20th Century Fox Hour*, the "live" shows were unable to do justice to their stories. Ann did two pro-grams for the Fox series, which had stand-out production values and talent. In "The Late George Apley"(1955), Ann's subtle presence as Mrs. Apley was incidental. John P. Marquand's story focuses on the conflict between Mrs. Apley's rebellious daughter (Joanne Wood-ward) and the stifling traditions forced upon his family by Mr. Ap-ley (Raymond Massey). Whenever the tension mounts, third-billed Ann tries to reconcile differences by directing people to the conserva-tory to "see the camellias," or announcing, "Tea is ready, dear!" By the finish, Mr. Apley can see that his "duty" to tradition has been nothing more than a burden. As an actor, Massey misses the satirical touch the author intended.

In Ann's repertoire of characters "not at all" like her, was a role from ABC's inter-faith program *Crossroads*. Producer Harry Joe

Brown (*Devotion, Prestige, Westward Passage*) told UP correspondent Vernon Scott, "I've never made a religious picture before in my life. We're not trying to prove anything with *Crossroads*, but we do believe it will help the various sects understand one another. The men in our stories are real people with problems. For a change clergymen will be humanized instead of lionized."[34] Lewis R. Foster, who had written *Mr. Smith Goes to Washington*, directed Ann in *Crossroads*' WWII episode, "With All My Love" (1955). As Philippines missionary Hulda Linn, Ann epitomizes someone who is unattached to physical life. Her sole concern is the spiritual well-being of the villagers in her parish. When an American army chaplain (Hugh Beaumont) arrives to "rescue" her from a war-torn area, Hulda seems more perturbed by his gesture than relieved. "I can't leave now," she says firmly, concerned over a young convert's loss of faith. With no sign of heroics, she is perfectly content to take whatever consequences befall her, even death. Although producer Brown was determined not to make the half-hour programs sound "preachy," the storyline had a decidedly contrived edge to it.

A month after the *Crossroads*' broadcast, Ann signed on for a TV adaptation of Oscar Wilde's *Lord Arthur Saville's Crime* for the CBS dramatic series *Climax!* (1955). Retitled "A Promise to Murder," Ann played the eccentric Lady Wetherby, the wealthy aunt of a barrister (Louis Hayward). She decides to sponsor Mr. Vorhees (Peter Lorre), a palm reader, going so far as to move him into her mansion. It isn't long before Lady Wetherby's reasoning ability is called into question. "I really think I'm past the age of having to justify my wishes to anyone!" she declares to her nephew-lawyer. "I want my will altered." $50,000 is to go to Vorhees, so that he may continue with his work.

A glamorous Ann co-starred with George Brent in Celebrity Playhouse's *"The Fleeting Years"* (1956).

Unbeknownst to Lady Wetherby, Vorhees' "work" involves a cleverly designed murder: *hers.* If anyone was deserving of being murdered it would have been Ann's make-up artist. The ghastly attempt to make her look older was amateurish, and it detracted from her performance. In 1956, Ann returned to the big screen, after claiming she had had enough of "live" TV. "That glazed look you see in the eyes of actors on 'live' TV," said Ann, "is not histrionic emotion, but inner panic. They're in a mental turmoil to remember their next lines." "Trying to speak in a normal tone after making a complete change of wardrobe in 48 seconds," she concluded, "[isn't] exactly conducive to delivering a good performance."[35]

The Corn Is Green

Ann began one of the most fulfilling roles of her stage career in the summer of 1952—Miss Moffat in *The Corn Is Green*. Emlyn Williams' poignant drama of a spinster teacher in a Welsh mining village was first created on stage by Ethel Barrymore in 1940. Bette Davis had played the role on screen. When Miss Moffat, an outsider and stranger, discovers among her students a young miner with a poetic soul, she is determined to make him "flower." How she nurtures young Morgan Evans toward the light of knowledge and a scholarship at Oxford is the plot of the play. Douglas Dick played the miner, and John Barrymore's daughter, Diana, played the mean-spirited young woman who attempts to ruin Miss Moffat's plans. The *Los Angeles Times* was impressed with actor/director Harry Ellerbe's direction, and the performances. "Miss Harding's spinster role assumes heroic proportions," stated the review. "She is the grand lady of the stage ... as she wrings to the fullest the pathos and occasional gentle humor of the play. Miss Barrymore is completely abandoned to her characterization of a shameless, mean adolescent. Douglas Dick is heart-warming as the young miner."[36] That winter Ann took the play to Palm Springs Playhouse. Los Angeles critic Edwin Schallert reported that Ann was the first "big name star" for the theatre, which was filled to capacity. "This singularly gifted actress," said Schallert, "brought to the role of Miss Moffat a unique warmth, which added measurably to the impact of the later scenes when she bid good-by to her young protégé, and undertakes to care for his illegitimate child. Miss Harding invested the role with that beautiful vocal quality for which she has long been celebrated and which lends special distinction to the production."[37]

Ann then took the play to the Sombrero Playhouse in Phoenix,

Arizona. The plight of miners had struck a chord in her. According to British political author Janet Coleman, Ann offered a script reading, in Chicago, of the blacklisted film *Salt of the Earth*, which was having problems being released. The film told about the exploitation of Mexican-American miners in the Southwest.[38] In 1955, Ann resumed her role in *The Corn is Green* for a memorable two-week run near Chicago, at Salt Creek Theater. Robert Brown, who had made his stage debut in *Skipper Next to God* (1948) under the direction of Lee Strasberg, played the role of Morgan Evans. When I contacted him in 2008, Brown was most enthusiastic about sharing his memories of working with Ann Harding. He had acted with other theatrical legends: Judith Anderson, Katharine Cornell, and Helen Hayes. Brown talked at length about what he felt to be a most memorable experience. He found Ann to be likeable and dignified without being stuffy. "You've chosen an unusual actor," he remarked to me during our conversation. He went on to explain why.

> I was playing this remarkable character. Ann was concerned about her own performance. She knew the play—she saw the original production with Ethel Barrymore. Ann had been struck by that performance. When she watched it, she felt the caution and anxiety that Barrymore's Miss Moffat had about her work with the children—she was there to help and bring them introspection as they came out of the darkness of their lives in Wales. Spiritually, they were frozen. Ann wanted to bring her experiences to it. She had a tough time. Most actors just learn the lines. Ann was working in a way that I was trained – trying to understand how to tell a story in a human, honest way.

When I met Ann at the lovely Salt Creek Theatre
in Hinsdale, Illinois, she wanted to talk about how
each of us got to be as we are. She asked me questions about my youth. Somehow it tied my life and
Ann's life together. [Brown mentioned the extensive traveling and military connection in both their
childhoods—and never having a "center."] We spent
a lot of time together. We spoke of many intimate
things. I'd listen to her stories about herself—her
loneliness—her desire to become an actor, which her
father didn't want. I remember she said she didn't
feel free—she wanted to break out. How she found
freedom as Miss Moffat in the play, was by touching
on another character who needed to find freedom—
herself! And that's what happened to me. That's
what happened to Morgan Evans—Miss Moffat gave
him the key to his brain and his talent. The thing
that got to Ann—we were so similar—was that I was
a stranger in a way in my own life. We were different,
yet similar. That's the thing that was like an improvi-
sation—and we locked in on it.

One of Ann's lovely things was never to talk about
how you are working. Find your own way and do it
yourself. That's the thing that Ann Harding did for
me. She recited this Edna St. Vincent Millay poem:
"All I could see from where I stood was three small
mountains and a wood; I turned and looked the
other way and saw three islands in a bay." She loved
St. Vincent Millay. [A passion Ann had shared with
Jasper Deeter.]³⁹When she did that, I spoke along
with her and it was a bonding. That's what happened in the performance. She gave me the cue that
we could bring our own lives into our work. We'd
look at each other across the stage during curtain

calls and some nights when it worked, when we
"caught it"—it was like there would be tears in her
eyes. I found her to be one of the special performers
that I played with. And I played with some of the
greats. I never ran into her again. I'm sorry I didn't,
because she was a gentle, creative force. She was really quite heroic in her way.

Ann's husband dropped in and wanted to ask questions of me. He wanted to know who the hell I was.
When he found out that I had lived in The Osborne
in New York, diagonally across from Carnegie Hall,
that made it seem possible for him to say, "He's a
good kid. Give him whatever he wants." He spent
hours with me everyday—perhaps because I had
some knowledge about the things that he knew
about and I did drop some names. [Brown, born on
Scotland's Isle of Skye, had grown up in New York.]
He was quite a bossy guy. I have a feeling that
Werner—there's something about a conductor. The
body language. I think Werner wanted to run the
show. Maybe that's why the marriage didn't work.[40]

In the fall of 1954, Ann and Werner traveled to Sweden, and didn't
arrive back in the US until mid-February. Jane Bannister had relocated from Hawaii to the San Francisco Bay Area where she got a job
at Saks Fifth Avenue. She met a young stockbroker by the name of
Alfred Paul Otto Jr., who was three years older. The couple married
on November 23, 1955, at San Francisco's Swedenborgian Church.
Paul Otto Jr. had been a pilot in the Naval Air Corps during WWII,

November 23, 1955. The wedding of Jane Harding to Al Otto in San Francisco. (l-r) Margarette Neuman (Marie Otto's sister), Marjorie Kimball (head turned, Al Otto's sister), Mary Pruett Gibson (maid of honor), Jane, Al, Ann, Werner, Al Sr. and Marie Otto (parents of the groom). (Courtesy of the Otto family)

and later resumed his studies at the University of California, where he was a member of Zeta Psi Fraternity. He was previously married to Vivian Gamble of Piedmont, California. By 1953, the couple, who had three children, divorced. Both Ann and Werner attended the wedding, but there was no mention of Harry Bannister being present. Janssen, Jane's stepfather, gave the bride away. Jane wore a short-skirted blue lace gown for the occasion and carried white orchids. A champagne supper party followed in the Phoenix Room of the Hotel Mark Hopkins. Ann received the guests at the reception, wearing a smoke-colored silk frock, and matching pillbox hat. She and Werner were registered at the Mark Hopkins.[41]

Jane and Ann at the reception held at San Francisco's
Hotel Mark Hopkins. (Courtesy of the Otto family)

On the set of *Celebrity Playhouse*, which had teamed her with George Brent as a pair of later-year lovers, Ann talked about aging and her own marriage. "I've never lied about my age," Ann told syndicated columnist Lydia Lane. "This clinging to youth desperately can be most unattractive. I watched an aging but once-famous star [Maude Adams] as *Peter Pan* when she was 65. She had so completely lost perspective that she felt she could play any age and I'm afraid there are a great many women like her. I find this attitude difficult to understand. There is so much of life to be lived and enjoyed beyond the youth years."[42] Ann had kept up with her exercise, determined not to put on weight. "I can still wear the dress I had on when I met my husband twenty years ago," she said. "In fact, I bring it out each anniversary and we laugh about it." As far as her diet, Ann gave all the credit to Werner. "My husband is the nutrition expert in our house. He knows all there is to know about food values and anyone who has dined at our home when he did the cooking …." Ann's expression indicated that these occasions were "sheer joy." "When I met Werner I met an angel," Ann told long-time Hollywood columnist Jimmy Fidler. "I've had no reason for 19 years to change that opinion."[43] Fidler's comment that the Janssen marriage was "one of the happiest in stage and screen history," would eventually become … history.

(Endnotes)

1   Debbie Reynolds, *Debbie Reynolds-My Life*, William Morrow, Inc. (NY), c. 1988, pg 68
2   "Ann Harding Resumes Pictures Career," *Evening Capitol (MD)*, 12/2/50
3   Debbie Reynolds, *Debbie Reynolds – My Life* ... pg. 69
4   Debbie Reynolds, *Debbie Reynolds—My Life* ...pg. 69
5   Review of *Two Weeks With Love*, Los Angeles Times, 12/18/50
6   Dudley Schnabel, *Load, Midland Magazine*, May 1931
7   James Padgitt, "Hollywood Newsreel," *Lebanon Daily News*, 7/26/50
8   "Hersholt Leaves Dr. Christian Part to Be Father in New Film," *Daily Interlake*, 3/20/55
9   E. Johnson, "In Hollywood," 12/15/51
10   Stuart Oderman, *Lillian Gish*, McFarland, c. 2000, pg 250
11   Scott Bettencourt, on , www.filmscoremonthly.com c. 2009
12   "Magnificent Yankee in Film," *Syracuse Herald*, 9/2/50
13   Letter to author from Jimmy Lydon, 3/17/2008
14   Bosley Crowther review of *The Magnificent Yankee*, New York Times, 1/19/1951
15   Sterling Sorensen review of *The Magnificent Yankee*, *The Capital Times (WI)*, 2/26/51
16   Review of *The Magnificent Yankee*, *The Saturday Review of Liberature*
17   Edwin Schallert review of *The Magnificent Yankee*, Los Angeles Times, 12/21/1950
18   Edwin Schallert, "Schallert Offers Oscar Forecasts," Los Angeles Times, 2/12/51
19   "Villa Riviera Set for Film," *Long Beach Press Telegram*, 1/14/51
20   John Robertson review of *The Unknown Man*, Cedar Rapids Gazette, 12/19/51
21   Review of *The Unknown Man*, New York Times, 11/17/51
22   "Ann Harding Impressed By New Talent," MGM Press Book for *The Unknown Man*, c. 1951
23   Erskine Johnson, "In Hollywood," *Fitchburg Sentinel*, 10/11/51
24   Ellis Walker, "Video Notes," *The Daily Review*, 4/26/55
25   Aline Mosby, "News-Notes From Hollywood," *Humboldt Standard*, 5/17/52
26   Walter Winchell, "The Broadway Line," 5/11/56
27   Steven H. Scheuer, "Ann Harding Is Not 'Sold' On Live TV," *Syracuse Herald*, 5/3/56
28   Letter from Peter Mark Richman, 6/25/2009
29   Jay Blotcher, "Interview with Veteran TV Writer Sam Hall," *Roll Magazine*, April 2009
30   Telephone conversation with writer Sam Hall, 6/16/2009
31   James Abbe review of *Progress Jr. and Minnie Sweeney*, Oakland Tribune, 11/7/55
32   Bill Bird, "Spotlight on, New Talent," *The Independent*, 2/7/56
33   Edwin Schallert, "Ann Harding Costars in *Intruder*," Los Angeles Times, 2/24/56
34   Vernon Scott, "Crossroads: Men of Cloth to Have Own Show on TV," news article, 11/15/55
35   Hal Humphrey, "Viewing TV," Oakland Tribune, 3/15/56
36   Review of *The Corn is Green*, Los Angeles Times, 8/14/52
37   Edwin Schallert review of *The Corn is Green*, Los Angeles Times, 1/30/53
38   Janet Coleman, *The Compass*, University of Chicago Pr., c. 1990, pg. 79
39   Conversation with director Paul Aaron, 7/15/2008, Aaron stated that Deeter enjoyed talking at length about Edna St. Vincent Millay
40   Conversation with Robert Brown, February 15, 2008
41   "Jane Harding Is Now Mrs. Alfred P. Otto, Jr.," *San Francisco Chronicle*, 11/24/55
42   Lydia Lane, "Ann Harding Makes No Effort to Hide Fact That She's Fifty Years Young," *San Antonio Express*, 1/30/56
43   Jimmy Fidler, "In Hollywood," *Nevada State Journal*, 3/17/56

19

On Playing
Tennessee Williams

"That got a lot out of my system*"*

—Ann Harding, 1963

Before Ann returned to the screen in 1956, she considered several film offers. Jimmy Fidler mentioned she was up for an important role in Cecil B. de Mille's *The Ten Commandments.* Louella Parsons confirmed that Ann was contemplating the role of Jane Wyman's mother for *Miracle in the Rain.* When Florence Eldridge backed out of playing the estranged wife of her real-life husband Fredric March in *The Man in the Gray Flannel Suit,* Ann happily accepted the opportunity to reunite with the leading man from her 1929 film debut, *Paris Bound.* After two more film roles in 1956, Ann's screen career came to a permanent halt. For various reasons she would back out of playing a society dowager in Debbie Reynolds' *Tammy and the Bachelor* (1957) and the innkeeper in *A Time to Love and a Time to Die* (1958). Ann would continue, however, to enjoy a steady mix of TV and stage opportunities after she and Werner relocated back east in the fall of

1957. As their marriage turned rocky, it was acting that proved therapeutic for Ann. The real highlight for her was playing characters created by Tennessee Williams.

Sloan Wilson's popular novel, *The Man in the Gray Flannel Suit*,
was brought to the screen by writer-director Nunnally Johnson (*The
Three Faces of Eve*) as a well-rounded version of the author's original work. In the years following WWII, millions of Americans had
migrated to the suburbs, commuting daily to major cities. Gregory
Peck, as Tom Rath, the man in gray flannel, typified the average,
$7,000-a-year commuter trying to cope in a geared-up, corporate
world. His petulant wife (Jennifer Jones) needles him toward a better paying job. Rath soon discovers that the "successful" people, such
as his ultra-wealthy employer Ralph Hopkins (Fredric March), are
really miserable. The accumulation of pressures that over-achiever
Hopkins has to contend with have cost him a great deal. He has failed
as a husband and a father. Rath faces the mounting pressures that
accompany "ambition," and bursts forth with honest opinions and
revelations that others may not want to hear. He rises to the occasion
to tell his boss what he *really* thinks, and tells Mrs. Rath about his illegitimate son in Italy—a result of an affair he had during WWII. As
the "honest" hero, Tom Rath appears to be the survivor.

Ann and Fredric March create the film's secondary theme, which
is touched on at intervals. As an estranged couple, they elevate their
scenes from standard soap opera with the sheer force and indelible
mark of talent. We are introduced to Ann's character (Helen Hopkins) when she calls her husband at work, insisting they talk in person. She is deeply concerned about their eighteen-year-old daughter
Susan (Gigi Perreau). "Don't fail me Ralph, please," she pleads be-

Man in the Gray Flannel Suit (1956) with Fredric March. (20th-Century-Fox)

fore he hangs up. In the scene that follows, Helen confronts Ralph regarding their daughter's obsessive nightclubbing, and declares, "She's a celebrity in that filthy crowd!" The family "riches" have made Susan an attraction to money-seekers—disreputable men, who are far older than she. "Who am I to offer advice," replies Hopkins. "You've got to do *something*," Helen demands. "You've got to give her at least the same time, thought, and attention that you give to a business proposition." Hopkins doesn't argue. However, his "talk" with Susan fizzles. After being notified by the press that Susan has married a much older lothario, he calls his wife to tell her the news. He also asks if she will take him back. "I don't want to see anybody," she tells him. "I don't want you to call me at all Ralph … please." She hangs up the phone—leaving Hopkins hanging in mid-air. The scene underscores that all he has left now is his relationship with the corporation, and a bad heart.

In 1946, March received an Oscar for his portrayal of the WWII vet re-adjusting to civilian life in the classic *Best Years of Our Lives*. Peck's WWII vet details the adjustment to the corporate culture that followed. Bosley Crowther, for *The New York Times*, observed, "Director Nunnally Johnson and producer Darryl F. Zanuck have fetched a mature, fascinating, and often quite tender and touching film. … All the actors are excellent. Mr. Peck is a human, troubled Tom Rath; Fredric March makes a glib but lonely boss; Jennifer Jones is warm and irritable as Tom's wife and Ann Harding is poignant as the worn-out wife of the boss."[1] Author James Robert Parish commented, "The mature and quiet authority Ann brought to her very few screen scenes was an excellent contrast to the mercurial emotionalism supplied by Jennifer Jones."[2] Drama critic Richard V. Happel concurred with Parish, saying, "Ann Harding, a star of other years, is excellent as the wealthy Mr. March's estranged wife. Rather miscast, we fear, is Jennifer Jones, whose best friends cannot accuse of being an actress. When her painfully honest husband tells her about the illegitimate son in Italy … she carries on fierce, and makes the worst faces."[3] *Variety's* review glowingly reported, "Ann Harding as March's neglected wife has the proper air of disillusionment and turns in a topnotch performance."[4]

Peck's commute in *The Man in the Gray Flannel Suit*, was from the coastal town of Westport, Connecticut, to New York City. Filming was done on location. Oddly enough, in the fall of 1957, just after Janssen completed his position as conductor for the Toronto Symphony Orchestra, he and Ann put their Los Angeles home up for sale in order to purchase a home in Westport. Their new address, 5 Tuck Lane, was a wooded area just off Lyons Plain Road (the same neighborhood where Paul Newman and Joanne Woodward would later reside). Few knew of the problems facing the Janssen marriage—problems Ann hoped would resolve themselves. In a divorce suit, four years later, Ann indicated that trouble in her marriage began *exactly* on January 1, 1955.[5] On that date, she and Werner were traveling in Germany and Scandinavia. Werner was bent on relocating to Europe. Ann was averse to the idea. Westport, Connecticut could well have been their compromise.

A former artist's colony on the Long Island sound, Westport was evolving into a thriving business center. Less than 50 miles from New York City, the affluent community boasted a long-time regional theater, a pavilion that provided free concerts, and a strong arts council. Westport seemed a logical location for people like Ann and Werner.

Ann's final two film assignments were decidedly offbeat. *Strange Intruder* (1956), co-starring Ida Lupino and Edmund Purdom, began filming on February 24. Jimmy Fidler caught Ann on the Allied Artists' set. "I talked with her this week," Fidler mentioned, "and I found her the same, calm, unexcitable, sensible, far-seeing woman of those earlier times."[6] Ann enacted Lupino's mother-in-law in an adaptation of the Helen Fowler novel, *The Intruder*. Irving Rapper (*Now Voyager*) directed this dark tale of a Korean War veteran Paul Quentin (Purdom), who keeps a promise to visit the family of his dead war buddy. After Quentin receives a warm welcome, Mary (Ann), the dead man's mother, is astonished by Quentin's ability to detail her son's life. "Did he send … a message?" she asks hesitantly. "There was one thing," replies Quentin. "It was just before he died. It was this …" (he places a kiss on her cheek). Mary is overcome. Moments later, she perceives that Quentin has some emotional problem. "You've been ill, haven't you?" she asks, deeply concerned. Indeed, the battle-fatigued man is hearing his dead buddy's "voice" instructing him to kill his two children in order to save them from their philandering mother, Alice (Lupino). Before you can dismiss the storyline, it must be pointed out that for some veterans such a scenario is not that far off target. In Paul M. Edwards' *A Guide to Film on the Korean War*, he calls *Strange Intruder*, "a harsh and depressing film … surprisingly well done."[7] Post-traumatic stress disorder makes for an uncomfortable film subject. *Strange Intruder* had some powerful elements, but the overall effect was uneven. *Variety* labeled this definite "B" film as a "fair meller," stating, "Purdom and Miss Lupino handle their roles acceptably, as does Miss Harding."[8]

Filmed after *Strange Intruder*, but released before, was the low-budget, reincarnation-themed Universal release, *I've Lived Before*. It was the first film to deal with the subject after the publication of Morey Bernstein's 1956 sensational best-seller, *The Search for Bridey Murphy* (later released as a film starring Teresa Wright). *Murphy* told of an amateur's attempt of using hypnotic regression on a Colorado housewife who, much to his surprise, began detailing her previous life in Cork, Ireland. The premise for these films is not necessarily fantastic. The 18th century French philosopher Voltaire (a favorite of Ann's) had stated, "It is not more surprising to be born twice than once." *I've Lived Before* offers a solid performance by Western star and ex-stunt man, Jock Mahoney, as airline pilot John Bolan. Before take-off, Bolan notices a middle-aged woman sitting among the passengers. She is the catalyst for a series of mental flashbacks that take place while Bolan is in the pilot's seat. He suddenly finds himself flying back in WWI … before he was born. In the scene that follows, Bolan wakes up in the hospital, convinced it is 1918, and claiming to be a deceased WWI pilot, Peter Stevens. Trying to solve the puzzle, Bolan is compelled to visit the lady passenger, Jane Stone (Ann), to see if she holds the key to his extraordinary experience. He locates her in Philadelphia. She is cordial at first, but becomes quite formidable when he tells her of his unexplained knowledge of Peter Stevens. "I don't want to hear any more," she declares. "I've heard quite

Tense scene from Allied Artists' *Strange Intruder* **(1956)**
with Edmund Purdom. (Allied Artists)

enough!" She asks him to leave. His story is an invasion of privacy—
hers. She was the fiancée of the deceased pilot.

Miss Stone reluctantly involves herself once more. In a psycholo-
gist's office Bolan details to her how Peter Stevens had proposed marriage. In the film's climactic moment, Miss Stone, who had claimed that
reincarnation was something "held out as a false hope to people in old
age and bereavement," changes her tune. "Something I believed impossible and foolish," she realizes, "is not impossible at all!" Although nothing
is resolved in this wordy and theoretical film, nothing is sensationalized
either. Any verdict is left to the viewer's discretion. Because of the subject matter, *I've Lived Before* is an easy film to criticize. Bosley Crowther,
for *The New York Times,* made his verdict clear. "Bridey Murphy can rest
easy," said Crowther. "*I've Lived Before* ... is a listless and colorless excur-

sion into the realms of the supernatural. It is made about as awesome and momentous as if the fellow discovered he was wearing somebody else's shoes."[9] *Variety* said, "For those who want to take the subject seriously, Mahoney turns in a credible performance … his sincerity is matched by the dignified portrayal of Miss Harding."[10] Ann's self-contained take on the role was certainly effective. The question is, was it worthy of her talent? John Robertson's syndicated review put it rather well, "*I've Lived Before* has Ann Harding in the cast, and she deserves better."[11]

Ann filmed her second hour-long teleplay for *The 20ᵗʰ Century Fox Hour* in 1957. "The Springfield Incident" was based on the studio's 1939 film, *Young Mr. Lincoln*, starring Henry Fonda. Capably filling Fonda's shoes was Tom Tryon. News items carried a photo of Ann beaming at the young actor, who would later abandon his career to become a successful novelist. Ann called at least one columnist to rave, "Tom Tryon is the finest young actor I've ever seen."[12] Playing Abigail Clay, Ann is hardly recognizable as the crusty and illiterate pioneer woman who

I've Lived Before (1956). Between takes, Ann shows Jock Mahoney photos of her family. (Universal)

makes a trade with young Abraham Lincoln (a storekeeper). She needs flannel to make shirts for her sons. As she can't read, she offers Abe a barrel of books. In the bargain was *Blackstone's Commentaries*. Lincoln is delighted. When he begins to talk about the book's content, Abigail brightens. "Law?" she says. "I always *knew* that book was 'bout somethin'!" The book provided the incentive for Lincoln's law career. Ironically, years later, in his first important case, Abe represents Abigail's sons wrongly accused of murder. Abigail's moment comes as she takes the witness stand, and refuses the prosecutor's offer to save at least one son by pointing out the "guilty" one.

Ann's second assignment on *Climax!* titled, "Trouble At No. 5," was as a conniving housekeeper-murderer. She reflected on her career to columnist Vernon Scott during rehearsals, saying, "All my life I've played straight leads and heroines. As time went on the roles got more and more noble. Finally, my appearance in a movie indicated that at least *one* character in the story would be terribly put-upon. It was awful. For years I played nothing but dear sweet, darling, frantic bores. I must accept some blame for my dull roles. I refused to do anything that was vulgar or in poor taste.[13]

The small screen continued to provide Ann with opportunities to act before the camera, as it did many stars from Hollywood's "Golden Age." One performance that fit snugly into Harding's "noble" genre was on the premier episode of *The Du Pont Show with June Allyson* (1959). "Those We Love," written by Arthur Ross, was touted as one of Ann's many "comebacks." Du Pont's first season also offered "comebacks" for Irene Dunne, Bette Davis, Ginger Rogers, Sylvia Sidney, and Myrna Loy. "How can I come back?" Ann queried to one reporter. "I never retired. What's happened is that my husband and I are country folks, and don't hit the night spots. So nobody sees me around and people think I'm dead. I don't get called unless somebody has an impulse and remembers me. Maybe I ought to hire a press agent so I could have somebody to blame for my obscurity." Ann pointed out with a sly smile, "While I would appear on live television, I don't think anybody's going to ask me to—not after the strong way I sounded off against it. And I'm still against it."[14]

Ann said she was flattered to be asked to be on the program's premier episode. "It's a pleasure to be working with June Allyson," Ann told columnist Harold Stern. Ann, with a dash of humor ... and foresight, summed up the plot, which was a variation on the biblical story of Ruth and Naomi. "The play is about a young widow," Ann began, "who feels her life has come to an end when her husband dies and that it would be unfaithful of her to love and marry again. When I first read it, I called and said, 'I didn't know that Du Pont sold soap.' But since then most of what I found objectionable has been written out. It's not half bad now."[15] According to critics it wasn't half good either. Cecil Smith's review in the *Los Angeles Times* was merciless. "This looks like the first chapter of a soap opera that will run for 27 years," said Smith. "By the time it was over, I thought it had lasted 27 years—a bad carbon copy of Loretta Young's weekly vale of tears."[16] TV reporter John Crosby barbed, "The nice thing about the *June Allyson Show* is that it's aimed at the nation's women. That means us fellows can get out of the house. There was endless soapy dialogue about the propriety of a widow ever having a finger laid on her again." Ann commented to the *Chicago Daily Tribune,* "In this play I'm not the star. I defer to Miss Allyson by soft peddling the mother's feeling about her son. I center my concern on her rather than on my own grief." Her rebuttal to Crosby was simply, "What the story offers is a plea against women like those in India who throw themselves on their husband's funeral pyre. We want to say that life can begin again after a person has suffered a great tragedy."

Director Jack Smight, who preferred more edgy subject matter (Rod Steiger's *No Way to Treat A Lady*), managed to pull off a few good scenes as Ann's "Naomi" encourages June's "Ruth" to give her new beau (Peter Mark Richman) a chance. Ruth refuses to talk about the budding romance, but Naomi is insistent. "Any subject that we evade this much," she tells her, "*must* be important." Naomi finally finds the words to set Ruth "free," and confronts her head on with them. "To love life," Naomi begins, "means to love someone who is *living*. Life needs the warmth of a human being. Life needs the sight of a human form; life is in the touch of the beloved." Call it "soap" if you will, but for many, Allyson's show was an oasis from the desert of hour-long westerns that had been corralled for TV consumption. *The New York Times* review was impressed with the final scene, saying, "Mr. Ross' final line on this relationship of love to the living and the dead reflected both penetration and understanding. And Miss Harding made the most of the scene without resorting to melodramatics."[18]

Peter Mark Richman, who had previously worked with Ann, gave a solid, impressive portrayal in "Those We Love." Richman told this author, "Ann was always warm and courteous to me. Of course, when I did the film with June Allyson, Ann and I were old acquaintances. I was a few years older, and we were shooting on film—not going "live" with all the ensuing pressures. There's a difference. Ann still had her gelatin with her and she was still beautiful, whatever age she was!"[19] At his request, I sent Richman a DVD of the program. "I dare say," wrote Richman, "I was surprised looking at a piece I had done so many years ago. Pretty good! Interesting to see Ann—remembering what a star she was."[20]

Like many well-seasoned actors who excel in their craft, Ann's TV performances, if not "fresh," were always technically impressive. It would be the stage that offered her challenges that proved more vivid. In the fall of 1953, she was set to play a woman who experiences the "hilarious" agonies of turning fifty in Andrew Rosenthal's *Red Letter Day*. The production, scheduled to open in Syracuse, New York, was cancelled. (Gloria Swanson later toured with success in this vehicle). The following year, Ann considered taking *Without Consent*, by the promising new playwright Jack Perry, to Broadway. In 1955, another new play, considered "pre-Broadway," *The Morgan Rock*, was to co-star Ann with Wendell Corey. It finally got off ground in 1959 (without Ann). Her next theatrical venture, however, was well worth waiting for.

In the spring of 1958, Ann returned to the stage in Tennessee Williams' *Garden District*, which consisted of two one-act plays: *Something Unspoken*, and *Suddenly, Last Summer*. The off-Broadway production played at the York Playhouse. On May 27, Ann, replacing Margaret Bannerman, took her audience by surprise. Walter Winchell observed in his column, "People who recall talented Ann Harding as the sweet, wholesome and long-suffering wife in the films, are amazed at the brutal force with which she projects the hard, ruthless mother in Tennessee Williams' *Garden District*. The drama critics should review the play (again) since she inherited the role."[21] Set in New Orleans, *Something Unspoken* presented Ann as the aging, egotistical Cornelia Scott. The affection-starved Cornelia has her heart set on being president of the Daughters of the Confederation. Her companion-secretary, Grace, refuses to talk about an awkward sexual moment the two had shared years previously—something unspoken. The issue remains dropped, and unresolved. Cornelia's rose garden is symbolically "not seen" and located off stage. Author Joe Falocco, in his article, "Gardens of Desire: Toward a Unified Vision of *Garden District*," states, "Each of these plays describes one of two major aspects of the behavioral dilemma facing American homosexuals in the 1950's. ... when read together, the two plays portray this dilemma in full."[22]

Critics recognized *Suddenly, Last Summer* as the major work in *Garden District*. It was basically two long monologues in which Ann, as the wheelchair-bound Violet Venable attempts to obscure the truth about her son Sebastian's homosexuality and violent death, by cannibalism, in Cabeza de Lobo. Sebastian was accompanied on this venture by his attractive cousin Catherine, who was used as bait for Sebastian's sexual appetites. As Catherine is aware of Sebastian's horrible end, Ann's character wants her lobotomized. For Mrs.Venable, Sebastian's legacy as a poet must remain unscathed by such scandal. While the lesbianism of Cornelia in *Something Unspoken* remains closeted in convention, the character of Sebastian, in *Suddenly, Last Summer*, refuses to conform to the same strictures. His exotic garden is located stage center. Sebastian's manipulations, however, indicate he hadn't completely liberated himself.

William's dark visions and compassionate heart were an unusual mix for the times, and for Ann Harding. Claudia Cassidy for *The Chicago Tribune* found *Suddenly, Last Summer* to be "the story of those who devour one another." Commenting on Ann's character and then Ann herself,

Cassidy wrote, "This twice-dispossessed mother, hoping to bribe the young doctor to silence the girl, pours out her own story, unaware that she was the first to devour her son. A bewigged Ann Harding [is] a new and strong contender as the furious woman in the wheelchair."[23] Ann relished her role, saying, "I read scripts that were dreary, disillusioned, dirty and often loaded with preachment, and then suddenly along came the wonderful opportunity in Mr. Williams' two short plays. I have a marvelous chance to prove myself. I couldn't find a better chance to get away from those noble women parts. I've been tired of them for years, and I know everyone else is too."[24] When the film version of *Suddenly, Last Summer* began several months later, Ann's RKO rival, Katharine Hepburn, was given the weighty assignment of Violet Venable. Ann took *Garden District* on a mid-summer tour in Chicago, the Playhouse-in-the-Park in Philadelphia and other key cities. Reflecting back on her role as Violet Venable in 1963, Ann laughed when she told columnist Larry Neely, "*That* got a lot out of my system." She said it was a great opportunity to vent the repressed villain in herself.[25]

In late July 1958, Ann signed on to star in Daphne Du Maurier's *September Tide.* Du Maurier, best known for her popular novel *Rebecca*, penned a tender and delicate tale of a lonely woman who falls in love late in life. The play originally opened at London's West End in 1948, starring Gertrude Lawrence, with whom Du Maurier was alleged to be having a passionate affair. On stage, Ann played Stella, a middle-aged widow living on the Cornish coast of England. She discovers that her bohemian artist son-in-law (Gig Young) is falling in love with her. By the play's end, Stella allows herself to surrender to the "unconventional." The 2007 BBC2 series, *Daphne*, pointed out that *September Tide* was based on Du Maurier's great love for Ellen Doubleday, the wife of

Bewigged Ann in Tennessee Williams'
The Garden District (1958).
(Courtesy of Photofest)

an American publisher. Although the two were very close, Doubleday made it clear that she was unable to reciprocate, sexually.[26] *September Tide* toured through August. That winter Ann paired with former co-stars Edward Everett Horton (*Holiday*) and Reginald Owen (*Enchanted April*), for the American premier of the London comedy-hit, *Not in the Book*. The play opened in Palm Beach, February 9, 1959, and told of an ordinary family-loving civil servant (Horton) who finds himself being blackmailed. He resolves his situation by attempting the "perfect murder" as laid out in a novel he had once read. Nothing turns out the way it did in the book, for hilarious results. Ann played Horton's wife, and she has no better luck concealing her series of traffic violations. While Horton and Owen continued on tour to the west coast with the play, Ann decided to drop out. She had come across what she thought to be an excellent drama about the early 19th century poet Charles Lamb and his insane sister, Mary. She failed in her attempt to find any backing for it. "I was told that because it's so well written it would never go on Broadway," Ann lamented. "I'll try for a London production first. I think it's deplorable the way standards in theater have been deteriorating. Maybe it might not be a bad idea to have critics pass on plays *before* they're produced."[27]

Ann became a grandmother in 1958, when Jane gave birth to a daughter, Diana. The Otto family had settled just north of San Francisco, in Marin County. Jane made annual visits to her mother in Westport, as Ann wasn't inclined to travel to the Bay Area. In the fall of 1959, Werner Janssen went to Austria where he served two years as conductor for the Vienna State Opera Orchestra. He returned home to Westport, and the Tuck Lane residence, intermittently. In 1960, Ann and author Faith Baldwin were on the 30th anniversary committee for the Westport Country Playhouse (where Ann had played *Yes, My Darling Daughter* in 1949). That same year, Ann busied herself with two television appearances, and local politics.

On NBC's *Sunday Showcase,* she played the mother of Oliver Wendell Holmes (Christopher Plummer) in the dramatic presentation, "Autocrat and Son." Sir Cedric Hardwicke played the egotistic poet-author Holmes Sr., and Anne Francis, as Fanny Dixwell, played the fiancée of his liberal and rebellious jurist son Oliver Jr. New York drama critic Harriet Van Horne commented, "Last night's play was honest, high-minded and gracefully written. ... But Sir Cedric Hardwicke seemed too dry, too bloodless. I am a staunch admirer of Mr. Plummer's work, but [Holmes had] none of the petulance, the arty, actorish quality that Mr. Plummer gave him last night. Ann Harding was an ideal Mrs. Holmes and Anne Francis gave us a gay spirited Fanny."[28]

Ann followed this with her first *Play of the Week* production, for the short-lived network, NTA. "Mornings at Seven," co-starred such veterans as Chester Morris, Dorothy Gish, and Beulah Bondi. Paul Osborn's 1939 play featured four sisters and a spinster (Eileen Heckart) who has been engaged to one of the sisters' sons—for fifteen years. Emotions are unleashed when the wedding is finally announced. As one critic joked, "Well now, let's not rush into anything."[29]

It was around this time that Ann had her short-lived "reunion" with former lover Gene Fowler. This was at the Beverly Hills Hotel bar and lounge, where Ann was most likely staying for the shoot, or promotion of "Autocrat and Son." During their brief encounter, Ann "murmured something about the impossibility of [Fowler] ever becoming an old man and then, exhibiting signs of emotional upset … turned and hurried away." Fowler's biographer, states that the scenarist was so stunned that he was unable to talk any further with his friend Thomas Mitchell who had joined him for a drink. He simply mumbled that he had to go home. Fowler later told his son,

> I've never had anything hit me as hard as this. My God, my knees gave out when she spoke to me. I called you because I had to have someone to talk to. I couldn't talk to Mother about it. She's always known about it but at this late date it would be almost too much for her. You should have seen her, Will. Still beautiful, still gorgeous.[30]

Fowler died three months later.

During the fall of 1960, Ann took an active interest in the Westport political scene. That October, she spoke for a bi-partisan fundraiser, along with Connecticut Democratic State Senator Gloria Schaffer at

Longshore Park. The "Politics and Fashion" themed event included luncheon, highlighted by a fashion show.[31] In December, The Fairfield County Republican Women's Association invited Ann to appear at the Southbury Training School, a rehabilitation facility for mentally challenged adults. Ann's remarks at these events made a lasting impression, and by the following April she was elected as vice-president of the Westport Republican Women's Association.[32] She was also chairman of its membership committee. The following year, Ann hosted a luncheon in New York City for former governor of Connecticut, John Davis Lodge (Ambassador to Spain) and his wife, upon their return from Europe. Lodge's wife, the former actress and ballet dancer, Francesca Braggiotti, had served as a founding member of the American Shakespeare Festival in Stratford, Connecticut. Lodge himself, to his family's dismay, had once been associated with the motion-picture industry, appearing in such films as *Little Women* and *The Scarlet Empress*. In June of 1962, Ann was a guest at the wedding of Lodge's daughter Lily, who had attended London's Royal Academy of Dramatic Art.

Two Queens of Love and Beauty was announced as Ann's return to Broadway for the fall of 1960, but she did not begin rehearsals for the play until July of the following year. In *Two Queens ...* , written by Bill Hoffman, Ann portrayed a former beauty contest winner who rebels against the violence in the world. Ralph Bell directed the all-female cast. During the play's run at Bucks County Playhouse, Ann had problems with her vocal chords and was not able to be in all the performances. Jan Miner, Ann's emergency understudy, performed a miracle and was able to fill in. The play never made it to Broadway. Ann took a month's rest before undergoing surgery on her vocal chords.

On February 26, 1961, Harry Bannister died at his home on West Ninth Street in New York. He was 73. A week later, a Pennsylvania columnist decided to offer his take on Harry's exploitation of Ann during the early part of their marriage. Drama critic for the *Pittsburgh Post*, Harold V. Cohen, claimed that from the beginning Harry saw Ann as nothing more than a meal-ticket. Titled, "Harry's Major Miscalculation," Cohen chronicled Bannister's shrewd maneuver to persuade Ann to leave producer George Sharpe behind and take over the Nixon Theatre for the summer of 1928. Cohen recalled,

NTA-TV's *Play of the Week* featured Ann and Beulah Bondi
in "Mornings at Seven"(1960).

> On his own, Mr. Bannister made a personal survey
> of the audience, and learned something he had long
> suspected, that the big draw was Miss Harding. She
> had built up a personal following that was loyal,
> demonstrative and even fantastic. Bannister began
> mapping a project of his own. In late 1927 ... he
> suggested a stock company to the Nixon people for
> the summer of 1928. Mr. Bannister clucked happily
> and began calculating what the joint bank account
> would look like on Labor Day.[33]

Of course, Ann's pregnancy put a damper on Harry's scheme ... temporarily. During her research, theater historian Gail Cohen discovered a similar situation existing between Ann and Werner. "The wife of Ann's dentist in Westport, Connecticut," Cohen told me, "implied that Werner Janssen went through Ann's money before leaving her."[34] This was also mentioned by Ann's step-granddaughter, Lynne Stickrod of San Francisco. Stickrod was the daughter from Alfred Otto Jr.'s first marriage. In the 1960's, after her mother and younger sister died tragically in a fire, Lynne and her two brothers went to live with Jane, Alfred and their daughter Diana just north of San Francisco. When this author talked to Lynne, she stated, "Ann didn't really have much money left when she died. What Jane had heard is that part of the reason Werner went to Europe right after [the divorce] was that Ann Harding was after him for money, because he went through her money."[35]

According to Ann, maintaining a peaceful home and relationship with Werner had proved challenging for a long time. Arguments and disagreements became the norm. The "angel" Ann had depicted Werner to be during interviews was more wishful thinking than reality. She finally filed for divorce on October 6, 1961, after Werner stormed out of their Westport residence, in a fury, yelling, "I want a divorce by Christmas!"[36] Ann's divorce petition charged "intolerable cruelty." Papers were served on Janssen the following day at the Commodore Hotel in New York City. He countered with a plea in abatement, as Ann sought alimony, and $500,000 in damages. She had good reason. Ann had financed some of Werner's musical ventures, and had taken a second mortgage on their home for $16,500. The funds were placed in Werner's account with his promise to make payments on the debt. He paid one installment and stopped. By October 10, Janssen was on a concert tour in Europe.

The issue wasn't only money. Janssen's persona and energy had the upper hand wherever they were. On February 7, 1963, during a thirty-minute hearing in Superior Court, Judge Herbert S. MacDonald granted Ann an uncontested divorce from Werner Janssen. She took the stand, describing Janssen's conduct as "literally intolerable." Ann claimed that during most of their 26-year-marriage, Janssen had dominated her life and "isolated" her from her friends. Janssen made it clear that her friends were not welcome in their home. "At first I thought it was the eccentricity of a genius I then believed him to be," Ann admitted. From early on in the marriage, when friends showed up at the door unexpectedly, Janssen instructed Ann and Jane "to hide until they left." "It never occurred to me to fail to accede in his wishes," Ann testified.

Two witnesses accompanied Ann, testifying that in their opinion, Janssen's treatment of Ann had "affected her health adversely." They were Ann's physician, Dr. Robert W. Nespor, of Westport, and the actress Leona Maricle. Maricle had stayed in touch with Ann since 1927. Ironically, she had played the Follies girl in *The Trial of Mary*

Promotional shot for *Two Queens of Love and Beauty* (1961).

Dugan, who came to Mary's defense. When the district attorney in the play ridiculed Mary's receiving a Rolls Royce for services rendered, Maricle's character snarled back at him, "Do you expect a girl to go to hell in a wheelbarrow?"

Werner Janssen, however, never had to reach into his own pocket. Several months before the judge's ruling, Ann withdrew her claims for alimony and damages of $500,000. She only asked for and was granted permission to resume the legal name of Ann Harding.

After 1958, Werner spent the bulk of his time in Europe. Ann pointed out that Werner, "loved, respected and revered everything German," and that when she did accompany him to West Germany, he kept her "incarcerated" in their hotel room, except when he sent her out alone on bus tours. While there, the stress from Werner's abusive behavior caused Ann to develop an ulcer, requiring hospitalization. Shortly before they separated in 1961, Janssen, recently returned from Germany, informed her that he wanted to live there. Ann stated, "I told him that divorce at our age, after 26 (sic) years of marriage, seemed rather undignified, but he insisted he wanted a divorce by Christmas."[37] She offered to accompany him to Germany, but he refused, saying he wanted to go alone. Ann testified that the day Werner left he had "raged and shouted until she became so ill she went to bed." Before leaving for the railroad station, Janssen shouted to her, "Get yourself to the Norwalk Hospital." The *Bridgeport Post* noted, "Miss Harding, who wept briefly after she left the witness stand, told Judge MacDonald she is not sure of her husband's present whereabouts, but believes he is living in West Germany."[38]

Time magazine's brief mention of the divorce referred to Ann as the "gracefully aging blonde cinema-actress," and Werner as the "world-traveling symphony conductor."[39]   Not surprisingly, Werner Janssen had become involved in a new relationship during his globe-trotting. A 29-year-old German airline stewardess from Dusseldorf had taken his fancy. Columnist Louis Sobol tracked down Werner's sister, Dorothy Szlapka, who had inherited the Janssen family restaurant in New York. "I don't even know what the girl's last name is," said Dorothy. "I hear she's beautiful—a sort of double for Ingrid Bergman. They were married all right—in Frankfurt, Germany—but it was all supposed to be so secret."[40] The new Mrs. Werner Janssen was Christina "Christa" Heintzmann. While residing in Germany in 1965, their daughter, Jennifer, was born. Werner and his new family did not relocate to the United States until 1971-72.[41]

As Robert Brown, Ann's co-star from *The Corn is Green*, observed, "There's something about a conductor … I think Werner wanted to run the show."[42]

(Endnotes)

1   Bosley Crowther review of *The Man in the Gray Flannel Suit*, *New York Times*, 4/13/56
2   James Robert Parish, *RKO Gals*, Rainbow Books, c. 1974, pg. 40
3   Richard V. Happel review of *The Man in the Gray Flannel Suit*, *Berkshire Eagle*, 5/10/56
4   Review of *The Man in the Gray Flannel Suit*, *Variety*, April 4, 1956
5   "Divorce Sought by Ann Harding," *Bridgeport Post*, 10/6/61
6   Jimmy Fidler, "In Hollywood," *Nevada State Journal*, 3/17/56
7   Paul M. Edwards, *A Guide to Films on the Korean War*, Greenwood Pub., c. 1997, pg 99
8   Review of *Strange Intruder*, *Variety*, 5/9/56
9   Bosley Crowther review of *I've Lived Before*, *New York Times*, 8/4/56
10   Review of *I've Lived Before*, *Variety*, 7/18/56
11   John Robertson review of *I've Lived Before*, *Cedar Rapids Gazette*, 1/31/57
12   Ellis Walker column, "Video Notes," 2/6/57
13   Vernon Scott, "TV Brings First Change of Pace for Ann Harding," *Amarillo Globe Times*, 1/31/57
14   Harold Stern, "Ann Harding Appears In Du Pont Premiere," *Troy Record*, 9/21/59
15   Harold Stern, "Ann Harding Appears In Du Pont Premiere," *Troy Record*, 9/21/59
16   Cecil Smith review of *Those We Love*, *Los Angeles Times*, 9/23/59
17   John Crosby, "Gals Soap Opera Boon to Men Folk," *Oakland Tribune*, 9/25/59
18   Jack Gould, "June Allyson Series," *The New York Times*, 9/27/59
19   Interview with Peter Mark Richman, 6/25/2009
20   Letter from Peter Mark Richman, dated 7/12/2009

21   Walter Winchell, "On Broadway," *Daily Time-News*, 6/6/58
22   Joe Falocco, "Gardens of Desire: Toward a Unified Vision of *Garden District*," *Tennessee Williams Annual Review*, c. 2005 www.tennesseewilliamsstudies.org
23   Claudia Cassidy, review of *Garden District*, *Chicago Tribune*, 6/19/58
24   James Robert Parish, *RKO Gals*, Rainbow Books, c. 1974, pg 41
25   Larry Neeley, "Ann Harding to Star In Next Arena Play," *Evening Independent (OH)*, 8/10/63
26   Locksley Hall, "BBC2's *Daphne* Explores Du Maurier's Bisexuality," afterellen.com, 5/21/2007
27   Harold Stern, "Ann Harding Appears In Du Pont Premiere," *Troy Record*, 9/21/59
28   Harriet Van Horne review of *Autocrat and Son*, *El Paso Herald-Post*, 3/21/60
29   *Los Angeles Times* comment 9/7/61
30   H. Allen Smith, *The Life and Legend of Gene Fowler*, William Morrow & Co., NY. c.1977, pg 311
31   "Westport News," *Bridgeport Post*, 10/16/60
32   Walter Winchell, "Winchell on Broadway," *Humboldt Standard (CA)*, 5/22/61
33   Harold V. Cohen, "Harry's Major Miscalculation," *Pittsburgh Post-Gazette*, 3/5/61
34   Conversation with Gail Cohen, November 28, 2008
35   Conversation with Lynne Stickrod, June 25, 2009
36   "Ann Harding Wins Divorce After Marriage of 26 Years," *Bridgeport Post*, 2/8/63
37   "Ann Harding Winds Divorce After Marriage of 26 Years," *Bridgeport Post*, 2/8/63
38   "Ann Harding Wins Divorce After Marriage of 26 Years," *Bridgeport Post*, 2/8/63
39   "Divorced" *Time Magazine*, 2/15/63
40   Louis Sobol, "New York Cavalcade," *Cedar Rapids Gazette*, 12/8/63
41   The Social Security Death Index shows that in 1971-72, Christina H. Janssen acquired her card in New York, and that she was born May 11, 1933
42   Conversation with Robert Brown, February 15, 2008

20

Her Final Bows

During a November 1961 taping in New York, Ann responded to news correspondent Terry Vernon's query about being a face that many people remember, "but few recall." "I have no regrets," said Ann thoughtfully. "People knew me in the 1930s when it was important to me that they did. Today it doesn't matter. I had fame and I enjoyed success. So few among us ever have the opportunity."[1] It was an attitude that Ann would carry with her into retirement. Vernon's interview, which took place a month after Ann filed for divorce, was on the set of the CBS series *Westinghouse Presents*. The alcoholic mother of a nun was a rather unusual role for Ann to be offered, but that is exactly what she had decided to tackle. The hour-long special, "Come Again to Carthage," pre-empted TV's rigid network programming on December 8, 1961. Columnist Vernon Scott said the program, "put the regular lineup to shame." Scott felt the cast excelled in the "forceful drama" about Sister Maria Joseph, a militant nun (Piper Laurie), who returns home, God's will or not, to save her dying father (Maurice Evans) and cure her alcoholic mother (Harding). In so doing, Sister Maria Joseph discovers that she has chosen her life's vocation for all the wrong reasons. Scott complimented Piper Laurie's "skillful acting," found Maurice Evans "exactly right," and Ann "convincing as the drunken mother."[2]

Piper Laurie confessed to this author, "I was so self-involved to the extreme at the time I was making 'Come Again to Carthage' that I have little if anything to recall about the beautiful and brilliant Ann Harding. I was trying hard to learn everything I could about being a nun in a few short weeks; walking around the city in my habit; spending time in the Bronx with real Sisters. Miss Harding was a benign presence. In the years since, I've had the opportunity to catch-up with her extraordinary work and gasp at her brilliance. Shame on me, back then, she was just an actress who plays mothers. I'm sure many young people view me that way today."[3]

Immediately after "… Carthage," Ann signed on for an episode of *Alfred Hitchcock Presents*. The teleplay was based on the Susan Glaspell one-act play *Trifles*. How fitting that the last chapter dealing with Ann's career takes a close look at her involvement in a piece inspired by the pen of the playwright who had put Ann's career in motion.

Trifles

French director Robert Florey (*Murders in the Rue Morgue*) managed to get striking performances from the cast of "Jury of Her Peers," based on the Glaspell play. Although cut down to thirty minutes and filmed in two days, the result was phenomenal. Author Oscar Cargill stated, "'Jury of Her Peers' was not merely superb, but a miracle considering the time in which it was given."[4] The story is that of a farmer's wife who is arrested for the death of her husband. He was found strangled in bed. While the sheriff and county attorney look over the crime scene, the sheriff's wife, Mary (Frances Reid), and a neighbor friend, Sarah Hale (Ann), gather belongings for the accused. The men make observations that are decidedly routine, but the women note the smaller details—the trifles— that tell of the abuse perpetrated on the wife by her husband.

Sarah, a longtime friend of the accused, makes her own assessment of the situation early on. She tells Mary, "It's wrong for them to come here like this and try to get her own house to turn against her." Sarah notices the stitching on a quilt panel the woman was working on, and remarks, "Looks as if she didn't know what she was doin'!" The woman was obviously upset about something. Sarah begins to pull out the tell-tale threads. Being the sheriff's wife, Mary protests, saying she'll have to tell her husband –and that Ann shouldn't tamper with "evidence." Sarah pays no attention, pulls out the remaining threads, and smiles, "Nothing to tell him, Mary ... about sewing that isn't there!" As the trifles mount up—a birdcage with a broken hinge—a canary with a broken neck, lovingly wrapped up in silk, the women realize that the wife did kill her husband, and more importantly *why.* "We've *got* to tell him!" Mary insists. Sarah picks up the dead bird and nods to herself suggesting, "I'll just put it in my bag and they'll never know a thing about it." She is remorseful about not being a better friend to the farmer's wife, someone she had been close to in her youth. "All the things he's been doin' to her for twenty years," Sarah shakes her head. "I should have come if I knew. *There's* a crime for you ... a real crime. Who's going to punish me?"

After the men announce there is a "lack of evidence," Sarah and the sheriff's wife remain silent. The sheriff's wife slyly places the dead bird inside Sarah's handbag. It must be remembered that in 1916, when the play was first produced, women could not vote and could not sit on juries. They *needed* to look out for each other. Together, Sarah and the sheriff's wife had reached an understanding: the farmer's wife was justified in her actions. Considering that in 1961 the Production Code still governed motion pictures as well as television, it is surprising that the aptly titled "A Jury of Her Peers" was broadcast. Crime, according to the code, could not go unpunished.

Glaspell's poignant play brings to the surface society's devaluation of women. The men in the play scoff at the conversation and concerns of females. Glaspell wasn't demeaning men. Her intention was to show that men and women communicate differently. In so doing, Glaspell deftly captures the reality that women were up against in the early 20th century. In the play's first performance in Providence, R.I., Glaspell played the part of Sarah Hale, which Ann would repeat so eloquently forty-five years later on television.

In early 1962, Ann prepared for a return to Broadway via Michigan. She returned to Detroit, where her career had made significant strides during the 1920s. George C. Scott and theatrical producer-director Theodore D. Mann headed the newly established Theater of Michigan Company, which was designed to break in new plays and allow the general public to invest in its stock. The venture in which Ann was asked to play in— the company's first— was titled *General Seeger*, written by Ira Levin (*A Kiss Before Dying*, *Rosemary's Baby*) and directed by Scott. *Seeger* told about a hard-bitten general who is disillusioned

General Seeger (1962) with Dolores Sutton and William Bendix. Bendix was fired after opening night. Director George C. Scott took over the lead.

when he learns that his son, who had grabbed a ticking grenade to save the lives of two GIs, did not die a hero's death. During the course of the play it is revealed that the younger Seeger had performed his "heroic" act to commit suicide. He hated army life. His death was now being used as an excuse to fund a memorial—a new recreation center at the Army post where his shrewd and self-satisfied father, General Seeger, is commanding officer. When Seeger discovers the truth about his son—a son he had bullied and demoralized, he calls off the dedication. His decision counters that of his superiors, which means the destruction of the general's life-long career. William Bendix was cast as Seeger, and Ann played his wife Rena—a grieving mother who spends her days in a darkened living room wrapped in an old bathrobe, watching television.

The world premier of *General Seeger*, on February 15, 1962, garnered headlines. The reason wasn't because of the drama on stage, but behind it. News items across the country reported that Ann had collapsed in her dressing room, between acts, and then finished her role before being rushed by police ambulance to the hospital. Dr. Irving Burton, an opening night patron, administered first aid to her backstage. Although the audience was unaware of the situation, Ann received an extended ovation after completing her last scene.[5] The following day, Harper Hospital officials reported her condition as "fair," saying she suffered from an "inflammation of the lining of the stomach and intestines." Stark Hesseltine, Ann's high-powered and respected agent, told reporters, "To me, it was the greatest case of 'the show must go on' showmanship I've ever seen."[6] The thirty-three-year-old Hesseltine, who is credited with discovering Robert Redford and Christopher Reeve, would represent such talents as Susan Sarandon and Richard Chamberlain before dying of AIDS in 1987. Hesseltine said that Ann was complaining that afternoon, but decided to go on. "She collapsed at the intermission," stated Hesseltine, "and it was a miracle she got through the second act. She fainted again before she made her second act entrance and was unable to take a curtain call when the play finished." Another ovation awaited Ann when she returned to the stage the following night. She disagreed with the doctor's diagnosis that she had "gastroenteritis" and left the hospital. Ann was facing a number of issues which affected her physically and emotionally: her divorce wasn't final; Werner's exact whereabouts were unknown; and she was struggling financially.

During rehearsals for *General Seeger*, George C. Scott became more and more dissatisfied with Bendix's performance. He was going to fire Bendix, but held off to see how things went. After the opening, producer Mann agreed that Bendix was not capable of tackling the role, so Scott immediately stepped into the leading man's shoes. He was riveting in the role. The play graduated to Broadway after its ten-day run at Detroit's Shubert Theatre. Mann later stated, "We had bright hopes when we opened at the Hudson Theater [it was the Lyceum Theatre] that we could keep our dream of the Theatre Company of Michigan alive. But those hopes were dashed when *The New York Times* and others, including the *Daily News* gave negative reviews to the play."[7]

Howard Taubman, for *The New York Times*, actually offered a fair assessment and pointed to the most effective scene, saying, "The truth finally emerges—the son was no hero. Mr. Levin has written this scene with sharpness, and Mr. Scott has staged it with economy and impact. Ann Harding as the general's wife brings dignity and feeling to her share of it. Having stripped the general of some of his illusions, Mr. Levin turns to the task of destroying his deepest ones about the honor of the Army. ... In a concluding scene it attempts to prove that the Army, intent on its chief mission—to defend the country—will not hesitate to trim and lie to keep its public image glamorous."[8] Taubman felt these final moments were too "drastic" a shift, appearing as "afterthoughts." *The Chicago Daily Tribune* praised the play's content as being, "well-blended, crisp and crunchy." "Levin has spun his tale expertly and tautly," said the review. "George C. Scott ... is acting the title role clearly and forcefully. There is a sweet, touching performance by Ann Harding in the role of the general's wife."[9] *General Seeger* closed at Broadway's Lyceum Theater after two performances, but paved the way for Scott's acclaimed Oscar-winning portrayal of another aggressive military icon, in *Patton* (1970). Typical of his intense personality, Scott, who felt that film was not an actor's medium, refused the Oscar, saying, "The whole thing is a goddamn meat parade. I don't want any part of it."[10]

Interestingly, Brigadier General Seeger's fate was similar to that of General George Grant Gatley. In the play, Seeger dies at San Francisco's Presidio hospital with his wife, Rena, at his side. While Gatley's rebel daughter Dorothy had a heart-felt reunion with her father,

Seeger's son was ultimately a victim of his father's iron will. Rena Seeger had memorized, word-for-word, the suicide note her son had left behind. *General Seeger's* most poignant moment is when Seeger acknowledges his despair, listening as Mrs. Seeger recites their son's message: "Goodbye, Mother, and forgive me. I know you will. I love you most of all, because you never expected me to be anything I wasn't."[11]

In May 1962, Ann signed on for another pre-Broadway engagement in the new Dore Schary play, *Banderol*. Schary, an ex-production boss at MGM, also directed this exposé of Hollywood power struggles. *Banderol* was inspired by his experiences with the studio (1948-1956). Schary was Ann's benefactor at MGM during her three-picture commitment in the early 1950s.[12] The cast also included Ed Begley, Betty Field and George Voskovec. On stage, Ann played the crippled and neglected wife of Begley, a Louis B. Mayer-like movie tycoon. The play opened at Wilmington's Playhouse Theatre in Delaware, September 13. It then played at Philadelphia's Forrest Theatre, closing after one week at a loss of $125,000. The scheduled October 9 opening at Broadway's Music Box Theatre was cancelled.[13] Schary admitted after reading the reviews in Philadelphia that *Banderol* was in need of a major overhaul.[14]

Shortly before Ann's uncontested divorce hearing, she was asked to participate in a series of readings and dramatic vignettes for the CBS-TV Special *The First Lady*. She was joined by Colleen Dewhurst (wife of actor George C. Scott) and Nancy Wickwire to recall the lives of First Ladies in the nation's capitol. Ann began the program with the words of Martha Washington, later stood by a portrait of Dolly Madi-

Ann, along with Nancy Wickwire and Colleen Dewhurst, offered readings and dramatic vignettes in the CBS special "The First Lady"(1963).

son for another reading, and ended the half-hour special with an impersonation of Mrs. Herbert Hoover. *The First Lady* was inspired by the acclaimed CBS program *A Tour of the White House with Jacqueline Kennedy.* The producer for both presentations was Emmy award-winning Perry Wolff. Critical response to Wolff's second effort was less than enthusiastic. "In frank terms," said UPI critic Rick Du Brow, "*The First Lady* was a stinker clear through. The readers, actresses Ann Harding, Colleen Dewhurst and Nancy Wickwire, along with narrator Harry Reasoner, are too worthy to be involved in such artificial silliness."[15] Du Brow had a point. Eleanor Roosevelt was finished off thusly: "Anna Eleanor Roosevelt was the most famous woman of the 20th century." Ann's own opinion of *The First Lady* was relayed in a rather sarcastic note to producer Wolff himself, congratulating him for "honoring forty-one women in 25 minutes."[16]

Ann did several TV guest-star appearances throughout 1963. In the popular law series *The Defenders* she played a grieving mother whose son has died of cancer. She accuses her daughter-in-law of intentionally giving him an overdose of morphine. The April 6 broadcast, "A Taste of Vengeance," emphasized the philosophical pros and cons of mercy killing. The following week, Ann was featured in "The Embezzler" for *Armstrong Circle Theatre*. She played the manipulative aunt of a bank president. Ann also filmed a segment for TV's homage to psychiatry, *The Eleventh Hour*. Before leaving Los Angeles, she told Louella Parsons that she anticipated a return to the film capital to "resume her career seriously."[17] Parsons indicated that Ann was hoping her agent would land her a running part in a TV series so she could move back to California permanently.

In the meantime, Ann resumed the role of Miss Moffat in a summer stock tour of *The Corn is Green*. She took the play cross-country from New Mexico to Ohio to New York. Ann's appearance at New Mexico State University's Corral Playhouse featured students who were studying dramatic arts. Dr. H. Lyle Hagan directed Ann in what was to be her first of several university productions. Ann was unduly impressed by the discipline, enthusiasm and talent in the middle of what she referred to as a "cattle range."[18] She then took Miss Moffat to Brockport State University's Campus Theater in New York. (Where she was less than impressed.) While Ann rehearsed for the Canal Fulton Summer Arena production in Ohio, she elaborated on *The Corn is Green* for reporter Larry Neeley. "*The Corn is Green* is actually more comedy than drama," said Ann. "It is a closely-woven play with delicate timing. It will never be dated ... they don't write plays that way anymore. I would rather play *The Corn is Green* in proscenium theater ... much of the play's timing depends on doors closing and locking within sight of the audience and others opening unexpectedly ... you have to lose some of this effect when the audience sees actors coming on stage through the aisles."[19]

Ann's off-the-cuff remarks to reporter Neeley reflected the opinions of many of her contemporaries in a world of bouffant hair-dos and bikinis. "You can't tell one of the new crop of Hollywood beauties from another," she protested. "I don't think any of them comb their hair." She followed this with, "We're all becoming a bunch of numbers ... social security, ZIP code, all-digit dialing, policy numbers, street numbers ... it's disgusting."[20] On a happier note, Ann mentioned her voracious appetite for reading. She was currently dwelling on the essays of Thomas Paine, Michel Montaigne and Voltaire, "with preference for the latter."

Ann took time out from her tour to guest on the popular *Mike Douglas Show*, originating in nearby Cleveland, Ohio. After her final bow as Miss Moffat, she returned to Hollywood, but not for the anticipated TV series. Producer Aaron Spelling coaxed her into playing a "nutty murderess" for an episode of *Burke's Law*. "Ann Harding is a wonderful actress," said Spelling, "and she should be seen a good deal more. I wrote a part for her and she's flying West." Spelling's aim, for what proved to be a popular program, was to "shoot for glamour [and] forget about being too believable."[21] The popular series employed a lot of "forgotten stars" from a bygone era: Mary Astor, ZaSu Pitts, Joan Bennett, Gloria Swanson, and Joan Blondell. Amid a display of cheesecake, martini-swilling babes, and male testosterone, Ann played an eccentric elderly woman living in the past—1929, to be exact — in the show, titled "Who Killed Mr. X?" Ann, as Annabelle Rogers, manages to pull off a quaint version of *Sunset Blvd.'s* Norma Desmond. She unwittingly shoots her former lover (Mr. X) when he shows up again after thirty years. She thought he was an intruder. Annabelle tells the debonair LA police detective Amos Burke (Gene Barry) that she couldn't figure out why an elderly, strange man came to see her. "An old man like that trying to kiss me!" she exclaims. "He looked at me as though he *knew* me!"   At the finis Burke has Annabelle hauled away, hopefully to an asylum with art deco décor. Barry was thrilled to be working with Ann. "I don't need a happiness pill to remind myself that my show, by its very design, has become a rendezvous for ... stars I have worshipped from afar," he said. "Ann Harding, that gracious lady of the theater ... Little did I dream, as a movie-struck kid in New York, that I would someday actually play opposite her."[22] Ann told Barry that she found her part rewarding. "She liked the laughs gleaned from her characterization," said Barry, "but there also was sympathy and a sort of sadness."[23]

When Ann's appearance on the more serious *Eleventh Hour* was broadcast that fall, she received generous critical acclaim, but garnered no Emmy nomination. In "Fear Begins at 40," Ann offered a brilliant performance as a woman who suffers "senile psychosis" (Alzheimer's) while her son (Robert Lansing) adjusts to her inevitable decline. Ann wavers between lucidity and childishness, stealing things and blaming others. The *Kansas City Star* raved, "Miss Harding is so good she makes the supporting players pale in comparison. If you're able to derive pleasure from the misfortune of others, you'll never see dotage more admirably portrayed."[24] The program's producer, Irving Elman, remarked, "She moves you to tears. I've seen it—or portions of it—a minimum of 50 times. And each time, tears. You'd think you'd get hardened to it, but you don't. Ann Harding gives one of the best performances of her life."[25] TV critic Ed Matesky found the episode disturbing, and commented, "It was uncomfortable to watch ... the deterioration of a human being, even if it was play-acting."[26]

Upon her return to Westport, Ann participated in a 29-hour-long radio-thon appeal for funds to aid Leukemia research. The joint broadcast originated from both Times Square and Westport. Other participating Connecticut celebrities were Richard Rodgers, David Wayne, Jackie Robinson, Dave Brubeck, and Ann's friend, former Ambassador John Davis Lodge.[27] The following month, Ann headed the TB Seal Drive for Norwalk County. As honorary chairman for the Christmas Seal campaign, Ann told reporters, "TB is not yet licked—but now that your purchase of Christmas Seals has brought this killer to its knees, your TB association is going after the greatest robber of health still at large—Respiratory diseases ... It ranks No. 4 ... taking the lives of ten per cent of all Americans."[28] Amid her civic duties, Ann found the time to star in a new play at Westport Country Playhouse.

The Moments of Love, by Westport playwright David Rogers, opened the Country Playhouse's Fall Festival. The setting for the romantic comedy-drama was a verdant garden on a Long Island estate. A gazebo was placed center stage. Two large urns, filled with lush blossoms, flanked the stairway to the structure, where Ann sat ever so poised. The urns ended up getting more publicity than she did. Leo B. Meyer, resident designer for the playhouse, recalled in 2005, "In this gazebo, Ann Harding, the production's aging star, would reenact love scenes from her past, using hired actors as her past amours. I'd asked the prop person to scout up two urns. The next morning two

exquisite metal urns graced the stage. The following morning the local radio newscasts screamed headlines about vandalism at the local
cemetery along Route 33 in Westport. The prop assistant had done
[his] deadly work in the gloom of night. The play, and the setting
with the urns in full view, were both well received."[29] Critic Fred Russell's review of the three-act play was mixed. Ann played a reclusive
widow who tries to keep the image of her war-killed husband alive.
She refers to the servants by numbers instead of names as she relives
her past. Russell found her methods of keeping her husband "alive"
were unorthodox, but novel. "It takes an actress of Miss Harding's
theatrical stature to make the role interesting and convincing," stated
Russell. "Unfortunately this unique idea is not constantly interesting and lively, but it does emerge as a theatrical work that can probably grow in impact as it is polished.[30] Indeed, the director Herbert
Machiz told the audience in a curtain speech of his difficulties. One
actress had broken her leg, and had to be replaced; another, Joanna
Pettet, had to leave the cast for surgery. Machiz, who had a long association with Tennessee Williams, had also directed Ann in *The Garden District*. Prior to *The Moments of Love*, Machiz was at the helm of
Williams' *The Milk Train Doesn't Stop Here Anymore* (1963), which
received mostly unfavorable notices.

In the fall of 1963, Ann flew to Los Angeles to film an episode of
the popular MGM-TV series *Dr. Kildare*, starring Richard Chamberlain and Raymond Massey. In "Never Too Old for the Circus" (which
aired January 1964), Ann played the wife of a retired doctor (Walter
Pidgeon). Charles E. Davis Jr., of the *Los Angeles Times*, interviewed
Ann, who was in good spirits. "I welcomed this role," she said. "I had
done three senile psychotics in a row on TV and I was beginning to

Dr. Kildare. In a 1964 episode, Ann played grandmother to Joey Scott.

get depressed."[31] Ann expressed her contentment with life in Connecticut. "I have a river nearby," she said, "and it has water in it. I love music and I play piano for hours. And I read a lot. I'm always involved in about five books." She talked about being an army brat, commenting with a smile, "I was born in a suitcase and I expect to die in one."

During filming, a death occurred that shook the world. On November 22, 1963, *Variety* columnist Army Archerd was at Metro scouting out stories for his column. He was on his way to give newlywed Robert Goulet a photograph of his wife Carol Lawrence at a luncheon with President John Kennedy. Before he got to Goulet, he heard that Kennedy had been shot. "The shattering news broke before we reached the studio's stages," wrote Archerd. "Big and bit players wept openly. On the studio streets, players in gay costumes sadly made their way to the gates. Ann Harding, her eyes flooded, slowly walked past."[32]

"Never Too Old for the Circus" focused on Dr. Priest (Pidgeon) and his failed comeback as a surgery consultant. He takes his bitterness out on an adoring grandson (Joey Scott), refusing to take him to the circus, telling him to "grow up." Ann's presence is strictly as the comforting grandma—she tries to fill Dr. Kildare with pie, and consoles her husband, who resents being out of touch with his profession. "Medicine isn't the only reason for living," she tells him. Although he has experienced a humiliating professional failure, Dr. Priest remains adamant

Broadway's ill-fated *Abraham Cochrane* (1964). Seen here with Bill Travers.

about working. As his wife, Ann puts it to him tenderly, "They're not going to let you, darling … and they're right." By the time he comes to his senses, the viewer has lost interest in Dr. Priest's plight and grown weary of the grandson's pouting. "The story is a bit too sticky," said the *Tucson Daily Citizen*. The review stated that Pidgeon was "sympathetically abetted by Ann Harding."[33] Never one to miss an opportunity for a cutting remark, Hedda Hopper commented on Ann's appearance in these recent TV outings. Hopper raved about actress Phyllis Thaxter. "She's changed less over the years than anybody I know," twittered Hopper. "You sure can't say that about Ann Harding whom I saw on TV the other night. She was so beautiful in *Holiday* with Mary Astor, Donald Ogden Stewart and me."[34] Hopper failed to mention that Thaxter was twenty years younger than Ann, and was mistaken about Donald Ogden Stewart, the film's scenarist. (Poor Hedda meant Edward Everett Horton.) Two years later, Hopper's nasty barbs would finally be put to rest.

Despite Ann's disappointments with *General Seeger* and *Banderol*, Broadway tempted her once more. In early 1964, she joined British film and stage star Bill Travers in the play *Abraham Cochrane*, slated to open at Broadway's Belasco Theater. This comedy about a modern-day Don Juan had Travers, a vagabond, showing up at the home of wealthy socialite Myra Holliday (Ann), only to seduce her daughter (Nancy Wickwire) … who is married. Ann's character is troubled with a heart ailment and concerned about her daughter's unhappy marriage. Her son-in-law has returned from a year in a mental institution. It was well into the second act, while Myra and her daughter indulge in toying with the scheming Travers, before audiences realized they were watching a comedy. The laughs came too late. After its February 17 opening, *Abraham Cochrane* was roundly panned by all the critics. In his review for UPI, Jack Gaver, thought the play's author, John Sherry, took, "a wordy and tortuous route to get to his point." The play was burdened with an abundance of long words from the dictionary. "It is a wonder the actors can say the sentences," said Gaver, "let alone give them meaning." Gaver took pity on the cast, saying, "Britain's charming Bill Travers, Nancy Wickwire and Ann Harding are a talented and personable trio, but the play is too much even for them."[35] William Glover for the Associated Press called the play a "three-act torture" and "a windy bore." [36] *New York Times* critic Howard Taubman felt Ann's Myra Holliday was "played intelligently," but observed that Sherry's play was "self-possessed, slow ... and lifeless."[37] *Abraham Cochrane* closed after one performance. When asked, Ann caustically commented on the closing, "Critics have made New York the only one-night stand in the country."[38]

"One-night stands" on Broadway weren't that uncommon. Claudette Colbert's *Julia, Jake and Uncle Joe* met a similar fate in 1961. But for Ann, *Abraham Cochrane* would be her last curtain call. Any disappointment was assuaged a few months later when Eastern New Mexico University in Portales invited Ann back as guest lecturer. She taught two classes during the summer months, and assisted the students, who were preparing for three productions scheduled between June 17 and July 27: *Come Blow Your Horn*, *See How They Run*, and *Come Back, Little Sheba*. ... *Sheba* featured guest star Betty Field, who had co-starred with Ann in 1962's *Banderol*.[39] Ann retreated to her home in Connecticut for the remainder of 1964. It was another year before she returned to Los Angeles for what would be her final acting assignment. She admitted to Jasper Deeter that she could not afford the luxury of turning TV offers down. When the opportunity to do an episode of *Ben Casey* arrived, Ann was undertaking a bridge-building project (30-ton capacity) in order to cross the river and create a private driveway onto her property. During this procedure, her Tuck Lane address became Lyons Plain Road. Ann was tired of the eight little brats who kept throwing rocks at her windshield whenever she drove down Tuck Lane. The project dug deep into her savings account, but her Banker (a top-ranking realtor) assured Ann that the bridge was an "inspiration." Her property value soared. It was this investment that enabled Ann to retire.[40]

Because of the Needle the Haystack was Lost

The needle in this instance is a titanium radioactive implant in the head of Edith Sommers (Ann). Neurosurgeon Ben Casey (Vince Edwards) places the removable object next to Edith's olfactory organ to halt the growth of a malignant tumor. "Because of the Needle ..." follows the familiar themes associated with the *Ben Casey* series—birth-death-infinity. Some described the medical drama series as "*Dr. Kildare* with attitude," which resulted in a stronger, more adult program than its competitor. The synopsis of "Because of the Needle ..." was nicely laid out in a script by John Meredyth Lucas (best known for his work on TV's *Star Trek*) and the once-blacklisted scenarist Howard Dims-

Career swansong. Ann on the set of *Ben Casey* (1965)
with co-star Franchot Tone.

dale. Alan Crosland Jr. directed. Wearing her famous chignon atop her head, Ann, as Edith, is first seen reminiscing with Casey about her father's flower garden. "Daddy used to say you'd have to watch me, or I'd get drunk on flower scent," she laughs. The new implant is also supposed to help revive Edith's sense of smell. Although her case involves a malignancy, Casey's bedside manner is optimistic.

The indomitable Gladys Cooper (whose stage career began in 1905) shows up as Dr. Brandt, a retired and bullheaded physician whose sharp opinions are the last word. When Casey first runs into Dr. Brandt, he innocently asks who she wants to see. "Most of the people I *want* to see are dead!" she snaps. When she learns who Casey is, she informs him of her intention to have him dismissed for malpractice. She also takes over Edith's case. In so doing, she places Edith's life in jeopardy.

When Dr. Brandt informs Edith that there *is* a malignancy involved, Edith waxes philosophical. "It's funny, the way things work," she says. "How life goes. It's like climbing a hill with a rise so gradual you don't notice it. You stop, and look back. And, you realize how high you've come." Dr. Brandt tells Edith, "We're born, and we die, one's no worse than the other. It's what we do in between that counts." Edith decides not to drag out the "inevitable," writes a farewell note, and leaves the hospital without telling anyone. Dr. Casey retrieves Edith's message. To his horror, he learns that she has disposed of the radioactive needle. It could have fatal consequences for anyone coming near it. The hospital (or, haystack in this case) becomes "lost" in a flurry of frantic searching by police and investigators. Edith is finally located, by Dr. Brandt, at an arboretum where she intends to have one last sniff of fragrant flowers before jumping off the balcony. "I meant that note to be goodbye!" announces Edith, calmly poised on the balcony edge. Brandt reassures her that no desperate measure such as suicide is necessary—that there is hope with Dr. Casey's procedure. The two return to the hospital where Edith apologizes. "I'm very ashamed of all the trouble I caused Dr. Casey," she says humbly. "I think Dr. Brandt is quite right about you! She says that you're ...." True to form, Dr. Brandt cuts Edith off, unwilling for Casey to hear any kind of compliment from her, even indirectly. She does assure him, however, that she is rescinding her decision for his dismissal.

Ann's softer edge deserved as much praise and attention as Cooper's feistiness. Their contrasting styles play off each other nicely. Still, Cooper's domineering character tends to overshadow the other players. The *San Antonio Express* found "Because of the Needle ..." "a crackling melodrama ... best remembered for the solid performance of Gladys Cooper. [There are] some excellent scenes, especially the ones with the two ladies confronting each other on old age."[41]

A subplot ran through the season, involving a young folk singer diagnosed with a mysterious virus. Marlyn Mason played the role, and although she had no scenes with Ann, she shared with this author her excitement about having such legends as Ann and Gladys Cooper on the set. "I had an 8mm movie camera with me," Mason told me, "and I took some footage of those two incredible ladies as they worked. I was sorry that I didn't have a scene with either one of them."[42] "Vince was sweet," said Mason, "but always on the phone to his bookie, or so I was told!" Mason said she "adored" Franchot Tone, who was on board as a physician for this sixth, and final, season.

In the mid-1960s publicist John Springer, an old acquaintance of Ann's, interviewed her for a *Screen Stories* article titled "Great Movie Stars—Where Are They Now?" He described her as living "quietly and alone" in Westport, and had asked her about her future plans. "How can you ask me if I have any future plans?" Ann smiled. "There was getting into the theater in the first place—not planned—really almost by accident. There was going out to the Coast after *Mary Dugan* to relax—not to get into films … the plans I made to do *Camille* in England never worked out—but did lead to *Candida*, my most thrilling experience. If I leave the future alone, I find that it takes care of me so much better than 'the best laid plans of mice and men' could possibly dream up!"[43] Her sentiment echoed what she had told writer Stephen Anders in 1931: "I've always believed in living in the *now*," Ann emphasized, "not in the future."[44]

(Endnotes)

1   Terry Vernon, "Star Film Actress of '30's in Drama on TV Tonight," *Press Telegram*, 12/8/61
2   Vernon Scott, "Story of Nun Is Done Well," *Albuquerque Tribune*, 12/9/61
3   Letter from Piper Laurie, 9/3/2009
4   Oscar Cargill, *Toward a Pluralistic Criticism*, Southern Illinois University Pr., c. 1967, pg 191
5   "Illness Fells Ann Harding," *Bridgeport Post*, 2/16/62
6   "Sick Actress Finishes Act," *Holland Evening Sentinel*, 2/16/62
7   Theodore Mann, *Journey's in the Night*, Applause Theater and Cinema Books, c 2007, pg 182
8   Howard Taubman review of *General Seeger*, *The New York Times*, 3/1/62
9   John Chapman review of *General Seeger*, *Chicago Daily Tribune*, 3/2/62
10   "Meat Parade," *Time*, 3/8/71
11   Ira Levin, *General Seeger*, c. 1962, Dramatists Play Service Inc., pg 52
12   James Robert Parish, *The RKO Gals*, Rainbow Books, c. 1974, pg 42
13   William T. Leonard, *Broadway Bound*, pg 45
14   Sam Zolotow, "*Banderol* to End During Road Tour," *New York Times*, 9/19/62
15   Rick Du Brow, "*First Lady* Show Did Nothing Right," *San Antonio Light*, 1/3/63
16   Harvey Pack, Famous First Ladies," *Waterloo Daily Courier (IA)*, 12/27/62
17   Louella Parsons column, *San Antonio Light*, 6/21/63
18   Based on letters from Ann to Jasper Deeter, Howard Gotlieb Archival Research Center, Boston University

19   Larry Neeley, "Ann Harding to Star in Next Arena Play," *Evening Independent*, 8/10/63

20   Larry Neeley, "Ann Harding to Star in Next Arena Play," *Evening Independent*, 8/10/63

21   Charles Witbeck, "Sophistication Aim of *Burke's Law*," *Hammond Times*, 8/11/63

22   "Gene's Got 'Genes' for Beauty," *Salt Lake Tribune*, 7/5/64

23   Gene Barry, "Big Stars Like to Romp," *Chronicle Telegram*, 6/29/64

24   Review of *Fear Begins at 40*, *Kansas City Star*, 10/16/63

25   Bert Resnik, "*11th Hour* Dramatizes Senility," *Independent Press Telegram (CA)*, 10/13/63

26   Ed Matesky, "Looking and Listening," *North Adams Transcript*, 10/19/63

27   "Area Residents to Aid WABC Leukemia Appeal," *Bridgeport Post*, 10/13/63

28   "Actress Heads TB Seal Drive," *Bridgeport Post*, 11/10/63

29   Richard Somerset, *The Story of Westport County Playhouse, 1931-2005*, Yale University Pr., c. 2005, pg 149

30   Fred Russell, review of *The Moments of Love*, *Bridgeport Post*, 10/30/63

31   Charles e. Davis Jr., "Ann Harding Recalls 'Hamming' by Shaw," *Los Angeles Times*, 12/8/63

32   Army Archerd, "1963: JFK Remembered," *Variety*, 11/25/63

33   Review of *Never Too Old for the Circus*, *Tucson Daily Citizen*, 1/30/64

34   Hedda Hopper column, *Los Angeles Times*, 1/13/64

35   Jack Gaver, review of *Abraham Cochrane*, *Cedar Rapids Gazette*, 2/19/64

36   William Glover, "Windy Play Opens on Broadway," *Oakland Tribune*, 2/20/64

37   Howard Taubman review of *Abraham Cochrane*, *New York Times*, 2/18/64

38   William T. Leonard, *Once Was Enough*, Scarecrow Press, c. 1986, pg. xv

39   "Guest Instructor," *Albuquerque Journal*, 6/14/64

40   Information from letters of Ann to Jasper Deeter. Howard Gotlieb Archival Research Center, Boston Univeristy.

41   TV Scout, "Highlights Tonight," *San Antonio Express*, 10/11/65

42   Email from Marlyn Mason, 7/21/2009

43   John Springer, "Great Movie Stars—Where Are They Now? Ann Harding," *Screen Stories*, February 1963

44   Stephen Anders, "It's No Crime to be Happy," *Hollywood*, November 1931

21

"I'm No Longer Involved"

By 1966, Ann considered herself retired from work, but "not from life." Content with her career, she avoided any special tributes that were offered her, and leaned towards reclusiveness. Ann continued her interest in local politics, and on at least one occasion was guest speaker at a meeting of the Liberty Amendment Committee of Connecticut. Her lecture was titled, "The Parent's Place in Teaching the Economic Story," accompanied by a film presentation.[1] Ann assisted the American Economic Foundation (est. 1939), which focused on US Currency, the Federal Reserve System, and particularly, the repeal of the Sixteenth Amendment: income tax. The Liberty Amendment, supported by an odd mix of Libertarian and right-wing conservatives, has remained focused on limiting the size and scope of the federal government. From 1959-1982, the controversial proposal was endorsed by nine "red" states. As Ann was financially strapped, she most likely came to the realization that the bulk of her salary over the years had either been consumed by husbands or by the government.

Ann also spent time in her garden and enjoyed the company of a small circle of friends. Among them was playwright George Kelly (favorite uncle of actress Grace Kelly and author of *Craig's Wife*). Kelly, another Broadway transplant to California after talkies arrived, had known Ann since 1924. Kelly's niece, Jeanne Turner, who lived not far from Ann, recalled, "Every time George came East he spent at least a week with me in Westport. He and Ann Harding, his friend, always came for high tea and the pair would have fun reminiscing about the good old days and the current decline of the theater. When they first met he had two hit shows playing on Broadway and Ann was making her professional New York debut."[2]

Ann hadn't completely put "theatrics" aside. With time on her hands and her professional "future" put to rest, she found new outlets for her dramatic persona. One example was a letter Ann wrote to William Porter, a fan who had forwarded her a photograph to sign. What ensued took on epic proportions—a battle of pens vs. glossy paper. After resolving the problem, Ann typed a letter using personal stationery, dating it August 6, 1968:

> Dear Mr. Porter,
>
> The reason for this note is that glossy prints will not take ordinary pens, so I have one that is made especially for this purpose. It functioned perfectly as far as: "to William Porter, With ….." and suddenly it ceased to operate at all. It still has plenty of ink and works perfectly on plain paper, but not on your glossy.
>
> I am taking the liberty of having a mat-finish print made from yours at an excellent camera shop here. It may take a week or so and I will then send them both to you, begging you to destroy the embarrass-

ingly messed-up inscription on the glossy print as a
result of my trying several pens. You will see why I
am having a mat made – and why I earnestly request
you to destroy the other – it looks as though it had
been signed by a half-wit! I would not want anyone
else to see it without this explanation, please. I am
trusting you to do as I ask.

Thank you for the stamped, addressed envelope. It
is remarkably seldom that anyone has the common
courtesy to do this.
Sorry for the delay – but I am sure you will find that
it was worth it.
Sincerely,
Ann Harding[3]

In 1972, scenarist Gene Ringgold wrote a career article on Ann for the
National Board of Review publication, *Films in Review*. He asked for
her definition of talent. "There's really no such thing in acting," Ann
told him. "To most people talent only means recognition and success.
And how successful you become depends on how hard you work, how
you profit from experience, and how much good luck you have."[4] After
Ann rejected the lead in *Of Human Bondage* in 1934, who is to say what
would have happened to Bette Davis if the role of Mildred had not fallen
into her lap? Luck and "talent" indeed go hand in hand. The legacy
of Davis became set in stone after Kay Francis, the Queen of Warners
from 1932-37, argued with her bosses. In the aftermath, Bette Davis
inherited several roles intended for Francis: *The Sisters, Dark Victory,*
and *Juarez*. These films catapulted the career of Davis. Lucky woman.
Ann's return to the screen in the 1940's was peppered with losses: *The
Yearling, Mrs. Miniver, Madame Curie,* and the lead in Warner's *Watch on
the Rhine*, which Davis herself managed to snatch from her.

In 1973, Publicist John Springer didn't have any luck either when he tried to persuade Ann to make an appearance for a film tribute, in her honor, to be held at New York City's Town Hall. Having recently recovered from an operation for a perforated ulcer, Ann replied in her "still cool, crisp voice, 'Thank you but no thank you. I am retired. I am no longer involved.'"[5] Ann wasn't interested in accolades. She had shown no interest in attending the Academy Awards after her own nomination for Best Actress in 1931. For Ann, acting and special recognition, were not necessarily a viable mix.

Undiscouraged, Springer lined up a successful and memorable film retrospective for other legendary stars: Bette Davis, Sylvia Sidney, Myrna Loy, and Lana Turner. Joan Crawford, Ann's old friend from early Hollywood, was so overwhelmed by the long standing ovation at her Town Hall tribute, she exclaimed to the audience, "I never knew there was so much … love!"[6] Following the Town Hall tributes, Springer offered Ann's telephone number to film historian James Robert Parish. Parish sought an interview with Ann for his homage to her former studio, titled, *The RKO Gals* (released in 1974). He told this author, "She came to the phone and said, 'I beg to be excused, but I am retired.'"[7] In this regard, Ann would remain set in her ways.

Ann recuperated from her 1972 ulcer operation while staying with friends in the Los Angeles area. (Possibly, her close friends film director George Seaton and his wife Phyllis Loughton. Loughton had directed Ann in *Candida* in 1938). Reportedly, Ann was considering relocating to Austria.[8] Instead, she ended up moving to Sherman

Oaks, California—an affluent, urbanized district in the San Fernando Valley. Along with her came a younger woman named Grace Kaye. Most likely the two had met at Norwalk Hospital where Ann's private physician, Dr. Robert W. Nespor, practiced. Grace had been on the staff since 1966, receiving her five-year service pin from the hospital in March 1971.[9] With Ann's various health issues, it appeared to be a practical move for Ann to have a congenial help-mate. Ann affectionately referred to her as "Gracie." Grace enjoyed Ann's world, and was impressed with her friends, particularly Jasper Deeter. She enjoyed Deeter's intelligence and was amazed at how much sense he had made about life during his occasional visits to Westport to see Ann.[10]

Shortly after relocating to Sherman Oaks (1973-74), Ann was approached by American journalist and humorist, H. Allen Smith, who was working on his book, *The Life and Legend of Gene Fowler*. As Ann played a significant role in Fowler's life, Smith was hoping for her cooperation. But, Ann demanded anonymity. In Chapter twenty-eight of his book, Smith wrote, "I refrain from calling her by name, because I do not have her permission to do so."[11] Ann was referred to throughout the Fowler biography as "Madame X." Smith was straightforward in introducing Fowler's mystery woman, saying, "It is known that the great love of Fowler's *own* life was a blond movie star, intelligent as well as distressingly beautiful, and that these two carried on for a while with galactic zest and abandon, causing a brief estrangement in the Fowler family."[12] Ann's demands for privacy, and her sense of propriety, precluded her involvement in Smith's project. Published posthumously (Smith died in 1976), Fowler's biography received mostly critical raves. Of the dozens of reviews this author read, none solved the riddle of "Madame X." Joan Bunke, long-time critic for the *Des Moines*

Register paid homage to Fowler's wife, Agnes, during Fowler's "flaming affair with a famous actress, unnamed here." "She stayed through some wearing times," wrote Bunke, "Fowler ... must have been worth the trouble that sticking to him entailed. Smith's biography brings his macho, ribald world to life again."[13] Jack Taylor, for the *Chicago Tribune* stated that Fowler was blessed with a "tolerant wife," and "an admiring biographer." "Of her husband's polygamous peccadilloes," said Taylor, "Agnes Fowler said, 'One woman would never have been enough for Fowler. If they looked good, and if they gave him so much as a flutter, he laid them. Then he came home.'"[14] Of course, Ann was a different story altogether. Agnes wasn't so sure of herself when it came to Fowler's great "romantic love" for Ann Harding.

While doing her research on Provincetown and Hedgerow, theater historian Gail Cohen didn't get any further with Ann than H. Allen Smith did. "I had some conversations with Ann," said Cohen. "Frankly, they didn't go too well. She refused to see me, saying she didn't want to see me, because I hadn't done my homework. She said, 'Do your homework.' She was probably correct. Even though I knew an awful lot about Hedgerow, I didn't know much about *her* at the time. So that was the first conversation. She wasn't real nasty. She had a point. I wrote her and said, 'You're right. I need to do further work.'"[15] Cohen then made a surprise visit to Ann's Sherman Oaks residence. "Grace came outside," said Cohen. "She said Ann wasn't there, but I wasn't sure. Grace talked to me for a long time." During her conversation with Grace, Cohen came to the understanding that Grace truly cared about Ann. "Grace appreciated and understood about Hedgerow and Jasper," said Cohen.[16] After Ann's death, Grace made a concerted effort to retrieve letters Ann had written to Jasper.

The letters were given to Boston University as part of the Hedgerow Collection. "She went berserk when she found out that the library had the Hedgerow letters," said Cohen.[17] Grace felt the letters were "mushy." According to Cohen, Deeter, who died a bachelor, was gay— so it seemed unlikely his and Ann's relationship went beyond mentor-pupil.[18] Still, Grace felt the letters might be misinterpreted.

Jasper Deeter died shortly before Ann relocated to California. He was 78. Deeter had stepped down from active teaching and directing in 1956, but continued as chief consultant of theatre training at the Hedgerow School. His unexpected death came in 1972, a few weeks before Hedgerow's July-August summer acting classes were to begin. He had been in the hospital following complications from a broken hip. His ashes were scattered in the garden of his home in Media, Pennsylvania.[19] Deeter's obituaries portrayed him as one of the greatest teachers of theater and theater artists. They mentioned his "unselfishness, his energy, knowledge and understanding of life."[20] Paul Aaron, who directed such veterans as Lillian Gish and Claudette Colbert, as well as the Emmy-winning adaptation of *The Miracle Worker (1979)*, studied under Deeter in the 1960's. He told this author, "Jasper Deeter— you're talking about my mentor. I saw a man who virtually lived in the world of the right brain and saw his longevity, his creativity and his wonderful view of the world from that place. He was a very magical character for that reason and influenced so many people."[21] Gail Cohen emphasized to me that Deeter, in creating Hedgerow, succeeded in establishing that rare thing: a true repertory theater.

At the time of his death, news reports made a point to say that Deeter "disliked intensely" sensationalism in theater, especially writers like Tennessee Williams. While Ann had found Williams therapeutic, Deeter had given up on adult theatrical direction due to the content of the newer plays. Toward the end, he "confined himself to children's theater."[22] Although Ann was no longer involved with Hedgerow, she let it be known that, in her opinion, "people at Hedgerow had taken the theater away from Jasper." [23] Ironically, Ann and Jasper had their own parting of the ways back in 1937. Ann requested that he come over to England and coach her in *Candida*. Deeter refused.[24] Prior to this, Ann had quit her annual treks to Hedgerow in 1933, and for good reason. "People from all over came to Rose Valley to look at the 'movie star,'" Ann commented. "They stormed the theater. It was necessary to summon state troopers to take care of the traffic—an unheard-of thing in that peaceful community. I had unwittingly brought a disturbing guest with me—Spectacular Publicity."[25]

By October 1942, Ann and Deeter were once again on friendlier terms. Ann had heard through the grapevine that Hedgerow's existence was being threatened. The armed forces had refused deferment for the small theatre's company of actors. Ann wrote to Deeter offering her support for those who were declaring their Conscientious Objection. She recalled that her father had nothing but contempt for the Artist "in any field." General Gatley felt the artistic temperament was "peculiarly ill-equipped for military service ... more of a burden than an asset after induction." Ann stated that the actor was "unquestionably of more value to his country as an artist than as a soldier." "Would love to be hearing from you again," Ann enthused. "Incidentally, I would appreciate reassurance that my last letter to you *has been destroyed* [underscored], since it would make me permanently ill to think there were a chance of anyone else ever coming across it. Please? Thank you."[26] (Glossy prints weren't the only thing on Ann's list of "things to be destroyed.") Yvonne Roseman, wife of former

Hedgerow board member Ralph Roseman, remembers Jasper burning some of Ann's personal letters.[27] Deeter undoubtedly had met his
share of temperamental performers, and had pegged Ann long ago.
"Miss Harding is one of the quickest actresses I have ever worked
with," said Deeter in 1930. "She is a gay, lively young woman with
a lot of temperament and personality. The quiet, reserved stage personality is not her own. She has learned that economy and restraint
are valuable assets in acting. So, wisely she has submerged the simple,
direct and almost childish Ann for a more matured one."[28]

Had Ann "submerged" her personality any differently for the
screen?   In my investigation of the Hedgerow Theatre Collection
at UC Berkeley, I came across an article by drama critic Robert Reiss, who claimed this to be the case. I was intrigued—and began to
wonder what I may have missed by not seeing her on stage. In his
article for the *Philadelphia Record*, Reiss stated that, on film, Ann had
masked her personality to the extreme. He made this assessment
while attending Ann's final performance at Hedgerow in 1933. After
witnessing her Madeline in Glaspell's *Inheritors*, Reiss commented:

> Everything that one misses on the screen in Ann
> Harding, the feeling and the fire, the meaning and the
> inspiration that should issue from a good player were
> there in her performance on the stage. The subtle
> shades of meaning, the grace of manner, the fluid
> motion—all that which goes to differentiate the good
> actress from the bad, differentiated Ann Harding the
> stage actress from Ann Harding the movie actress.[29]

According to Reiss, it was Ann's "intellectuality" that compromised her
on-screen performances. "But to one sitting only a few feet from the
actress on the stage at the Rose Valley playhouse," wrote Reiss, "it was

evident at all times that she has all the warmth required, and perhaps even more than enough. ... so it must be that the screen does not show her to her best advantage, bringing out the intellectuality and hiding the warmth and tenderness and sensitivity that reveal themselves on the stage. She has never achieved in the movies the heights she attained the other night in the old barn near Media when she played the impassioned apostle of liberty, the college girl, in Susan Glaspell's *Inheritors*."[30] Regardless of Reiss' assessment, Ann's impact on cinema acting was a godsend. Her influence on other actors cannot be underestimated. Ann's characters were full of reflection, and brought to the screen what author Mick LaSalle refers to as "an entire life."

Ann and Grace lived at 4747 Sepulveda Blvd., in Sherman Oaks. Biographer David Chierichetti (*Mitchell Leisen-Hollywood Director*) had the opportunity to meet them both (c. 1974) after Ann had requested a private screening of her MGM film, *Magnificent Yankee*. Chierichetti was involved in making arrangements with the studio. "We sat up when she arrived," recalled Chierichetti. "She was very ... a *very* strong woman. On screen she seemed ethereal, delicate. In reality she wasn't at all." Walter Plunkett, who had designed costumes for ...*Yankee*, *The Fountain*, and ...*Vergie Winters*, also attended the screening. Upon seeing Plunkett, Ann slowly cried out in her deepest vibrato, "Walll-ter!" (Plunkett's most famous design was Scarlet O'Hara's dress made from green velvet drapes). "I tried to talk to Ann," said Chierichetti. "Here was this big opportunity for me, and she didn't have much to say. The one quote I got out of her was:

'When RKO couldn't find a script in the trash can for me, Harry Edington would arrange a loan out.'"[31] As for Grace, Chierichetti said,
"This person she introduced as her daughter ... she really wasn't her
daughter." Grace, a small woman, cautioned Chierichetti that it was
difficult for Ann to write after he had asked for an autograph. "She
gave me one anyway," he recalled, "and it took her a long time to do.
Grace Kaye didn't make much of an impression on me."[32]

It came as a surprise in my correspondence with author James
Robert Parish, to learn of the rumors surrounding Ann. Parish told me,
"My late friend DeWitt Bodeen (the scriptwriter/historian), when he
lived at the Motion Picture Country Home in the late 1970's, said that
his next door neighbor, Mary Astor, told him that she stopped speaking to Ann Harding, because she had turned lesbian."[33] Bodeen began
his career as a script reader at RKO in the late 1930's. A respected
researcher and scenarist, Bodeen wrote screenplays for such successful films as Cat People (1942) and The Enchanted Cottage (1945). Was
there any real substance to Astor's catty remark? Personally, I found
the Ann-as-lesbian scenario, if puzzling, unlikely. When I related the
Bodeen-Astor story to Gail Cohen, she replied, "He was talking about
Ann? That's really strange. I was so confused about Grace."[34] Prior
to my message from Parish, Cohen had told me that when she met
Grace Kaye outside Ann's Sherman Oaks residence in the 1970's, she
was puzzled by the way Grace explained her connection to Ann. "She
always referred to herself as Ann's 'ward,'" said Cohen. "I never asked
about their relationship, and I guess I didn't, because she confused
me by the term 'ward' and for all I knew they were lovers. She looked
old then to me. [Grace would have been in her mid 40's—Ann, in her
70's]. After Ann died, Grace lived in Van Nuys."[35]

I contacted Mary Astor's daughter, Marylyn Thorpe Roh, to ask if Astor would have made such a remark regarding Ann's sexuality. Marylyn was straightforward with her opinion on Astor's reputed comment. "My snobby mother!" Marylyn remarked. "Of all the gay and lesbian friends in the 'business' she knew and surrounded herself with in her life—I have often wondered if she were not a 'Bi' herself—no proof. To give up a friend for that reason is pitiful. Possible jealousy involved in there. The past is past, and Ann isn't around to speak for herself with her own story."[36] Marylyn is the daughter from Astor's marriage to Dr. Franklyn Thorpe. She was four years old in 1936, during the time of Astor's sensational divorce trial. It had been at Ann's suggestion that Astor employ lawyer Roland "Rich" Wooley to help with the custody battle. Marylyn knew nothing about Ann's support in Astor's attempt to regain custody, but stated, "I never knew Ann or her daughter. I can only remember Mom saying some rather catty remarks about her which I don't recall these umpteen years later."[37] According to Marylyn, Astor wasn't in the best of spirits during her stay at the Motion Picture Country Home (MPCH), which was located in the San Fernando Valley. "In those final years," said Marylyn, "Mom was very private, and very unsociable. Her family members had to always phone and make an appointment to see her on HER turf at her time. Ergo, busy with families, we didn't get to see her much. I can remember her saying, 'all my peers around me are dying—I hate living around these ol' farts.' She was in her 80's!"[38]

It wasn't long after Ann and Grace relocated to California, that Ann had an extended stay at Sepulveda Convalescent Hospital. A Van Nuys news item from December 1974, reported of her participation in a 103rd birthday celebration for one of the residents. Columnist

Couples night out. (c. 1931) Ann and Harry Bannister are joined by
Mary Astor and husband Dr. Franklyn Thorpe, a gynecologist.

Agnes Dow wrote, "Ann Harding, retired actress of stage and screen, recited 'The Night Before Christmas' in the deep, clear voice which brought back memories of the actress at the height of her career."[39] Ann's contribution for this event was her final public "performance." Veteran columnist-author Jess L. Hoaglin, who lived in nearby Santa Monica, stated that while Ann was in ill health and confined to her home, she remained "vibrant." "She doted on visits from her friends," said Hoaglin, "and delighted in relating stories of her past. She would never dwell on the unhappy events of her life, but always made her listeners leave with a glow of good feelings and inspiration."[40] Hoaglin was privy to get one of the last interviews Ann gave. In a 1976 issue of *Hollywood Studio Magazine*, he wrote about his visit to Ann's home in the San Fernando Valley. Ann stated that she had loved her farm home in Westport. "When I first bought it," said Ann, "my adopted daughter, Grace Kaye and I enjoyed the serene surroundings but later it became a veritable nightmare … progress began crowding in and our home no longer held the security and privacy we wanted."[41] So, somewhere along the line, Ann had adopted Grace.

For the longest time, I was getting nowhere in solving the mystery of Grace Kaye. After trying several phone listings for "Grace Kaye" in the Los Angeles area, I gave up. What I did learn provided some idea as to her background. Like Ann, Grace was born in Texas. Her parents, Basil Lyons Kaye and Grace Bowker Kaye, were living in San Antonio when their daughter Grace Florence Kaye was born in 1930. Basil had immigrated from England, and his wife, a Texas native, grew up in San Antonio. Mrs. Kaye had graduated from the San Antonio College of Music, where she studied voice and piano. Her specialties were Haydn, Bach and Beethoven. She also acted for the Optimist Club and occasionally performed on the radio.[42] After completing her schooling in Texas, daughter Grace Kaye eventually relocated to Westport.

Gail Cohen, who had lost contact with Grace and was desperate to find her, kept encouraging me not to give up the search. So, I made one last effort while finishing my manuscript. I wrote to six addresses listed for the name Grace Kaye from various internet search engines. On each envelope, under Grace's name, I put in parentheses, "Or Current Resident." My letter stated that I was trying to locate Grace Kaye, a companion of the actress Ann Harding. (At that time, I wasn't aware that Ann had adopted Grace). I hoped that Grace would be willing to tell me something about herself and share anecdotes about Ann. Whoever read the letter might know of Grace's whereabouts, or, better yet, it would be Grace herself who opened one of the six envelopes. Three days later I received a phone call. The woman on the other end of the line was not Grace, but a close friend of hers. She was concerned how I got her address, and emphasized that Grace was not Ann's "companion," but her daughter. "My husband and I knew Ann very well," the woman said. "We were very, very close. When we got this letter, I thought, 'Oh my goodness sakes! Here we go! She's long gone and somebody wants to bring all this out.'" I suddenly felt as if I had opened a can of worms. "It's just so funny that all this is starting to come out when she has passed on," the woman continued. "You mean Grace?" I asked. "Grace is living," she answered. "It is just so weird after all these years. It's sort of like bringing back the dead. Hold on one minute." I held on.

The raspy tone of another woman's voice greeted me. "Good morning, Scott. How are you?" It was Grace herself, as formidable as Ann, and as fascinating. I asked if she had ever seen Ann on stage. "Well, of course I've seen her on the stage, I'm her daughter!" she stated indignantly. Wondering what plays she had seen Ann appear in, I asked if she would like to comment on Ann's performances. "Oh, no, no, no! I would not go into that! I don't want *any* book published on my mother. I have one I could have published a long time ago, but I didn't do it. I would never put any stuff in a book that, you know … I'm not a Joan Crawford daughter." (An obvious reference to *Mommie Dearest* written by Crawford's adopted daughter, Christina). As I was uncertain as to where they had met, I made the big mistake of asking Grace if she had known Ann in Connecticut. "She was my mother Scott! You talk to me like I'm some sort of a maid! So, I don't appreciate this conversation. I think we'd better end it right now." Dead silence. Grace did not hang up, so I decided to brave new territory. I asked what Ann's retirement years were like. "Everything was fine!" she snapped. "You found all this stuff out now like a detective. So, I guess you can find out all the rest, can't you?" I was beginning to like this woman. She was on a roll. "All this gossip! All these people going around looking for me," she railed. "I had a call the other day from a friend of mine in Pennsylvania, somebody looking for me. Somebody from the theatre [Hedgerow]. Well, I haven't seen that theatre in years. Jasper Deeter, I haven't seen since before he died, about a year before he passed away. Well, you found me, and I don't know what you want, still. I know there is really something else that is wanted. Something about some *letters*."

As Gail Cohen had mentioned Grace's paranoia about Ann's letters to Jasper, I assumed this is what Grace referred to. I told Grace that the letters didn't matter. "It matters!" she emphasized. "Yes, it *does* matter!"[43] I began to wonder what shocking things were contained in these letters? Had Ann and Jasper bumped someone off? Did they produce an illegitimate child? I never heard such a fuss. I began to think of Ann's portrayals of unwed mothers in her biggest box-office hits, *The Life of Vergie Winters* and *Gallant Lady*. I had to remember that older generations still carry the legacy of shame and suffering perpetrated by outdated social mores and religious indoctrination. Nowadays, having a child out of wedlock doesn't carry the same sting, or stigma.

Although Grace offered no clue as to what the controversy was all about, she revealed far more than she probably intended to. The whole tone of our conversation underscored the fact that there was something to hide. There was some dark secret waiting to be uncovered, as Grace's friend had said, "after all these years." Grace did clarify that she was Ann's "adoptive" daughter and that Jane was Ann's "natural" daughter. She then asked for Gail Cohen's phone number. I offered it to her. Grace told me to let Gail know that she would be calling her. "I'll let her know that you are well," I said. "Yes," Grace replied. "I'm alive and well. I'm in there kickin'!" Like a mule. There was something I admired about her feisty character.

When I finally got a hold of them, I found nothing scandalous in the Harding-Deeter letters. In the earliest seven-page letter (fall of 1928), Ann was missing Harry (who was in New York), and she details that her energy registered at "zero" while playing *The Trial of Mary Dugan* in Chicago. She rhapsodizes about baby Jane, calling her "a healthy, merry little soul." Before leaving for California, Ann again wrote to Deeter, saying she was looking forward to a long rest. She curiously refers to Harry's tour in *Strange Interlude* (which she amusingly calls "Up in Nina's Womb") as the "Six Day Bi-Sexual Race."[44] Once in Hollywood, Ann shared with Deeter her enthusiasm for working at Pathe, saying she was "enjoying it too much." If anything, the letters reflect Ann's reliance on Deeter's opinions and his ability to help her focus on what she refers to as the "fundamentals." The deep love and gentle friendship between the two is undeniable. Aside from their dry spell (1937-42), Ann relied on Deeter's support through retirement. While she was grabbing at TV opportunities in 1963, she wrote to her "revered Teacher," asking the reason for facing each day. Ann felt that Deeter had discovered it, she hadn't. "All I want is OUT," wrote Ann. She reassured him that she had not lost the gift of laughter, and not to worry. "It might amuse you to know," Ann added, "that I am still capable of a 'pick-up.' At my age! Who else could 'pick-up' a Jesuit Priest in a very exclusive restaurant in New York? Give me credit, no kidding!"[45] If Ann had once confided some dark secret to Deeter via the US Postal Services, the letters were most likely among those that Deeter turned to ashes.

Five months after our conversation, I received another surprise call from Grace Kaye. This took place shortly after I had sent her my copies of Ann's letters to Deeter, with the intent of putting Grace's mind at ease. Grace apologized for her previous phone call, saying, "I didn't intend to be so mean. I wish you a lot of luck with your book. I'm looking forward to reading it."[46] I told her that I bet Ann would have treated me the same way. We had a good laugh about that.

Unfortunately, when Ann passed away, she and her daughter Jane were estranged. Forty years had passed since writer/scenarist Katherine Albert (who penned the Bette Davis vehicle, *The Star*) visited Ann and Jane at their hilltop home on Pyramid Place. Albert recalled watching Ann kiss little Jane, and stand away from her marveling, "Isn't she amazing? I can't believe that I am responsible for that— that I should have had a part in the creating of anything so lovely."[47] What exactly caused the rift between mother and daughter is unclear. One wonders about Jane's reaction to her mother adopting Grace, who was only two years Jane's junior. Had Ann's decision jeopardized her relationship with Jane? Gail Cohen said Grace told her that Jane had not spoken to her mother for several years. Ann's step-granddaughter, Lynne Stickrod, confirmed this, saying Ann and Jane never reconciled their differences. "By the time we came into the picture [1963]," said Lynne, "Ann was kind of … not close to her daughter. They kept in touch somewhat, but they were not that close. We don't really know what Ann was doing when she moved to San Fernando Valley. She wasn't really ... how do I describe it ... she became more reclusive. Obviously, if she was reclusive she was depressed. Jane didn't have contact with her per se during those final years."[48]

Reclusiveness in old-age is a familiar scenario for many screen legends. Mary Astor's daughter described her mother's final years as being similar to Ann's. "Mom didn't like visitors," said Marylyn, "even at the MPCH where she lived for 10+ years. Very reclusive. She didn't keep any 'famous' people as friends. So many had died!"[49] When Astor passed away in 1987 (age 81), she had also alienated her daughter. "She had 'dismissed' me from her life the last time I saw her," said Marylyn. "There was a slight tiff between us. I was just leaving after a visit at the MPCH hospital. I had told her I would be thinking of her. She said, 'Well, don't get too sentimental.' Somehow she pushed one of my buttons, and I told her she never allowed me to love her as I wanted to—that everything always had to be her way. I was miffed and frustrated. I shouldn't have been, because she was elderly and possibly on the fringe of dementia—but I didn't know about that then. All she said after my few sentences was, 'Go!' I looked at her in disbelief, and she repeated, 'Go.' I walked out slowly. She died four months later."[50]

Ann had not only crossed off Jane, but also her sister Edith. According to Gail Cohen, it had been many years since the two sisters had spoken. "Something really weird happened," said Cohen, "and Ann never spoke to her again."[51] (Edith MacKenzie passed away in 1985, while residing in Albuquerque, New Mexico). Cutting people off from her life in the grand tradition of her own Brigadier General father appears to have been Ann's way of dealing with conflict. Long ago she had once emphasized that life was a journey that one takes *alone*. The award-winning author Elizabeth Borton de Trevino, talked to Ann shortly before the Bannister divorce headlines in 1932. A few years later, de Trevino reflected back to their conversation, taking into consideration what Ann was going through at that time. The writer could see poignancy in what Ann had to say. "I have only one wish for my little daughter," Ann told her, "I wish for her that she will never love anyone too much ... I hope that I can teach her, in time, the deep truth of our essential loneliness, of everyone's. We die, alone, you know. But also, we live alone."[52] De Trevino was struck by a special quality of Ann's—the impression to be "speaking from spirit." "I want to give my child a weapon ... a sort of protection," Ann candidly stated. "I want her never to live with a longing to love and be loved. I believe the wish for love, and the hope of love, is the cause of most unhappiness. It's caused by thinking that love cancels loneliness. I want my Jane never to put her trust into a fleeting thing, like love ... I want her to know that there is only one person she can really always count on ... Jane, herself."[53]

Jane Bannister Harding Otto

I began my research on Ann Harding shortly after Jane Otto passed away. Ann's step-granddaughter Lynne Stickrod mentioned Jane's occasional visits to Westport, but stated that Ann never came to the Bay Area to see them. "She wasn't part of our lives," said Lynne. Jane did not talk about Hollywood, or her mother's film and stage work. "She talked about the different houses they had while she was growing up," Lynne recalled, "because it was so different. She mentioned her bodyguard after the Lindbergh kidnapping. I just think Jane and her mother, I don't know why, but sometimes kids are close to their parents and sometimes they aren't. As time went on they weren't close."[54]

One thing Jane Otto did maintain throughout her life was a bright and resilient spirit. Her friends concur that Ann remained distant. This was quite evident during the time Jane attended UC Berkeley. Mary Pruett Gibson, Jane's wedding attendant and San Francisco roommate, told me, "I don't know how close Jane was to her mother. My guess would be that it was difficult growing up with a mother who was, obviously quite lovely, but also in the movies. Jane didn't talk a lot about that."[55] Jeanie Barry, a close friend and former sorority sister of Jane, was more blunt, "Jane was raised by a very detached mother ... I don't know whether the word 'estranged' would apply. They just sort of went their own way, because that was the way it was."[56] Ann's statement, "I want [Jane] to know that there is only one person she can really always count on ... Jane, herself," would turned prophetic.

After close to thirty years of marriage, Jane and Alfred Otto separated. In 1985, the year following their separation, Alfred passed away after a brief illness.[57] Jane's step-children remained fond of her. Otto provided handsomely for Jane, who was actively involved with the world around her. She is listed in *Who's Who of American Women, 6th ed., 1970-71.* Among her interests were the Junior League of San Francisco, the Episcopal Sanctuary, the San Francisco Zoo, SPCA, and ARCS Foundation. From 1976-78, she was president of ARCS, which provided scholarships for outstanding individuals in the fields of science and technology. Her connection with ARCS was inspired by her close friend, the wealthy San Francisco socialite, Ann Russell Miller, a tireless fundraiser and do-gooder. After raising ten children,

Miller gained a great deal of notoriety in 1989, when she abandoned her gregarious life, her season tickets to the opera, shopping sprees at Saks Fifth Avenue—and joined a convent.[58] Not just any convent, but one of the strictest—a Carmelite monastery—a cloistered and ascetic order. Miller's decision had a profound effect on Jane. "Ann and Jane were terribly close." said Jeanie Barry, "When Ann entered the convent, I think that actually just sort of broke Jane's link to the world."[59]

Jeanie Barry commented that one of the men in Jane's social circle, Bill Goulet, a former executive of Gump's (the famous San Francisco luxury store) suggested that Jane move to Sante Fe. "He convinced Jane that was the place for her to set up camp," said Barry. "That's why she moved." New Mexico's capital city is a well-known center for the arts. "Jane was interested in the arts and sponsored different artists," said Barry. "I think she had a very nice, superficial life in Sante Fe. We had dinner with her there one night. Her spirit was good ... a very keen mind. She was terribly crippled, because she always had dreadful posture—the arthritis. She was in a wheelchair or a walker, I forget. However, she was able to live nicely in Santa Fe."[60] Lynne Stickrod emphasized that when Jane relocated, there was already a sizable group of San Francisco "ex-pats" who had retired to Sante Fe. "Jane was in good company," said Lynne.[61]

When I asked Jeanie about Ann's granddaughter, Diana Otto, Barry mentioned that she, too, had a daughter Diana's age. "The girls had different outlooks, but they exchanged birthday parties," recalled Barry. "Diana was a cute little girl. I know that her life was turned upside down because her father's children (after their mother died) were transported from the East Bay to Marin County. Jane and Al took over. They instantly had a family of four. They had just com-

pleted building this house in Ross, and had to enlarge it to accommo-
date the other three children. So Diana's life became much different.
I think she was a problem in high school. I do remember she married
a hippie. She had a baby. You know what I'm talking about—she suffered from being the only child to being one of four."[62] Barry stated
that Jane handled Diana's plight intelligently, but let it be known she
was worried about her.

Diana Harding Otto (as she is listed in the California Birth Index)
was going by the name of Diana Laurent at the time of her father's
death (1985). Her son, Aaron Daniel Perillat, (Ann's great-grandson)
was born July 24, 1979. Aaron's father, William Perillat, a respected
artist and wood sculptor, raised his son as a single parent from 1982-
2000.[63] Aaron completed his degree in computer science from Southern Oregon University. He currently has a position with a computer
company. I asked Aaron about his famous great-grandmother and his
impressions of her films. "I don't have a lot to tell," he offered. "I was
very close with Jane, but she never talked about her mother. Obviously, I never met Ann. I have not seen any of her films, sadly. As
for my mother, she has not said much about Ann either. She is sadly
unavailable to talk to. As for me, I was born in Sante Fe, and have lived
in Ashland since I was two-years-old. I am sorry I do not have more
information to give."[64] Aaron is the last in the line of Ann's legacy.

Jane Otto died on November 19, 2005 in Sante Fe, where she had
resided since 1990. "Jane's one of the people I miss … very much," said
her friend Jeanie. "She was a wonderful character. We first met when
she came to Berkeley and joined my sorority. Jane was raised … very
loosely. Her mother was the star of the family. Jane spent a lot of time
in hotel rooms and as a consequence never made a bed. Things like that

didn't bother her, but she was a wonderful cook. She was very, very smart. She just seemed to make the most of her world. Sometimes her mother would be in the money and sometimes she wouldn't. Sometimes Jane would have $300 formal dresses. Sometimes she'd have to borrow one. We always had to bring up the subject of Jane's mother. She rarely talked about her, but she'd often mention her step-father, Werner Janssen, she was very close to him."[65] Barry talked about skiing trips up to Portland in the late 1940's, while Janssen was conducting the Portland Symphony. Jane invited several from her Berkeley group to come and stay with them in Oregon. Jane's step-daughter, Lynne Stickrod, also mentioned Jane's affection for Werner. "When [Janssen] was in Europe," said Lynne, "Jane would always check with the musical critic for the *San Francisco Chronicle* to find out what he had heard about Werner Janssen. She had great affection for him, because he was the one who was there for her when she was growing up."[66]

Ann rarely mentioned her own mother. It was always her father, the father that had disowned her, that meant the most to her. By nineteen, Ann was on her own, permanently. By the time Jane entered UC Berkeley, she too came to the realization that she was on her own—creating her reality, with no mother's shoulder to cry on. Jane's real confidant, according to friends, was her stepfather. Either Ann had complete confidence that Jane could do it on her own, or she was too consumed with other issues to take time for her daughter. Even at the height of her career, Ann was burning her candle at both ends—filming; involvement with the Screen Actor's Guild; treks to Hedgerow; directing Little Theatre; divorce proceedings; the fiasco in Cuba; Hawaii trips; not to mention love affairs with Dudley Murphy, General Sawbridge, and Gene Fowler.

Stinson Beach (1980). The progeny of Ann Harding. The girl with the long tresses is Ann's granddaughter, Diana. Jane is holding Ann's great-grandson Aaron. "Jane never talked about her mother," said Aaron in 2009. "I have not seen any of Ann's films, sadly." (Courtesy of the Otto family)

On the first day of September, 1981, at 8:15 in the morning, Ann Harding passed away. She was 79. UPI reported that she had been ill for a long time and that her death occurred at a hospital in the San Fernando Valley. *The New York Times* stated that Ann died at her home in Sherman Oaks. The actual location was the Sepulveda Convalescent Hospital, where she had been a frequent patient since moving to Sherman Oaks. Her physician, M. Sheila Beirne, M.D., indicated that Ann had died from "acute myocardial infarction," commonly known as a heart attack. Ann suffered from arteriosclerosis for "many years," according to her Certificate of Death.[67] After cremation, Ann's ashes were interred at Forest Lawn Hollywood Hills. No funeral or memorial service was planned.[68]

The New York Times write-up by Carol Lawson, said that Ann did not speak of Hollywood in flattering terms. "I loathed the stupidity in the handling of the material in Hollywood," Ann was quoted as saying. "If you're under contract when you're making pictures you may get the plums but they own your soul."[69] Her obituaries inevitably mentioned Ann's patrician good-looks, and her long blond hair tied in a bun at the nape of her neck. Ann was hailed for her roles as elegant women. In 1983, the British publication, *The Illustrated Who's Who of the Cinema*, summed up what has been widely considered Ann's screen legacy: "She established herself as a leading lady of repute, but this willowy, poised, elegant actress never did fulfill her potential. She was always the honor-bound heroine, emotional and caring, and always ready to sacrifice herself. In the Forties she was back playing older, grander versions of the ladies she seemed unable to escape from."[70]

After Ann's death, Gail Cohen sent a telegram to Grace which she appreciated. The message talked about Ann, Glaspell's *Inheritors* and Jasper Deeter. "Grace really liked me, and we talked a lot," said Cohen. "She said mine was the most important message she received."[71] Cohen also stated that Ann, with someone's assistance, had made a series of audio tapes regarding her life and career. Grace told Cohen that the quality of the tapes were very poor—"useless." "When I last spoke to her in 2000," said Cohen, "I told her that technology can now improve the quality. She was discouraged, and I had the sense she had gotten rid of the tapes. I begged her to save them."[72] It is likely that Ann had the intention of writing her memoirs—the tapes being the first step. The only consolation is a book in the works about Ann and her sister Edith. Ann's grandniece, Faeylyn Walker of Tucson, has been researching the lives of her grandmother (Edith) and famous great-aunt for several years. Apparently, a considerable amount of emotion is tied up in this project about the two sisters. Due to contractual agreement, Walker was unable to talk with this author. Faeylyn talked with Jane Otto shortly before she died (2005), so, hopefully, for those desiring more insight into the turbulence behind Ann's family life, this new volume will prove worthwhile.[73]

According to family members, it was only following her mother's death that Jane Otto learned that Grace Kaye considered herself to be Ann's adopted daughter. On Ann's Certificate of Death, under "Name and Address of Informant," appears: "Grace K. Harding – Daughter."[74] It is not uncommon for an older individual to adopt a younger adult. Legally, it allows inheritance rights within a relationship. Probate courts handle such petitions all the time.

Ann's step-granddaughter, Lynne Stickrod, said the news of Jane's brand-new 50-year-old sister came as a complete surprise to Jane and her family. "It was a joke among us," said Stickrod. "Apparently, this woman was the housekeeper to Ann Harding. I think Ann adopted her at the end to try to ... I don't know what ... to get her money for taking care of her? Ann didn't really have much money left when she died. The only thing I know is that when Ann died, they didn't recognize the adopted daughter, Grace Kaye. (If she *was* the adopted daughter). But I know that Jane had to sign off on it and she was the legal next of kin. As a family joke, when the obituary came out, we were going to have a party for Jane's new 'sister.' Which, of course, we didn't. And we never ... she never came up here. It wasn't like 'families reunited.'"[75] Although none of the Ann Harding obituaries I read mention her, it was adopted daughter Grace who was there for Ann during her final years.

The ashes of Ann Harding are placed in a tiny crypt, discreetly located in an unassuming niche, at the Forest Lawn Memorial Park in Hollywood Hills (not to be confused with the original Forest Lawn in Glendale). Other famous contemporaries of Ann's interred at Hollywood Hills include Bette Davis and Charles Laughton. The massive marble tomb of Bette Davis is like a shrine designed for the pilgrimages of her many followers. When I was interviewed for the documentary, *Queer Icon, the Cult of Bette Davis* (2009), the film's photographer, Car-

Forest Lawn, Hollywood Hills.
A gigantic wall containing over a
thousand grave markers, places
Ann Harding on the bottom row.
(Courtesy of Carole Summers)

ole Summers, upon learning I was working on an Ann Harding biography, made a point of taking a photograph of Ann's crypt. Ann's diminutive vault is located on the bottom row in the back section of Forest Lawn's Court of Remembrance— an enormous wall with well over 1,000 markers. At the film's premier I was struck by the size of Davis' tomb—even from a distance. And then I thought of Ann's, tucked away in an obscure location for only the determined to find.

The difference between the memorials of Davis and that of Harding seems to reflect their contrasting style on screen. Davis was always larger than life. Harding was never bigger than the story being told. Being a star, for Harding, was not a priority. It was barely a consideration. While working in the ensemble spirit, her gracious presence captured the imagination of the viewer. As her co-star Robert Brown said, "she was a gentle creative force."[76] Thanks to Turner Classic Movies and film revivals, Ann continues to be a "creative force" well worth re-discovering.

Ann Harding came from a group of innovators in the 1920's—the Provincetown Players, Jasper Deeter and Hedgerow, Eugene O'Neill, Paul Robeson, and Susan Glaspell. Their combined influences helped redefine theatre arts, and reinforce the age-old tradition of creating the "magic of illusion." As mentioned, both Deeter and Ann were fueled

Ann Harding—a legacy worth remembering.

with admiration for their friend and contemporary, the Pulitzer-Prize winning poet, Edna St. Vincent Millay. Her classic poem, "Renascence"—which bonded Ann and her young co-star, Robert Brown, from *The Corn is Green*, delved into the workings of the inner spirit in touch with the Universe. "The world stands out on either side, no wider than the heart is wide," wrote Millay.[77] In creating her characters for stage and screen, Ann opened her heart and *connected*. For her, the phenomenon of death and rebirth became a lived, and felt experience, not a theological problem. "In playing a role," Ann had once stated, "I get to intimately understand another's point of view. I learn that circumstances may alter cases—and for the time being, to think as another thinks."[78] Thanks to her unique contribution to the cinematic arts, the inner flame of Ann Harding, to paraphrase the words of St. Vincent Millay, continues "to give a lovely light."[79]

(Endnotes)

1   "Ann Harding to Talk in Trumbull Monday," *Bridgeport Post*, 4/21/66
2   Arthur H. Lewis, *Those Philadelphia Kellys*, William Morrow and Co., N.Y., c. 1977, pg 92
3   Letter to William Porter, 8/6/68
4   Gene Ringgold, "Ann Harding," *Films in Review*, March 1972
5   James Robert Parish, *The RKO Gals*, Rainbow Books, c.1974, pg 42
6   Charlotte Chandler, *Not the Girl Next Door*, Applause Books, c. 2009, pg 267
7   Email from James Robert Parish, 7/8/2008
8   James Robert Parish, *The RKO Gals*, Rainbow Books, c. 1974, pg 42
9   "116 Employees Honored at Norwalk Hospital," *The Bridgeport Post*, 3/27/71
10   From Ann's letters to Jasper Deeter, Howard Gotlieb Archival Research Center, Boston University
11   H. Allen Smith, *The Life and Legend of Gene Fowler*, William Morrow and Co., N.Y., c. 1977, pg 221
12   H. Allen Smith, *The Life and Legend* ... pg 17
13   Joan Bunke, "Life, legend and laughter—Gene Fowler," *Des Moines Register*, 6/26/77
14   Jack Taylor, review of *The Life and Legend of Gene Fowler*, *Chicago Tribune*, 6/5/77
15   Conversation with Gail Cohen, 7/14/2008
16   Conversation with Gail Cohen, 7/27/2009
17   Conversation with Gail Cohen, 8/15/2009
18   Conversation with Gail Cohen, 7/14/2008
19   "Jasper Deeter of Theater Dies," *Bridgeport Post*, 6/1/72
20   Gerry Oliver, "Hedgerow's Jasper Deeter Didn't Die Unappreciated," *Delaware County Daily Times (PA)*, 6/1/72
21   Conversation with Paul Aaron, 7/15/2008 (Aaron is the former step-father of actor Keanu Reeves)

22   Gerry Oliver, Hedgerow's Jasper Deeter ..."
23   Conversation with Gail Cohen, 7/14/2008
24   Gail Cohen stated that Ann's request for Deeter to come to England is documented in *The Hedgerow Collection* at Boston University
25   Elza Schallert, "Why I Have Kept Silent for Two Years," magazine article, circa 1934, Hedgerow Theatre Collection, UC Berkeley, Bancroft Library
26   Letter on microfilm at UC Berkeley, Bancroft Library c. 1942
27   Email from Gail Cohen, 8/17/2009
28   Elsie Finn, "Talkies and Talkers," *Philadelphia Record*, 8/1/1930
29   Robert Reiss, "Return of Ann Harding," *Philadelphia Record*, 1/22/33, from Hedgerow Theatre Collection, UC Berkeley, Bancroft Library
30   Robert Reiss, "Return ..."
31   Phone conversation with David Chierichetti, 9/21/2009
32   Email from David Chierichetti, 9/26/2009
33   Email from James Robert Parish, 7/8/2008
34   Conversation with Gail Cohen, 7/14/2008
35   Email from Gail Cohen, 6/25/2008
36   Email from Marylyn Roh, 4/22/2009
37   Email from Marylyn Roh, 4/23/2009
38   Email from Marylyn Roh, 4/24/2009
39   Agnes Viola Dow, The Sounding Board," *The Valley News*, 12/22/1974
40   Jess L. Hoaglin, "In Memoriam – Ann Harding," *Hollywood Studio Magazine*, December 1981
41   Jess L. Hoaglin, "Ann Harding – Portrait of a Lady," *Hollywood Studio Magazine*, October 1976
42   Information on Grace Bowker Kaye - from articles in *The San Antonio Light*, January 1923-Feb. 1930
43   Conversation with Grace Kaye Harding, 9/12/2009
44   Letter from Ann to Jasper Deeter, January, 1929. Howard Gotlieb Archival Research Center, Boston U.
45   Letter from Ann to Jasper Deeter, 9/10/63. Howard Gotlieb Archival Research Center, Boston U.
46   Conversation with Grace Kaye Harding, 2/15/2010
47   Katherine Albert, "Ann Harding's Menace," *Modern Screen*, March 1933
48   Conversation with Lynne Stickrod, 6/26/2009
49   Email from Marylyn Roh, 7/2/2009
50   Email from Marylyn Roh, 4/29/2009
51   Conversation with Gail Cohen, 7/27/2009
52   Elizabeth Borton, "Ann Harding Talks About Her Child," *Motion Picture*, January 1936
53   Elizabeth Borton, "Ann Harding Talks ..."
54   Conversation with Lynne Stickrod, 6/25/2009
55   Conversation with Mary Pruett Gibson, 8/4/2009
56   Conversation with Jeanie Barry, 8/4/2009
57   Email from Lynne Stickrod, 8/11/2009
58   Julia Prodis, "Socialite Gives Away Wealth to Become A Cloistered Nun," *The Seattle Times*, 10/20/94
      Adair Lara, "From High Society to a Higher Calling," *San Francisco Chronicle*, 3/27/2005
59   Conversation with Jeanie Barry, 8/4/2009
60   Conversation with Jeanie Barry, 8/4/2009
61   Email from Lynne Stickrod, 8/11/2009
62   Conversation with Jeanie Barry, 8/5/2009
63   William Perillat Wood Sculptor, www.wperillatwood.com
64   Email from Aaron Perillat, 8/17/2009
65   Conversation with Jeanie Barry, 8/4/2009
66   Conversation with Lynne Stickrod, 6/25/2009
67   Ann Harding, State of California, "Certificate of Death," (informational copy) item no. 22, 9/4/81

68   UPI, "Long Illness Fatal to Ann Harding," *Syracuse Herald-Journal (NY)*, 9/3/81

69   Carol Lawson, "Ann Harding, Actress Hailed for Roles as Elegant Women," *New York Times*, 9/4/81

70   "Ann Harding," *The Illustrated Who's Who of the Cinema*," Orbis Pub. Ltd (London). c.1983 pg 192

71   Conversation with Gail Cohen, 7/14/2008

72   Emails from Gail Cohen, 6/25/2008, 6/26/2008

73   Email from Gail Cohen, 7/27/2009- Cohen stated that Faelyn Wylder indicated that her publisher would not allow her to talk about her biography project on Ann Harding and Edith.

74   Ann Harding, State of California, "Certificate of Death," (informational copy) item no. 20, 9/4/81

75   Conversation with Lynne Stickrod, 6/25/2009

76   Conversation with Robert Brown, 2/15/2008

77   Edna St. Vincent Millay, *Renascence*, from *Renascence and Other Poems*, c. 1917

78   "Animal Kingdom," *Nevada State Journal*, 3/19/33

79   Edna St. Vincent Millay, *First Fig*, from *A Few Figs From Thistles*, c. 1922

Ann Harding

in

"CANDIDA"

by

GEORGE BERNARD SHAW

Program for *Candida* (1938)

Credits

Ann Harding on Stage

(Note: The titles from Ann's engagements with Jessie Bonstelle, Hedgerow, and smaller companies may not be complete listings)

1921:

(Off Broadway) *Inheritors* (Susan Glaspell) March 1921, Provincetown Players, New York. Cast: Ann Harding (Madeline)

(Summer stock) Jessie Bonstelle Company (plays unknown)

(Broadway) *Like a King* (John Hunter Booth) October 1921, 39th Street Theatre (16 performances) Adolph Klauber (producer) Cast: Ann Harding (Phyllis Weston), James Gleason, Mina Gleason, Arthur Allen, E.L. Duane, Charles Esdale, Frances Howard - (In April 1921, the play had a tryout in Trenton, N.J.)

The Lonely Heart (Edward Sheldon) November 1921, Tryout in Baltimore. Cast: Basil Sydney, Ann Harding

1922:

(Winter Stock) Jessie Bonstelle Company, 1921-22, Providence, Rhode Island. Plays included:
  The Tiger Woman
  Little Women (Louisa May Alcott - adapted for the stage by Marian de Forest) Ann played Amy
  Mis' Nelly of N'Orleans (Laurence Eyre) Ann played Melanie Cardanne
  Seventeen (Booth Tarkington)
  (Summer Stock) Jessie Bonstelle Company – Detroit, Michigan. Plays included: *Peter Pan*
  (James M. Barrie) Ann played Peter
  The Bird of Paradise (Richard Walton Tully) Ann played Luana
  The Man Who Came Back (John Fleming Wilson – adapted for stage by J. E. Goodman)

1923:

Hedgerow Theatre, July - October 1923, Plays include:

Inheritors (Susan Glaspell) Cast: Ann Harding (Madeline)

The Master Builder (Henrik Ibsen) Cast: Ann Harding (Hilda), William Price

Mr. Pim Passes By (A.A. Milnes) Cast: Ann Harding (Dinah), Will Walton, Virginia Farmer, William Price, Sydney Machet, Ruth Deeter, Gretchen Myleeraine

(Broadway) *Tarnish* (Gilbert Emery) October 1923 - May 1924, Belmont Theatre (248 performances)

Produced and directed by John Cromwell – Cast: Ann Harding (Letitia Tevis), Tom Powers, Fania Marinoff, Marion Lord, Mildred MacLeod, Albert Gran - (In the summer of 1923, *Tarnish* had tryouts in Stamford, CT. and other cities)

1924:

Hedgerow Theatre, June - December 1924 (Several Fall performances were held at Philadelphia's Players Club) Plays included:

Candida (George Bernard Shaw) Cast: Ann Harding (Candida), William Price, Dorothy Kite, Louis Leverett, Ferd Nofer

Inheritors (Susan Glaspell) Cast: Ann Harding (Madeline), Jasper Deeter

Misalliance (George Bernard Shaw) Cast: Ann Harding (Lina), Sydney Machet, William Whitney

The Master Builder (Henrik Ibsen) Cast: Ann Harding (Hilda), William Price, Dorothy Yockel, William Berry, Margaret Scott Oliver

Paolo and Francesca (Stephen Phillips) Marguerite Robinson (director) Cast: Ann Harding (Francesca), Kirah Markham, Jasper Deeter, Elizabeth Ross, Morgan Farley/Ferd Nofer (alternating as Paolo)

Captain Brassbound's Conversion (George Bernard Shaw) Cast: Ann Harding (Lady Cecily)

The Dreamers (Barry Conners) Cast: Ann Harding, Jasper Deeter

King Hunger (Leonid Andreyev) Marc Blitzen (incidental music) Mordecai Gorelik (set design) Cast: Jasper Deeter (actor/director), Ann Harding, Edward Biberman, Dorothy Yockel, William Price

The Dragon (Lady Gregory) (Colorful Irish story about a King, Queen, Princess and a dragon) Cast: Ann Harding (the Princess), William Berry, Howard Earling

(Summer Season) *Mary the Third* (Rachel Crothers) August 1924, Garrick Theatre, Detroit, Michigan. (In this comedy Ann played a flapper who is determined to "live in sin" rather than repeat her mother's marital woes) Cast: Ann Harding (Mary)

(Broadway) *Thoroughbreds* (Sam Forrest and Lewis B. Ely) September 1924, Vanderbilt Theatre (16 performances) Cast: Ann Harding (Sue), George Marion, John Litel, William Corbett, Katherine Emmett, Kathleen Graham, J.K. Hutchinson, Calvin Thomas - (Spring tryouts for this play, originally titled *The Horse Thief*, were in Chicago)

1925:

The Green Hat (Michael Arlen) played in Detroit and Chicago – Cast: Katharine Cornell, Leslie Howard, Ann Harding

(Broadway) *Stolen Fruit* (Dario Nicodemi) October – December 1925, Eltinge 42nd Street Theatre (96 performances) Produced by Henry W. Savage (in association with A.H. Woods) Rollo Lloyd (director) Cast: Ann Harding (Marie Millias), Rollo Peters, Harry Beresford, Vera Dunn, Lawrence Eddinger, Virginia Farmer, John R. Hamilton, Felix Krembs, Helen Strickland - (*Stolen Fruit* had tryouts along the East coast under the title *The School Mistress*. The cast tour included: Ann Harding, Morris McKay, Elizabeth Patterson, and Douglass Dumbrille)

Hedgerow Theatre, January - August 1925

Misalliance (George Bernard Shaw) Cast: Ann Harding (Lina), William Whitney, Virginia Farrar, William Parry, Ferd Nofer, Dorothy Yockel

Welded (Eugene O'Neill) (story tells of conflict between a playwright and his actress-wife) Cast: Ann Harding, Jasper Deeter, Dorothy Yockel

Beyond the Horizon (Eugene O'Neill) Cast: Ann Harding, William Kirkland

Captain Brassbound's Conversion (George Bernard Shaw) Cast: Ann Harding (Lady Cecily), Lynn Joslyn *Mary the Third* (Rachel Crothers)

(Broadway) *Taming of the Shrew* (Shakespeare) December 18-27, 1925, Klaw Theatre – Richard

Boleslawski (director) Cast: Ann Harding (Bianca), Estelle Winwood, Rollo Peters, Jessie Ralph, Allan Joslyn, Walter Abel

1926:
(Broadway) *Schweiger* (Franz Werfel) March - April 1926, Mansfield Theatre (30 performances) Jacob
    Ben-Ami (director) Cast: Jacob Ben-Ami, Ann Harding (Anna Schweiger), Hugh Buckler, Minnie
    Dupree, Edward Forbes, Philip Leigh, Herbert Ranson, Samuel Rosen, Georgina Tilden, Edward
    Van Sloan
(Broadway) *The Woman Disputed* (Denison Cliff) September 1926 – January 1927, Forrest Theatre
    (87 performances) A. H. Woods (producer) Crane Wilbur (director) Cast: Ann Harding
    (Marie-Ange), Lowell Sherman, Louis Calhern, Viola Roche, Joseph Burton, Crane Wilbur,
    Andrew Corday, Louise Quinn, Royal Thayer
Hedgerow Theater, July 1926 (Plays held at Philadelphia's Broad Street Theatre)
Misalliance (George Bernard Shaw) Cast: Ann Harding (Lina), Mary Law, Allan Joslyn, William Berry,
    Dorothy Yockel, Paul Rosenbaum, David Delnker
In a Garden (Philip Barry) Cast: Ann Harding
(Summer Stock) Garrick Theatre, Detroit, Michigan – Plays included:
Bluebird's Eighth Wife (Alfred Savoir) Cast: Ann Harding
The Eskimo (Gene Markey and Samuel Hoffenstein) Cast: Ann Harding, Rollo Peters
In a Garden (Philip Barry) Cast: Ann Harding

1927:
The Woman Disputed (Denison Cliff) March 1927 – April 1927, Chicago (The play closed after Ann
    fell ill from exhaustion)
(Broadway) *Trial of Mary Dugan* (Bayard Veiller) September 1927 – June 1928, National Theatre (437
    performances) A. H. Woods (producer) A.H. Van Buren (director) Cast: Ann Harding (Mary
    Dugan), Rex Cherryman, Michelette Baroni, Robert Beggs, Robert Cummings, Robert Wil-
    liams, Leona Maricle, Arthur Hohl, Charles Edwards, Marie Santas, John Ravold, Oscar Polk,
    Dennie Moore, Barton MacLane, Julia Ralph, Dean Raymond, Merle Maddern, Edward West,
    Jasper Mangione, Rita Kane

1928:
Pittsburgh Stock Company (George Sharpe producer) 1928
Plays may have included: *Rain* (W. Somerset Maugham), *Constant Wife* (W. Somerset Maugham)
(Summer Season) August 1928, Nixon Theatre, Pittsburgh, Pa. (Harry Bannister - manager) *Smilin'
    Through* (Jane Cowl and Jane Murfin) Cast: Ann Harding (Kathleen/Moonyean)
Trial of Mary Dugan (Bayard Veiller) October – January 1929, Adelphi Theatre, Chicago. Cast: Ann
    Harding (Mary Dugan) – after Chicago, Ann took the play to Pittsburgh, and then to the Broad
    Street Theatre in Newark, N.J.

1931:
Hedgerow Theatre, April 1931
Inheritors (Susan Glaspell) Cast: Ann Harding, Jasper Deeter

1933:

Hedgerow Theatre, January 14, 1933 – January 16, 1933
Misalliance (George Bernard Shaw) Cast: Ann Harding (Lina)
Inheritors (Susan Glaspell) Cast: Ann Harding

1936-37:

Candida (George Bernard Shaw) 11/12/36 – 2/22/37, (Tour included Blackpool, and London's
   Globe Theatre) Irene Hentschel (director) – Cast: Ann Harding (Candida), Nicholas Hannen,
   Athene Seyler, Edward Chapman, Stephen Haggard

1938:

Candida (George Bernard Shaw) September – October 1938 (Played at San Francisco's Curran
   Theater and at Los Angeles' Biltmore Theatre) Homer Curran and Luther Greene (producers),
   Phyllis Loughton (director) – Cast: Ann Harding (Candida), Rafaela Ottiano, Paul Cavanagh,
   Clay Mercer, Ian Purvis, Ernest Cossart

1948:

The Glass Menagerie (Tennessee Williams) July – August, 1948, Lo Jolla Playhouse, California. James
   W. Neilson (director) Cast: Ann Harding (Amanda), Richard Basehart, John Ireland, Betsy Blair

1949:

(Summer Stock) *Yes, My Darling Daughter* (Mark Reed) June – September 1949 (Played in: Sea Cliff,
   Long Island; Westport, CT; Boston, MA.; Dennis, MA; Fitchburg, MA.; Fairhaven, MA.; Ivoryton,
   CT.; Mountain Home, PA.; Stockbridge, MA.) Cast: (In Westport production) Ann Harding (Ann
   Whitman Murray), E.G. Marshall, Phyllis Kirk, Muriel Hutchinson, Lawrence Fletcher
(Broadway) *Goodbye, My Fancy* (Fay Kanin) October – November 1949, Martin Beck Theatre.
   December 1949, John Golden Theatre. Sam Wanamaker (director) Cast: Ann Harding (Agatha
   Reed), Conrad Nagel, Donald Curtis, Bethel Leslie, Marie Phillips

1950:

Goodbye, My Fancy (Fay Kanin) December 1949- February 1950, Harris Theatre, Chicago, Illinois.
   Sam Wanamaker (director) Cast: Ann Harding (Agatha Reed), Bramwell Fletcher, Phillip Reed,
   Jean Casto

1952:

The Corn is Green (Emlyn Williams) August 1952, La Jolla Playhouse, California. Harry Ellerbe (director) Cast: Ann Harding (Miss Moffat), Diana Barrymore, Douglas Dick, George Macready, Cora
   Witherspoon, Larry Dobkin

1953:

The Corn is Green (Emlyn Williams) January 1953, Palm Springs Playhouse, California. Michael Fer-
   rall (director) Cast: Ann Harding (Miss Moffat), Tim O'Connor, Mary Foskett, Michael Hayes,
   Wanda Lynn, Helen Stenborg, Barnard Hughes

The Corn is Green (Emlyn Williams) February 1953. Sombrero Playhouse, Phoenix, Arizona. Lester Vail (director) Cast: Ann Harding (Miss Moffat), Douglas Dick, Russell Lewis

1955:

The Corn is Green (Emlyn Williams) August 1955, Salt Creek Theatre, Hinsdale, Illinois. Cast: Ann Harding (Miss Moffat), Robert Brown

1958:

Garden District: Something Unspoken, Suddenly, Last Summer (Tennessee Williams) May-June 1958, York Theatre, New York, N.Y. Herbert Machiz (director) – Cast: Ann Harding (Cornelia/ Violet Venable), Robert Lansing, Hortense Alden, Donna Cameron, Ann Meacham, Alan Nixon, Patricia Ripley

September Tide (Daphne Du Maurier) July – August 1958, Pocono Playhouse, Mountain Home, Pa., Matunuck, R.I., Ogunquit, Maine. Rowena Stevens (producer) John O'Shaunessy (director) Cast: Ann Harding (Stella), Gig Young, Doris Rich, Diann Wyland

1959:

Not in the Book (Arthur Watkyn) February 1959, Royal Poinciana Playhouse, Palm Beach, Florida. Gilbert Miller (producer) Richard Bender (director) Cast: Ann Harding, Edward Everett Horton, Reginald Owen, Ralph Purdum, John Irving, Herbert Voland, Val Avery, Claude Horton

1961:

Two Queens of Love and Beauty (Bill Hoffman) July 1961, Bucks County Playhouse, New Hope, Pa. Jay Julien (producer), Ralph Bell (director) Cast: Ann Harding (Amelia Damper), Georgia Burke, Jan Miner (understudy)

1962:

General Seeger (Ira Levin) February 1962, Schubert Theatre, Detroit, Michigan. Theodore D. Mann (producer) George C. Scott (director) Cast: William Bendix (replaced by George C. Scott after opening night), Ann Harding (Rena Seeger)

(Broadway) *General Seeger* (Ira Levin) March 1962, Lyceum Theatre (2 performances) Theodore D. Mann (producer) George C. Scott (director) Cast: George C. Scott, Ann Harding (Rena Seeger), Roscoe Lee Browne, Dolores Sutton, Gerald Richards, Paul Stevens, Lonny Chapman, John Leslie, Tim O'Connor

Banderol (Dore Schary) September 1962, Playhouse Theatre, Wilmington, Delaware; Forrest Theatre, Philadelphia, Pa. Robert Whitehead and Roger L. Stevens (producers), Dore Schary (director) Cast: Ed Begley, Betty Field, Ann Harding (Charlotte Banderol), George Voskovec, Staats Cotsworth, Alan Bunce, Michael Tolan

1963:

The Corn is Green (Emlyn Williams) July – August 1963, Corral Playhouse, Portales, New Mexico; Canal Fulton Summer Arena, Massillon, Ohio; College Theatre, Brockport, N.Y. – Cast: Ann Harding (Miss Moffat), George Reinholt (Morgan Evans – in the Canal Fulton production)

Moments of Love (David Rogers) October – November 1963, Westport Country Playhouse, Ct. James McKenzie (producer), Herbert Machiz (director) Cast: Ann Harding, Dorothy Sands, Nicholas Pryor, Ina Niemela, Leo Lucker, Roy Shuman

1964:

(Broadway) *Abraham Cochrane* (John Sherry) February 1964, Belasco Theatre (1 performance)
Walter Fried and Helen Jacobson (producers), Harold Stone (director) Cast: Bill Travers, Ann
Harding (Myra Holliday), Audrey Ward, Richard Nicholls, John Griggs, Nancy Wickwire, Peter
Adams, Franklin Cover, Olympia Dukakis

Ad for *Gallant Lady* (1934) (United Artists)

Ann Harding on Film

1. *Paris Bound* (1929) – Pathé – 73m (based on the play by Philip Barry) Arthur Hopkins (d)
    Cast: Ann Harding (*Mary Hutton*), Fredric March, George Irving, Leslie Fenton, Hallam Cooley,
    Juliette Crosby, Charlotte Walker, Carmelita Geraghty, Ika Chase, Frank Reicher
2. *Her Private Affair* (1929) – Pathé – 71m (based on the play *The Right to Kill* by Leo Urvantzov)
    Paul Stein (d), Rollo Lloyd (director for silent version) Cast: Ann Harding (*Vera Kessler*), Harry
    Bannister, John Loder, Kay Hammond, Arthur Hoyt, William Orlamond, Lawford Davidson,
    Elmer Ballard, Frank Reicher
3. *Condemned* (1929) – United Artists – 91m (suggested by the book *Condemned to Devil's Island*
    by Blair Niles) Samuel Goldwyn (p), Wesley Ruggles (d) Cast: Ronald Colman, Ann Harding
    (*Madame Vidal*), Dudley Digges, Louis Wolheim, William Elmer, William Vaughn, Albert
    Kingsley, Constantine Romanoff, Harry Ginsberg, Bud Somers, Stephen Selznick, Baldy Biddle
    (reissued as *Condemned to Devil's Island* in the 1940s) – 1930 Nominated for Oscar: Ronald Col-
    man (Best Actor)
4. *Holiday* (1930) – Pathé – 99m (based on the play by Philip Barry) Edward H. Griffith (d) Cast:
    Ann Harding (*Linda Seton*), Mary Astor, Edward Everett Horton, Robert Ames, Hedda Hopper,

Monroe Owsley (repeating his Broadway role as Ned), William Holden, Elizabeth Forrester, Mabel Forrest, Creighton Hale, Hallam Cooley (Edward Everett Horton would repeat his role as Nick in the 1938 remake starring Katharine Hepburn and Cary Grant) – 1931 Nominated for Oscar: Ann Harding (Best Actress); Horace Jackson (Best Writing, Adaptation)

5. *Girl of the Golden West* (1930) – First National – 81m (based on the play by David Belasco) John Francis Dillon (d) Cast: Ann Harding (*Minnie*), James Rennie, Harry Bannister, Ben Hendricks, Jr., J. Farrell MacDonald, George Cooper, Johnny Walker, Richard Carlyle, Arthur Stone (Remade as musical in 1938 with Jeanette MacDonald and Nelson Eddy) – Film is believed to be lost

6. *East Lynne* (1931) – Fox – 102m (based on the play by Mrs. Henry Wood) Cast: Clive Brook, Ann Harding (*Lady Isabel Severn*), Conrad Nagel, Cecilia Loftus, Beryl Mercer, O.P. Heggie, Flora Sheffield, David Torrence, J. Gunnis Davis, Ronald Cosbey, Wally Albright, Eric Mayne (Filmed a dozen times before the 1930 version) - 1931 Nominated for Oscar: Best Picture

7. *Devotion* (1931) – RKO-Pathé – 84m (based on the novel *A Little Flat in the Temple* by Pamela Wynne) Robert Milton (d) Cast: Ann Harding (*Shirley Mortimer*), Leslie Howard, Robert Williams, O.P. Heggie, Louise Closser Hale, Dudley Digges, Alison Skipworth, Doris Lloyd, Ruth Weston, Joan Carr, Joyce Coad, Douglas Scott, Tempe Pigott, Forrester Harvey, Pat Somerset, Olive Tell

8. *Prestige* (1932) – RKO-Pathé – 71m (from the novel *Lips of Steel* by Harry Hervey) Tay Garnett (d) Cast: Ann Harding (*Therese Du Flos*), Adolphe Menjou, Melvyn Douglas, Guy Bates Post, Carmelita Geraghty, Rollo Lloyd, Clarence Muse

9. *Westward Passage* (1932) – RKO-Pathé – 73m (based on the novel by Margaret Ayer Barnes) David O. Selznick (p), Robert Milton (d) Cast: Ann Harding (*Olivia Van Tyne*), Laurence Olivier, ZaSu Pitts, Irving Pichel, Juliette Compton, Irene Purcell, Emmett King, Florence Roberts, Ethel Griffies, Bonita Granville, Don Alvarado, Florence Lake, Edgar Kennedy, Herman Bing, Julie Haydon, Joyce Compton, Nance O'Neil

10. *The Conquerors* (1932) – RKO – 88m (based on the story by Howard Estabrook) David O. Selznick (p), William A. Wellman (d) Cast: Richard Dix, Ann Harding (*Caroline Ogden Standish*), Edna May Oliver, Guy Kibbee, Donald Cook, Walter Walker, Wally Albright Jr., Marilyn Knowlden, Julie Haydon, Harry Holman

11. *Animal Kingdom* (1932) – RKO – 95m (based on the Philip Barry play) Edward H. Griffith (d) Cast: Ann Harding (*Daisy Sage*), Leslie Howard, Myrna Loy, Neil Hamilton, William Gargan, Henry Stephenson, Ilka Chase, Leni Stengel, Donald Dillaway (Leslie Howard, William Gargan, and Ilka Chase repeated their Broadway roles) – Remade in 1946 as *One More Tomorrow*

12. *When Ladies Meet* (1933) – MGM – 73m (based on the play by Rachel Crothers) Harry Beaumont (d) Cast: Ann Harding (*Clare Woodruf*), Robert Montgomery, Myrna Loy, Alice Brady, Frank Morgan, Martin Burton, Luis Alberni (Remade in 1941 with Joan Crawford and Greer Garson in the Loy/Harding roles) 1934 Nominated for Oscar: Cedric Gibbons (Best Art Direction)

13. *Double Harness* (1933) – RKO – 70m (based on the play by Edward P. Montgomery) Merian C. Cooper (p), John Cromwell (d) Cast: Ann Harding (*Joan Colby*), William Powell, Henry Stephenson, Lilian Bond, George Meeker, Lucile Brown, Reginald Owen, Kay Hammond, Leigh Allen, Hugh Huntley

14. *The Right to Romance* (1933) – RKO – 70m (story by Myles Connolly) Merian C. Cooper (p), Alfred Santell (d) Cast: Ann Harding (*Dr. Margaret Simmons*), Robert Young, Irving Pichel, Alden "Stephen" Chase, Nils Asther, Sari Maritza, Helen Freeman, Delmar Watson

15. *Gallant Lady* (1933) – United Artists – 81m (story by Gilbert Emery) Darryl F. Zanuck (p), Gregory LaCava (d) Cast: Ann Harding (*Sally Wyndham*), Clive Brook, Otto Kruger, Tullio Carminati, Dickie Moore, Janet Beecher, Betty Lawford, Gilbert Emery, Scotty Beckett (Remade in 1938 as *Always Goodbye*, starring Barbara Stanwyck)

16. *The Life of Vergie Winters* (1934) – RKO – 82m (based on the story by Louis Bromfield) Pandro S. Berman (p), Alfred Santell (d) Cast: Ann Harding (*Vergie Winters*), John Boles, Helen Vinson, Betty Furness, Frank Albertson, Lon Chaney, Jr., Sara Haden, Molly O'Day, Ben Alexander, Donald Crisp, Maidel Turner, Cecil Cunningham, Josephine Whittell, Wesley Barry, Edward Van Sloan, Wallis Clark, Edwin Stanley, Bonita Granville, Walter Brennan

17. *The Fountain* (1934) – RKO – 84m (based on the novel by Charles Morgan), Pandro S. Berman (p), John Cromwell (d) Cast: Ann Harding (*Julie von Narwitz*), Brian Aherne, Paul Lukas, Jean Hersholt, Ralph Forbes, Violett Kemble-Cooper, Sara Haden, Richard Abbott, Rudolph Anders, Barbara Barondess, Betty Alden, Ian Wolfe, Douglas Wood, Frank Reicher, Ferike Boros, William Stack

18. *Biography of a Bachelor Girl* (1934) – MGM – 84m (based on the play by S.N. Behrman; Anita Loos, screenplay) Edward H. Griffith (d), James Wong Howe (camera) Cast: Ann Harding (*Marion*), Robert Montgomery, Edward Everett Horton, Edward Arnold, Una Merkel, Charles Richman, Greta Meyer, Donald Meek, Willard Robertson

19. *Enchanted April* (1935) – RKO – 66m (based on the novel by Elizabeth von Arnim) Harry Beaumont (d) Cast: Ann Harding (*Lotty Wilkins*), Frank Morgan, Reginald Owen, Katharine Alexander, Ralph Forbes, Jane Baxter, Jessie Ralph, Charles Judels, Rafaela Ottiano (One of RKO's biggest box-office failures for 1935 – credited as expediting Ann's decline at the studio) The 1992 British remake was a critical and box-office success

20. *The Flame Within* (1935) – MGM – 72m (screenplay by Edmund Goulding) Edmund Goulding (p,d), James Wong Howe (camera) Cast: Ann Harding (*Dr. Mary White*), Herbert Marshall, Maureen O'Sullivan, Louis Hayward, Henry Stephenson, Margaret Seddon, George Hassell, Eily Malyon, Claudelle Kaye

21. *Peter Ibbetson* (1935) – Paramount – 88m (based on the novel by George du Maurier and the play by John Nathaniel Raphael) Henry Hathaway (d) Charles Lang (camera) Cast: Gary Cooper, Ann Harding (*Mary, Duchess of Towers*), John Halliday, Ida Lupino, Douglass Dumbrille, Virginia Weidler, Dickie Moore, Doris Lloyd, Elsa Buchanan, Christian Rub, Donald Meek, Gilbert Emery, Marguerite Namara, Marcelle Corday, Adrienne D'Ambricourt (remake of the 1921 film *Forever*) - 1936 Nominated for Oscar: Irvin Talbot (Best Music Score) (Score by Ernst Toch)

22. *The Lady Consents* (1936) – RKO – 77m (based on the story *The Indestructible Mrs. Talbot* by P.J. Wolfson) Stephen Roberts (d) Cast: Ann Harding (*Anne Talbot*), Herbert Marshall, Margaret Lindsay, Walter Abel, Edward Ellis, Hobart Cavanaugh, Ilka Chase

23. *The Witness Chair* (1936) – RKO – 64m (based on the novella by Rita Weiman) George Nicholls, Jr. (d) Cast: Ann Harding (*Paula Young*), Walter Abel, Douglass Dumbrille, Frances Sage, Moroni Olsen, Margaret Hamilton, Maxine Jennings, William Benedict, Paul Harvey, Murray Kinnell, Charles Arnt

24. *Love From a Stranger* (1937) – United Artists – 87m (based on a story by Agatha Christie and the play by Frank Vosper; screenplay by Francis Marion) Rowland V. Lee (d) Cast: Ann Harding (*Carol Howard*), Basil Rathbone, Binnie Hale, Bruce Seton, Jean Cadell, Bryan Powley, Joan Hickson, Donald Calthrop (Remade in 1947 with Sylvia Sidney in Ann's role)

25. *Eyes in the Night* (1942) – MGM – 79m (based on the novel *Odor of Violets* by Bayard Kendrick) Fred Zinnemann (d) Cast: Edward Arnold, Ann Harding (*Norma Lawry*), Donna Reed, Allen Jenkins, John Emery, Stephen McNally, Katherine Emery, Reginald Denny, Rosemary de Camp, Stanley Ridges, Barry Nelson, Steve Geray, Erik Rolf, Reginald Sheffield, Milburn Stone, Frances Rafferty, Edward Kilroy, John Butler, William Nye, Fred Walburn, Robert Winkler, Walter Tetley, Frank Thomas, Marie Windsor (bit)

26. *Mission to Moscow* (1943) – Warner Brothers – 112m (based on the book by Joseph E. Davies; Howard Koch, screenplay) Michael Curtiz (d) Cast: Walter Huston, Ann Harding (*Mrs. Davies*), Oscar Homolka, George Tobias, Gene Lockhart, Eleanor Parker, Richard Travis, Helmut Dantine, Victor Francen, Henry Daniell, Barbara Everest, Dudley Field Malone, Maria Palmer, Moroni Olsen, Minor Watson, Jerome Cowan, Doris Lloyd, Mike Mazurki, Cyd Charisse, Michel Panaiess – 1944 Nominated for Oscar: Carl Jules Weyl and George James Hopkins (Best Art Direction - Interior Decoration, Black and White)

27. *The North Star* (1943) – RKO – 106m (screenplay, Lillian Helman) Samuel Goldwyn (p), Lewis Milestone (d), James Wong Howe (camera) Cast: Anne Baxter, Farley Granger, Jane Withers, Eric Roberts, Dana Andrews, Walter Brennan, Dean Jagger, Ann Harding (*Sophia*), Carl Benton, Ann Carter, Walter Huston, Erich Von Stroheim, Esther Dale, Ruth Nelson, Paul Guilfoyle – 1944 Nominated for Oscars: James Wong Howe (Cinematography - Black and White); Lillian

Hellman (Best Writing – Original Screenplay); Thomas T. Moulton (Best Sound, Recording); Aaron Copland (Best Music – Scoring of a Drama or Comedy); Perry Ferguson and Howard Bristol (Best Art Direction – Interior Decoration, Black and White); Clarence Slifer, Ray Binger, Thomas T. Moulton (Best Effects, Special Effects)

28. *Janie* (1944) – Warner Brothers – 106m (based on the play by Josephine Bentham) Michael Curtiz (d) Cast: Joyce Reynolds, Robert Hutton, Edward Arnold, Ann Harding (*Lucille Conway*), Robert Benchley, Clare Foley, Barbara Brown, Hattie McDaniel, Jackie Moran, Ann Gillis, Russell Hicks, Ruth Tobey, Virginia Patton, Colleen Townsend, William Frambes, Sunset Carson, Jimmy Dodd, Keefe Brasselle – 1944 Oscar Winner: Owen Marks (Best Film Editing)

29. *Nine Girls* (1944) – Columbia – 75m (based on the play by Wilfred H. Pettitt) Leigh Jason (d) Cast: Ann Harding (*Grace Thornton*), Evelyn Keyes, Jinx Falkenburg, Anita Louise, Leslie Brooks, Lynn Merrick, Jeff Donnell, Nina Foch, Shirley Mills, Marcia Mae Jones, Willard Robertson, William Demarest, Lester Mathews, Grady Sutton

30. *Those Endearing Young Charms* (1945) – RKO – 81m (based on the play by Edward Chodorov) Bert Granet (d) Cast: Robert Young, Laraine Day, Ann Harding (*Mrs. Brandt*), Marc Cramer, Anne Jeffreys, Bill Williams, Glenn Vernon, Norma Varden, Lawrence Tierney, Vera Marshe, Larry Burke

31. *Janie Gets Married* (1946) – Warner Brothers – 89m (screenplay Agnes Christine Johnston) Vincent Sherman (d) Cast: Joan Leslie, Robert Hutton, Edward Arnold, Ann Harding (*Lucille Conway*), Robert Benchley, Dorothy Malone, Dick Erdmann, Clare Foley, Donald Meek, Hattie McDaniel, Barbara Brown, Margaret Hamilton, Ann Gillis, Ruth Tobey, William Frambes, Theo Washington, Monte Blue, Mel Torme

32. *It Happened on Fifth Avenue* (1947) – Allied Artists – 116m (story by Herbert Clyde Lewis and Frederick Stephani) Roy Del Ruth (p), Joe Kaufman (d) Cast: Victor Moore, Charlie Ruggles, Don DeFore, Gale Storm, Ann Harding (*Mary O'Connor*), Alan Hale Jr., Dorothea Kent, Cathy Carter, Ed Brophy, Arthur Hohl, Anthony Sydes, Edward Ryan, Jr., Grant Mitchell – 1948 Oscar Winner: Herbert Clyde Lewis and Frederick Stephani (Best Writing, Original Story)

33. *Christmas Eve* (1947) – United Artists – 90m (based on stories by Lawrence Stallings) Edwin Marin (d) Cast: George Raft, George Brent, Randolph Scott, Joan Blondell, Virginia Field, Dolores Moran, Ann Harding (*Matilda Reid*), Reginald Denny, Carl Harbord, Clarence Kolb, John Litel, Joe Sawyer, Douglas Dumbrille, Dennis Hoey, Molly Lamont, Walter Sand, Marie Blake (Remade for TV in 1986 with Loretta Young)

34. *Two Weeks With Love* (1950) – MGM – 92m (story by John Larkin) Roy Rowland (d) Cast: Jane Powell, Ricardo Montalban, Louis Calhern, Ann Harding (*Katherine Robinson*), Phyllis Kirk, Carleton Carpenter, Debbie Reynolds, Clinton Sundberg, Gary Gray, Tommy Rettig, Charles Smith - Featured in *That's Entertainment* (1974)

35. *The Magnificent Yankee* (1950) – MGM – 90m (based on the book *Mr. Justice Holmes* by Francis Biddle and the play by Emmett Lavery) John Sturges (d) Cast: Louis Calhern, Ann Harding (*Fanny Holmes*), Eduard Franz, Philip Ober, Ian Wolfe, Edith Evanson, Richard Anderson, Guy Anderson, James Lydon, Robert Sherwood, Hugh Sanders, Harlan Warde, Charles Evans, John R. Hamilton – 1951 Oscar Nomination: Louis Calhern (Best Actor); 1951 Oscar Winner: Walter Plunkett (Best Costume Design, Black and White)

36. *It's a Big Country* (1951) – MGM – 89m (The original film consisted of nine episodes. The one featuring Ann, *Load*, based on a short story by Dudley Schnabel, was deleted upon release) *Load* was directed by Anthony Mann, Cast: Jean Hersholt, Ann Harding (*Mrs. Anderson*)

37. *The Unknown Man* (1951) – MGM – 86m (story and screenplay by Ronald Milar and George Froeschel) Richard Thorpe (d) Cast: Walter Pidgeon, Ann Harding (*Stella Masen*), Barry Sullivan, Keefe Brasselle, Lewis Stone, Eduard Franz, Richard Anderson, Dawn Addams, Phil Ober, Mari Blanchard, Dabs Greer, Anna Q. Nilsson, Bess Flowers, Mae Clarke

38. *The Man in the Gray Flannel Suit* (1956) – 20ᵗʰ-Century Fox – 153m (based on the novel by Sloan Wilson) Darryl F. Zanuck (p), Nunnally Johnson (d) Cast: Gregory Peck, Jennifer Jones, Fredric March, Marisa Pavan, Lee J. Cobb, Ann Harding (*Mrs. Hopkins*), Keenan Wynne, Gene Lockhart, Gigi Perreau, Portland Mason, Arthur O'Connell, Henry Daniell, Connie Gilchrist,

Joseph Sweeney
39.   *I've Lived Before* (1956) – Universal – 82m (screenplay by Norman Jolley) Richard Bartlett
      (d) Cast: Jock Mahoney, Leigh Snowden, Ann Harding (*Jane Stone*), John McIntire, Raymond
      Bailey, Jerry Paris, Simon Scott, April Kent
40.   *Strange Intruder* (1957) – Allied Artists – 82m (based on the novel *The Intruder* by Helen Fowler)
      Irving Rapper (d) Cast: Edmund Purdom, Ida Lupino, Ann Harding (*Mary Carmichael*), Jacques
      Bergerac, Gloria Talbot, Carl Benton, Douglas Kennedy, Donald Murphy, Ruby Goodwin, Mimi
      Gibson, Eric Anderson

Film Shorts

1.   *The Hollywood Gad-About* (1934) – Louis Lewyn Productions – 11m (Footage from the Screen
      Actor's Guild's Film Stars Frolic, hosted by Walter Winchell) Features: Ann Harding (on a
      horse), Mary Astor, Gary Cooper, Alice Faye, William S. Hart, James Cagney, Shirley Temple,
      Wallace Ford, Eddie Cantor, Chester Morris, Alice White, May Robson, William Gargan, Stuart
      Erwin, Billy Barty, Lee Moran, Kenneth Thomson
2.   *Screen Snapshots* (1936) (Series 16, Number 1) – Columbia – 10m (Vignettes include Ken May-
      nard's private circus, Bette Davis posing for a portrait, Frank McHugh playing with his children, and
      a visit to the West Side Tennis Club) Ralph Staub (d) Features: Ann Harding, Virginia Bruce, Errol
      Flynn, Elissa Landi, Bette Davis, Frank McHugh, James Cagney, Lili Damita, Betty Furness, Madge
      Evans, Marian Marsh, Ken Maynard, Cesar Romero, Rosalind Russell, Ann Sothern, Johnny Weiss-
      muller, Eleanore Whitney

Ann Harding on Radio

1930:

Women's Achievement Program: KHJ (October 10, 1930) (10 am) guests: Ann Harding (first radio ap-
      pearance), Mrs. Thomas G. Winter (former president of the General Federation of Women's Clubs),
      Florence L. Kahn, Mrs. Helen B. Cooper (President of the LA Advertising Association of Women),
      Martha Logan- Women occupying prominent positions in world affairs since World War I
All-Star Special: KFI (November 3, 1930) (11-12pm) guests: Ann Harding, songwriters: DeSylva,
      Brown & Henderson, Cliff Edwards, Reginald Denny, Dorothy Jordan, Rubinoff, Frank Fay
      (Master of Ceremonies)

1931:

Sunkist Musical Cocktail: KHJ (CBS) (March 11, 1931) (5:30pm) Ann Harding (guest of honor–
      interview), Raymond Paige, conductor, Hallelujah Chorus, Chili Peppers, Ted White
Hoover Relief Special: NBC (November 15, 1931) (7:45pm) "Parade of Stars" (from three major
      cities) for the motion picture industry's aid to unemployment relief – From Hollywood: Ann
      Harding (guest), Jeanette MacDonald, Bebe Daniels, Marie Dressler, Lionel Barrymore, Tom
      Mix, Maurice Chevalier, John Boles, Will H. Hays, Irene Dunne, George Arliss, Conrad Nagel
      (master of ceremonies)

1932:

Program: "Washington," WJZ (New York) (7:15pm) Ann Harding
Hollywood on the Air: NBC (October 27, 1932) (9:00 pm) Ann Harding (guest), Leslie Howard
Hollywood on the Air: NBC (December 15, 1932) (9:30 pm) Ann Harding and Leslie Howard play scenes
      from *The Animal Kingdom*; with William Gargan, Ilka Chase, Neil Hamilton, Henry Stephenson

**Ann and John Boles enacting scenes from *The Life of Vergie Winters*
(June 24, 1934). NBC's Hollywood on the Air**

1933:

Hollywood on the Air: NBC (August 21, 1933) Ann Harding (guest), with Dolores Del Rio, John
Boles, Margaret Sullavan, Merian C. Cooper, W.C. Fields, William Gargan

1934:

Hollywood on the Air: NBC (June 24, 1934) Fred Astaire (Master of Ceremonies), Ann Harding,
John Boles, enact scene from *Life of Vergie Winters*

Hollywood on the Air: NBC (August 19, 1934) (8:30 pm) "The Laughing Journey" Ann Harding
and Tom Lennon (author)

1935:

Hollywood Hotel: CBS (April 19, 1935) Host: Dick Powell, Ann Harding, Herbert Marshall (miniature edition of *The Flame Within*-Edmund Goulding narrates)

Hollywood Hotel: CBS (September 13, 1935) Host: Dick Powell (scenes from *Peter Ibbetson*- with
Gary Cooper and Ann Harding)

Conversations: (KHJ) (October 6, 1935) (10:15 pm) Ann chats with columnist Read Kendall

1936:

Hollywood Hotel: CBS (January 10, 1936) Host: Dick Powell – scenes from *A Lady Consents*- with Ann Harding, Herbert Marshall. Other guests: Frances Langord, Igor Gorin

Shell Chateau Hour: NBC (April 25, 1936) (8:30 pm) Ann Harding – scenes from *Holiday*. Other guests: Monroe Owsley, Lillian Emerson, Yacht Club Boys

1937:

Chase and Sanborn Hour: Red. net.(May 7, 1937)"The Guardsman" (scene) Ann Harding (as Marie), Don Ameche (as Tony), W.C. Fields, Bergen & McCarthy, Dorothy Lamour, Rodgers & Hart, Werner Janssen and His Orchestra

Lux Radio Theatre: CBS (June 14, 1937) "Madame X" Ann Harding (as Jacqueline Cartwright), James Stewart (as Raymond Cartwright), Conway Tearle (as Alan Cartwright) with: Janet Beecher, George Coulouris, Bea Benaderet, Regis Toomey, Clara Blandick - Pulitzer Prize-winning play, Cecil B. DeMille (host)

Edwin Schallert: KFAC (August 1, 1937) Ann Harding and Basil Rathbone join the columnist to converse about the making of *Love from a Stranger*

1939:

Rudy Vallee Variety Hour (WEAF) (May 11, 1939) Ann Harding appeared in a one-act dramatic sketch, "Until Tomorrow." Rudy Vallee (host). Arthur Treacher

1940:

Campbell Playhouse: CBS (March 10, 1940) "Craig's Wife" Ann Harding (as Harriet Craig), Orson Welles (as Walter Craig) – with Janet Beecher, George Coulouris, Bea Benaderet, Regis Toomey

1945:

Cavalcade of America: Red net. (January 1, 1945) "Westward the Women" Ann Harding (as Abigail Scott Dunaway), Walter Huston (host)

Lux Radio Theatre: CBS (November 19, 1945) "The Keys of the Kingdom" Ronald Colman (as Father Francis Chisholm), Ann Harding (as Mother Maria-Veronica) with Lal Chand Mehra – William Keighley (host)

1946:

Cavalcade of America: CBS (December 2, 1946) "Mother of Freedom" Ann Harding (as Anna Zenger), William Conrad (as John Zenger) with Francis X. Bushman, Joseph Kearns

1949:

Hi Jinks: (November 8, 1949) interview: Ann Harding

1951:

Hallmark Playhouse: CBS (November 22, 1951) "The Widened Heart" Ann Harding (Fannie Kilbourne story)

1952:

Lux Radio Theatre: CBS (April 7, 1952) "The Magnificent Yankee" Louis Calhern, Ann Harding

1958:

Sally Ferrebee Show: WVPO (July 29, 1958) Interview with Ann Harding and Gig Young

1963:

WABC Leukemia Radiothon: (October 18-20, 1963) 29-hour appeal for funds to aid national leukemia research. Guests: Ann Harding, David Wayne, Richard Rodgers, John Davis Lodge, Peggy Wood

Ann Harding on TV

1950:

December 2, 1950- *Don McNeill's TV Club*—Ann Harding

1951:

1951- (ABC)-"Washington Lady"—Ann Harding, John Litel

1952:

January 30, 1952-*Pulitzer Prize Playhouse* (ABC)-"Years of Grace" –Ann Harding, Lucille Watson, Joan Chandler, Bramwell Fletcher, Scott McKay, Mary Howard, from Ayer Barnes novel (author of *Westward Passage*) – story concerns an emotional crises between a mother (Ann) and daughter (Chandler)

October 27, 1952-*Hollywood Opening Night* (CBS) (Live)-"Somebody I Know" –Ann Harding, James Dunn, Peggy Ann Garner, Natalie Wood (The first anthology series to originate in Hollywood)

1953:

June 4, 1953-*Ford Television Theatre* (NBC) (Live) –"There's No Place Like Home" –Ann Harding, Walter Abel, Jimmy Lydon, Mary Ellen Kay-a newspaper exposé stars a violent quarrel between a writer and his family

August 14, 1953-*Schlitz Playhouse of Stars* (CBS)-"Miracle in the Night"—Ann Harding (as Nettie Hallett), Charles Cane – story about an unbending penny-pincher (Ann) who is contemptuous of the poor.

1954:

March 5, 1954-*Schlitz Playhouse of Stars* (CBS)-"The Great Lady"—Ann Harding (as Julia Courtney), Vera Miles, Douglas Kennedy, Ann O'Neal, Maudie Prickett, Roy Kellino(director), Dorothy Cummins (writer) – a retired actress (Ann) solves the murder of a younger actress who lives in the same boarding house-(Note: this unsold "pilot" show was repeated in 1956, as part of ABC's *General Electric Summer Originals*)

May 13, 1954-*Lux Video Theatre* (CBS) (Live)-"The Queen's English"—Ann Harding (as Henrietta Mekker), Gene Lockhart, Erik Rhodes, Earl Eby (director), Joseph Cochran (writer) – story of a spinster teacher (Ann) who flunks the son of a wealthy man (Lockhart) who had done her an injustice years earlier

Ann and actor-dancer Gene Nelson discuss the script for "Tryout"
General Electric Theatre (October 2, 1955).

October 14, 1954-*Lux Video Theatre* (CBS) (Live)-"A Visit from Evelyn"—Ann Harding (as Nora Wall-
ing), Lynn Bari, Margaret Lindsay (host), Richard Goode (director), Turner Bullock (writer) – a
famous novelist returns to her alma mater only to be met with vengeance from the widow of a
former professor

1955:

April 10, 1955-*Stage 7* (CBS)-"Young Girl in an Apple Tree"—Ann Harding (as Vanessa), Regis
Toomey, Whit Bissell, John Hoyt, Peter Camlin, Peter Godfrey (director), Wells Root (story)
April 21, 1955-*Lux Video Theatre* (CBS) (Live)-"An Act of Murder"—Ann Harding (as Cathy Cook),
Thomas Mitchell, Ray Danton, Buzz Kulik (director) Ernst Lothar (novel) (TV adaptation of
the Fredric March-Florence Eldridge 1948 MGM film)-Ann is the terminally ill wife of Mitchell.
Mitchell decides they'll die together in an auto wreck.

May 12, 1955 – *Hollywood Half Hour*, "The Honeymoon is Over"—Ann Harding, Joyce Reynolds

June 2, 1955-*Ford Television Theatre* (NBC)-"P.J. and the Lady"—Ann Harding (as Louise Potter), Vera Miles, Thomas Mitchell, Elliot Reid – ex-vaudeville hoofer (Mitchell) is determined to see his daughter (Miles) marry the man who loves her rather than encourage her stage career. Ann plays Mitchell's friend.

June 4, 1955-*Damon Runyon Theater* (CBS)- "Lonely Heart"—Ann Harding (as Amelia Crumb), Donald Woods, Allen Jenkins, Steven Geray – A many-time widow (Ann) keeps losing her heavily insured husbands to violent "accidents"

October 2, 1955-*General Electric Theater* (CBS) (Live)-"Tryout"—Ann Harding, Gene Nelson – an aging actress (Ann), who is slowly losing her eyesight, is determined to make one last stage appearance. (Jasper Deeter wrote to Ann that he was especially impressed with her performance in this short film)

October 4, 1955-*Matinee Theatre* (NBC) (Live)-"Progress Jr. and Minnie Sweeney"—Ann Harding, Angie Dickinson, Larry Schwab (director), Edmond Kelso (story)-a school teacher (Ann) is pressured to retire by proponents of progressive education.

October 28, 1955-*Crossroads* (ABC)-"With All My Love"—Ann Harding (Hulda Lind), Hugh Beaumont, Leo Gordon, Jerry Paris, Bryon Keith, Robert Cabal, George Huerta, Frank Fenton, Lewis R. Foster (director) Tom Reed (story)-a missionary (Ann) is rescued by an army chaplain (Beaumont) during WWII

October 30, 1955-*Studio 57* (Dumont)-"Vacation with Pay"—Ann Harding (as Martha Halstead), Joan Leslie, Claude Akins, DeForrest Kelly, Richard Irving (director) Fenton Earnshaw (writer)-several warnings fail to keep a secretary (Leslie) from taking a job with an eccentric writer (Harding) (filmed at Republic Studios)

November 7, 1955-*Climax!* (CBS) (Live)-"A Promise to Murder"—Ann Harding (as Lady Bertha Wetherby), Louis Hayward, Peter Lorre, William Lundigan (host), Allen Reisner (director), Oscar Wilde (story) – Palm reader (Lorre) makes startling prophesies for a lawyer (Hayward). Ann plays Hayward's eccentric Aunt Bertha.

November 16, 1955- *The 20th Century-Fox Hour* (CBS)-"The Late George Apley"—Ann Harding (as Mrs. Apley), Raymond Massey, JoAnne Woodward, Arthur Franz, Barry Coe, Joseph Cotton (host), Jules Bricken (director) George S. Kaufman (play) John P. Marquand (novel), (TV adaptation of Ronald Colman's 1947 film) – an irascible Bostonian (Massey) dominates his family until his daughter (Woodward) challenges him. Ann plays the understanding wife. Also known as *Back Bay Romance*. (This series was mastered and restored in 2002)

1956:

January 15, 1956-*Front Row Center* (CBS) (Live)-"Strange Suspicion"—Ann Harding (as Grammie), Betsy Palmer, Sidney Blackmer, Byron Foulger, Frank Cady, James Daly – in a decadent New England town, people band together to aid one of their friends suspected of homicide

February 7, 1956 – *Matinee Theatre* (NBC) (color) (Live)– "As Young As You Feel"—Ann Harding – A Broadway actress who has married four times, twice to the same man

March 23, 1956 – *Matinee Theater* (NBC) (color) (Live)-"M is for the Many"—Ann Harding, Lewis Harton, Carole Nugent, Livia Granito (director), Joan Cunningham (story)

April 24, 1956-*Playwrights '56* (NBC) (Live)-"The Center of the Maze"—Ann Harding (as Augusta), Dina Merrill, John McGiver, Peter Mark Richman, William Hanson, Russell Hicks, Gina Petrushka, Vincent J. Donehue (director), Sam Hall (writer)-A popular clubwoman (Ann) whose professed liberalism meets an unexpected challenge when her daughter (Merrill) wants to marry a gardener

May 1, 1956-*Celebrity Playhouse*-"The Fleeting Years"—Ann Harding, George Brent, May Wynn, William Leslie – After Ann is introduced to her daughter's future wealthy father-in-law (George Brent), his son accuses her of being a fortune hunter. (Filmed *before* the "live" presentation of *The Center of the Maze*, but broadcast afterwards)

1957:

January 8, 1957-*Cavalcade of America* (a.k.a. Dupont Theater) (ABC)-"The House of Empty Rooms"-Ann
Harding (Mrs. Milgrim), Rachel Ames, Robert Crosson, Ross Ford, Helen Westcott-A lonely widow
(Ann) almost gives up hope of leading a useful life, until she befriends a shy young burglar in need of
a piano.

January 31, 1957-*Climax!* (CBS)-"The Trouble at No. 5"—Ann Harding (Nora Roach), Patricia
Collinge, Jacques Sernas, Reginald Owen, Lisa Daniels, Shelley Smith (novel)-Ann is a hard-
hearted housekeeper out to destroy her employer (Patricia Collinge). She weaves a web of deceit
to cast doubt on her employer's sanity.

February 6, 1957-*The 20th Century Fox Hour* (CBS)-"Springfield Incident" (a.k.a. *Young Man From Kentucky*)—Ann Harding (Abigail Clay), Marshall Thompson, Tom Tyron, Alan Hale Jr., Robert
Sterling (host), Lewis Allen (director) (TV adaptation of Lamar Trotti's *Young Mr. Lincoln*)

December 11, 1957-*Kraft Television Theatre* (NBC) (Live) (color)-"Heroes Walk on Sand"—Ann Harding, Basil Rathbone, Walter Abel, Elliott Nugent, Gene Rayburn, George Dyslin (teleplay)- Behind the Iron Curtain, a man's heroism places his family in jeopardy. In his review of *Heroes Walk
on Sand*, columnist William E. Wald commented, "Like so many Krafts, it fizzled—it also had
a competent cast: Elliott Nugent, Walter Abel, Basil Rathbone, Ann Harding. There is an air of
cheapness about each *Kraft Theatre*, an atmosphere of insufficient rehearsals, dull stage, choppy
writing. I suspect the limpness of the show is not so much the fault of its creative personnel, but
rather of its comparatively meager budget." (*Weirton Daily Times* -12/12/1957)

1958:

February 18, 1958-*Matinee Theater* (NBC) (color) (Live) – "The Tenth Muse"—Ann Harding,
Kathleen Crowley, Donald Murphy, Sam Hall (story)-Ann is a poetess whose shady past is
investigated by her idealistic biographer.

1959:

September 21, 1959-*Dupont Show with June Allyson* (CBS)-"Ruth and Naomi-Those We Love"—Ann
Harding (as Naomi), June Allyson, Peter Mark Richman, Jack Smight (director), Arthur A. Ross
(writer)-Grieving widow Allyson lives with mother-in-law (Ann)

1960:

March 20, 1960-*Sunday Showcase* (NBC) (color)-"Autocrat and Son"—Ann Harding (as Mrs. Holmes), Christopher Plummer, Anne Francis, Cedric Hardwick, Bramwell Fletcher, Ernest Kinoy
(writer)-dramatic story about the great American jurist, Oliver Wendell Holmes Jr.

September 30, 1960 – *Play of the Week* (NTA)- "Mornings At Seven"—Ann Harding (Cora), Chester
Morris, Dorothy Gish, Ruth White, Russell Collins, Eileen Heckart, Beulah Bondi, Paul Osborn
(story), Jack Ragotzy (director)-varying emotions unleash when the 15-year engagement of a
spinster (Heckart) is about to result in marriage

1961:

January 9, 1961-*Play of the Week* (NTA)-"The Potting Shed"—Ann Harding, Frank Conroy, Fritz Weaver,
Zina Bethune, Paul Bogart (director), Graham Greene (play) (the 1957 play received a Tony Award
nomination)-Ann plays the mother of a young man (Weaver) who is desperately searching for his
forgotten past and the reasons he was denied audience during the last moments of his father's life.

December 8, 1961-*Westinghouse Presents* (CBS)-"Come Again to Carthage"—Ann Harding (Mother), Piper Laurie, Maurice Evans, Ina Balin, Joan Hackett, Robert Crean (story), Jack Smight (director)-A nun (Laurie) returns home for the death of her father (Evans), only to learn she has chosen her way of life for all the wrong reasons

December 26, 1961-*Alfred Hitchcock Presents* (NBC)-"A Jury of Her Peers"—Ann Harding (as Sarah Hale), Philip Bourneoff, Robert Bray, Frances Reid, June Walker, Robert Florey (director), Susan Glaspell (story)

1963:

January 2, 1963-*The First Lady* (CBS Special)—Ann Harding, Colleen Dewhurst, Nancy Wickwire, Perry Wolff (producer)-three actresses portray ladies who have lived in the White House – Ann was offered Martha Washington, Dolly Madison, Lucy Hayes, Edith Roosevelt, Edith Wilson, and Lou Henry Hoover

April 6, 1963-*The Defenders* (CBS)-"A Taste for Vengeance"—Ann Harding (as Helen Bernard), Robert Reed, Marc Connelly, Ed Binns, Don Richardson (director), A. J. Russell (writer)-the mother (Ann) of an incurably ill man charges that her daughter-in-law murdered him with an overdose of morphine

April 10, 1963-*Armstrong Circle Theatre* (NBC)-"The Embezzler"—Ann Harding, Gene Saks, Alvin Boretz (director)-a bank president, manipulated by a domineering aunt (Harding), embezzles the books to offer a helping hand to those in need

August 14, 1963-*Mike Douglas Show* (NBC) – Ann Harding (guest)

September 27, 1963-*Burke's Law* (ABC)-"Who Killed Mr. X?"—Ann Harding (as Annabelle Rogers), Elizabeth Montgomery, Gene Barry, Charles Ruggles, Soupy Sales, Gary Conway, Regis Toomey, Jim Backus, Barrie Chase, Dina Merrill, Don Weis (director), Lewis Reed (writer)-Ann plays a daffy ex-film star who murders her ex-leading man

October 16, 1963- *The Eleventh Hour* (NBC)-"Fear Begins at 40"—Ann Harding (as Mrs. Green), Ralph Bellamy, Robert Lansing, Jacqueline Scott, Leonard Horn (director)-a woman (Ann) approaches senility

1964:

January 30, 1964-*Dr. Kildare* (NBC)-"Never Too Old for the Circus"—Ann Harding (as Mae Priest), Walter Pidgeon, Joey Scott, Richard Chamberlain, Raymond Massey, Paul Wendkos (director), Jameson Brewer and Eric Peters (writers)-an elderly doctor (Pidgeon) feels worthless during retirement. Ann plays his understanding wife

1965:

October 11, 1965-*Ben Casey* (ABC)-"Because of the Needle, the Haystack Was Lost"—Ann Harding (as Edith Sommers), Gladys Cooper, Vince Edwards, Marlyn Mason, Alan Crosland Jr. (director), Howard Dimsdale (writer)- A retired doctor (Cooper) returns to the hospital to quarrel with Dr. Casey on how to care for her old friend (Ann)

Index

Photo Credits

Every effort has been made to trace the copyright holders of the photographs included in this book; if any have been inadvertently overlooked, the author and publisher will be pleased to make the necessary changes.

All photos, unless otherwise noted, are from the author's collection. The author would like to express his thanks to the following individuals for the lending of photos: Howard Mandelbaum (of Photofest), Wisconsin Center for Film and Theater Research, The family of Al and Jane Otto, Jenny Paxson and Larry Smith, Carole Summers, and Joseph Worrell.

About the Author

S cott O'Brien has written two previous film biographies: *Kay Fran-cis – I Can't Wait to be Forgotten* (2006) and *Virginia Bruce – Under My Skin* (2008). Scott has penned articles for such publications as *Films of the Golden Age, Classic Images,* and *Filmfax.* He has been a guest author on such film websites as Turner Classic Movies' Movie Morlocks and Silver Screen Oasis, and was an interviewee for the film-documentary *Queer Icon – the Cult of Bette Davis* (2009). Scott appeared on Bay Area Emmy-winning producer Jan Wahl's *Inside Entertainment,* for KRON-TV. Radio's *Silver Screen Audio* and KRCB's *A Novel Idea* have also invited Scott to talk about his research and writing. Scott lives in Northern California's Sonoma County with his partner Joel. Websites: www.kayfrancisbiography.com, www.virginiabrucebiography.com, www.annhardingbiography.com

KAY FRANCIS
I CAN'T WAIT TO BE FORGOTTEN

HER LIFE ON FILM AND STAGE

SCOTT O'BRIEN
Foreword by Robert Osborne

"Best of Year"
Laura Wagner · Classic Images
EXPANDED 2ND EDITION

Virginia Bruce

I'VE GOT YOU UNDER MY SKIN

by
Scott
O'Brien

Foreword by
James Robert Parish

CPSIA information can be obtained at www.ICGtesting.com
Printed in the USA
BVOW010836300113

311954BV00010B/879/P